Coming of Age in New Jersey

Coming of Age in New Jersey
College and American Culture

MICHAEL MOFFATT

RUTGERS UNIVERSITY PRESS
New Brunswick and London

Illustrations in front matter by Lisa David

Library of Congress Cataloging-in-Publication Data

Moffatt, Michael, 1944–
    Coming of age in New Jersey :   college and American culture   /   Michael Moffatt.
      p.   cm.
    Bibliography: p.
    Includes index.
    ISBN 0-8135-1358-8 ISBN 0-8135-1359-6 (pbk.)
      1. Rutgers University—Students.   2. College students—New Jersey—New Brunswick—Social
life and customs.   3. College students—New Jersey—New Brunswick—Sexual Behavior.   4. Educational anthropology—New Jersey—New Brunswick.   5. Ethnology—New Jersey—New Brunswick.   6. Participant observation.   I. Title.
    LD4756.M62   1989
    378'.198'0974942—dc19   88-10124
                                                                                                    CIP

British Cataloging-in-Publication information available

For Alan

Contents

Figures

Maps

Acknowledgments

Thanks, first of all, to the hundred and eighty Rutgers students who allowed me to live among them over the years on "Gates Third," "Erewhon Third," and "Hasbrouck Fourth." Special thanks to my roommates (real first names only): Rich and Mike and Chris and Hank and (another) Chris. Not to mention, slightly farther afield, Sue and Sally and Venita and Lisa and Beth and Renata and Julie and Jeannie and Estelle and Jill and Shelley and Katrina; Mike and Spanky and Lee and T. J. and Greg and A. J. and Jeff and David and Joe and Scott and Kenny and Stan and John and Bill and Alex and Howdy and Kelvin and ("you look maahvelous") Mike and Lou. And who could ever forget Dapper?

My collective gratitude to the thousand or more students who wrote self-reports for me, or who commented on earlier drafts of these essays. My specific thanks to Louis Miller 1987, William Brahms 1989, Christine Brandel 1986, and Anne Devine 1988 for the materials in figure 1, map 2, map 3, and map 4, respectively.

I am particularly grateful to Susan Gal for her anthropological and linguistic insights and her good friendship during the entire decade of this research. Janet Baldares gave me an equally incisive long-term commentary and the support of a loved one and a family member. Andrew Abbott, D. Randall Smith, Karen Predow, Sarane Boocock, Robert Gutman, Benjamin Zablocki, Anne Foner, and Ann Parelius of the late lamented Department of Sociology and Anthropology at Rutgers College encouraged and advised me in my early years on Gates Third and Erewhon Third—and Abbott and Smith have gone on being my sociological gurus throughout. George Kearns and Cleo McNelly in the Department of English were also early friends of this project.

More recently, I am very grateful to many members of the splendid Department of History at Rutgers University. John Gillis introduced me to the social history of youth and gave me valued friendship and much supportive encouragement over the years. Richard P. McCormick kindly introduced me to the pleasures and mysteries of local historical research using primary sources. Judith Walkowitz did excellent readings of chapters 5 and 6. David Oshinsky thought up my title and did me other kindnesses. (Thanks also to Margaret Mead, her reputation bloodied but still unbowed after the attacks of pygmies, for her original title, which inspired mine.) T. J. Jackson Lears provided me with the last-minute expertise of, in one anthropologist's opinion, a very perfect cultural historian.

Historian and Dean Mary Hartman gave me advice and encouragement. Historian and Dean Tilden Edelstein and linguist and Associate Dean Robert Jeffers bestowed an ethnographically invaluable temporary job on me *as* an academic dean. James McLachlan (New York University) made all the right encouraging noises about an early draft of my dorm ethnography. Helen Lefkowitz Horowitz made similar remarks about other initial writings.

The Social History Group at Rutgers allowed me to practice my first historical fumblings on them. The Gender Group (History and English) helped me cope with the contents of chapters 5 and 6. Dean Catharine Stimpson gave me an encouraging reading of an early draft of chapter 7. Bruce Robbins of the Department of English commented fruitfully on half of these essays. George Levine talked to me so gracefully and intelligently during most of the later period of this research and write-up that he *had* to have had some impact on the results. Joseph Harris, peripatetic English writing pro, read and offered helpful comments on many chapters. And Kurt Spellmeyer, the Rutgers writing director, has expressed more good ideas about the undergraduates in my hearing than the average twenty-five over-specialized Rutgers professors combined.

Anthropologist Hervé Varenne gave me many useful critiques and much encouragement over the course of this research and helped me to remember, surrounded by all these historians and literary folk, what it is that we anthropologists do. John Kirkpatrick gave me one good reading and an inspiring pitch to keep my results fluid and dialogic. Thanks to Roy D'Andrade and Naomi Quinn for other anthropological kindnesses. Linda Nelson and Mwalimu Shujaa gave me invaluable assistance with chapter 4. And in 1986, I greatly benefited from a long talk with James Clifford about the new ethnographic experimentalism in cultural anthropology.

It may be a mixed blessing for administrative or student-life personnel to be thanked in the acknowledgments of this particular book. Thanks, nevertheless, to former Dean of Students Howard Crosby and to present Dean Stayton Wood for facilitating my research and for being always unfailingly courteous and helpful about everything I needed. Thanks also to Reginald Bishop, Elsa Vineberg, Eve Sachs, Charles Coogan, Roberta Parkinson, Marie Logg, Patricia Wilder, Dwight Smith, Joan Carbone, Bernadine Calkins, Barbara Bender, Charles Waldie, Fred Clark, Louise Duus, and Barbara Schroder. And thanks to the Institutional Review Board of the Office of Research and Sponsored Programs at Rutgers, which reviewed my research in the dorms and also checked over my approach to the elicitation of the anonymous sexual self-reports used in chapters 5 and 6.

Assistant Vice-President David Burns has read and extensively commented on earlier drafts of much of this research and has been generous in sharing his own considerable insights into Rutgers and Rutgers students with me. Like everyone else mentioned here, of course, he bears no responsibility for my results.

Special thanks to historian and Dean of Rutgers College James Reed for very generous practical help and encouragement during the two years I was writing this book and for exceptionally savvy readings of everything between these covers.

Lisa David painted the striking illustrations at the front of this volume for an undergraduate project in Art History unrelated to this research. My gratitude to her for making these paintings available and to Elizabeth McLachlan of the Art History Department for drawing my attention to them.

Alan Dalsass has given me increasingly expert assistance with the nuances of adolescent culture as he has grown from a cute little kid to a cute big one during the years of this research. Dayan Rosen, Scott Page, and Steve Freiman have been helpful in the same way more recently.

And finally, Marlie Wasserman, editor extraordinaire, has nurtured and advised me on this project down through the years. For better or for worse, this book would not exist without her.

Preface

Coming of Age in New Jersey is an anthropological study of students at Rutgers College, based on participant observation in the Rutgers dorms and on other types of research carried out between 1977 and 1987. This book is more than just a case study of Rutgers, however. It is also about college, late-adolescence, and certain general American cultural notions—individualism, friendship, community, bureaucracy, diversity, race, sex, intellect, work, and play—in the thought and experience of the under-graduates. The essays that follow attempt to grasp the students' mentalities. But ultimately, of course, the story here is my own; it is my attempt as a cultural anthropologist, a college professor, and a middle-aged American male to explicate, simplify, and give a certain form to the undergraduates' often more inchoate or tacitly held ideas about the subjects I chose to treat.

Conventional accounts of American college students rely on the anecdotal knowledge their professors have of them—a dubious source—or on questionnaires or structured or unstructured interviews. Questionnaires usually require their subjects to respond to predetermined topics, how-ever; with students, they are about what adult investigators have decided should be relevant to youths in advance. Interviews give subjects a better chance to talk and think in their own terms. But interviews with adolescents, especially with glib college adolescents, also encourage subjects to talk in their most formal, adult-sounding ways. Participant observation with the undergraduates, on the other hand, amounts to hanging around with one's subjects for a long enough time to start hearing them in their more natural adolescent tones—very different ones—and to start sensing their own priorities as they understand them. I have tried to capture these distinctive adolescent voices and mentalities below. They are frequently impolite and vigorously vulgar. But they introduce us to realities that other, loftier points of view about college and modern adolescence often miss or obscure.

A collaborative technique also used in this research provided another source of student voices in this book. For two years after the completion of participant observation in the dorms, I taught my preliminary results to many Rutgers undergraduates, and they wrote me papers in reply, correcting and refining my initial conclusions about them and providing me with new interpretations and new information about themselves.

The seven chapters that follow have been written so they can be read as separate essays about different aspects of the students' lives in college. But they have also been written to be read one after another. Later chapters go deeper into the details of things touched on in passing in earlier chapters. And, with the exception of chapter 4, the order of the chapters is roughly the order in which I figured out what I am presenting here.

I have tried to keep the focus on the students; thus, the more specialized academic commentary in this book will be found in the Further Comments section following each chapter. I have done my best to keep my tone neutral, to try to describe the students' lives from something like their own attitudinal stances. But occasionally my own moral tone does break through, I think, especially in chapters 5 and 7 and whenever the subject of fraternities comes up. Finally, following recent realizations in anthropology that what you describe is strongly conditioned by how you choose to describe it, I have tried to write different chapters in different ways.

Thus, chapter 1 is an attempt to evoke my first naive responses to undergraduate society at Rutgers in the late 1970s and to introduce my readers to my research relationship with the students. Chapter 2 is an overview of some general themes treated in more detail or in other ways in later chapters. It is also where the busy reader who does not want to wade through yet another ethnographer's "entry tale" might wish to begin this book. Chapter 3 is intended to be a slice of life, a comment on "community," and it brings the anthropologist back into the text. Chapter 4 tells about my other year of fieldwork in the dorms, and it also tries to lay out some implications of contemporary American individualism in a context where these usually sacred American values did not turn out all that well.

Chapters 5, 6, and 7 move to other levels of description and analysis. The large number of student texts on which they are based permits more attention to important issues of typicality and variation among the undergraduates than was possible in small-group research in the dorms. These later chapters also contain more self-consciously self-interpretative student voices and rich new sources of information about the private lives of the students. Self-reports and texts have their limitations as well, however. Some of them I think I have been able to deal with through my independent sense of undergraduate culture from my years in the dorms. Other questions about the truthfulness of the most sensitive of the student self-reports I discuss in detail in chapter 5. Finally, in the appendixes, I discuss my methods and approach to ethnography in greater detail, and the probable typicality of this Rutgers research.

What do all these essays add up to in the end? To no single simple conclusion that can be stated in twenty-five words or less. And I have deliberately avoided writing an authoritative-sounding conclusion to this book, or to most of its individual chapters. American adolescents and American college students in particular are perennially remonstrated with by their elders for not being what *they* were at their youthful bests (as they remember their youthful bests, of course), or for not being even better. For youths are, as the commencement speech cliché goes, "our future." There is quite enough of this moralizing literature on students and colleges floating around at present. I would be happy if this set of essays contributed a different kind of understanding of what college, college adolescence, and contemporary American culture are all about, from a less-than-elite undergraduate perspective. I would also be happy if the conclusions to these essays could remain as open as the state of adolescence itself ideally ought to be.

Coming of Age in New Jersey

ONE / Orientation

I n 1977, on a whim, I decided to try passing as an overage, out-of-state freshman for the first few days of the fall semester at Rutgers College. I had been on the Rutgers faculty for four years at the time. My serious anthropological interests then lay in south India, but it would be some years before I could get back into the field. Meanwhile I wanted to practice my professional skills. I was curious what a big, confusing institution like Rutgers looked like from a worm's-eye view, and I wanted to know more about the undergraduates I was teaching in large, often impersonal classes. For already, by the age of thirty-three, I no longer understood my students. By 1977, my own college years, the early and mid-sixties, were beginning to feel like very distant times indeed.

My little foray into the dorms was not likely to develop into serious research, I thought. It really would not be wise if it did, for in cultural anthropology, your professional prestige depends on how distant, exotic, and uncomfortable your research site is.[1] But what harm could a little underground investigation of the undergraduates do? At the very least, it would be fun to see if I could get away with it.[2]

I made my arrangements, and on a hot Saturday morning in early September I showed up at one Gates Hall, in the main cluster of dormitories on the old College Avenue Campus of Rutgers (see map 1), dressed in jeans, a T-shirt, and sneakers and carrying a battered old suitcase.[3] Nobody in the dorm would know who I was, I'd been told. I was typically late sixties in appearance at the time—long-haired, with a moustache and wire-rimmed glasses. I was alone. All around me were students in similarly casual dress, with somewhat shorter hair, accompanied by their better-dressed parents, unloading carfuls of clothes, stereos, and other personal possessions. As I waited for the elevator to take me up to my floor, I began to have second thoughts. I would never get away with this. Perhaps I should just confess my real identity from the beginning: Hi, I'm a Rutgers professor, here to study you for a few days. Please don't pay any attention to me. But when I arrived on the third floor, a nice-looking young woman greeted me in a friendly but practiced manner: "Welcome to Rutgers! Are you a new student? Tell me your name and I'll tell you what room you're in. My name is Melanie. I'll be your preceptor this year."[4] "Mike, Mike

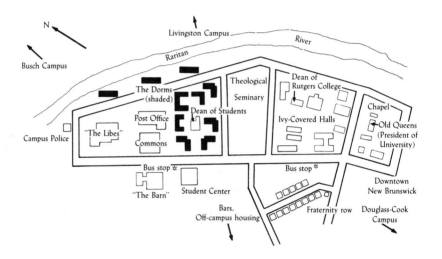

N

Livingston Campus

Raritan River

Busch Campus

Theological Seminary

Dean of Rutgers College

The Dorms (shaded)

Chapel

Dean of Students

Ivy-Covered Halls

Old Queens (President of University)

Post Office

Campus Police

"The Libes"

Commons

Bus stop ✳

Bus stop ✳

Downtown New Brunswick

"The Barn"

Student Center

Bars, Off-campus housing

Fraternity row

Douglass-Cook Campus

MAP 1 / The College Avenue Campus

Moffatt," I replied. And, like it or not, I was launched into my temporarily fraudulent role.

I walked into the "staging area" to which I had been assigned, a room that usually served as the lounge between the two "sections" of fourteen double and triple student rooms on one floor in this particular dorm plan.[5] Our floor was "coed by sections"—the females on one side, the males on the other. The more popular arrangement was "coed by alternating rooms." My staging area looked like a small army barracks: six temporary cots lined up side by side, with a few of my new roommates already moving in. We exchanged hi's and first names, and I shoved my suitcase under one bed, flopped down, and started doing research. That is, I started eavesdropping.

My roommates continued to trickle in with various family members in tow. One had a mother who was vigorously acting out "mother": setting up his little refrigerator, explaining what food he had and what clothes she had packed, instructing him mock-seriously to be "nice to his roommates, they look like nice boys." Another came with a pipe-smoking older brother who speculated in a worldly way about the sex life of the residence counselor downstairs, an older male in a coed dorm. Soon we were all there, however, and soon all the family members had taken themselves away. And immediately, good Americans that we were, we started making friends. We started exchanging the innocent biodata that Americans spontaneously verbalize under such circumstances—a few personal and academic interests, idle stories about home and coming to Rutgers, initial sketches of likes and dislikes.

Or more precisely, my five roommates immediately started exchanging initial confidences. I threw in the occasional friendly remark, but I mostly listened, fascinated and slightly nervous about my acceptance by them. Also, I could not think up details of high school life quickly enough to play. It had been too long to remember about parents and old buddies and girlfriends and high school capers and summer camps and regional travels . . .

All five of my new roommates on Gates Third in 1977 were eighteen years old. All five were white, like many Rutgers students the children or grandchildren of white ethnics who had entered the United States in the twentieth century. All five were males; the sexual integration of the Rutgers dorms had not yet extended into individual rooms, nor has it done so by the late 1980s. And all five were recent graduates of high schools in suburban towns in northern New Jersey. None of them lived more than

3

fifty miles from New Brunswick, and two could easily have commuted. But they had all "gone away to college," as you are supposed to do after high school in the United States in the late twentieth century if you have middle-class career goals and if you can afford it.

Four of my new roommates had well-defined vocational goals linked to their college educations, to their intended majors in particular: premed, engineering, criminal justice, and "junior high math teaching with coaching on the side." The fifth didn't know—"something in the liberal arts," he said dismissively. Two had hometown girlfriends to whom they hoped to remain faithful. All five talked about their families casually and fondly ("My mother sewed my name on the bottoms of all my socks!"). And all but one apparently took me at face value, as an older, out-of-state freshman. The exception was John, a handsome young man with a friendly, half-aggressive manner—the intended cop, interestingly enough. Just after introductions, when no one else was in the room, he suddenly asked me, "Are you a freshman, Mike?" I inwardly cursed him for making me tell my first overt lie, and I told him that I was. But he obviously continued to regard me with suspicion.

Our preceptor, Melanie, put her head into our room and told us to go get our student handbooks and course registration materials at "the barn," the old gym on College Avenue, have lunch, and be back at 1:30 for the first meeting with all the first-year students on our floor. I went off as instructed, on my own—practicing my act as a dumb freshman, trying to walk familiar paths unfamiliarly, enjoying the surprising thrills of an apparently successful con—and reported back to Gates Third just before the meeting. Now orientation was really beginning.

Orientation is the well-scripted routine by which anyone who has gone away to college since about 1925 has probably first experienced American higher education. Historically, it replaced the older, hairier student-to-student initiations of the late nineteenth century: hazing and some of the other colorful customs of the old undergraduate college life.[6] Modern orientation can be seen as a firmly entrenched college custom as well, however—in this case, as a deans' ritual. It is the one institutional moment during which the student-life specialists who run the nonacademic side of undergraduate Rutgers have a chance to tell *their* version of college to the freshmen, to try to represent Rutgers as a rational, well-ordered institution that cares about the individual student and, through a series of student-life specialists, sees to her or his health, welfare, and personal development.

Except that, as the deans themselves know, Rutgers is not really quite so caring, so orderly, or so personal. Accordingly, deanly orientation, as experienced by the freshmen, was shot full of contradictions and double messages. Some of these double messages might have been intentional. Others were inevitable. Still others were, as far as I could tell, unplanned and probably unknown to the deans.

Ours began in 1977 with the first of what were to prove the invariant subrituals of intimacy of the contemporary deanly routines: "boundary-breakers" or "icebreakers." The friendliness of roommates was being left to private enterprise at the moment, but the friendliness of new floor members was not about to be left to chance.[7] Our preceptor asked us to form a circle and introduce ourselves one by one, each with a personal detail or two that would help others remember us. Everyone began with, "Hi, I'm [first name, short form; no last name]." Everyone indicated their hometown, almost all north Jersey towns. A few mentioned their intended academic majors. And everyone provided some cute personal taste or characteristic—a hobby, a favorite kind of music, and so on. That year no one mentioned anything remotely intellectual during this first exercise. My own introduction passed muster: "Hi, I'm Mike. I'm from Connecticut. I like to eat, and I canoe sometimes." When I added, "I've also been out of school for a few years," I saw Melanie nod as though I had confirmed something she had been wondering about.

After our icebreaker, our residence counselor (RC) stopped in and said a few breezy words, first articulating what was to be the fundamental sociological dichotomy in the daily lives of the students at Rutgers, the strong contrast between the personal world of the students and the impersonal qualities of the official college. The RC put it vividly. Higher education Rutgers-style, he said, was no longer "a few students sitting under a fig tree with a professor." It was a giant business. "*We're* here," he said, "to help you, to give you support against that factory system out there." He recommended that we use college to work on our "social skills," which might help us get jobs out there after graduation more than anything we learned in the classroom. He told us our preceptor was a great person, but he said we could also always bring our problems to him: "My door is always open." Then he withdrew.

Melanie then carefully delineated her relationship to us, denying in loco parentis but not her formal authority in the dorms: "I'm not your mommy. I *want* to be your friend. But there *are* some mean things I have to do." She went on to the nitty-gritty of life on the floor. Keep marijuana out of sight, in the rooms. Liquor was OK anywhere on the floor (this was to change, drastically and controversially, in the mid-1980s), but the "boys" had to clean up their own messes. Firearms were out of the question, and hot plates were technically illegal because of fire regulations, though preceptors were to tolerate them in every dorm I was in, warning students when the fire inspectors were due on their "surprise" visits. Get to recognize one another and look out for one another, Melanie continued. Look out for strangers on the floor or in the dorm—"people who look like they are much older, or who aren't dressed well." I glanced around to see if anyone was looking at me. No one was.

A good thing about coed floors, Melanie generalized, was that "the boys can protect the girls." Boys, she warned, watch out for female cleaning ladies who walk suddenly into the men's bathrooms in the mornings. Girls—to a gasp of collective embarrassment—no used sanitary napkins on the floors or in the toilets in your bathroom. And sorry for the urinals in *your* bathroom; this was once an all-male college. Rutgers had "gone coed" five years earlier, but the bathrooms still all contained urinals. According to Melanie, the females on another floor of Gates Hall had neutralized theirs the year before by planting flowers in them.

Then on to academic advice. The technicalities of academic registration and the "drop-add period," a little inaccurately. Study time. Melanie, who had identified herself as a physical education major, looked around to make sure no one but the other preceptor and the freshmen were in the room and gave us her opinion of the lowdown on this important topic. Her first year at Rutgers, she said, she had been very upset by a preceptor who told her that she would be OK at Rutgers if she studied five hours a day. But this was nonsense, she told us: "You have to make up your mind what you want here. If you want to enjoy yourself, if you want to have any social life at all, two hours a day is plenty, one in the morning and one in the evening. A 'B' or a 'C' isn't a disaster. Of course," she amended, alluding to the great status divide among undergraduate majors, "you bio-sci people are different . . ." Biological science majors were premeds, the most respected undergraduates on academic grounds, then and later in the mid-1980s.

A penultimate exhortation: we could have lots of fun on our floor this year if we brought our freshman enthusiasm to the formal dorm programs fostered by the deans, if we counteracted the possibly more blasé returning upperclassmen, and so on. And a final plug for the sophisticated adult pleasures of urban New Brunswick, for two nearby bar-and-grills.

My freshmen peers listened quietly to this presentation and asked a few routine questions. More privately a few minutes later, however, they were talking about it in a voice I soon came to think of as Undergraduate Cynical:

It's all bullshit.—Freshman female

What they said was, you can do whatever you want as long as you don't get caught.—Freshman male

My roommates and I retired to our room for another hour or so of idle chat, and then four of us went off to dinner together. On the way, I reminded myself again that I was not supposed to know my way around. I told myself to keep my mouth under control, to keep the polysyllabic words in my vocabulary to a minimum, and to avoid initiating conversation or collective actions as much as I could. John took charge and got us across a street and through an outdoor concrete mall surrounded by un-distinguished dorm architecture—brick high-rises built in the 1950s, more collegiate-looking brick dorms from the 1920s, one impressive old nineteenth-century pile—to Brower Commons. In that vast, half-underground undergraduate dining area, with six separate cafeteria lines debouching into the drinks, condiments, and salad dispenser area, around which several hundred students danced, I didn't have to remember to try to look like a novice. Like virtually all my faculty peers, I had never dined at these depths before.

At our table, my roommates and I fell into the light banter that marks American male friendliness. I was enjoying myself tremendously. It was not all that hard to keep up with them—to think, at thirty-three years old, of a line or two that might be amusing to eighteen-year-olds. Just as I had to watch my high or academic talk among the freshmen, however, I discov-ered that I had to watch my low talk as well. Maybe intimate sex-talk was more explicit among people my own age; maybe I was making the wrong assumptions about "college men." In any case, I found myself being smut-tier than they were if I wasn't careful.

After dinner we walked out amiably together on a very hot night and eventually made our way back to the barn for a class meeting with a thou-sand and a half of our peers.[8] Inside the temperature had risen to over a hundred degrees. I almost told off a snotty upperclassman who ordered me impolitely to go sit in a particularly hot freshman location. And I laughed,

I was told later, much too appreciatively at the sophisticated collegiate jokes of the guest speaker, the newscaster Dave Marrish. Marrish was the only adult, besides the dean of instruction two days later, who tried to evoke the possible intellectual values of college during that orientation. ("Marrish's law: Buy any secondhand paperback you see in college that costs fifty cents or less and throw it under your bed. Eventually you'll read it.")

Later that evening at the student center, John—still suspicious of me—managed to snatch my student pub ID card out of my hand when I took it out of my wallet to compare photos with my roommates. I was afraid he would see the checkoff for faculty. He missed it, but he did not miss my birthdate: "1944??!!" he burst out incredulously. He and my other roommates had been born in 1959 and 1960. I got mad at him and yelled back, "You bastard! What's the matter, aren't I a nice guy any more?" Then I saw a little kid hanging around the student center and half-apologized with a quip: "See, they're letting some people in a little younger these days. And they're letting others in a little older." But I did not give him or my other roommates any further explanation of my near senescence. And for another few days, by manipulating our developing loyalty as roommates, I managed to get them to keep the secret of my actual age from others on the floor. John did challenge Judy, a hometown friend of his, a freshman who happened to live on Gates Third, to "guess how old Mike is":

Judy: I thought you were a little older. Oh, dear, I don't know which way to go. Either way you'll be offended. Listen, I have some older friends. One of my sisters is thirty! . . . I'll guess you're twenty-three! No? Then twenty-four!

The next morning was a Sunday. John and one roommate went off to Catholic church. With another roommate, Chuck, I accidentally wandered to a newsstand I knew in downtown New Brunswick and picked up the Sunday New York Times I was after. That afternoon I began going on my own to some of the informational programs we were advised to attend. One was a fraternity-sorority promotion run by students. ("Fraternities are not just social groups. We also do important community services.") Another was a careers presentation run by an adult authority. "Is he a professor?" a girl asked me afterwards. I said I didn't know (he wasn't). "I'd hate to have him," she commented. "He's not very interesting."

Back in our room some of my roommates were doing their laundry. Others were just hanging out and trying to get to know the other "kids" on the floor, especially some of the "girls." College adults usually tried to show their respect for the students by referring to them as "women" and "men," but these terms did not come naturally to the students in the dorms, especially to the freshmen and sophomores. The words were too old for their senses of self. "Kids" was a good colloquial compromise. Between the sexes, "boys" sounded too young. The usual asymmetric solution was that the males were "guys," but the females were "girls."

Other freshmen stopped by our door regularly and peered in, looking away in embarrassment if they happened to catch one of us in our underwear. Total nudity, I noticed, was generally masked even between male roommates. Then and later, undergraduates claimed that living in a coed dorm was "no big deal." But in my first couple of days in the dorm, I was finding the generally suppressed sexuality of the coed dorms, which I had never experienced in my own college years, a steamy business, more than a little stressful for my thirty-three-year-old libido. Sexuality was something students alluded to a great deal in dorm chitchat and in other forms of expression—in musical lyrics, for instance, or in the human icons that decorated the walls of their rooms. But the students only discussed sexuality honestly with close friends, if they discussed it honestly at all. And they were even less likely to discuss it with me once they knew I was an adult anthropologist.

At my unthinking instigation, my roommates and I now began to give a little thought to our relationships with the upperclassmen who were moving back into the dorm. My roommate Fred suggested that we pass the time with a small bet on how many upperclassmen were back. I asked him how we were going to find out: "We can't go down the hall knocking on doors asking people if they're upperclassmen." The others asked why not? I was wondering about norms of deference toward the upperclassmen, as in my own college days and in earlier American college traditions of interclass hierarchy, and I said something to that effect. "Oh, no," John objected, "do you mean I have to worry about some upperclassman looking down on me?" I kicked myself for planting ideas in my roommates' apparently egalitarian little minds, but they knew what I was talking about. Fred later told me that he had had a nightmare just before he had come to Rutgers "of big upperclassmen throwing me in the Raritan river." But such norms were no longer mandatory at Rutgers in the late twentieth century. Interclass relationships were now considerably more informal, though they were not entirely egalitarian.

Meanwhile I was back up against the sexual conundrums of the new coed dorms. All Sunday I had been trying to get to know a few girls on the floor for research reasons. Other males had been doing the same thing with other ends in mind, however, and there was no reason my overtures should have been interpreted any differently by the women. But I hadn't figured this out yet. I was trying to attach to one of the all-female groups that had started going off to Commons together, the evolving female friendship groups on the floor, I had decided. I was not having much luck. I asked Stephanie, a pleasant extrovert, but she stalled me and then slipped off on her own. Later I saw her in Commons in the company of six males, some from Gates Third, others from elsewhere. Then I saw John's friend Judy, and she said I could go to dinner with her. I hoped she meant with her and some female friends, but it slowly dawned on me that such a request from a male was taken as a one-to-one proposal, and off Judy and I went on what seemed to me almost like a date.

We talked a little uncomfortably over dinner, and then on an impulse— perhaps correctly sensing that my time was running out—I asked her if it would amuse her to hear something very surprising about me. She looked guarded, but said OK, so I handed her my letter of identification from the deans, my research permission ("Mr. Michael Moffatt is conducting research on freshman orientation. . . ."). She gaped at it for a moment, and then expostulated: "Does this mean you've already *been* to college? . . . You have your Ph.D.?! . . . You're a pROFESSOR?! . . . You're writing a book about us? Are you going to write about *me*? Wait till I tell my mother!" She was very pleased I had told her first and promised to keep my secret ("You really don't *look* 33!"). But it was not entirely keepable for much longer.

When we arrived back at Gates Third, John greeted me at the door of our room and asked me to come in alone. My other roommates were sitting on their beds looking serious and slightly embarrassed. John told me that they had started comparing notes about me in my absence, over dinner, and they had realized they knew nothing about me: "You've been witty and charming, Mike, and you've found out a great deal about us, but we don't know a thing about you. What's the story?" The jig was up. I had let the required verbal reciprocities of friendship slip too far out of balance. So I did with John what I had just done with Judy. I showed him my deanly letter. He looked at it, thought for a moment, and then exclaimed, "*I get it! You're a* T . . . *I!*" I explained that I was not a TA (a graduate student teaching assistant) but a "real professor," and John appealed to the same offstage parental audience as Judy: "Wait till I tell my mother!"

I asked John and my other roommates to help me keep my secret from the rest of the floor for another day or so, and they did so with glee. At one point, a couple of them put their heads into preceptor Melanie's room and teasingly said to her, "We've got a surprise for yooooooo!" John told me that he had been so paranoid the night before that he had wondered if he dared to sleep in the same room with me. He told me his fantasy about me. I was a "returned Vietnam vet infiltrating the system to take knowledge back to the Vietcong." My long hair and wire-rimmed glasses had looked "radical" to him. I had slept a lot. (I had really been listening in on them with my eyes closed.) I had been quiet and apparently relaxed when everyone else had been zinging with nervous tension. "Vets can sleep under fire in foxholes," John explained.

Chuck told me that my vocabulary had been too advanced despite my quietness, and he had thought it odd that I read the *New York Times* every day (though he told me a few years later that he picked up the habit from me that year). Another roommate, on the other hand, said he had not noticed anything specially strange about me: "I've had other things on my mind for the last two days."

None of my five roommates seemed ethically concerned that I had violated their privacy. None of them voiced any formal protest against my methods. They were thrilled when I told them I might write about them, but they seemed a little disappointed when I assured them I would change all their names to protect them. They did feel, a lot less theoretically, that I *had* tricked them, however; and in the next two days they pulled four practical jokes on me. Noticing that I clutched a pillow to my head at night to sleep in the noisy dorm, they inserted an empty quart-sized glass juice bottle inside the same pillow; it was much less soft the next time I threw it over my ear. They stole my clothes when I was sleeping, and I had to run naked onto a balcony to recover them. They spritzed shaving cream into my shoes. Etcetera. And they made the social dynamic of their jokes abundantly clear to me. "We're just getting you back! You're getting off light."

I was very happy to have this explained to me. Though I had not yet figured it out at the level of cultural analysis, I knew implicitly that in modern American male conventions, you "bust on" your friends. We were still friends! They were not suddenly going to give me a lot of distancing respect because they now knew that I was a professor.

For another two days I continued to venture out of my room alone as a cryptofreshman. I experienced some of the impersonality and hassle of being an undergraduate in the college. I took an English test and a math test. A graduate student administering one test told us to watch out; he knew we were all "programmed to cheat," he said. The room for the other test was, like the gym two nights before, over a hundred degrees in the late-summer heat. I theorized to myself that the long lines and other procedural ordeals of orientation at Rutgers were the modern functional equivalents of the older, suppressed practices of student hazing, an inadvertent way in which the bureaucracy, rather than the upperclassmen, now bonded us together in mild solidarity as common fellow sufferers.

I attended student-life orientation and listened to local samples of American psychobabble: "Ask yourself, 'Who am I?' 'Where am I going?' 'What are my relationships like?'" I went to talks on professional and peer counseling, on student health, and on financial aid. And I sat through academic orientation, where the dean of the college told us we were a "select group" (a small exaggeration), an assistant dean of instruction reviewed the complex details of course scheduling and rescheduling, and the dean of instruction delivered what were to be the only official remarks I heard during all of freshman orientation in 1977 on the meaning of college as a place of learning. I listened to this dean carefully, for he did know how to articulate a value.

The "liberal" in liberal arts, the dean began by saying, meant "free," and the liberal arts had been devised back in the days of the Greeks to educate free citizens, which we would soon be. Man was a feeble thing, a "reed in the wind," quoting Pascal. But (still quoting Pascal) he was also a reed who *thinks*; thought was what gave him his power—his ability, like the reed, to resist natural forces much stronger than himself. And it was this power we should work on in ourselves during our four years at Rutgers, the dean proclaimed; we should try to use our God-given intelligence to the best of our ability.

College should also be a time to learn new things. Take a course in a subject we had never heard of before, the dean suggested. And do not forget the foreign languages; language competence could be one of the most useful skills we acquired in college. (The dean was also a professor in a modern-languages department, which he admitted to us while making this pitch.) The dean recommended we pay more attention to the substance of what we were learning than to our grades. We shouldn't hassle our professors about grades; "grades are the professional judgment *by* a professional *about* the professional quality of your work," he informed us. Then he lightened up a little with an elaborate joke he had swiped from another dean, which illustrated, he said, the difference between really understanding a subject and "bullshitting" the professor to get a good grade.[9]

Now the dean was into his peroration, back up in his high ethical stance. College, finally, was a time for self-sacrifice, he instructed us. Our parents were making sacrifices to send us to college. We should repay them by working as hard as we could while we were in college. How hard should we work? He recommended two hours of preparation for every classroom hour of instruction. For the average student, this would work out to seventeen hours of classes and thirty-three hours of studying every week, he calculated, "leaving you plenty of time for fun on the weekends." The dean's advice amounted to over three times the academic work that Melanie had recommended to our freshman group two days earlier. An audible murmur arose from the freshman audience. The dean was aware that official culture and student culture were at odds on this issue and others in college. "Beware the advice," the dean warned us in conclusion, "of those sidewalk philosophers who will be showing up soon, the sophomores and the juniors." Ignore the peer group. Figure college out for yourselves!

Ignoring the peer group was about the last thing the new college freshmen I was living among were doing at the time, however. They were going to far fewer of these orientation programs than I was, and many of them were skipping them altogether. The official presentations were about things that were not yet relevant to most of them and might never be. It is possible that when and if they had a problem, the presentations would come to mean, There's someone out there who can help. But for the more typical freshman listener, the presentations were soon amalgamated into undergraduate cynicism, into the idea of bureaucratic Rutgers as a set of complex rules and regulations just waiting to catch you off your guard—into Rutgers as "The Rutgers Screw."

"The Rutgers Screw" had been in Rutgers student vernacular for about ten years, and it was still current in the 1980s. It was originally part of the rhetoric of student radicals in the late 1960s, and then mainstream undergraduates had adopted it. In the mid-1980s, I even heard administrators allude to it, though most faculty members were too distant from the undergraduates to have picked it up after even twenty years. It was the way the students turned the perceived impersonality of bureaucratic Rutgers around on the bureaucracy, rereading at the same time the deanly assertion that "Rutgers cares" into a much more vulgar putative relationship. From this undergraduate point of view, Rutgers officialdom was not a personal entity. Just as it did not treat the students as individuals, it was not a "you" or a "we," and it was only sometimes a "they"; more often, it was an "it." And if you gave it half a chance, what would it do for you? It would certainly not care for you. Rather, it would fornicate with you.

Faculty members were not usually seen as impersonal institutional antagonists, however. Unfortunately, they were also almost not seen at all. They were curious, mildly respected personages, but they were distinctly peripheral; they were very much offstage in the consciousness of the undergraduates. No adult figure had appeared during orientation so far who was what I thought of as a real faculty member. No faculty members were present who did not have to be there in their capacity as deans.

In later orientations in the 1980s, the deans invented a new activity that did feature a faculty member: convocation, a supposed revival of Rutgers tradition. It was staged in the pretty Gothic-revival chapel on old College Hill, in the original block of nineteenth-century buildings that had once housed all of the old Rutgers College. The first year that convocation was held, 1984, an upperclassman told my group of freshmen to show up dressed "kinda nice, no tank tops or shorts, or the priest will get stressed." No priest or clergyman was actually involved. After we students had sat down in the chapel pews, the "faculty"—three-quarters of whom were actually nonacademic student-life personnel—processed in, in robes, mimicking rather nicely the older ecclesiastically derived ritual of the academic college. First the dean of the college and then the dean of students addressed us. Then a token faculty member gave a brief academic talk, followed by a few old Rutgers songs sung by members of the glee club.

I enjoyed the event myself both times I attended it, in 1984 as a pseudo-freshman and in 1985 as the token faculty speaker, talking to the freshmen about the history of undergraduate culture at Rutgers. But freshman opinion was much more mixed. It cut too much against the collective attitudes of orientation as they had already been established. Most of the freshmen were not receptive to "serious stuff" at this juncture in their introductions to college: "The songs weren't bad, but that faculty talk was BORING!" "That faculty member got me right in the mood for next week. He said the simplest things in the most complicated way!"

Back in 1977 I went from the last of the formal orientation presentations to my small group. Here, about fifteen freshmen were brought together randomly, apparently so that we would get to know other freshmen who lived somewhere besides our own dorm floors. And we were led by two of the red-shirted sophomores who had volunteered to help the deans' office with orientation. First we had to play four more icebreakers intended to speed up the process of our acquaintanceship. In one, we were given colored pencils and a large sheet of paper and asked to cover it with the images that occurred to us when we thought of Rutgers. I collected the sheet afterwards ("for my wall," I said, to curious stares). Drawings on it included a "joint" (a marijuana cigarette) labeled "hooch"; a No-Doz bottle, a toilet, a bottle of beer, and an open book; a stick figure saying, "chem is for nerds—aughh!"; a dorm window with a cactus in it and the sun in the distance; an elegantly drawn comparison of a tall, complex "ideal hamburger" alongside the flat "actual hamburger" served by Commons; and the word *chaos* written chaotically (my contribution). As in our first introductions in the dorm, positively presented academic imagery was not central in these drawings.

In another icebreaker, we were asked to write our greatest hope and our greatest fear about Rutgers on a slip of paper and to throw the slips into the center of the room, where they would be scrambled and read out randomly. They were amazingly similar, apparently indicating the simple pragmatic orientations of most incoming freshmen *and* the simple bifurcation of "college" in unreflective student notions into two halves: "academics" and "social life." The hopes were either academic, in the narrow sense, or social: To succeed, To get good grades, To pass courses, To get into med school or To make friends, To find people like me. The fears were the other side of the same coin, all variants of "to fail" academically or socially. My own entries were very heterodox: "To attain true enlightenment" and "To be found out." The sophomore group leader who read them out looked around speculatively when he came to mine.

The small-group leaders went on to give us the least official—the most cynical—advice we had heard during all of orientation: how to beat campus traffic tickets, how to survive the allegedly deteriorating food in Commons, how to save money on the used-book market, what the best "gut courses" (the easiest undergraduate classes) were. One of the leaders heard me say to my freshman partner during an icebreaker, "You're not sure of your identity?" My word choice was apparently too advanced: "Are you an English major, Mike?" he interjected. I said I wasn't sure, that I was thinking about anthropology. His face lit up, and he told me that anthropology was an interesting subject and an easy one, that he himself was a joint English-anthropology major hoping to be a travel writer. Since I had taught the only big introductory anthropology course in the college his freshman year, I wondered why he did not recognize me. When I met him a few weeks later as a professor, however, I found out that he had not in fact taken anthropology yet. He was passing on the ratings of other students as his own experience.

Back in our room, my roommates seemed more relaxed with me now that they knew my real identity, and they talked to me about many more topics. They asked me practical questions about the college and the university. Despite their orientation experiences to date, they were surprised at the size and complexity of Rutgers in my tellings of it. I had never met the president!? I didn't know Professor X or Dean Y!? I had less idea than they did of the intricacies of student course registration!? In tones of friendly male banter, they asked me about my own colleges and college experiences, or I reminisced about them spontaneously:

> *Anthropologist* (looking at roommates poring over course schedules): I'm sure glad I don't have to go through all this shit again.

> *Roommates:* You're not supposed to *say* that!

They speculated about the future of our odd relationship. "What are we supposed to call you when we bump into you around campus, 'Professor Mike'?" And now that I was a safe elder rather than a competitive peer, they confided in me more about certain things. As high school students with moderately good academic records, they were aware that they were likely to be overconfident about college. They all expected to get A's and B's. They all knew that not everyone did, and each one worried about how he himself might do. One evening I made a tape recording with all of them ("suddenly you sound different, Mike, more like a professor"), and they grew intense about religion (two were Catholics, one was a Baptist, and two were agnostics) and—in much more coded talk—about "going all the way" in sexual relationships.

John and I also extended our established friendly-aggressive relationship into new areas. Thinking about my being an anthropologist, John asked me if "blacks have a better survival instinct than whites?" "Well, for a start," I replied, "the question is a racist one." John blushed and hedged: "We could change the *words* . . ." And he labeled the college students of the late 1960s "rebels without a cause" who liked to smoke dope and burn down buildings. "Rebels *without* a cause?" I asked, taken aback. His own college generation, he maintained, was more mature. Stung, I shot back, "How about more quiescent, more apathetic, and more apolitical?" He looked embarrassed and asked me to tell him what those words meant.

That same evening, my roommates sat around working on last-minute details of their class schedules and then went to bed early, around eleven o'clock, mildly excited. The following morning, a Tuesday, three days after we had arrived, classes were starting. I went off with one roommate to his very first class (*Roommate:* "I feel like I can *dominate* all of this. I'm sure that's the wrong attitude"). Still wearing my student garb, I sneaked in easily. I did not know the young professor. Back at our room after class my roomie told our other roomies that I had laughed much too loudly at the professor's little jokes.

I finally went to see our preceptor, Melanie, and told her who I really was. She was less amused by the revelation than my roommates had been. Naturally, she feared I might report on her job performance to the deans: "I'm so naive! I never suspect anything! But I thought you looked a little older. I felt a little sorry for you." She agreed with my request that she announce me as a surprise speaker at the end of the first general floor meeting that evening, so I could explain myself to everyone on the floor.

That evening, I wondered as I stood up from the floor, where I had been lounging with my freshmen roommates, whether any of the upperclassmen who were now back on the floor might recognize me as a faculty member. So I started by asking, "Does anybody here know me?" Someone yelled out, "Yeah, you're Mike the freshman! Siddown!" But I persevered:

I'm an anthropologist, a faculty member at Rutgers. Anthropologists believe that when you study someone you live with them, like them. You get to know them personally. That's what I've been doing with you for the last few days. I wanted to see what Rutgers looked like from a student's point of view. I may write something about my findings, but I'll change your names and all the details so your confidentiality will be protected. . . . I hope you're not too mad at me for doing this. I'll be leaving the dorm soon. Please stay in touch. If any of you ever need a friend on the faculty, please come and see me.

There was a buzz from the students, and after the meeting a number of the students, mostly freshmen women, came up to give me their reactions. Some said I had been "kinda scary"—I had been rather silent and I had often smiled mysteriously. Several said I had looked older to them. One had imagined I was a "parolee." Stephanie, the woman who had stood me up for the dinner date two nights earlier, told me:

> I figured you were a burnt-out [drug-using] high school case who'd worked in a garage and then taken his little high school equivalency and come to college. You talked fancy because you read a lot on the side. I was *sure* you'd turn out to be the pusher on the floor. I was also sure you'd be good with cars, that I could get you to work on my car.

Half an hour later she came to my room to ask me to help her with her first freshman composition exercise.

Off and on for the next couple of days, with breaks to go home to my family, I hung around Gates Third. But my initial research in the dorms was really over. It had been surprisingly fun and interesting while it lasted. Compared to previous ethnographic research eight thousand miles from home, it was handy to have my natives right next door, to be able to go in and out of "the field" with the movement of a couple of miles and the change of a few articles of clothing. After trying to work in a difficult south Indian language, Tamil, it was a relief to know the language, or at least one age-dialect of it. It was interesting to attempt to apply, imaginatively, the anthropological outsider's perspective to something at once so familiar (my "own" culture) and so exotic (the subculture of contemporary late-adolescents). I remembered my own college adolescence as a time of uptight workaholism. It was undeniably fun to go back and experience vicariously what I had never really enjoyed when I was eighteen: college fun and games, peer-group sociability.

I also felt that I had a chance to look at some other, more serious, more generally American cultural notions and dilemmas in the late twentieth century among the students—individualism, friendship, adolescence, racism, sex, and sexism—with perhaps just the right amount of distance from the adult concepts of the same. And my faculty colleagues and other college adults seemed fascinated with my preliminary findings. They apparently felt as far from the worlds of the undergraduates as the undergraduates felt from theirs.

I visited my five roommates regularly that year and invited them to my home from time to time. And I stayed friends with four of them in ways I have never been friends with youths I have known only as a professor at Rutgers. Eight years later, Chuck, now with twin degrees in engineering and law and a job with a New York patent-law firm, married the Rutgers undergraduate whom he had met in the second week of his freshman year in 1977. Fred, working in biomedical engineering in a nearby corporation, was at the wedding. He had married the year before and Chuck had been his best man. Also at Chuck's wedding were myself and Ron, the liberal arts major. Ron had majored in political science and worked on the campus radio station. He was now doing video work for television in New York City. John, at present a junior officer in the Air Force overseas, sent his felicitations by mail. We had all lost track of Ed, the intended junior high math teacher, in 1978. He had gone somewhere else or dropped out, according to my old roommates.

But back in 1977, I discovered that I could not really keep up with my roommates' complicated late-adolescent lives when I visited them or they visited me. Most of what I was interested in they were learning or experiencing tacitly or implicitly. They could not redescribe these things to me. Now that I was no longer with them, I did not know what to ask them, and they could not have told me even if they had wanted to. There were no shortcuts available, no easy ways to pursue my new anthropological interests in a local culture. Ultimately, research among students in New Jersey—if it was to be done with any competence—was going to be as much work as research among villagers in south India. And it had some extra wrinkles. How do you write anthropologically for audiences who may already know a great deal about the "exotic" culture you are describing? How do you achieve the distancing that anthropologists strive for elsewhere in describing a culture very close to the one in which you yourself have grown up?[10]

In any case, more research was clearly necessary, a great deal more participant observation. In 1978, I arranged to live with John and Fred, now sophomores, a day and night a week all academic year on the third floor of Erewhon Hall (see chapter 4). And six years later, in 1984, I repeated the same yearlong field season in the dorms, on the fourth floor of Hasbrouck Hall (see chapter 3). What follows—the rest of this book—is my attempt to convey some of the things I found out about college life, adolescence, and American culture in the late twentieth century at Rutgers, on the basis of two more years of fieldwork in the dorms, and on the basis of other research methods as well.

Further Comments

1 / I later encountered an only half-joking inversion of this prejudice, however. At several professional meetings, where cultural anthropologists routinely and matter-of-factly sit around exchanging details of daily life in the last poor Indian village or remote South Sea island where they did research, I told colleagues that I had spent a year or two living among undergraduates in the local dorms where I taught. "You lived in dorms with the *under*graduates!" they would say. "What was it like?" Most American anthropologists spend most of their working lives in colleges and universities, yet no one else has ever applied intensive participant observation to these most local of natives. Could it be that, to these anthropologists, their undergraduate students are the ultimate unfathomable aliens?

2 / Anthropologists do not usually operate undercover in this way. In other cultures they often simply cannot pass themselves off as one of the natives. They look too different; their language skills are too poor. But "spy" also goes against the ethics of the profession. According to the code of the American Anthropological Association, you are expected to always let your subjects know as honestly as possible who you really are and what you are really up to.

I knew this in 1977. But, as I argued to colleagues on a university review committee concerning research using human subjects, I might seriously disorient the incoming freshmen by immediately introducing myself to them as a professor. I thought I could operate more unobtrusively if they thought I was one of them at first. Then, I promised, I would "come out" and tell everyone I had fooled who I really was and what I was doing. And if I did more research in the dorms after that, I would tell new student acquaintances who I was and what I was doing as soon as possible, I promised. I would explain who I was before any formal interviewing. I would use a tape recorder only with my subjects' knowledge and permission, and so on. Students who objected to my research could then avoid me and not be part of it. The committee accepted my methodology—and this was the way I operated during all my subsequent research in the dorms.

3 / Gates is a fabricated name, as are the names of the other two Rutgers dorms studied here: Hasbrouck Hall (chapter 3) and Erewhon Hall (chapter 4). Merrill Edwards Gates and A. Bruyn Hasbrouck are the only two nineteenth-century Rutgers presidents who, due to obscurity or incompetence, do not have buildings or other parts of the sacred landscape named after them at modern Rutgers. They are honored here at last, if only fictitiously. Readers who don't recognize the source of the "Erewhon" in Erewhon Hall have only themselves and their shoddy educations to blame.

I have altered the architecture of all three dorms in minor ways to make it more difficult for local people to identify them. These changes aside, however, all three dorms are real places.

4 / Like some building names, all personal names in this book are fictitious. I have also changed minor personal details here and there to make identifications more difficult, and I have made several major changes in the identity of one actor. Otherwise, however, everything described here is as accurate as I have been able to make it.

Student quotes in this book that are taken from student papers are left exactly as they were written, without corrections. Dialogue from tape recordings will be identified as such in the notes. All other student quotes are dialogue as I remembered it, usually writing it down within a half-hour or hour of hearing it.

5 / Rutgers had fouled up that year and taken more students for housing than it could accommodate. Excess students would be relocated from the staging areas into real rooms as soon as the rooms opened up through attrition in the early weeks of the fall semester.

6 / In fact, I discovered during subsequent historical research, the deans' orientation and a cleaned-up version of undergraduate hazing coexisted at Rutgers and at other American colleges for half a century. Hazing suited the deans' purposes admirably: it stitched the students together; it taught them conformity to conservative student "traditions." Only after the undergraduates laughed such practices out of currency in the late 1960s did the deans discover that hazing was illegal and

beneath the dignity of college youths.

7 / The preceptors followed common orientation routines on all dorm floors because they had been carefully trained in them during a week of workshops held on campus in the late summer by residence-life specialists in the deans' office.

8 / The freshman class numbered about two thousand individuals. Not all of them had made it to orientation, however.

9 / The other dean in turn may have swiped the joke from *Saturday Review:*

> On a physics exam, a student was asked how to determine the height of a tall building using a barometer. He answered, take the barometer to the top of the building, tie a rope to it, lower it to the ground, pull it back up and measure how much rope was let out. For this he was flunked, on the grounds that, though his answer was correct, he had not demonstrated any knowledge of physics.
>
> When the student protested his grade, his professor agreed to re-examine him on the question. The second time round the student gave five answers (still managing to resist the obvious rote response, differential barometric pressures at the top and bottom of the tower): drop the barometer off the roof, time its fall and calculate the height with a particular formula; take the

barometer out on a sunny day, hold it upright, measure the length of its shadow, measure the length of the shadow of the tower, and determine the height of the building with a simple proportion; measure the length of the barometer, climb the tower marking off lengths of the barometer on the inside wall, and multiply; tie the barometer to a string, swing it as a pendulum at the street level and at the top of the tower, measure the value of "g" at both points and calculate the height from the difference in the two values; and, the best and easiest way, take the barometer to the superintendent of the building and bargain with him thus:

> > "Mr Superintendent, here I have a fine barometer. If you tell me the height of this building, I will give you this barometer."
>
> For these answers, the student received an A.

Our dean concluded with the simple observation that the student had now demonstrated not just rote knowledge but also a wide grasp of the subject, the point of higher education. He did not confuse us with the more critical moral of the tale as it was originally published: the student gave his original answer, he said, because he was fed up with the "pedantry" of high school and college instruction, which expected certain routine answers and seldom encouraged students to learn the real structure of a subject (Calandra 1968). See chapter 7 below to guess what this student critic would have thought of most of the teaching that undergraduates received at Rutgers.

10 / One answer is to have a foreigner study *you*. Another is to conduct research in an alien culture, as I had done, and to try to bring that distant comparative sensibility back into your research at home. A third is to use social historical methods to achieve distance on the cultural present, which I subsequently tried to do. A fourth is simply to attempt to locate that tone and attitude of relativistic detachment often (but not always) adopted by anthropologists with respect to other cultures. For the best example I know of an "at-home" study that successfully solves all these problems—without, in this exemplary case, adopting a morally neutral tone—see Barbara Myerhoff's modern classic, *Number Our Days* (1978).

As for what it is an ethnographer does when she or he works at home, two types of findings seem possible. One is shared with good reporting—making unknown or partly known subcultures (here, contemporary late-adolescent culture) more widely known. Another has to do with making tacit knowledge explicit, with bringing the taken-for-granted of daily life to the surface, where it can presumably be looked at with greater clarity. Closely related to this is a third ethnographic goal I have tried to accomplish, at least sketchily, here—relating the local knowledge of the students to some of the much bigger concepts, notions, themes, attitudes, and values in general American culture in the 1970s and 1980s.

T W O / "What College is REALLY Like"

M y first, most vivid impression from the dorms was how different college looked from the point of view of the undergraduates. The students' Rutgers was obviously not the same institution the professors and other campus authorities thought they knew. The college was a very complicated place, made more complicated by its inclusion in a bigger and even more confusing university. Very few administrators understood all of it—even its formal organization—let alone how it actually worked. Most campus adults did not even try; they simply did their best to grasp those small parts of the college and the university that they needed to understand. The students did the same. And the undergraduates and the professors—and the janitors and the buildings and grounds men and the campus police and the campus bus drivers and the secretaries and the graduate students and the librarians and the deans and the administrators and the public relations staff and the president— were all in contact with very different bits of institutional Rutgers.[1]

Thus, to highlight only those differences I knew best, the students had no idea of most of what the professors spent their time doing and thinking about: research, publication, and department politics. Student friends in the dorms who knew I was a faculty member were surprised to discover that I had written a book, or even that I had my Ph.D. Two sophomore friends once admitted to me that they had always privately thought that "tenure" meant a faculty member had been around for "ten years." Most students were not sure of the relation between the two most immediate authorities in their lives, the dean of students and the dean of Rutgers College. And very few of them could name any of the higher-level university officials between these two deans at the bottom of the administration and the president of Rutgers University at the top.

Most Rutgers professors, on the other hand, would not have known how to do what the students had to accomplish successfully every semester—how to balance college and major requirements against the time and space demands of Rutgers classrooms, how to get to their classes on time on the overcrowded campus bus system, and how to push their academic needs through a half-efficient, sometimes impolite university bureaucracy. Most faculty members no longer possessed the ability to sit passively through long lectures without ever once getting a chance to open their own mouths. Few faculty members could have named the dean of students at Rutgers College. Most of them had never heard of some of the commoner terms in undergraduate slang in the 1980s. Almost all of them would have been confused and uncomfortable in the average dorm talk session, and none of them would have had any inkling of how to go about locating a good party on the College Avenue Campus on a Thursday night.

The different perspectives of the students and of campus adults were also rooted in generation, of course. Professors and other campus authorities were not in the same position in the typical American middle-class life cycle as college adolescents. College was a profession for most campus adults. It was the way station to a hoped-for profession—not to an academic one, in most cases—for most students. Presumably you had already come of age if you were a campus adult. Usually you were still coming of age if you were a student.

And generational differences, finally, were historical differences. In an effort to empathize with the students, campus authorities sometimes tried to think back to when they were college youths. They almost always got it wrong. Memory was selective, of course. But aside from this, student culture and youth culture have changed every ten or twenty years in two centuries of the history of higher education in the United States. And the relation of every undergraduate generation to historical and social events in the wider world has always been different. One's own past student experience never serves as an adequate map for the present.

I came of age in college in the early 1960s, for example. I was on the peak of the postwar baby boom wave. Everything was always cresting for my generation. The economy was always growing; our schools were always expanding; our SATs were always going up. I knew I could study whatever I was interested in; I would always get a good job after college. In college my first year at Dartmouth, we still observed some of the old traditions established in the late nineteenth century—hats, hazing, college patriotism, and so on. I was in graduate school during the late sixties. That was the first time I had ever allowed myself to pay attention to noncollegiate youth culture, to rock-and-roll. I was also grateful for the onset of the second American sexual revolution in the twentieth century during those years, my early twenties. And, though I was not particularly active politically, I found the late sixties exciting times to be young and on campus. It seemed like something new was always going on. It was difficult to be bored.

My student friends at Rutgers in the late seventies and early eighties, on the other hand, had been on the downside of the same demographic wave from which my own generation had benefited. They had grown up in much more uncertain, cynical-making times than I had, during the Vietnam collapse, Watergate, and the pallid years of Jimmy Carter's America. The economy was tighter. If your college education did not get you into the job market, what would? In high school, almost none of them would have dared to neglect the sort of universal youth culture centering on music that had thoroughly established itself in the sixties. They had also lived in a more extensively sexualized culture than I had. In college, the late sixties were ancient history to them. The occasional campus demonstrations were exciting events, part of college life as they expected to find it in the late seventies and early eighties. But students in the 1980s also expected the ambience of the typical college demonstration to be slightly archaic—to be a culture capsule from the sixties, as it were. And most of them had never heard of the quaint old customs of college life whose last vestiges I had experienced at Dartmouth in the early sixties.

There were continuities as well as changes from generation to generation in undergraduate student culture. Some aspects of the students' college as I discovered them during my dorm research were identical or similar to those from my own undergraduate days; living among the students simply served to remind me of what they were. Other things were brand new, and at first they were often very hard to see. Much of the effort involved in this research was descriptive in the most basic sense of the term: learning to notice what one did not normally notice given one's original assumptions, in this case about the students.

Thus, in my first full year in the dorms, on Erewhon Third in 1978–1979, I was most aware of what was missing from student culture in the late seventies. Student life did not remind me of the late sixties. Nor did it remind me of older, more "traditional," American college life either. After my first ethnographic year among the students, I improved my imagination about the present through historical research into past forms of student culture and western youth culture.[2] And when I returned to the dorms in 1984–1985, I began to perceive things that I had entirely missed—that I had literally not looked at—in the late seventies.

For most faculty members, *the* purpose of higher education is what goes on in the classroom: learning critical thinking, how to read a text, mathematical and scientific skills, expert appreciation and technique in the arts, and so on. Some educational theorists propose broader, more humanistic goals for a college education, especially for the liberal arts: to produce "more competent, more concerned, more complete human being[s]" (Boyer 1987:1); to give students a "hope of a higher life . . . civilization" (Bloom 1987:336). And, almost all college authorities assume, whatever is valuable about college for the undergraduates is or ought to be the result of the deliberate impact, direct or indirect, of college adults such as themselves on the students.

Professors and other campus authorities do know, of course, that the students get up to other things in college. Many of them remember that they themselves got up to other things in college. But, in their present mature opinions, the "other things" that contemporary students are getting up to at the moment are either to be ignored or to be discouraged. Or they are, at best, the trimmings of a higher education. The main course— the essence of college—is its serious, high-minded goals as articulated and understood by its adult leaders.

The Rutgers students I knew in my research agreed that classroom learning was an important part of their college educations. College would not be college, after all, without "academics"—professors, grades, requirements, and a bachelor's degree after four years. Most students also agreed that college should be a broadening experience, that it should make you a better, more open, more liberal, more knowledgeable person. But, in the students' view of things, not all this broadening happened through the formal curriculum. At least half of college was what went on outside the classroom, among the students, with no adults around.

Beyond formal education, college as the students saw it was also about coming of age. It was where you went to break away from home, to learn responsibility and maturity, and to do some growing up.[3] College was about being on your own, about autonomy, about freedom from the authority of adults, however benign their intentions. And last but hardly least, college was about fun, about unique forms of peer-group fun—before, in student conceptions, the grayer actualities of adult life in the real world began to close in on you.

About the middle of the nineteenth century, American undergraduates started calling this side of college—the side that belonged to them, the side that corresponded to late-adolescent development in college the way *they* wanted to experience it—"college life" (Horowitz 1987:23–55, Kett 1977:174–182, Moffatt 1985a). And so they still referred to it in the late twentieth century. American college life was originally a new adolescent culture entirely of the students' own creation, arguably the first of the modern age-graded youth cultures that were to proliferate down to preteens by the late twentieth century. It was a boisterous, pleasure-filled, group-oriented way of life: hazing and rushing, fraternities and football, class loyalty, college loyalty, and all the other "old traditions" celebrated in later alumni reminiscences.

College life had changed almost out of recognition a century later, however. By the 1980s, it was much closer to the private lives of the students. It no longer centered on the older organized extracurriculum. Nor was it an elite culture of youth any longer. Now it was populistically available to almost all students on campus, and it was for "coed" rather than for strictly masculine pleasures. But college life was still very much at the heart of college as the undergraduates thought of it in the late twentieth century. Together with the career credential conferred on them by their bachelor's degree, it was their most important reason for coming to college in the first place, their central pleasure while in it, and what they often remembered most fondly about college after they graduated. Let us look at its contours in more detail, as the students thought of it and experienced it at Rutgers in the late 1970s and mid-1980s.

WORK AND PLAY

College life, first of all, involved an understanding among the students about the proper relationship between work and play in college, about the relative value of inside-the-classroom education versus extracurricular fun. A century ago, the evaluation was a simple one. Extracurricular fun and games and the lessons learned in the vigorous student-to-student competitions that "made men"—athletics, class warfare, fraternity rushing—were obviously much more important than anything that happened to you in the classroom, as far as the students were concerned.

College students could not make the same aggressive anti-intellectual judgments in the late twentieth century, however. Most modern Rutgers students, like undergraduates elsewhere in the United States, instinctively knew what historian Helen Lefkowitz Horowitz has pointed out in an important new book on American undergraduate culture. Despite periodic crises of confidence in higher education in the United States (one is occurring as I write, in 1987), American parents have sent higher proportions of their children to college every single decade since 1890, and the trend continues in the 1980s. Why? Because, in the increasingly bureaucratic, impersonal, modern American economy, a college baccalaureate—and a good one with good grades—has become the indispensable initial qualification leading to the choicest occupations and professions via law school, business school, medical school, graduate school, and other types of professional postgraduate education. Once there were several routes to comfortable upper-middle-class status in the United States. And once, college could be a lazy affair. You could drift elegantly through Harvard as a "gentleman C" and still wind up in a prime law firm thanks to your family connections. No longer for other than a tiny portion of the American elite (Horowitz 1987:4–10).

What was the relation between work and play in contemporary student culture, then, and what were the preferred forms of play? Consider an unsophisticated but evocative image entitled "What College is REALLY Like" (figure 1). It comes from a scrapbook a Rutgers freshman put together privately in 1983 for his own enjoyment and apparently for later reminiscence, one of many montages of words and pictures the student had cut out of magazines and newspapers and arranged into his own designs.

Most of the image is obviously about college fun—sexuality, drinking, and entertainment—and, implicitly, about being on one's own to enjoy such things, away from parental controls. Its exemplars, comedian Bill Murray and rock musician Billy Idol, are not collegiate types as they might have been in the early twentieth century, young men in raccoon coats or football players. They are drawn from the national and international youth culture to which most American college students orient their sense of generation in the late twentieth century, a culture that comes to them

What College is REALLY Like

FIGURE 1

through popular music, the movies, TV, and certain mass-market maga-zines. The image also contains references to more local undergraduate cul-ture at Rutgers. The Santa Claus stands for "Secret Santa," a favorite student festivity in the Rutgers dorms in the early 1980s (see chapter 3). "TKE" is the name of the student's fraternity. One of the two references to institutional Rutgers is to its least attractive feature in student opinion, to its bureaucratic inefficiency ("RU Screw"; "Three Wrong Classes!"). The other depicts "Rutgers," together with "'83' Academics," under a mushroom-shaped cloud.

This last image needs interpretation. It did not mean, the student told me a year later, that he had wanted to "blow away" academics during his first year in college. Rather, it depicted what he had feared might happen to his grades when he decided to pledge his fraternity as a freshman. But, he told me proudly, he had kept his "cum" up to a B+. We cannot say, therefore, that the academic side of college was irrelevant to this fun-loving freshman. But it was obviously not a central part of college in his imagery. It was necessary but peripheral, at least at this point in his young college career.

How typical was this college youth? One way to figure out actual un-dergraduate priorities was to examine a crucial set of student actions: how they budgeted their time in college. Both years in the dorms, I asked hun-dreds of students to fill out simple time reports: "Please tell me, as pre-cisely as possible, what things you have done, and how long each has taken, since this time twenty-four hours ago." Most of the reports were made on weekdays in the middle of the semester. On these reports, 60 to 70 percent of the students suggested that they studied about two hours a day. Another 10 to 15 percent indicated harder academic work, up to six or seven hours a day—usually, but not always, students in the more diffi-cult majors. And the rest, about a quarter of those who filled out the time reports, hardly studied at all on a day-to-day basis, but relied on frenetic cramming before exams.

How did the students spend the rest of their time in college? They did a surprising amount of sleeping, an average of just over eight hours a day. They spent about four hours a day in classes, on buses, or dealing with Rutgers bureaucracy. A quarter of them devoted small amounts of their remaining free time, one or two hours a day, to organized extracurricular activities, mostly to fraternities or sororities, less often to other student groups. One-eighth worked at jobs between one and four hours a day.

One-tenth engaged in intramural or personal athletics. And two-fifths mentioned small amounts of TV watching, less than the average for American children or adults.

The students' remaining free time was given over to friendly fun with peers, to the endless verbal banter by which maturing American youths polish their personalities all through adolescence, trying on new roles, discarding old ones, learning the amiable, flexible social skills that constitute American middle-class manners in the late twentieth century. Friendly fun was thus the bread and butter of college life as the undergraduates enjoyed it at Rutgers in the 1980s. It consisted almost entirely of spur-of-the-moment pleasures; with the exception of one type of campus organization (fraternities and sororities—see below), very little of it had to do with the older extracurriculum. Friendly fun included such easy pleasures as hanging out in a dorm lounge or a fraternity or a sorority, gossiping, wrestling and fooling around, going to dinner with friends, having a late-night pizza or a late-night chat, visiting other dorms, going out to a bar, and flirting and more serious erotic activities, usually with members of the opposite sex. And the students managed to find an impressive amount of time for such diversions in college. Across my entire sample, the average time spent on friendly fun on weekdays in the middle of the semester was a little over four hours a day.

On the face of it, then, the students were fooling around about twice as much as they were studying in college. But this is a deceptive conclusion. For from their point of view, college work also included going to classes, and the total of their classroom time plus their study time was about six hours a day. They also almost all worked more and played less around exams or when big papers or other projects were due. It was fairer to say instead that the students acted as if they assumed that academic work and friendly fun were, or ought to be, about equally important activities during one's undergraduate years.

In many ways, they also said that this was the case. Incoming freshmen usually had two goals for their first year in college: to do well in classes and to have fun (or to make friends, or to have a good social life). Older students looked back on college as either an even or a shifting mixture of work and fun. And students *in* college who were deviating from the ideal balance almost always knew that they were, and sounded defensive about it. Here are two female deviants, in papers written for me in 1986, confessing to the studying styles of a grind and a "blow-it-off," respectively:

33

The Grind: I am a little too serious about my studies. . . . I often give up extra-curricular activities to stay home and study. . . . A few of my friends sent me a "personal" in a recent [student newspaper] which read: "What's more difficult—to get Jane Doe to stop flirting or [name of writer] to stop studying?" This is not to say that I am a "nerd" or some kind of Poindexter.[4] I have a variety of good friends, and I party as much as is feasible. . . . [But] I am the type of person who *has* to study. . . . This inner force or drive has been contained in me since childhood.

The Blow-it-off: I am a female freshman, a once level-headed, driven, and, above all, studious girl [who in college] has become a loafer . . . totally preoccupied with my social life. . . . I spend the great majority of my day in the [dorm] lounge, resulting in my nickname; "lounge lizzette." . . . My new, urgent goal is to combine my old, intellectual self (study habits) with my new social self so I can be a happy, well-rounded person.

What was the happy, well-rounded student in the late twentieth century, by contrast? Someone who maintained a healthy balance between academics and college life, obviously. The two halves of college ought to be *complementary* ones in the opinion of modern college students. You came to college for the challenge, for the work, and to do your best in order to qualify for a good career later in life, most students assumed. College life was the play that made the work possible and that made college personally memorable.

AUTONOMY

Modern college life, like college life in the mid-nineteenth century, was also about autonomy, about experiencing college one's own way, independent of the influence and the intentions of adults. At first in the dorms, however, it was more difficult to figure out where the students were not autonomous than where they were. On initial impressions, they did not really seem to be oppressed or controlled by adults in any part of their lives.

Most of them had led peer-centered existences for years before arriving at college. In their public high schools and in their homes and families, they had become masters at avoiding the close scrutiny of adults, or at manipulating adult authority when they could not avoid it. Incoming freshmen women and men also typically said that their parents had voluntarily given them more freedom—later nighttime curfews, fewer questions about their private behavior—in their last few years at home, in anticipation of their leaving daily parental authority when they did go away to college.[5] Once they arrived at Rutgers, most of them really felt that they were on their own on a daily basis. And, in the dorms, the authority of the deans as mediated through the student preceptors did not exactly weigh heavily on their shoulders.

Looked at more carefully, however, the students actually lived in three different zones of relative autonomy and control in college in the 1980s. They were freest in their private lives. Rutgers, like other American colleges, had officially renounced in loco parentis authority over the personal conduct and moral behavior of its students in the late 1960s. Many of the other reforms that the protesting students of the sixties had tried to make in higher education had long since been rolled back by the late seventies and early eighties. But this fundamental change in college authority had endured for a generation.[6]

It had not been an uncontested change, however. Since the sixties, adult critics had regularly deplored the new arrangements, often imagining that good old American college life had now degenerated into a noisy, dirty, hedonistic world of sex and drugs.[7] And in the mid-1980s, with renewed public concern about teen alcoholism and, more recently, about a possible heterosexual AIDS epidemic, deans of students all over the country were thinking about new ways of intervening more directly in the personal lives of the students once again. At Rutgers in the late 1980s, however, the basic redefinition of undergraduate autonomy arrived at in the late sixties was still holding. In the dormitories, the authority of the deans stopped at the doors to the students' rooms.[8]

The students were least free, on the other hand, when it came to their formal education at Rutgers. Here, they had to submit in certain ways to adult authority—to professors, who gave them grades, their fundamental institutional pay. They had to sit passively in scheduled classes. They had to learn the material the professors thought was important. They often felt that they had to think like their professors to get a good grade, whether they agreed with them or not. They had to meet "requirements."

However, the students also had a degree of autonomy and of choice even in this least free side of college. College was not mandatory like high school. The undergraduates had chosen to come to college in the first place, knowing that it would be full of academic work. In college, they did not have to get to know their professors on a personal basis; they usually could not get to know them at Rutgers even if they had wanted to. So faculty authorities were not breathing down their necks. General academic requirements at Rutgers in the mid-1980s were exceptionally loose and open-ended ones. Once the students chose majors, they often had a tighter, more demanding set of academic things they had to do. But at least they had chosen those requirements. And, despite the ideal balance of work and play outlined above, there were also many ways to get through college in the 1980s with very little academic work, if that was the way you chose to balance college life against probable academic success during your four years at Rutgers (see chapter 7).

Between their private lives, on the one hand, and academics on the other, lay a third, intermediate zone, an area where the authority of the dean of students was still intact after the liberalization of the late 1960s. The students literally walked into this zone in the dorms whenever they left the privacy of their rooms. Their dorm floors were supervised by student preceptors, at the bottom of the chain of deanly command. The dorms as a whole belonged to residence counselors, one link up the chain. Sets of dorms had full-time, adult area coordinators looking after them. Extracurricular organizations and student government were "developed" and "guided" by an associate dean with a staff of seven people, and there was an assistant dean who tried to "work with" the fraternities and sororities. A student guilty of cheating in class or a troublemaker in the dorms who could not be handled at lower levels of the system went through a judicial procedure run by yet another assistant dean. And so on up to the dean of students himself. And behind him stood the university police, wielding physical force.

How did the average student, outside a private room, experience the power of the deans at Rutgers in the 1980s? Most of the time, not at all. When they ruled India, the British used to marvel—and tremble—at having control of a nation of several hundred million peasants with a white ruling caste that numbered only in the thousands. The deans of students at Rutgers in the 1980s had the same fragile sense of their own power, for similar numerical reasons. Ultimately, about seven thousand residential students were held in check by a full-time professional staff that numbered twenty-seven individuals.[9] Like the British in India, the deans had their own loyal natives, their hundred or so preceptors, plus other students whose "personal development" they were "fostering" by coopting them to their purposes. But they never knew just how loyal their natives were. For their part, just as Indian peasants rarely laid eyes on their white rulers, the students hardly ever saw a dean in the flesh outside of orientation and the odd official function. Consequently, most students led most of their college lives at Rutgers without thinking much about the deans at all.

But the students did know that the deans were there. And, as the residents of Hasbrouck Fourth discovered in 1984 when it came to public drinking and Secret Santa (see chapter 3), the deans could enforce their will even within the cozy student dorm-floor groups when they really chose to do so. The students usually resented deanly power when it was directly brought to bear on them. When this happened, they typically imagined the deans as far more powerful personages than they actually were—stereotypically, as small-minded, power-hungry, dictatorial autocrats. In the fall of 1984, when the deans were insisting that some of the more run-down fraternities clean up their acts, I listened as three fraternity brothers directly compared the dean of students of Rutgers College to "Dean Wormer," the villainous college authority in that modern college-life classic *Animal House*. In the spring of 1985, as another student on the floor I had been studying confessed to me that for some months she had believed I was a spy for the deans, she added, in self-defense (perhaps revealing a post-Watergate mentality): "But when you think about it, they *could* do anything they wanted to here. I mean, they could have all these rooms wired for sound. They could be listening in on us all the time!"

PRIVATE PLEASURES AND THE EXTRACURRICULUM

Late-nineteenth-century college life had been a group-oriented way of life. The students had claimed that college life did teach individualism, the "rugged individualism" of the era, the ability to impose one's character and one's will on other people. But it had done so through collective activities, through an extracurriculum of organized groups created and run entirely by the students: college classes, fraternities, glee clubs, campus newspapers, yearbooks, intramural and intercollegiate sports teams, and other student organizations. Not one college authority had had anything to do with these extracurricular student groups for forty or fifty years. Despite the claims of college officials that the professors and good bourgeois families in college towns kept an eye on the private lives of the undergraduates, the students in most American colleges were actually almost entirely on their own outside the classroom before about 1900. Hence the lifelong love of early-twentieth-century alumni for the old extracurriculum. It really had belonged to them (see Moffatt 1985a, 1985b:38–99).

In the early twentieth century, however, American social psychologists invented the modern concept of adolescence (Gillis 1974:133–183; Kett 1977:215–244), and the leaders of American colleges borrowed from the students the notion that college was about adolescent development. They added whole new layers of staff to their burgeoning administrations: deans of students, directors of residence life, directors of student activities, athletic directors and coaches, musical directors, health specialists, psychological counselors, career counselors, and so on. They moved many of the undergraduates into newer college housing, into dormitories on the expanding campuses. The new deans of students proceeded to tame the undergraduates and college life in its original form. They made the extracurricular student their professional specialty. The nineteenth-century students' "college life" became the twentieth-century deans' "student life" (Moffatt 1985b:101–169; Horowitz 1987:118–150). As this occurred, the students progressively lost interest in the old extracurriculum they had created, and they revised their own notions of college life so that it still belonged to them. To do so, they had to move its essential pleasures closer and closer to their private lives—hence the dominance in the 1980s of informal, ad hoc forms of student fun.

Rutgers students in the 1980s gave considerably less energy to organized extracurricular groups than they did to their private pleasures. The Rutgers Student Activities Office was proud that there were 155 duly constituted student groups on the campus in 1987, not counting the fraternities and the sororities.[10] Most undergraduates probably had a formal affiliation with one or two of them. But, according to student time reports and the estimates of knowledgeable undergraduates, no more than one in ten of the students were really active in any of them. Freshmen often said that they intended to concentrate on their studies and their social life during their first year in college, and then possibly to "go out for something" in later years. In their accounts, an extracurricular involvement sounded like a duty that they felt might be good for them, somewhere between the fun of their private pleasures and the work of academics. Most students managed to avoid this duty entirely.[11]

The students did make distinctions among the organized extracurricular activities in the 1980s, however. The radio station was so focal to the interests of American youth culture that it was a prestigious involvement, even if the deans ultimately oversaw its operations. So, too, was the Concerts Committee of the Program Council, the student committee that selected musical performers on campus. Another respected student organization, however, the campus newspaper, had made itself independent of college oversight.[12] Student government, on the other hand, was a joke in the opinion of most students. The undergraduates voted for its representatives in the tiniest of turnouts. Student leaders must be lackeys of the administration, the students imagined. Even if they were not, they had no chance of accomplishing anything against the weight of deanly bureaucratic power. The only reason to become a student leader was to get to know some dean for reasons of your own, many students assumed.

The undergraduates had also invented intercollegiate athletics in the late nineteenth century. In the Original Football Game, in fact, played between Rutgers and Princeton in 1869, Rutgers undergraduates had legendarily been in on the very creation both of intercollegiate athletics and of American football (see Moffatt 1985b:30–31, 75–81). In the twentieth century, however, following nationwide trends, the alumni and a growing professional coaching staff had taken sports out of the hands of the students. Rutgers had more recently gone big time in intercollegiate sports. By the 1980s, most students in the dorms did not know any Rutgers varsity athletes personally. (Football players were carefully housed separately from other undergraduates.) Some students enjoyed intramural athletics. Others jogged or worked out. Most of them were as likely to be fans of nearby professional teams as of any of the college teams.

There was one exception to the students' generally casual interest in the organized extracurriculum in the late twentieth century, however, an exception that proved the rule. Rutgers students in the 1980s were strongly split in their opinions of the fraternities and the sororities. But for those of them who liked them, a quarter to a third of the students, the fraternities and sororities were going strong in the mid-1980s and getting stronger by the year. Why? Because, though the deans had attempted to "work with" the fraternities and sororities as much as with the rest of the extracurriculum, they had not really succeeded in penetrating and controlling them despite seventy years of trying. In their ritual constitutions, the fraternities were intrinsically secret, and the intense peer solidarity created by their initiations could be extended into other aspects of their operations. The members also held their houses in private ownership; the deans did not have the same right to place preceptorlike supervisors inside them as they did in the dorms. And the fraternities often produced loyal alumni who could, as influential adults in the college, counteract deans or other authorities possibly unfriendly to the Greek community.

Thus, in the late twentieth century, the fraternities still gave undergraduates an opportunity for real autonomy in a group setting rather than only in their informal private lives. Such a zone of collective autonomy had not been available elsewhere in student culture at Rutgers or at other American colleges since about 1900. What fraternity and sorority members chose to do with this autonomy, however—unfortunately—was not likely to warm the hearts of many adults who believed in freedom and autonomy for college youths.[13]

INDIVIDUALISM, THE REAL WORLD, AND THE FRIENDLY SELF

The students' general preference for private pleasures over group involvements was also related to tendencies in the wider culture, to the shape of American individualism in the late twentieth century in particular. Real satisfaction and fulfillment, most middle-class Americans assume in the 1980s, are personal matters. You may choose to commit yourself to some larger social cause, but this is only one of many culturally legitimate choices you can make. There are other acceptable, more private paths to culturally meaningful fulfillment as well. And many of the students implicitly shared with their elders their sense that the American public world, which the students commonly referred to as "the *real* world," was as hopelessly complex, impersonal, and bureaucratized as, at a more local level, institutional Rutgers was.[14] If you were capable and well-educated, you might still carve out a satisfying career in some narrow, chosen part of it, especially in one of the professions. But you rarely assumed that you could affect it or change it in any fundamental way. So if you were sensible, you learned to base your values on more private expectations and satisfactions.

The recent American individualistic self, in other words, is, as many cultural critics have observed, a "privatized" self, an inward, psychological entity of personal beliefs, values, and feelings.[15] Unlike the rugged individualists of a century ago, Americans today do not feel that they can impose their will on the larger society. But the self still remains at the heart of their values, at the center of their felt authenticity. The true self desires or ought to desire autonomy, choice, and equal "natural" relationships with other selves, most Americans assume. And it does so by strictly sealing itself off from other known realities of the real world. As sociologist Robert Bellah and his colleagues have recently written: "We [Americans still] insist . . . on finding our true selves independent of any cultural or social influence . . . while [spending] much of our time navigating through immense bureaucratic structures . . . manipulating and being manipulated by others" (Bellah et al. 1985:150).

Rutgers undergraduates did not ignore the real world in conceptualizing the self, however. They simply saw it as a different place, requiring a different, more artificial social self. The true self had to disguise itself in the wider world, they believed. It had to wear masks. It had to play roles. It had to manipulate other people. Personal development of the sort that most students expected to accomplish in college was thus a complicated business. A well-socialized current American adult was neither inner-directed nor other-directed; she or he was both. Therefore, you had to come to know, or to construct, your "real" personal identity as you came of age. At the same time, you had to polish the practical skills of masking this same true self in the public world. You had to refine your ability to influence others if you wanted to get ahead in life.

Much of what the students did among themselves in the dorms, especially in the long talk sessions held in Undergraduate Cynical (see chapter 3), was related to the less authentic aspects of their social selves: joking, play, and ad hoc performances that taught them how to hustle and how to "operate" when necessary. Other parts of modern American college life, however, especially at more private levels with good friends and sometimes with lovers, had to do with the authentic, real self as the students thought of it in the 1980s.

And friendship as a relationship was about the self in the most fundamental way. Friendship had been the core relationship in undergraduate culture for two centuries. Since the mid-nineteenth century, the intensities of college friendships in particular have been celebrated in American culture; in the mid-1980s, the movie *The Big Chill* was their most recent sentimentalization. With your college friends, middle-class Americans believed, you left childhood behind; you became a young adult. When you graduated from college, you might never have the time or the opportunity for so many real friendships again. I noticed the centrality of friendship from my first days in the Rutgers dorms in the late 1970s—and, occasionally, the students' anticipatory nostalgia for their college friendships while they were still in the midst of them.[16]

Though many incoming students had hometown friends at Rutgers, almost all of them believed that they would not benefit from higher education unless they also made new friends in college. And most of them did so very quickly. After a month at Rutgers, the average freshman already considered half a dozen new college acquaintances to be friends or close friends. Within two months, the average dorm resident named almost one-third of the other sixty residents on her or his dorm floor as friends or as close friends. In one longitudinal sample, freshmen and sophomores indicated that almost half of their five best friends in the world were friends they had made since they had come to college. The percentage of best college friends then rose to about three in five for juniors and seniors.[17] And most seniors believed that they would stay in touch with their best college friends for years to come after graduation.[18]

If anything, friendship was even more central in undergraduate culture in the 1980s than it had been in the past. For it was the only culturally unproblematic tie with another human being that still existed in the late twentieth century, given the fundamental assumptions of current American individualism strictly construed. All other social connections—the relationships of work, family, class, race, and ethnicity—were imposed on your true self from without (you did not choose what family you were born into, who you worked with, etc). Even love and sexual lust often chose you rather than you choosing them. (Love and lust can "overwhelm you," according to American folk psychology; see D'Andrade 1987). Your friends, on the other hand, were freely chosen, mutually chosen, egalitarian others whom you trusted with the secrets of your self. A true friend was, definitionally, someone who was close to your true self. Friendship was, in fact, simply the social side of the late-twentieth-century American individualistic self, which "naturally" desired to "relate" to freely chosen others.[19]

Friendship as the students thought of it actually had its own dilemmas and uncertainties, however.[20] Since it was about the true self, a definitionally inward entity, its ultimate proofs were entirely invisible. No external actions or rituals could constitute it. You and I are true friends if and only if both of us consider the other to be a true friend "in our hearts." And I am never entirely certain about what you really feel in your heart. The students therefore spent endless amounts of time discussing and thinking about the sincerity and authenticity of their own friendships and of those of other people whom they knew well.

Busting—aggressive mockery of one another—was important in the very definition of undergraduate friendship in the 1980s, as well as being an expression of its uncertainties.[21] A friend was someone who knew and accepted your real self. Polite talk was inauthentic behavior appropriate to the social self. Therefore, vulgar talk and mutual mockery were natural ways in which true friends related to one another. Busting was also the way in which the undergraduates tested who their true friends really were. "Only a real friend would let you bust on them; anyone else would get mad," as one student explained it to me in 1984.

Between the two spheres into which the students (like their elders) divided life, the private world of the true self and the real world of the manipulative social self, lay a third behavior and value, perhaps the central mediating value in American daily life in the 1980s. It is one that is so taken-for-granted by most Americans that it is virtually invisible as cultural behavior. And it is virtually undescribed in analyses of contemporary American culture. It is the late-twentieth-century American social value of "friend*liness*." [22]

In the assumptions of most Americans, the contemporary self is neither self-contained nor exclusive in its affiliations. It is or it should be potentially open to other selves in its most authentic form; if you are a good, normal American human being in the 1980s, you should be ready, under certain unstated circumstances, to extend friendship to any other human being regardless of the artificial distinctions that divide people in the real world. To be otherwise is to be something other than a properly egalitarian American; it is to be "snobbish"; it is to "think you are better than other people." Americans know perfectly well that they cannot actually be friends with everyone, but in many daily contexts most of them still feel obliged to act as if they might be, to act friend*ly*. To act friend*ly* is to give regular abbreviated performances of the standard behaviors of real friendship—to look pleased and happy when you meet someone, to put on the all-American friendly smile,[23] to acknowledge the person you are meeting by name (preferably by the first name, shortened version), to make casual body contact, to greet the person with one of the two or three conventional queries about the state of their 'whole self' ("How are you?" "How's it goin'?" "What's new?").

The knowledge that "friendly" is often social etiquette, that it does not always mean that the person who is acting friendly wants or expects to be friends, can be a subtle matter. Foreigners, especially from closely related Western European cultures in which similar behavior is only produced under more genuinely intimate circumstances, have to learn to distinguish American friendliness from real friendship before they can function smoothly in the United States (see Varenne 1986a). Well-raised Americans, on the other hand, usually understand the distinction without thinking about it consciously. They know that the correct response to a friend*ly* How are you? is Fine or Not bad; only with a true friend do you perhaps sit down and talk for half an hour about how you are actually feeling at the moment. They know what five of my sophomore friends from Hasbrouck Fourth knew when, in 1985, I introduced them to the president of Rutgers University, an official so lofty that most Rutgers faculty members had never met him.

The president, in charge of a university comprising thirteen undergraduate colleges and twelve graduate schools at New Brunswick, Newark, and Camden, with a combined total of about forty-five thousand students, chose to act friendly to them for five or ten minutes: (Pointing) "There's the window to my office, over there in that next building. Stop in and visit me some time!" The sophomores knew enough not to believe him. They were impressed that he had had the good manners to act friend*ly*, however. And for several days, back in the dorms, they bragged about their classy encounter to their real friends.

Friendliness was the fundamental code of etiquette among the students in the 1980s, the one courtesy that they expected of each other in daily life. It had its rules. You were not friendly to everyone, but you ought to be friendly to anyone you had met more than once or twice. When the students complained about the impersonality of Rutgers bureaucrats, they often meant that they treated them brusquely instead of in a friendly fashion. And, among groups of students who knew one another personally, friendliness could be virtually mandatory. To violate "friendly" in an apparently deliberate way was to arouse some of the strongest sentiments of distrust and dislike in Rutgers student culture (see chapter 4).

BOYS AND GIRLS TOGETHER

Until recently in American culture, friendships usually formed between men and men or between women and women; they did not ordinarily occur between the sexes, especially for youths over ten or eleven years old. As late as 1970 a sociologist could generalize about American gender relations: "Except during courtship, [American] men and women are not expected to pursue interaction voluntarily with one another. And they are not expected to form friendships with one another, but to try to find a marriage partner, thus the assertion that 'men and women can be lovers but never friends'" (Kurth 1970:145). By the late 1970s and mid-1980s, however, over a third of hundreds of reciprocated close friendships reported to me by students in the Rutgers coed dorms were cross-sex relationships. Most students carefully distinguished these friendships from erotic or "romantic" ties, though stable girlfriend-boyfriend unions were also usually considered close friendships as well. And most students made it clear that they valued their cross-sex friends for their personalities, for the perceived closeness of their true selves, rather than for their sexual attractiveness:

> *Sophomore male:* My best friend is a girl named Debby. She is really *special.* I first met Debby two days after I got here [my freshman year]. . . . I like her 'cause she's different from a lot of other girls. We seem to be on the same level. She understands what I'm saying and I understand what she's saying. Towards the end of the first semester we became good friends. Even over the summer we kept in touch. Even after I graduate and we go our separate ways, I think we still will keep in touch.
>
> *Anthropologist:* We're not talking about a romantic relationship here, are we?
>
> *Sophomore:* No. She's just someone I always know will be there to talk to.[24]

It was true that students of both sexes sometimes made friends with persons of the opposite sex in hopes that something closer would develop between them. Cross-sex friendships could include an erotic interest, usually unilaterally. But eroticism was not an invariant part of such connections, most students insisted; and if lust was all that was going on, then the relationship was not really a friendship. The students not only distinguished between friendships and sexual relationships at a formal, definitional level; they also observed cross-sex codes of conduct toward "girls-who-were-friends" and "guys-who-were-friends" different from the behavioral codes that signaled predominantly erotic or romantic attraction. The details of these codes varied from friendship group to friendship group, but they tended to be based on older male-friendship conventions. One of them was busting. Male friends usually initiated busting, but many female undergraduates in the 1980s were adept at busting back. Busting typically marked friendship rather than romance.

American friends of either sex were also supposed to be physically as well as emotionally close. Heterosexual males dealt with mainstream homophobia by putting their physical contacts in certain acceptable frames (cf. Goffman 1974). One of these was 'athletic': wrestling or horsing around together. Another was 'alcoholic': falling down drunk together. A third might be called 'homosexual ironic,' in which male friends implied that they were so manly that they could act "gay," for fun, because no one would ever believe that *they* were really homosexual.

Cross-sex friends did not have to worry that their physical contacts would brand them as homosexuals, but they did have to handle closeness in such a way as to rule out the possibility that they were heterosexually interested in one another. 'Brother-sister' and 'little kids at play' were handy frames for friendship between women and men among the students—tickle fights, pillow fights, and the like. And, unlike American male friends past the age of puberty, cross-sex friends could sit with companionable arms around one another, but not for too long. Or one of them could lie with her or his head in the other's lap. But they generally could not hold hands; holding hands meant 'romance.' More provocatively, males might pretend-assault female friends, usually in the presence of a protective audience of peers, being careful about where they placed their hands. Females, conversely, might pretend-seduce male friends in the same stagy manner.

Cross-sex friendships in the Rutgers dorms were thus relatively mutual, egalitarian relationships. Their high incidence suggests how far what historian Mary Hartman calls "gender crackup" had proceeded in contemporary middle-class American culture by the 1980s (Hartman n.d.). In ways for which there are no real parallels in the American past or in other cultures and societies,[25] these young American women and men were trying to deal with one another as persons rather than as sexually defined human beings, at least some of the time. But there were also limits to contemporary American sexual egalitarianism as it was practiced in Rutgers dorms in the 1980s.

One of them had to do with which sex's patterns were being used to be egalitarian in. Gender convergence had taken place in some instances. According to common undergraduate stereotypes about different sorts of dorm floors, for example, all-men's floors were often said to be dirty, noisy, and "rowdy." All-women's floors, conversely, were considered "uptight" and "catty"; women supposedly had a harder time dealing with their hostilities than men did. But on coed floors, the students said, the more commendable traits of each sex were typically brought into a new combination. Coed floors were quieter and cleaner "because of the girls," and they were more amiable and relaxed "because of the guys."

But more often, the price that the women had had to pay for being treated as near equals in the coed dorms was to act like the men, to move more in the direction of older male gender patterns than males had moved toward older female patterns. The standard convention for daily banter on coed dorm floors in the 1980s, for example—competitive busting—was an old male norm rather than a female one (see Maltz and Borker 1982). And males still took the lead in busting on the coed dorm floors, and thus, with some exceptions, unmistakably dominated informal social processes among the students (see chapter 3).

Likewise, the unisex style of dress common on the average coed dorm floor, one that served to minimize erotic awareness between the sexes, was a relatively masculine style. Girls wore pants and jeans and T-shirts and sweats. Guys did not, on the average dorm floor in the late 1970s or mid-1980s, ordinarily wear jewelry or other detectably feminized fashions. Finally, many of the fundamental pleasures in contemporary student life were also older male pleasures. "Partying," drinking to excess, and sexual "scoring," now done somewhat mutually by women and men, were stereotypically masculine pleasures or desires a college generation or two ago.

Another limitation to modern gender egalitarianism among the undergraduates was that in private, among themselves, many of the men simply did not go along with it at all. Perhaps a third of them were obviously happier among their all-male peers, still viewing women as physical objects, still thinking of them in traditional locker-room sensibilities. They were happier with the older, more traditional American double standard. They were threatened by "women who acted like men." And they often found the combination of asexual friendship and sexual tension on coed dorm floors particularly difficult to deal with. They wanted the women to be sex objects again, and they resented them for not automatically "giving" them sexual satisfaction. Yet they would not have "respected" them if they had.

Their generally more liberal peers usually kept these males in line on the coed dorm floors. But many of them moved as quickly as possible into their more natural habitats in late-twentieth-century undergraduate society—the fraternities. At the worst, their attitudes became actions; incidents of sexual abuse and "acquaintance rape" continued to blight the female undergraduate's college experience at Rutgers and at other American colleges in the 1980s.

Aside from these male traditionalists, however, Rutgers students had not somehow lost erotic interest in persons of the opposite sex just because they were able to define some of them as coequal persons and friends. Quite the contrary. If relaxed, friendly fun was the private pleasure to which students devoted most of their free time in the late twentieth century, sexual and erotic fun were the even-more-private pleasures that they found most intensely interesting and enjoyable. Older college authorities had been sure they knew exactly what late-adolescent college females and males would get up to if they were given the chance, if they were not carefully sequestered from one another. In the 1980s, the students were living the unsupervised private lives that the older authorities had feared. And the authorities had been right in their premises if not in their judgments that adolescent sex was immoral and corrupting. Rutgers students in the 1980s did have a great deal of sexual fun with each other. Sexual fun, in fact, could be said to be at the very core of college life as the students defined it in the late twentieth century.

Females had access to about as much sexual pleasure as males. Perhaps because of this and perhaps because they had not yet encountered modern American gender asymmetry in the real world—occupational inequities, the special women's problems of combining career and family, the changing sexual balance between women and men as they grew older—most women undergraduates were not especially impressed by feminist or other political critiques of gender inequality.

Undergraduate women sometimes implied that such arguments sounded dated to them. Most of them apparently assumed that there were a few "natural" differences between the sexes: "naturally" girls had to be more careful about sexual danger than guys, "naturally" girls had a more direct investment in birth control than guys, and so on. But, judging by their replies when asked about their political attitudes toward sex and gender in the 1980s, most of them seemed to feel that these natural differences were no big deal compared to the real sexual autonomy they now enjoyed and to their near equality with undergraduate males in most other aspects of their daily lives in college. In my two years in the dorms, I never heard an undergraduate woman spontaneously complain that she had been subjected to sexism by her professors or by other college authorities—and most women, when I asked them about this directly, said such things had never happened to them. In the opinion of most female undergraduates in the dorms, apparently, the political battles for the equality of the sexes had largely been won.[26]

If Rutgers students enjoyed a considerable amount of sexual fun and sexual freedom in modern college life, there were also many limits to their sexual behavior. Considering the potential, the late-adolescent women and men who lived together on most coed dorm floors maintained remarkably discreet, self-monitored sexual codes among themselves without adult supervision. In the dorms and in the student body more widely, a significant minority of both sexes were probably sexually inactive at any given time, either out of choice, out of lack of opportunity, or out of ineptitude. And most of the students who were sexually active were guided by the same sexual moralities that most middle-class Americans under the age of forty-five followed or preached in the 1980s (for more on the complicated relation of sex and gender in the lives of the students, see chapters 5 and 6).

The principal peer-group activity associated with student sexuality at Rutgers in the 1980s was "partying." Through parties, students tried to meet new erotic partners or got in the mood for sexual pleasures with partners they already knew. A party could be a scheduled event with a time and a place. Or it could be any time that a few students gathered together with the necessary ingredients: liquor, music, and members of the opposite sex—or of the same sex, for homosexuals—who were not "just friends," who were erotically interested in one another. And the students evidently did quite a bit of partying. One sample of twenty-eight students from Hasbrouck Fourth, for instance, quizzed about their use of time over the past week in the middle of the fall semester in 1984, reported an average of 2.5 parties a person, 11.5 hours of partying time. The champion was a young woman—not a bad student—who claimed to have partied for a total of 40 hours, 8 hours every evening, Wednesday through Sunday inclusive.

Liquor lubricated undergraduate partying, and restoring the minimum drinking age to twenty-one at Rutgers in the fall of 1984, mandated by the state of New Jersey, did nothing to alter this fact. To ask the students to stop drinking was about as popular as it would have been to ask the professors to stop reading books—or to stop drinking. Soft and hard drugs were used in smaller amounts and by fewer Rutgers students, in frequencies on which I have no good information.[27]

YOUTH CULTURE AND COLLEGE CULTURE

In its nineteenth-century origins, college life was a specifically collegiate culture. And up through the middle of the twentieth century, less-privileged American youths knew it as the subculture of a college elite—of the more affluent undergraduates, typically from older WASP backgrounds. As Horowitz points out, college life did not just distinguish college students from the great masses of less-fortunate young women and men who did not attend college in those days. Many undergraduates were also excluded from it—from the "best" fraternities, for example. Horowitz calls these students "the outsiders," poorer undergraduates who were in college in order to achieve the middle-class status that the more-prosperous students who were enjoying college life took for granted. The outsiders tended to work hard at their studies and to view their professors with respect. Students in the college-life elite often stigmatized them as "grinds" (Horowitz 1987:56–81).

The original college-life culture slowly faded on American campuses during the twentieth century, however, and it virtually disappeared in the sea change that swept over American youth culture in the late 1960s. Between about 1964 and 1968, the casually well-dressed college man (and woman) suddenly became archaic at Rutgers and at other American colleges. All at once the students were part of a common, classless, internationally defined youth culture. And in their new tastes in clothing and in music, they unmistakably stated their new antielitist sentiments. Blue jeans had once been working-class garb. Long hair and beards had distinguished cultural bohemians, as had casual drug use. Rock-and-roll music—supplanting collegiate musical tastes such as Peter, Paul, and Mary or "cool jazz"—was recently transformed black music. Army jackets were the clothing of poor draftees into the unpopular Vietnam War (Moffatt 1985b: 174–176, 221–234, 241–243).

Students in the mid-1980s no longer looked like students from the late 1960s. But in the way in which a general youth culture rather than a specifically collegiate one dominated their lives, and in the way in which this youth culture was available to everyone, not just to an elite, they were still very much the children of the sixties. The old extracurriculum was almost gone. The most fundamental student pleasures were the pleasures of other adolescents: friendship and erotic fun. The students' musical tastes came directly to them out of popular culture, and they recognized the sixties, whose music they now revered as "classic rock," as the *fons et origo* of music as they knew it.

The nearest thing to the older collegiate look in clothing among the students in the 1980s was "preppie," named, with obvious irony, for prep school students rather than for college students. Preppie was one step more formal than 'student casual': loafers rather than sneakers, slacks rather than blue jeans, and an Oxford shirt or an Izod shirt rather than a T-shirt or a sweatshirt. Undergraduates said that it was the look of student leaders and of academic straight-arrows. Other clothing fashions—"punk," "gay," "GQ,"[28] "jock"—had nothing to do with college; like music, fashions in clothes also originated in mass adolescent culture. College iconography was only incidentally visible on the walls of student rooms and on their clothing. Most Rutgers students guessed that no one in a crowd of strangers their own age would be able to guess that they were college students simply by looking at them.

There were some collegiate nuances in their otherwise mass-cultural-defined lives, however. Although the students did not show their college identity in any obvious way—that wouldn't be cool, they implied—most of them guessed that other members of their own generation would probably be able to identify them as college students after talking to them for a few minutes. They were likely to sound more intelligent, they thought. They were likely to "talk better." The college transformation was a subtle, inward one, the students implied, not an outer identity to be flashed like a beacon. But almost all of them said that it was important to them that they were in college; privately, "college student" was an identity in which most of them took considerable pride.

Another type of collegiate nuance was exemplified by a category of popular music in the trend-defining periodical *Rolling Stone*: "college albums." College albums were the most sophisticated contemporary popular music—new wave, post−new wave, punk, hard core—the antithesis of Top 40. College albums received their biggest play on college radio stations. What marked them as collegiate was not some class-differentiated identity of their performers, however; they were not sung by buttoned-down preppies, for instance. It was their relatively difficult accessibility as art. Their actual content could be even raunchier than conventional popular music.

In *Campus Life*, Horowitz argues that American undergraduate culture in the 1980s is the product of two older student subcultures inherited internally on American campuses. Modern students are the "new insiders," she suggests—joyless workaholics like the old outsiders *and* nonintellectuals in their basic orientations toward higher education, like students in the old college-life elite (Horowitz 1987:263−288). As a summation of an average student attitude toward the life of the mind in American colleges in the late twentieth century, there is more than a grain of truth in Horowitz's typification (see chapter 7). She is dead wrong about the joylessness of the students, however. At Rutgers at least, in their own opinions at least, the students had lots of fun.

Moreover, though Horowitz is aware of the transformations in college youth culture that took place in the 1960s, she does not give enough weight to the impact that these changes have continued to have in the 1980s, of the degree to which contemporary popular youth culture continues to dominate the sensibilities of American undergraduates. The internal inheritance of campus traditions has not since the 1960s been the cultural force that she suggests it has been. Undergraduates at Rutgers—and elsewhere, on tangential evidence—only knew a few things about older college cultures. They knew that college was about adolescent autonomy. They knew that it was about fun and games: elaborate college pranks, and so on. They knew that they would find such typical college institutions as dormitories and fraternities on most campuses. Since the sixties, they had also expected to find political protesters and cultural radicals in college. But the images of "college" that the average under-graduate carried around in her or his head were probably conditioned much more by contemporary American mass culture in its adolescent version than by any of the older student traditions indigenous to American colleges. A short list of popular adolescent movies about American college life in the late 1970s and mid-1980s, for example, would begin with the type specimen *Animal House*, progress through favorites such as *Fraternity Vacation*, *Spring Break*, *The Sure Thing*, *Revenge of the Nerds*, *Real Genius*, and *Soul Man*, and culminate in Rodney Dangerfield's recent *Back to School*.

Otherwise, almost everything in the private lives of students on American campuses in the 1980s was in fact a projection of contemporary late-adolescent culture *into* the particular institutions of youth that colleges now represented—places where everyone else was fairly intelligent, places where you were on your own with a considerable amount of free time, and places where adult authorities had a minimum knowledge of and impact on your private life.

COMING OF AGE

The age grading that characterized most of American childhood and adolescence in the 1980s first developed for small numbers of middle-class college students a century and a quarter ago (see Kett 1977:126–128). And with age grading, college students also formulated stereotypical notions of their own physical and mental maturation in college. Drawing on older images of the Ages of Man, late-nineteenth-century undergraduates pretended that they progressed from infancy to maturity during their four short years in higher education. One typical image from Rutgers in the 1880s showed the freshman as a precocious baby, the sophomore as a drunken youth, the junior as a suave ladies' man and the senior as a care-worn, middle-aged bourgeois (Moffatt 1985b:57). And for two-thirds of a century, college class histories repeated the same conceits. Freshmen and sophomores were carefree, childish pranksters; juniors and seniors were more manly in body and in mind.

Rutgers students no longer drew such drawings or wrote such histories in the 1980s.[29] But they still had similar concepts of the typical stages of their personal development in college, which they still enacted with some faithfulness. Freshmen were foolish and inexperienced. Sophomores were wild men (and women), the leading troublemakers in the dorms. Then, with a predictability that resembled that of some form of pupating insect, juniors almost always discovered that they had matured beyond the juvenilities of dorm culture. Dorm fun was now dorm foolishness. And the inescapable intimacies of collective living—everyone else knowing almost everything about you—had grown tiresome with time (for changing student images of college in early and later undergraduate years, see maps 2, 3, and 4).

Juniors usually decided that they were ready for something closer to an independent adult existence in the real world, usually an off-campus apartment. Seniors often wanted a maturer life-style still. Or they might typically consider themselves to be "burned out," victims of mild or severe cases of "senioritis," weary of college, apprehensive about what came next. Sexual maturity was no longer peculiar to college upperclassmen in the 1980s. Now it could characterize students in any of the four college classes. But the older you were, the more likely you were to be sexually active.

In student opinion, you were pushed through these stages of development in college in the 1980s by the various formal and informal learning experiences that characterized modern undergraduate college life. Students sometimes felt that college adults did have some impact on them in college. Four out of five students in a large class in 1987 said they thought that looking back twenty years after college they would remember a professor or two as people who had inspired them in college, who had made a real difference in what they were today as adults in the real world. But most of the time the students believed that they came of age in college thanks to what they learned among themselves on their own, student to student, or, paradoxically, thanks to what they learned from dealing with precisely the least personal, most uncaring sides of official Rutgers.

College from the students' point of view was a combination of academic and outside-the-classroom education. Academic learning gave you the credentials you needed to progress toward a good career, and perhaps it made you a broader, more knowledgeable person. Outside-the-classroom education, on the other hand, was often the greater influence on your personal development, many of the students believed. About half the same large class in 1987 said that academic and extracurricular education had been "different, but equally important" aspects of college learning for

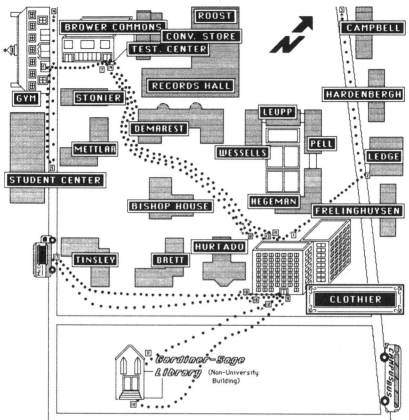

My Personal Rutgers Map illustrates an average daily route (in this case, a Friday) which is indicative of any other day aside from the classes -- usually more on College Ave on other days. • • represents my path. ☐ (box with numbers) are used to show the chronological order of events. Everyday I begin by going to class, in this case on Busch and Livingston. If there is free time available during the day I will go to work at one at one of my part time jobs (at Van Nest Hall or The Barn), in this case The Barn. After work I usually eat lunch and head on to my dorm -- Clothier, sometimes stopping at my RPO. My afternoons are generally free, I use this time to hang out in my lounge or to study--at Gar.-Sage Lib. in this case. I would then go to the rest of my classes, none in this case and dinner spending most of my free time in my dorm lounge, with maybe a trip to the Grease trucks, depending on how good dinner in the Commons was. I choose only to include the part of the CAC because the large majority of my time is spent in this small area.

MAP 2 / Personal Map of Rutgers, by a Freshman Male

In a class taught in 1986, undergraduates drew college as they knew it at the moment. This younger male's college is typically small in scale and centers on the dorms and the campus buildings immediately surrounding them. It is also clear from his map that this student is an unusually precise, academically oriented youth—the Gardiner-Sage Library is his favorite study spot—and a whiz on the computer.

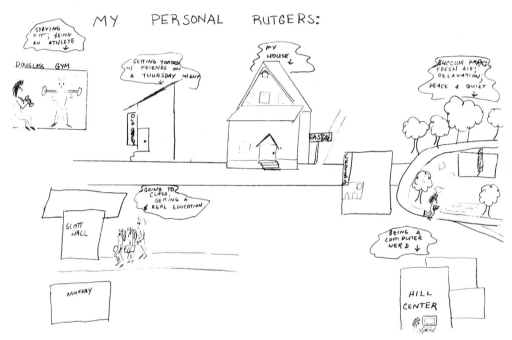

MAP 3 / Personal Map of Rutgers, by a Senior Female

This older female, on the other hand, draws an upperclassman's image of college, a cute, apparently intentionally naive view centered on off-campus life. Her extra-curricular pleasures include athletics, drinking, and relaxing in nature. When she uses the campus, she uses many different parts of it: the gym at Douglass, the computer center at Busch, and only two classrooms on the College Avenue Campus —where she does, despite off-campus distractions, still "get a real education."

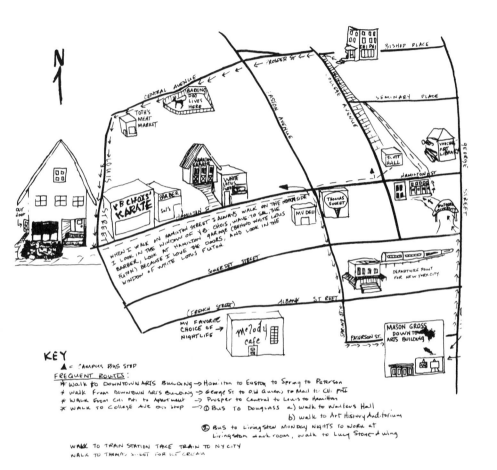

MAP 4 / Personal Map of Rutgers, by a Sophomore Female

A more cosmopolitan upperclassman, old for a sophomore. She lives farther down-town, goes to a trendier bar (the Melody Cafe), has a sweet tooth, looks at the city more visually, and apparently bugs out regularly for New York. Her College Avenue Campus centers on one classroom, the Art Library, and one fraternity (Chi Phi, *top*).

them so far. About one in five of the remaining students considered academic learning more important than extracurricular learning, and about four in five made the opposite judgment. So, for about 40 percent of these students, the do-it-yourself side of college was the most significant educational experience. And for all but 10 percent, extracurricular learning had been at least half of what had contributed to their maturation so far in college.

One form of outside-the-classroom education in college, according to the students, resembled academic learning in content but not in context: the extracurricular intellectual learning that they did among themselves. Like the rest of college life as the students enjoyed it in the 1980s, most of this intellectual fun took place in private, in long talks about philosophy, morality, politics, and other serious interests, usually with friends. Some of it also took place due to the extracurricular programming available on campus, the students said, thanks to speakers, concerts, and other performances, thanks to an intellectual environment richer than anything they had typically known in their hometowns and high schools before college (see chapter 7).

The students sometimes referred to the rest of extracurricular learning in college as "social learning," as the things you had to know in order to be a competent adult in the real world as you would find it after graduation. And the students' college did prepare them for the real world as well, many of them firmly believed. Moreover, they added, a relatively cheap public college such as Rutgers often did a much better job of this than fancier private colleges were likely to do. You were, first of all, on your own in college, the students pointed out—much more so at Rutgers than at smaller, more personal colleges—and learning to take real responsibility for yourself helped you to grow up as an individual:

> Rutgers has helped me to learn what it is like to be on my own and take responsibility for my own actions. . . . The majority of college students find drinking to be of second nature . . . [but] I do not abuse the freedom obtained by living in college.—Freshman female [30]

> It is up to the individual. No one else at Rutgers cares how he does.—Sophomore male

The academic work was more difficult than it had been in high school. Your teachers no longer knew you personally or cared about you. Guidance counselors were not tracking your every move any longer. Your parents were not sure what you were doing on a daily basis. You had a more flexible schedule and more free time than you had ever had in high school—and more distractions all around you. It was not easy under these circumstances to remember the serious purposes for which you had probably come to college in the first place. Learning to balance college work against college play was one of the tougher challenges of your college years, the students maintained.

Second, college, and Rutgers in particular, was more like the real world than hometown and high school had been. A century ago the student apologists for college life had claimed that the rich associational activities of the undergraduates had prepared them to be movers and shakers after college, to build business organizations and other voluntary organizations in adult life. Now, in the 1980s, student associations were in eclipse in college, but so, too, were similar activities in the real world beyond the groves of Academe. Now the real world, especially at the professional and middle-management levels toward which most Rutgers graduates were headed, was already highly organized. Now it was an impersonal and bureaucratically complicated place. And now, conveniently, thanks to Rutgers' impersonality and bureaucratic complexity, college prepared you for this aspect of life after college. Smaller, more elite colleges were cloisters compared to Rutgers, the students commonly argued. Rutgers, on the other hand, got you ready for the real world with a vengeance:

> How did Rutgers teach me to deal with the real world? The answer, as ironic as it seems, is through the "RU Screw" . . . through that tortuous, roundabout way of making everything three times more difficult to accomplish, I learned the skills of persistence and determination which I would need for the rest of my days . . .—Junior female

Rutgers also mirrored the real world in the diversity of its undergraduate student body, the students often asserted. As a public institution, it brought students together from suburban hometowns and high schools that were often more homogeneous by class, by race, and by ethnic group. And here again, Rutgers resembled the real world much more than fancier colleges did:

> I have an old girlfriend from high school who now goes to Mt. Holyoke. Its all like "high-up Suzie Sorority" there. Like they're all just the *same*. My girlfriend

is sheltered from life. I have to deal with more. Because this is a state university, they have to let in all kinds of people. You just can't imagine the *friends* you have at a place like this!—Sophomore male, 1985

The actual ability of Rutgers students to deal with real cultural diversity as I observed it in the dorms was often very limited. Many students could not tolerate it at all, but sealed themselves into little friendship groups of people as much like themselves as they could find (see chapter 4). Virtually all the undergraduates believed in the value of diversity, however. For "diversity"—like "friendship" and "community" as they were ideologically defined—was simply one more entailment of late-twentieth-century American individualism (on "community," see chapter 3). What was the point of being an individualist if everyone and everything was the same? Real choice required a diverse universe within which to choose.

Diversity, moreover, was an easily shared value because it was almost empty of content. Real cultural diversity to an anthropologist might mean the difference between an American middle-class youth from a white ethnic background raised in northern New Jersey and a student who had recently arrived in the United States from a small city in south Asia. To an undergraduate, on the other hand, it might mean a roommate who liked mellow music while you yourself liked punk, a nerdy roommate while you yourself were a jock, or (somewhat more culturally) a friend whose third-generation white ethnic identity was different from yours—Italian versus Irish, for instance.

Nevertheless, undergraduate Rutgers was almost inevitably more diverse than anything most students had known to date, and was probably more diverse than the world in which most of the professors and other college adults lived.[31] At the very least, the students at Rutgers had to learn to get along with people they did not like for reasons of cultural differences. "Archie Bunker would never make it as a Rutgers student," one student commented on a paper in 1987. At best, the students sometimes did learn valuable things at Rutgers about themselves and the world from other students who were really different from themselves.

All in all I am very glad I came to Rutgers. Many people say it's too big. However, I really believe that is an advantage. There are so many different opportunities here . . . [Also,] being somewhat of a conservative, it was great being exposed to those "damn liberals."—Senior male

In high school, everyone in my classes was either Irish, Italian or Polish. Here, I go to classes with Asians, Indians, Blacks, Puerto Ricans and many others, from whom I get different viewpoints.—Senior male

Above all else, college is a breeding ground for interrelationships between students. If nothing else, a college student learns how to interact with his or her peers. The ability to form lasting relationships is of great value to the graduating adult. College is a step in the mental and psychological development of an individual.—Senior female

One attribute of mine . . . that was well developed through the years I spent at Rutgers . . . is that of being a true partier. . . .—Senior female

My social development [in college] seemed to help me as much, if not more, than my academic development into shaping me into what I am today. . . .
—Senior male

In the end, the students claimed, even the fun of college life was a learning experience. And with this claim, the dichotomy between formal education (work, learning) and college life (fun, relaxation) collapsed entirely for the students. In the end, you learned from everything that happened to you in college, the students asserted. And, anthropologically speaking, they were not far from wrong. For they did spend those four hours a day in informal friendly fun, working on their real identities through such activities and practicing the "bullshit" necessary to the well-tuned American social self in the real world in the late twentieth century. And they did devote about the same amount of imaginative and real energy to "learning to pick up girls or guys" as they did to seeking out "meaningful relationships" during their college years. All these personal skills would undoubtedly continue to be useful to them long after they graduated from college. In their refinement, in their opinion—as much as in the intellectual learning that they acquired in college—they came of age, they progressed toward something like adult maturity during their four years at Rutgers.[32]

But how and where did this all happen? How did particular students act out, negotiate, and modify these cultural conceptions and values at Rutgers in the 1980s? What sorts of variations were there among the somewhat variable late-adolescent youths who attended Rutgers? The best place to start looking for answers is back in the dorms.

Further Comments

1 / This language suggests that Rutgers is a big institutional thing existing independently of any particular actor's perception of it. Rutgers might be redefined more phenomenologically, however, as the sum total of all those imprecise partial understandings that all the actors who make it up have of it, as the negotiated and changing product of their combined understandings. (Power plays a role, of course; the president's understanding has considerably more impact on the sum total than some untenured assistant professor's. And wider definitions are involved as well. One thing most administrators do when planning any big change, for instance, is to call their opposite numbers at half a dozen similar institutions to find out how they do the thing in question.) For my summary sketch of some of the structural complexities of contemporary Rutgers, see appendix two.

2 / See Moffatt 1985b, especially pages ix–x and 261, for a summary of some of my historical sources.

3 / The subjects of these essays are "traditional" college students—in the "college-age" cohort (seventeen to twenty-two years old), residing on campus or, usually as upperclassmen, independently off-campus. Rutgers College served mostly late-adolescent students; adults who attended Rutgers-New Brunswick usually went to University College, the "night school." About one-fifth of the undergraduates at Rutgers College, on the other hand, were commuters with far less access to the pleasures of modern college life than residential students had.

4 / *Poindexter* and *nerd* are two negative stereotypes for socially inept youths. *Poindexter* ("dexter" for short) was the name of a character on a favorite children's TV show, which most of the students had watched when they were much younger. In the late 1980s, the campy musical performer Buster Poindexter had taken his second (stage) name from this old youth cultural meaning. The origins of *nerd* are unknown (but see chapter 7, note 36).

Note that both terms, by the way, come out of the wider youth culture. They are not specifically collegiate. In past generations, there were college-specific words for such stigmatized students— "throat" at Rutgers in the 1970s, for instance (see chapter 7, note 12).

5 / One freshman woman on Hasbrouck Fourth in 1984–1985, on the other hand, reported

a mother who was still struggling with her daughter's autonomy after she had gone away to college. (The mother had not attended college herself.) Toward the end of her freshman year, the daughter alarmed the mother by some rumored or reported behavior, and the mother told the daughter that she was "grounded," restricted to her room with no social life. "I'm *grounded*, Ma?" the daughter told me she had replied in stupefaction. "But I don't live at *home* any more! I've lived in a room in a dorm in the college all year. How are you gonna know?!" The mother had reportedly retreated in confusion.

6 / It may be deceptive to say that the colleges abandoned in loco parentis in the 1960s, as is generally said. What the colleges actually did was to stop trying to exercise increasingly archaic kinds of parentlike authority. For, with the rapid shifts in sexual norms and youth culture that were occurring in the sixties, American middle-class parents themselves were no longer able or willing to supervise their own late-adolescent children according to older Victorian norms. In this sense, the colleges were simply going along with the parents. And in the 1980s, the colleges' approach to the personal morality of their late-adolescent undergraduates resembles that of contemporary middle-class parents. In this sense, modern American colleges might still be said to be in loco parentis. They take the same approach that most American parents have to take toward children in their late teenage years. They try to be rational. They teach birth control and health hazards. They are available with help if youths get into trouble. And they hope that late-adolescents will make the "right" choices, whatever these might be.

7 / For instance, "The conventional [coed] dormitory can be the worst of all worlds, providing a grim, noisy, prison-like atmosphere, setting the students loose on each other without adult supervision or faculty influence, providing little more than a setting for the exchange of drugs and casual sexual encounters" (Rebecca Vreeland, *Journal of Higher Education*, no. 1 (1973): 78).

8 / Most fundamentally, of course, moral supervision meant sexual supervision. And the deans had actually been retreating for two-thirds of a century on the question of where precisely they drew the sexual boundary between female and male undergraduates. First it was separate campuses. Then it was separate dorms. Then it was various regulations about "intervisitation" of women to men's dorms and vice versa. The doors to student rooms were the

last lines at which the deans fought their losing battle at Rutgers College in the mid-1960s. One Rutgers dean from that era remembers one curious final regulation, which I also remember from undergraduate days at Dartmouth in the early 1960s: "If a girl is in a boy's room during intervisitation, they both have to have at least one foot on the floor at all times, and the door must be open." "How wide open?" student legalists asked. "At least as wide as a book," the deans ruled, in their Solomonic wisdom. "But then when one student came in and argued that he had been in compliance because his door had been open as wide as a *match*book," the dean concluded his reminiscence, "we decided the time had come to drop the whole business."

9 / These seven thousand students included Rutgers College students who did not commute or live off-campus, plus undergraduates from "affiliated" nonresidential colleges living in the Rutgers dorms (see appendix two). At least twice as many undergraduates had a right to be on the Rutgers College campus beyond these residential students, and thus also fell under the deans' area of responsibility—as did, to a poorly defined degree, the students living in the fraternities. The twenty-seven responsible adults consisted of the dean of students and the twenty-six individuals who reported to him: three associate deans, six assistant deans, and seventeen other full-time "professional staff" members ("Organizational Chart, Office of the Dean of Students, Rutgers College," unpublished document dated November 1986).

10 / Twenty-six were preprofessional, twenty-two had to do with sports, fourteen were college or class related, twelve had to do with minority identity, twenty-one had to do with other ethnic identities, twelve were hobby clubs, nine were military, eight were political (Republican, Democratic, Democratic Socialist, Zionist, prolife, El Salvador-related, environmental, and antinuclear), eight were religious, seven were service organizations, five had to do with music, four were literary, three were theater-related, and the last four were a feminist association, a lesbian-gay alliance, a handicapped association, and a group for student peer-counseling.

11 / In his recent nationwide survey of American colleges, Ernest Boyer reports a similar, very widespread uninterest in the older extracurricular organizations (see Boyer 1987:177–195). His assumption that they can be rebuilt by college authorities, however—

that deanly notions of "community" are likely to strike many chords with contemporary undergraduates—strikes me as somewhat naive.

12 / It had been incorporated and had a board of trustees composed of Rutgers graduates who used to work at the paper, on which the dean of students sat as a nonvoting member.

13 / At best, the fraternities gave young men an environment for single-sex peer solidarity that some of them found richer than anywhere else except on sports teams. There was a great deal on the other side of the ledger, however. First, though hazing was and is illegal under New Jersey state law, physical and psychological abuse continued to be virtually universal in the half-dozen fraternities on which I had good information in the 1980s; fraternities without hazing were almost a contradiction in terms. Second, to the degree that drinking was pushed underground in the dorms, it became even more central in the fraternities—whose members were, thanks to the peer solidarity produced by their hazing and to private ownership of their facilities, better able to conceal drinking from adult authorities. (These two systematic properties of the fraternities were apparently

the context for the very unfortunate death from alcohol toxicity of a young fraternity initiate at Lambda Chi fraternity in February 1988. And third, the fraternities regularly attracted the least progressive male students on campus—the most reactionary and the most sexist. For details on sexual attitudes and behaviors in the fraternities, see chapters 5 and 6.

14 / "The real world" is a common American idiom in the 1980s, of course. I first noticed it when a student made it linguistically productive. Four or five undergraduates were walking back to Hasbrouck Fourth after an intramural football game in a nearby park in the fall of 1984. They passed a pretty block of houses quite close to the college. Thinking ahead about off-campus housing for the following year, a sophomore said to an older and wiser junior, "Hey, there's some nice houses. Do students live there?" "No," the junior replied discouragingly. "*Real* people live in *those* houses."

15 / For a small sampler of different interpretations of the contemporary American privatized self, see Lasch 1977 and 1978; Sennett 1978; and Bellah et al. 1985.

16 / Komarovsky's recent

study of an unnamed elite women's college, probably Barnard, suggests that friendship was similarly salient there (see Komarovsky 1985: 72–82).

17 / I asked the students in a large college class in 1985 to identify their own college class, to list the "five best friends in your life at present, at Rutgers or elsewhere," and then briefly to indicate when, where, and how they had made each friend. The 114 students who responded listed over 560 friends (a few listed fewer than five). College friends made up 44 percent of the freshmen choices; most of the remainder were hometown friends from high school years and earlier. Predictably, the percentage of college friends then rose for sophomores (47 percent), juniors (59 percent), and seniors (61 percent). The relatively big jump in college friends between sophomore and junior year may be significant. It is in these years that many students stop thinking of themselves as "kids" who need the support of dorm living and visits to home and family on weekends, and decide to try off-campus housing and an independent life-style more like that of adults in the "real world." The declining proportion of hometown friends during these years may then indicate a jump in detachment from home and family.

The salience of dorm living in college friendship making also emerged on the same questionnaire. For those students who had lived at Rutgers at all (20 percent of the respondents were commuters), 13 percent of all college friends had been made in classes, 8 percent had been introduced by mutual friends, 4 percent had met through extracurricular organizations including fraternities and sororities, 4 percent had met in "social life," 2 percent had met in off-campus jobs, and 1 percent had met as roommates in off-campus housing. The remainder, two-thirds (68 percent) of all reported college friends, had been made through common dorm residence, usually through common dorm-floor living groups.

18 / As Horowitz points out, college friendships were once of more-than-sentimental value; your "old school ties" often got you a good job in the real world after college. No longer in the late twentieth century, however, for the most part. The American economy is too vast and bureaucratized, and credentials rather than personal connections get you into the professions and into most other status-bearing occupations. See Horowitz 1987:81.

19 / The literature on friendship is a very mixed one in the social sciences; and, oddly,

given what seems to be its salience in Western culture compared to among many non-Western peoples, social and cultural historians have barely touched it. Empirical sociologists love to map it, but rarely look into its meaning. The three best accounts of friendship as a cultural concept are Paine 1969; Suttles 1970; and Allan 1979. Barkas 1985 is also useful; see Brain 1976 for an interesting but analytically unfocused cross-cultural survey; and see Baker 1980 for an interesting ethnography of friendship and politics in the United States Senate.

Most accounts of American friendship tend to be highly value-laden ones. They tend to assume that the true self as contemporary Americans unreflectively believe in it really exists and that friendship is a naturally good relationship because it concerns the true self. My own approach, sketched below, is more agnostic. I see friendship and the self as two cultural mysteries— no more objectively verifiable than the odd deities believed in by many "primitive" peoples—which mutually constitute one another and which are both, in their fundamental definitions in modern American culture, intrinsically problematic.

20 / For an interesting note by two psychologists who, atypically, perceive some of the dilemmas embedded in modern American friendship concepts, and who have some psychological evidence for the existence of these dilemmas, see Roll and Millen 1979.

21 / Bust, or bust on (someone): to deflate their pretensions by means of aggressive verbal mockery. In male locker-room talk, the term was short for "to bust their chops" or "to bust their balls." The connection between friendship and busting was a particularly male connection. I didn't have much access to woman-to-woman friendship talk; in the coed dorms, women often played by male rules in any case. In 1987, I had a report from one of the allegedly better fraternities at Rutgers, which polishes off its secret initiation with a paddling done in such a way as to deliberately make the initiate's testicles ache; and see also chapter 3 on the "wedgie patrol."

22 / The only literature on "friendly" of which I am aware is Kurth 1970, an unperspicacious treatment, and Hervé Varenne's interesting refusal to analyze its meaning (Varenne 1986a).

23 / The cultural history of the American family smile also remains to be written. The years of Franklin Delano Roosevelt (the soothing patrician smile) and Dwight David Eisenhower (the

powerful-man-as-a-regular-guy smile) were obvious watersheds. To grasp the historical specificity of these looks, try to imagine Abraham Lincoln, Woodrow Wilson, or even Calvin Coolidge grinning the modern American friendly grin. Or consider whether Richard Nixon might have survived Watergate if he could have put it on as convincingly as Ike and Ronald Reagan have worn it. Or, conversely, try to imagine Miss America without it.

The relation of the smile to other social concepts can be read in some photos of Rutgers undergraduates over the years. A common genre of informal student group photo in the late nineteenth century was a painterly composition: young men in various relaxed postures, standing or sitting, intertwined or separate, looking in a carefully composed set of directions, framing themselves by their postures and their looks (see, for example, Moffatt 1985b:47, 49, or 54–55). They rarely smiled. They only incidentally looked directly at the camera. These photos say, Here is our amiable group of young men. You may gaze upon it.

The equivalent informal student group photo in the 1980s, on the other hand, virtually requires its American subjects to compose themselves into looser, more spontaneous-looking collectivities (a ragged row of youths, possibly with an arm or two around one another's shoulders), to laugh or put on the friendly smile, and to look directly into the eye of the camera (see Moffatt 1985b:243; or, for an older, deanly version, 201). These photos say, We're open friendly people. We're friendly to each other. If you were here with us, we'd be friendly to *you* too!

24 / This student, whose eulogy to a cross-sex friendship was especially fervent, happened to be black. White males—and white females and black females—said similar things, however.

25 / Most cross-cultural evidence suggests that the equivalent of friendship in non-Western cultures—disinterested, chosen relationships of diffuse emotional regard and mutual support—is most often an intrasex bond and rarely a cross-sex one. Robert Brain tries to argue for some incidence of asexual amity between persons of different sexes in African tribal cultures. His examples are highly impressionistic, however, and he does not cite many instances of these relationships (Brain 1976:50–54).

26 / This typification is based as much on what most undergraduate females did not say as on what they did say—on their apparent boredom or lack of interest when the topic of sexism was

raised. There were smaller numbers of undergraduate women in my classes in the social sciences who thought about American culture more politically and who generally had more critical views of gender. The only person I knew in the dorms who might have felt this way was Carrie (chapter 3). Komarovsky found the same sort of indifference at the women's college she studied in the early 1980s, particularly among freshmen women, with some movement away from it among certain upperclass women (see Komarovsky 1985, chapters 4 and 5).

27 / This was deliberate. I never asked about drugs in the dorms. The last thing I wanted the students to suspect me of being was a "narc."

28 / A layered, somewhat European look characteristic of the male fashion magazine "GQ," *Gentleman's Quarterly*.

29 / On the deans' initiative rather than the students', the class history was revived in the early 1980s in the form of a student commencement address. It was no longer a collective biography, however, for who could write a biography of about two thousand students? Instead it tended to be a review of local, national, and international events in the four years the class had been at Rutgers and a sanitized account of the ways in which the realities of Rutgers had helped members of the class to grow up in college.

30 / Unless otherwise indicated, these quotes are taken from self-reports that Rutgers students wrote for me in large classes taught in 1986 and 1987.

31 / The diversity of the undergraduate population at Rutgers in the 1980s is suggested by the identity of some of the extracurricular organizations in the college. There were a number of groups for blacks and for Hispanic students; and, beyond groups for these minorities, the ethnic associations included Arab, Armenian, Luso-Brazilian, Chinese, Cuban, Greek, Indian, Islamic, Korean, Lebanese, Pakistani, Filipino, Polish, Turkish, Ukrainian, Vietnamese, and West Indian clubs. (Even if most students were not very active extracurricularly, as was argued above, someone had to care enough about each of these cultural affiliations to serve as officers, to put in regular funding requests to the deans, and to talk faculty members into being advisers.)

32 / Actually, only about half of the incoming freshmen at Rutgers passed through college in just four years. Another 20 percent took five to seven years, and about 30 percent never finished—at Rutgers at least.

THREE / A Year on Hasbrouck Fourth

A DORMITORY IS A PLACE TO STORE POSSESSIONS AND SLEEP AT NIGHT—BUT A RESIDENCE HALL IS MUCH MORE. IT IS AN INTERDEPENDENT COMMUNITY WHERE STUDENTS CARE ABOUT AND RESPECT ONE ANOTHER AND A PLACE WHERE PEOPLE CAN SHARE AND LEARN FROM ONE ANOTHER.—Shaping a Community: A Guide to Residence Life at Rutgers College

COMMUNITY?

Rutgers students enjoyed much of the fun of college life, especially in their freshman and sophomore years, on their coed dorm floors among the sixty other young women and men with whom they happened to share the same level of a college residence hall in any given year. They did not need to form personal groups with these particular youths. The students could have lived anonymously in the dorms, side by side like strangers in a New York apartment house.[1] But their own peer culture, and the deans, encouraged them to link up with everyone else on their floor. And on nearly one hundred dorm floors at Rutgers every year, they almost invariably did so.

The deans characterized these student groups in an officialese that was uniquely their own. It emphasized student choice and it obfuscated deanly authority. Dorm floors should be "interdependent communities of caring individuals" who "enhanced their college experiences" together, the deans recommended. The deans "fostered" student "community-building" through the "residence life" infrastructure, through "role-models," "mediation," "programming," "non-credit courses," and "hall government." Power did not really exist in this voluntaristic world of deanly fantasy. Collective standards somehow emerged without agents; the deans were simply the custodians of an impersonal democratic process:

To protect the rights of all students, community standards have been developed. The Residence Life staff strives to uphold these standards. They provide constraints for those students who demonstrate an unwillingness to monitor their own behavior without unduly inhibiting the freedoms of those students who do. With the support of all community members, behavior problems can be kept to a minimum.[2]

The students thought about these same groups in somewhat different ways.[3] They recognized deanly authority and power, to begin with. As my student preceptor on Gate Third in 1977 put it, "There are some mean things I have to do." But if the deans believed that *they* "developed" the undergraduates through residence life—that the shaping of the students' extracurricular values was their expert task—the undergraduates, conversely, saw the dorms at their best as places for real student autonomy. The less a given dorm activity was obviously influenced by the deans, the better the undergraduates in the residence halls tended to enjoy it.

Like the deans, the students also wanted the dorm floors to be amiable places without lots of personal conflict on them. But the term "community," like "residence hall," rarely passed from their lips. Somehow "community" made the dorm floor groups sound much more earnest and intentional than they really were in student experience. A good dorm floor, most students believed, should be a relaxed place full of girls and guys who "got along," who were able to enjoy the informal pleasures of college life in an easy, personal atmosphere of their own making. Rather than being communities, dorm floors, according to student conceptions, should simply be "friendly places."

"Community" was a suspect term for another reason: its established position in the official rhetoric of late-twentieth-century American individualism. For, in addition to being open, friendly individuals (see chapter 2), well-socialized American adults in the 1980s are supposed to desire community. Real communities in Western or Third World societies consist of people who have to get along with one another on a daily basis. They usually do not have much choice about the matter. Real communities thus constrain or even define the individual. A village in south India is one example; a department of tenured faculty members in an American university is another. "Community," in its contemporary American ideological sense, on the other hand, is often an individualistic concept masquerading as a sociological one. It usually means something like "people who choose to live together or work together due to common interests." Moreover, it is a word used by leaders, spokespersons, and publicists much more often than it is by ordinary folk. The late-twentieth-century political meaning of "community" tends to be "people who *ought* to choose to live or work together due to some common interest, as defined by me."

These meanings aside, "community," like "diversity" and the other key phrases of modern American individualism, is almost empty of specific content. It no longer even necessarily has to refer to a face-to-face group with a small, well-defined territorial base. Thus, cartoonist Gary Trudeau can make one of his characters belong to "the homeless community." Thus, Rutgers undergraduates can live in the "greater New York community," the "Rutgers community," the "undergraduate community" and their own "dorm communities."[4]

Communities or not, the friendly groups of students who formed on every dorm floor every year at Rutgers did have certain recurrent sociological characteristics in common, however. Their human ingredients: undergraduates from similar provincial suburban hometowns of central and northern New Jersey. Their cultural contexts: contemporary American popular culture in its late-adolescent version, "college life" and American individualism as sources of shared interests and values among many of the residents. Their ecologies: similar spatial layouts for student sociability. Their micropolitical structures: standard bureaucratized systems of local control under the supervision of the deans (residence counselors, preceptors, and so on). And an ideal: a loosely formulated but very pervasive one concerning collective harmony or friendliness.

No two dorm floors ever worked out alike, however, and neither floor community nor floor friendliness was easily achieved. Most actual dorm floor groups amounted to varying mixes of collective success and failure. The members of every dorm floor acted out, over the course of a year of common residence and personal acquaintanceship, their own collective dramas, which they themselves reviewed and summed up now and again. This chapter is the story of one such annual student collectivity as I was able to know it, on the fourth floor of Hasbrouck Hall, where I did research a day and night a week in the academic year starting in 1984. Who were the main actors? What was the stage on which they performed? And what collective script did they write, half-deliberately and half-accidentally, in collaboration with one another all year long?[5]

DRAMATIS PERSONAE

By the time I moved onto Hasbrouck Fourth in early September 1984, I was an old pro in the dorms, a veteran of three freshman orientations and one previous full year of day-a-week residence. I knew one other dorm-floor group through intensive firsthand participant observation (see chapter 4); I knew another dozen or more through more casual observations and through research papers written by my students in cultural anthropology. And, at first in 1984, Hasbrouck Fourth seemed to be loaded with potential for the best kind of lively, sociable relationships among its student residents.

The Preceptor

The leading actor, Pete, the senior preceptor, appeared to be a capable and experienced student leader. He initiated residence life on the floor at the beginning of the year with some esprit, putting the new freshmen through the required deanly rituals of orientation, "icebreakers" and the rest, more vigorously than many other preceptors did. And he promoted the floor with what sounded like real enthusiasm. He had lived in Hasbrouck Hall all four years at Rutgers, he told the freshmen, and the year before he had also been the preceptor on Hasbrouck Fourth. And the floor had been lots of fun last year. It had had great parties; it had organized its own spring "semiformal" at a nearby hotel; it had even designed its own T-shirt. Pete held up an example, a bright red shirt bearing a vigorous, crudely drawn King Kong who danced on the roof of the dorm (Hasbrouck Fourth was the top floor of Hasbrouck Hall), partying and terrorizing passing students in the street below. This year, Pete promised the new students, they could have just as good a floor if they worked at it. Many of last year's residents were coming back. "Wait till you meet them," Pete promised the freshmen. "They're *crazy!* They're also very di*verse!*"

In my first few days on Hasbrouck Fourth, I was so impressed with Pete that I kidded a residence life dean about him. The dean had placed me on a floor with a preceptor this good, I claimed, so that the Rutgers residence life program would look particularly good in my research.[6]

More privately a few days later, however, Pete expressed some reservations about his job in 1984. Last year, though he had been the local authority, he had also been very much one of the boys—enjoying floor fun himself, keeping the lid on it, making sure that no one on Hasbrouck Fourth got in trouble with any higher authorities. Over the summer, however, he said he felt he'd "grown up a lot." He had gone off to a summer program in France (posters of the French countryside adorned his walls) and had established a serious romance with a woman from a nearby college, who would be staying with him in his room on weekends. "I don't know if I can take all this any more," he said in a moment of meditation about what now seemed to him like the juvenilities of dorm culture. "I want to get on with my life."

Pete also had ambitious academic plans for his senior year: a senior honors thesis in his major, psychology, and a good graduate school subsequently; or, if that did not work out, high school teaching as a "fallback strategy." He was also finishing up a certificate in education and was scheduled for practice teaching in a nearby public high school in the fall. Hasbrouck Fourth would have to be a mature floor, Pete warned the freshmen during orientation. The residents would have to learn to get along with one another without having a preceptor around all the time to mind them.

Other Upperclassmen

Many of the returning students soon lived up to their notices. Most of them were sophomores. In 1984–1985, 85 percent of residents of Hasbrouck Fourth were freshmen and sophomores, not uncommon percentages in the Rutgers dorms. But, more atypically, the sophomores outnumbered the freshmen, thirty-five to eighteen.[7] The two college classes were also skewed by sex. Thirteen of the eighteen freshmen on the floor were females, while twenty-three of the thirty-five sophomores were males. A rowdy year seemed possible. The sexual year was more difficult to predict.

Among the returning residents, it was difficult to miss Dan and his friends, six variously extroverted, assertive, and physically big sophomore males.[8] Dan was a good-looking young man from a north Jersey city, a major in economics; but he studied so little in his sophomore year that he almost flunked out. He had a vivid personal style, a strong white ethnic identity, and his first love was theater; he was minoring in it. A poster of the young Marlon Brando had pride-of-place on his wall. Dan and four of his friends lived on the same side of the floor as I did, on the "low side," named for its lower room numbers, 401 through 414. A sixth friend, Tim,

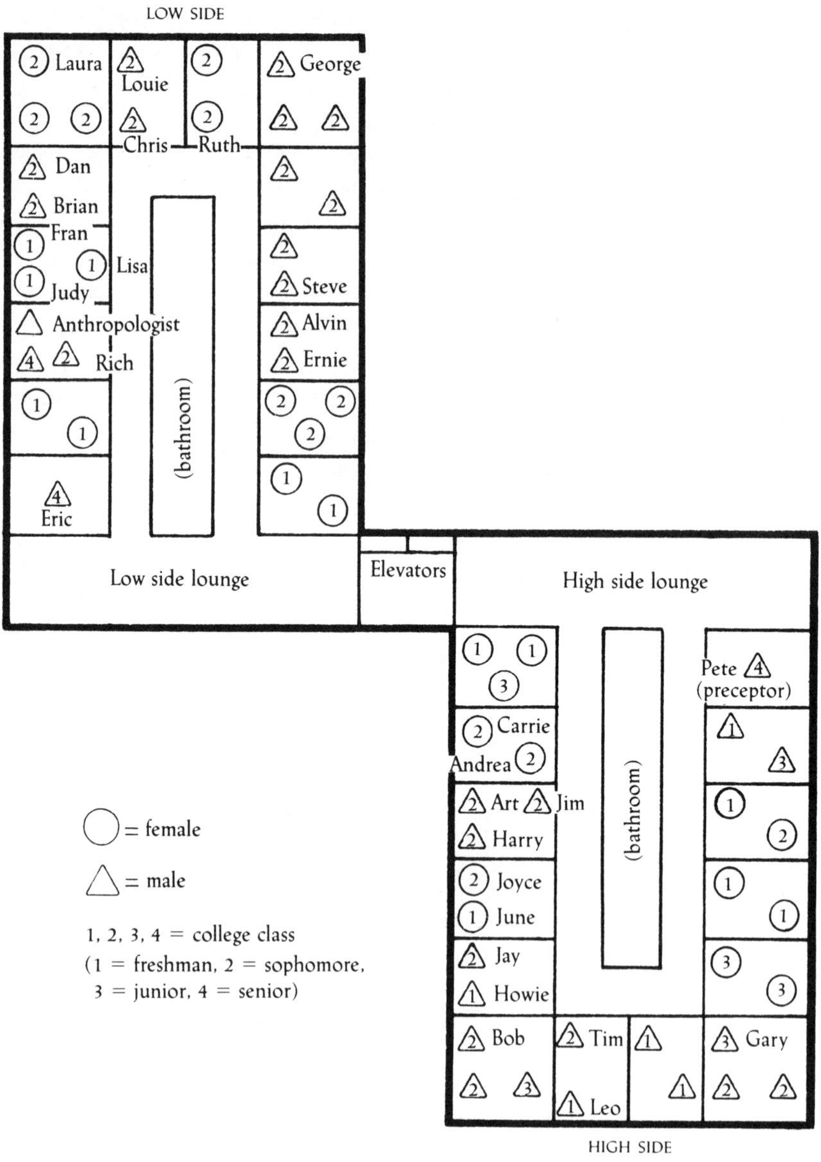

LOW SIDE

HIGH SIDE

◯ = female

△ = male

1, 2, 3, 4 = college class
(1 = freshman, 2 = sophomore,
3 = junior, 4 = senior)

FIGURE 2 / Hasbrouck Fourth, 1984–1985 (not to scale)
(some architectural details changed or omitted)

a second-generation Japanese-American, had been stranded over on the "high side" (rooms 415 through 428) by the luck of the room lottery. All these youths had lived next to one another on Hasbrouck Fourth the year before (see figure 2).[9]

Dan and his friends were very friendly toward the new freshmen, especially toward some of the new freshman females. Only one of them had any erotic success with any of these young women, however, and a few months later they were noticeably less friendly. Among themselves, Dan and his friends spoke in a colorful, ever-changing argot that marked the boundaries of their clique. Dumb people or losers were "Zekes"—but by an odd linguistic inversion, they themselves were also Zekes. Anything inauthentic was "bogus." "Good-bye" was "I'm outta here" or "I'm history." Being certain about anything was being "etched" on it (from the expression "etched in stone"). Napping was "catchin' zees."[10]

Living near these characters were Louie and his roommate Chris. Louie was a charming hustler, a self-proclaimed womanizer, and another economics major.[11] Louie also made some early attempts to date several of the new women on the floor but then lost interest. Chris was quieter and had an old high-school girlfriend to whom he was trying to be faithful. Louie and Chris had won the Best Roommates award on Hasbrouck Fourth the previous year. They posed for my camera one day in the fall, holding their award, taking the male 'homosexual ironic' stance (see chapter 2)—dressed only in shorts, Louie up against Chris, dollar bills stuffed in his shorts like a go-go dancer, a leg thrown intimately over Chris's thigh. They spent much of their leisure time in the first few months in the company of the girls in the next room, two pretty young women who smiled a lot and almost always allowed themselves to be dominated in public by Louie.

On the high side, I also noticed Bob and his roommates early in the semester, two sophomores and a junior, all of them new to Hasbrouck Fourth. Everyone on the floor soon referred to them as the "DUK brothers," for their fraternity, whose activities filled their talk and whose emblems filled their room. Bob was brash and friendly; his roommates kept more to themselves. Also on the high side were Gary and his two roommates, two more returning sophomores and one junior. They seemed rather self-contained, though two of them did sit around regularly in the lounge in a friendly fashion. But they looked tough; they looked as if they lifted weights. The third, whom we hardly ever saw, spent a great deal of time in ROTC activities. Since the year before, he had been known on Hasbrouck Fourth as "Soldier Sam." Uniquely among the residents of the

77

floor, Soldier Sam never consented to be interviewed and never filled out any of the eight or nine brief questionnaires that I circulated to the residents over the nine months of my research on Hasbrouck Fourth. Over the year, I found myself developing a certain respect for the purity of his attitude toward being a subject of research.

One last sophomore friendship group was very visible on Hasbrouck Fourth from early September. One member was Carrie, a lively black woman with a punk haircut. She was unusually assertive and outspoken for a woman in the dorms, as likely to initiate "busting" as any male (see chapter 2)—a politically aware student who seemed to enjoy challenging conventional opinions wherever she encountered them. Andrea, her white roommate, was a very close friend. The two of them shared artistic interests and, at the beginning of the year, an active, unattached social life. To my male eyes, Andrea was also an exceptionally sexy young woman; and in the first month or two, she flaunted her sexuality more openly than most females did in the ordinary erotic etiquette of the coed living group, I thought (see chapter 5).

Art, one of their next-door neighbors, was tall, intense, unpredictable, and every bit as vivid a personality as Carrie. He liked to play mental games with people, defending his ego with frequent, well-performed comic routines, many of them based on characters created by comedians Eddie Murphy and Joe Piscopo on the TV show "Saturday Night Live." His roommate Harry was quieter but no more conventional. Harry's central personal value was what he called "bizarrity." He enjoyed wearing odd clothing combinations and saying odd things, and he patronized movies with names like Skin Heads, Moving Men from Outer Space, and Repo Man. Jim, their roommate, seemed to be just a pleasant, regular guy with a good word for everyone.

Joyce and June, their next-door neighbors, struck me as similarly uncomplicated. June, the only freshman in this friendship group, simply seemed happy to be included in a sophomore clique at all. Joyce was a pretty kid with a sunny disposition. She had a boyfriend somewhere else, but she seemed fond of Harry, and he appeared to like her in return.

There were also some free-floaters among the sophomores on Hasbrouck Fourth, I realized in early September, residents who were not part of any of the larger cliques on the floor. One of my favorites was Ruth, who had switched to Rutgers after her freshman year at Douglass, Rutgers's old sister school. Ruth evidently studied all the time—in her room, in the library, or half-seriously in the low-side lounge. Another free-floater was Steve, also a low-sider, who had achieved a straight A average as a freshman but as a sophomore was shifting his energies away from academics and into student journalism, on which he said he was spending forty hours a week in the fall. At the end of my first month on Hasbrouck Fourth, Steve published a well-written story about my research in one of the student newspapers, which made it easier for me to introduce myself to new undergraduate subjects for some weeks to come. ("Did you read about that professor in the *Review* who's studying students? Well, I'm him.") He wore a neat beard and looked older than the average Hasbrouck Fourth resident; he looked a little like a young assistant professor. And I found out later that, in the early days of the semester before I had met everyone personally on the floor, he had told a few residents that *he* was the rumored anthropologist on the floor and that they should tell *him* all their secrets.

A third free-floater was Jay, a returning sophomore on the high side. Jay worked very hard at his joint majors, English and political science. I sometimes read over his papers for him, and he did good work. He tended to dress preppie, he had the style of a smart know-it-all, and he bragged occasionally about his rich, well-traveled father. Jay was not the most popular resident of Hasbrouck Fourth in 1984–1985, but as far as I could tell, the other students did not actively discriminate against him, not in the friendly ambience of the floor lounges, at least. He was often right there at the center of the informal talk sessions, expressing himself as forcefully as anyone else.

THE STAGE

The residents of Hasbrouck Fourth were housed as they were on most dorm floors at Rutgers in the 1980s, two and three to a room, alternating by sex as one moved along the corridors (see figure 2). The rooms were small and utilitarian. Their tile floors were uncarpeted; each contained a desk, a chair, a dresser, and a bed for each resident, plus a few lights; and the residents had between about fifty and eighty square feet of floor space per person.[12] There was no air conditioning, and in the muggy heat of the early fall and the late spring, I sometimes caught myself thinking back fondly on my field site, on my comfortable, airy thatched hut in a south Indian low-caste hamlet.

Each room looked out on the world through an aluminum-framed double window (see map 1, chapter 1). For me, the view ameliorated the crowding within. Nearby were other high-rise dorms, all built in the 1950s in a style that could be called Low-rent Institutional Modern. Only the red brick in their rectilinear walls referred to older types of American college architecture. To the southeast were prettier parts of the campus: the lovely Federalist and Gothic Revival buildings of the original college, now monopolized by the upper administration of "Rutgers, The State University of New Jersey"; early-twentieth-century classroom buildings covered with ivy; and fraternity row, rather a tacky one by the standards of most older American colleges. Just north ran the Raritan river—gulls and Canada geese and ducks all year long, egrets and other waterfowl in the spring—and the greener park and suburban treeline beyond. Down the river to the right was the bridge to my hometown. From the top floor of a nearby dorm, I could almost see the roof of my little two-story house a mile and a half away.

Back in the dorm, the interiors of the student rooms did not remain institutional looking for long. Soon they were full of astonishing amounts of personal paraphernalia: rugs, stereos, tape decks, record and tape collections, TVs and VCRs, small refrigerators, hot plates, hot pots, microwave ovens, beer bottle collections, bars for liquor, athletic equipment, stuffed-animal collections and other juvenile items—a rubber ducky and a small plastic train set in one male's room on Hasbrouck Fourth—the occasional illegal waterbed. Even books! Individualism penetrated the rooms. Roommates expected each other to respect personal property; roommates who were close friends still almost always decorated their walls separately ("This wall's mine, that one's yours").

No two rooms were identical in decor, but recurrent motifs included good-looking, minimally-clad young adults of the opposite sex, which were about as common and about as near-nude in women's rooms as in men's, and favorite stars of music, television, and the movies. Males were more likely to display athletic equipment, the paraphernalia of drinking, and other emblems of youthful bravado in their rooms. The stolen road sign, for instance, dates back at least a hundred years in Rutgers student culture. Females were more likely to mount evidence of artistic tastes and of continuing childlike qualities. Stuffed-animal collections were much more common with "girls" than with "guys." One young man on Hasbrouck Fourth did have a single teddy bear on display, usually sitting in the middle of his neatly made bed. He also lifted weights, however, and he was careful to explain to the interested visitor that the teddy bear was a gift from his girlfriend.

Some residents put only a little effort into the personalization of their rooms. My sophomore roommate Rich pledged a fraternity in 1984, and he was around on Hasbrouck Fourth so little all year long that he periodically had to ask *me* who was who and what was going on. His wall iconography consisted entirely of a large Mickey Mouse logo, a photo of a favorite sports car, and a poster of Ronald Reagan with a missile through his head. He had an excellent tape deck and a fine collection of contemporary popular music, however, which I enjoyed listening to with him late at night.

Carrie and Andrea, on the other hand, were known on the floor for their "interesting" room. Early in the fall, it combined daily clutter equal to that of the most stereotypically messy male rooms—open dresser drawers, clothing of every sort strewn on the floor, unmade beds—with intricate wall design. Though Carrie and Andrea had decorated different walls, the room looked coherent as a whole, like what it was, the single space shared by two good friends. One evening Carrie spent half an hour annotating one of her walls for me. Up and down its twelve-foot length were dozens of different emblems of her tastes in poetry and popular music, her regional origins in New Jersey, and her sexuality. It was hard to miss the enormous pharmaceutical poster advertising a birth control device directly over her bed or the "Who's for sex?" scrawled near the top. The wall also displayed cryptic references to local incidents that had already occurred on Hasbrouck Fourth, including a pair of panties hung up to spoof the "wedgie patrol" (see below), and references to the use of an illegal substance. Perhaps as interesting as what the wall did show was what it did not. You probably wouldn't have known from the wall alone that Carrie was black. But you would have known that she was proud of her punk identity.

The doors to the rooms almost always carried the erasable message boards by which the students kept track of their callers, and occasionally there were collages or other visual displays. But once across their thresholds, the personal imagery dropped abruptly away. Once out into the corridors, one moved into the semipublic area of the floor. And here the walls were all almost entirely unadorned: brick or cinder block on Hasbrouck Fourth, with a few half-tended bulletin boards, and thermostats that seemed to work on the placebo principle. There was a public phone booth in the corridor on each side of the floor, and students in perhaps a third of the rooms quickly had their own private phones installed. A collection of utilitarian furniture squatted bleakly in each lounge: a formica table and plastic chairs, butcher-block easy chairs and a sofa chained together against theft. And more aluminum windows from which to look out onto the world.

The lounges and the corridors may have appeared impersonal, but in the tacit social conventions among the undergraduates, they were only semipublic spaces. If, as a stranger, you walked confidently through or directly to a private room, no one would challenge your presence on the floor. But if you hung around uncertainly or sat down in one of the lounges, a resident would usually ask you who you were and what you wanted within a few minutes. The lounges and the corridors were spaces for friendly behavior between known floor residents. Much of the more amiable fooling around on the floor occurred in them: wrestling between friends of either sex, golf and floor football among some males on Hasbrouck Fourth—the latter played on hands and knees, with a foam rubber ball—and endless talk.

Hasbrouck Fourth, like other floors in Rutgers dorms of this design, was divided into two sections, each with fourteen rooms, one lounge, and one big bathroom. Like virtually all Americans, according to almost all sociometric research, Rutgers dorm residents tended to make their best friends from among those persons closest to them in space. So you were more likely to know and to be friends with the residents of your own section than with those of the other side of the floor. But this was only a tendency. There were many exceptions. Two things encouraged friendliness and real friendships across the sections: the preceptorial system, expressly designed to foster floor community through common floor meetings, programming, counseling, mediation, and so on; and—far earthier—the bathrooms. In any semester, one of the two bathrooms on the floor was for women only and the other was for men, with a reversal of assignments the following semester. Thus you met people from the opposite section every day under very intimate circumstances, either walking past the opposite lounge in your bathrobe or being walked past, or, with same-sex persons, dishabille in the showers or around the washbasins in the bathrooms.

The bathrooms (three toilets, three urinals, five washbasins, and four showers) were the least-pleasant areas on the floor, often smelly and dirty, especially after liquor-laden weekends. Professional janitors did their best to keep them clean. They were the only adults who were around the floor on a daily basis. In the 1980s, they were usually working-class Latin women and men who lived in the slums of downtown New Brunswick.[13]

OPENING SCENES

The preceptor, Pete, raised the curtain on Hasbrouck Fourth with the first floor meeting of the year, held on a Wednesday evening in early September. Pete made a series of announcements, and, sounding a demented basso profoundo, Dan's clique and a few of the other returning sophomore men busted on him, loudly and incessantly, all through the meeting. With the new residents as an audience, they were clearly laying claim to their old friendly male connections with Pete, established the year before:

> *Visiting Residence Counselor:* Pete is a great preceptor. I know him from last year. I guarantee you, if you help him out, you'll have a great floor this year. If you help him, Pete, Pete will do *anything* for you.

> *Sophomores:* Yeah, especially you *girls!* You do anything for Pete, he won't forget you. Pete *loves* girls who do anything for him!

Pete took the sophomores' mockery in apparent good humor. But, along with his new, private ambivalence about his job, he had another problem, which was not his own doing. He had some bad news for his old friends, some new dorm regulations they were not going to like at all.

College Drinking

For a decade, liquor had flowed freely among American college students. The liberalization of the late 1960s had driven minimum drinking ages down all across the country. Rutgers was no exception; the college had even had its own student pub, the Rusty Screw, open to anyone eighteen years old or older. And in the dorms, the single most popular event by which the students had built their notion of floor "community" had been the floor party, usually thrown once a semester on every dorm floor for many guests—with beer kegs and highly potent punch and other liquor in the lounges. But now things were about to change drastically, back toward older pre-1960s college alcohol protocols outside the memory of modern students. For the state of New Jersey had raised the minimum drinking age back up to the age of twenty-one. And university officials had ruled that liquor was now forbidden to underage drinkers—to about two-thirds of the undergraduates and to all but a few of the residents of the dormitories—anywhere "in public" in the college.

Still respecting more recent understandings about the demise of in loco parentis, the officials had declared that whatever the students did behind the closed doors of their own private dorm rooms was their own business. "In public," however, explicitly included those parts of the dorm that the students tended to think of as their own collective private spaces, the corridors and lounges of the dorm floors. Pete explained this very clearly as he announced the new policies in the first meeting, to catcalls and hoots of contempt from the sophomores. "They" really meant it this time, Pete said. He would *have* to write up any residents he caught even walking from one dorm room to another with open beers in their hands; he would have to report them to higher authorities for possible disciplinary action. There were also imprecise guidelines about the point at which a few friends in a dorm room turned into a more public, more illegal party, he tried to explain—fifteen people to a room, or twenty-five, he was not really sure.[14]

Pete sounded angry about these announcements, and a grouchy tone that I had not heard from him before crept into his voice, almost as if he resented the Hasbrouck Fourth residents for making it necessary for him to enforce such dumb, unpopular rulings. The sophomores wondered how the deans expected them to make the floor a friendly place, on the one hand, while taking away their favorite collective activity on the other. Pete delivered the deans' line in response—there were other things the residents could do together. They could have other kinds of parties ("How can you have a *party* without liquor?" some students asked in disbelief).[15] They could hold interesting programs. Money was available for a bus trip to New York City. The sophomores were not convinced, however, and the first floor meeting of the year on Hasbrouck Fourth ended in cacophony.

The sophomores apparently took Pete at his word about the toughness of the new drinking regulations, but they also immediately began scheming about ways to circumvent them. The very next evening, some ex-residents of Hasbrouck Fourth from the year before—a group of seniors with a big house on Henry Street, a half-mile from campus—threw a big off-campus party, a "three-kegger." Dan and his friends saw to it that everyone from Hasbrouck Fourth was invited. Some of the new freshmen drank so much that they had to be helped back to the dorm afterward, the sophomores reported contentedly later. Many students also drank all the harder in their rooms. Perhaps a dozen had little refrigerators for cold beer, and there was at least one private bar among the students on the floor. Many of the men and some of the women possessed fake identification cards for use in public places and exchanged information about which off-campus bars were easiest which nights of the week. One evening I nursed a beer at a favorite college hangout and had the genuine pleasure of being "carded" myself, at the age of forty-one, while four underage friends put away drinks with names like Zombie and Red Death and Kamikaze.

And two months later, in early November, after extensive planning, Dan and Louie and Chris collaborated on a de facto floor party one Thursday evening when they had determined that Pete would be out. They emptied Dan's room entirely of furniture and equipped it with a bar, a stereo, and two kegs of beer. They established Louie and Chris's room as a quiet room for talk and for extra guests, and the girls next door donated their room for even more intimate pleasures. They invited a dozen select guests to come early, to warm up on "[Bloody] Marys." And they invited over ninety guests to come later on, counting on them to show up at different hours and to move in and out of the drinking-and-dancing room so that it would never have more than about thirty people in it at any one time. They kept an eye on its door and monitored the noise level. No one got written up. Dan, Louie, and Chris were very pleased with themselves for several weeks after the party.

Hazing: The Wedgie Patrol

The new liquor regulations provided the first dramatic tension on Hasbrouck Fourth in 1984, early plot complications inflicted upon the floor by higher authorities. The next challenge to the floor's equanimity, however, came from within. I had only lived on Hasbrouck Fourth for a few days when I began to hear rumors of activities that reminded me of some of the cruder customs in older American undergraduate culture. I had thought such things had entirely died out or had been suppressed by the deans. And, in fact, I never heard any stories of similar carryings-on anywhere else in the college in the 1980s. Something called the "wedgie patrol" was abroad in the late hours of the night on Hasbrouck Fourth, I was told.

Soon I heard a lot more,[16] and one day I was directed to a display of ritual objects: five or six pairs of torn white men's underwear tacked up on

Dan's door. The perpetrators, once again, were the rowdiest of the returning sophomore males, Dan and his friends. At two or three in the morning, when most of the night owls on the floor had finally gone to sleep, the marauders insinuated their way into the rooms of other males on the floor ("Jay, there's a phone call for you out here . . ."). New male students and unpopular older ones were snatched from their beds, usually sleeping only in their underwear,[17] and "hoisted" by the tops of their "'wares" until the garments shredded, leaving them naked and confused, sometimes with cloth burns on intimate parts of their anatomy, at the center of a circle of laughing attackers. In vulgar male talk among the students of the 1980s, to "bust someone's balls" was usually metaphoric: to make verbal fun of them in an aggressive way. The wedgie as an action collapsed the metaphor, making the phrase very literal indeed.

The correct manly response to a wedgie attack, according to its perpetrators, was to take it in good humor. The patrol had started the previous year, some of the sophomores said, when Hasbrouck Fourth had had lots of freshmen men on it. It had been initiated by a junior clique on the floor, guys all from the same New Jersey hometown who had stuck together for three years at Rutgers. They were still together in 1984. They were the "Henry Street guys," the hosts of the off-campus party above. Last year's juniors had wedgied last year's freshmen, and then each freshman victim had happily joined the patrol, its aficionados claimed. "Last year, the patrol brought us all together!" This year, in 1984, the old freshmen, now returning sophomores, were seeking to make the patrol into a tradition on Hasbrouck Fourth. They were, of course, also following the old principle of asymmetric reciprocity in undergraduate hazing: What was done to me last year *I* get to do to someone else this year.

The patrol was not popular on Hasbrouck Fourth in 1984, however. For one thing, the demographics of the floor were very different; there were only five freshmen males on it in 1984. ("We would *never* wedgie a girl!" one sophomore said in shocked response to an anthropological query about the fundamental rules of the game.) And the first two freshmen men the patrol attacked did not enjoy the experience at all. One was Howie, a pleasant, nervous young man who had expected "more academic types like me" at Rutgers than he found. The second was Tim's freshman roommate Leo. Leo appeared to be an ordinary fun-loving New Jersey adolescent, and he did love drinking and partying. He was actually Argentinean, but without a detectable accent because he had come to the United States at the age of ten. His early Latin American socialization might not have prepared him for collegiate assaults on his genitals; he was, in any case, extremely angry about his nighttime wedgie attack. He made it very clear that he had no desire whatsoever to join the patrol, and he tried to find a new roommate for a week or two until the patrol cooled off and left him alone.

Other members of Hasbrouck Fourth also profoundly disapproved of the patrol in 1984. Its activities, which had apparently originated in early-adolescent male locker-room culture, were "high school stuff" in the opinions of most of the residents of the floor. Carrie really wanted to be friends with Tim, but she simply couldn't, she said, for in his heart all Tim really was was the "wedgiemaster." Which was a fundamentally stupid thing to be, Carrie thought. Art, Jim, and Harry thought that the patrol was equally dumb.

Other stories began to be told about Hasbrouck Fourth the year before. The wedgie patrol had been a favorite activity on the high side that year, according to Chris. (Room assignments had been different the previous year.) "They were like a fraternity over there last year," Chris added. He and Louie had lived on the low side, "where we were more individualistic." Chris and Louie were not close friends with Dan and his friends in 1984, in part because of their disapproval of the patrol originating from the previous year. "They're really a bunch of bozos," Louie declared, "not that I don't get along with them or anything." Ditto, in the opinion of Gary and his roommates; ditto, in the opinion of Jay. George, one of the patrollers in 1984, inadvertently confirmed these stories of floor conflict the previous year. One night last year, he said, a very big, muscular junior male from the other side had, for some reason, "gone berserk" and tried to beat down George's door, shouting, "No more of this patrol *bull*shit!!"—while George and one of his friends had cowered inside in fear.

In 1984, Dan and his friends declared that the other residents of Hasbrouck Fourth were not going to "bully" them into giving up their nocturnal fun. But they took the patrol elsewhere (down to the third floor, where there happened to be many more freshmen men in 1984), and by mid-October the patrol had died out as a visible activity on Hasbrouck Fourth, apparently killed off by the collective disapproval of most of the residents of the floor. Though I did not notice it at the time, however, the preceptor, Pete, was oddly absent from all the stories—old ones and new ones alike—that were told about the wedgie patrol on Hasbrouck Fourth.

INTERLUDE

Despite these early conflicts, daily routines and ordinary sociability became established among the residents of Hasbrouck Fourth in the first two months of 1984 much as they had on other college dorm floors in other years. The sophomore males tried to teach the freshmen the underside of college life by telling them stories of the wild and crazy things they had done the year before. They had stolen Pete's stereo after he lectured them all on the importance of locking up and then walked out of his own room leaving the door unlocked; they had thrown flaming paper airplanes off the roof; they had carried out some particularly legendary Secret Santa stunts (see below). Early this year, they had lugged a drunken, passed-out friend in his underwear into one of the two elevators in the dorm, to go up and down all night grossing out the other dorm residents.[18] The sophomores also passed on a few pieces of nonsensical student folklore. "Do you know that if your roommate commits suicide, the deans have to give you 4.0 [a straight A average] that semester?"

Occasionally a few upperclassmen engaged in a little light, ad hoc hazing. Irritated by a loud, especially naive freshman, Gary and his roommates invited him into their room one evening for a few glasses of the fruit punch they had mixed up. They warned him with a wink to watch out for it. After he rapidly began to show signs of intoxication, they told him, and everyone else on the floor for a few days, that it had contained nothing but fruit juice and club soda. He quieted down for a few weeks.

Floor Friendliness

Most of the freshmen on Hasbrouck Fourth, interviewed privately in the first weeks of the semester, said they were impressed and relieved by the general friendliness of the other students on the floor, especially of the knowledgeable upperclassmen. They were grateful for the chance to establish personal relationships so quickly in college, particularly given the size, impersonality, and confusion of most of Rutgers outside the dorms. A few of them also said, however, that the ambience of the dorms was more juvenile than they had expected in college, and a few others were surprised at how little studying some of their upperclass exemplars appeared to do. Half a dozen freshmen said they were particularly surprised at the amount of drinking that went on.

The sophomores and some of the other upperclassmen also set examples for the sensible use of daily and weekly time for the freshmen. Avoid classes before eleven or so in the morning. Look for floor friends for lunches and dinners; nap in the afternoon if a morning schedule was absolutely necessary; spend some friendly time in the lounge every day, especially before an early dinner (around four in the afternoon) and after an evening of studying. To bed at one or two in the morning after quieter talks with closer friends, or perhaps after a little "David Letterman" or some other late-night TV comic. Avoid Friday classes. Thursday nights were the big party nights; then home or somewhere else for the long weekend, and back to campus Sunday afternoon, perhaps warming up for the next week with the first real studying of the weekend.

Not everyone followed these routines. They were only a kind of well-known average. And not all students oriented themselves to Hasbrouck Fourth as their main unit of college sociability. Sixteen of the sixty-two residents in 1984–1985 were not part of everyday society on the floor. About half of them were juniors and seniors, many of whom had special dispensation. "Who's that guy who lives in 401?" a freshman asked the sophomore Steve in October. "Oh, that's Eric," Steve explained: "He's a senior. He's a good guy. But he's very busy. He's on the campus fee board. That's an important position. He's also working his butt off on an honors thesis in economics. He's a hotshot. He's gonna get into Harvard law school." Other absentees were freshmen and sophomores with their commitments elsewhere—my fraternity roommate Rich, a girl with a boyfriend in another dorm, a kid from a nearby hometown who had never really made the break from home.

You were not a bad person if you did not hang out on the floor; you were just a nonperson. A much worse thing to be was a person who was around a lot but not friendly. Then you were in trouble. Then you were a snob. If you didn't watch it, you might open your door one day to find some local vigilantes "mooning" you in disapproval, or someone might fill a large garbage can with water, balance it against your door, knock, and disappear.[19]

Accordingly, most of the remaining forty-six residents of Hasbrouck Fourth spent varying amounts of time together in the fall of 1984 in the lounges, in private rooms, at Commons, going out visiting or partying with one another at night, going to classes together when they happened to have them in common, and so on. This was friendly time. You necessarily spent some of it with floor acquaintances you were not especially crazy about as individuals, but you tried to spend more of it with your "real" friends on the floor.[20]

The Discourse of the Dorm

In the lounges, the sophomores also soon taught the freshmen to talk the dominant mode of discourse in the undergraduate peer group. It might be labeled "Undergraduate Cynical." In different forms, it is probably a very old speech genre in American college culture.[21] It can be seen as the polar opposite of Deanly Officialese, or of Faculty Lofty. Its attitudinal stance is "wise to the ways of the world." In it, moral, ethical, and intellectual positions are rapidly reduced to the earthiest possible motives of those who articulate them; in it, everyone who participates or is referred to is treated in the same way—leveled—made equal by the joke-and-insult-impregnated discourse of contemporary American friendly busting.

As the students spoke Undergraduate Cynical in the dorms, friends and acquaintances and one's own self were mocked at firsthand, and other people and other kinds of pretension were made fun of at a distance.[22] The students might complain to one another about the rigors of higher education:

> I really hate the teaching in my poly sci classes. They give you a lot of reading and lectures and then tell you to figure things out for yourself. There's a thousand questions the professor can ask. "Relate this to that." . . . I wish they'd have textbooks that just told you everything you need to know. Enough of this enlightened bullshit!—Freshman male, Erewhon Third, 1978

Or they might discuss among themselves various ways of beating the system, as did two upperclassmen on Hasbrouck Fourth in the spring of 1985.

> *Al:* Hey, John, how was that exam? Was it a cake exam?[23]

> *John:* Yeah. The prof said up to five answers were correct for every question.

> *Al:* Good, good. That means you can definitely argue points with him.[24]

At first I mistook Undergraduate Cynical for a privileged form of truth, for what the undergraduates really thought among themselves when all their defenses were down. Eventually I realized that, as a code of spoken discourse, Undergraduate Cynical could be just as mandatory and just as coercive as other forms of discourse. You could say some very important things in it, things that you really were not allowed to say elsewhere. It was definitely fun to talk it once you learned its rules, and I certainly enjoyed my regular bouts of it throughout my research. But you could not necessarily say everything that you really thought in it, any more than a dean speaking in public could easily stop emphasizing consensus and community among all those who "worked together" at Rutgers and suddenly start ventilating her or his personal animosities toward a particular administrative rival.

Imagine, for instance, that you were an undergraduate who had been reading a sonnet by the poet Shelley for a classroom assignment, and that it had really swept you away. Unless you enjoyed being a figure of fun, you would not have dared to articulate your feelings for the poem with any honesty in the average peer-group talk in the average dorm lounge. You might, on the other hand, have discussed such sentiments more privately with trusted friends. Ordinarily, the dorm lounge and its near-mandatory code did not allow you to say what the "real you" believed, either intellectually or in other ways. The dorm lounge was more often an arena for peer-group posing in which, acting friend*ly*, you presented the "as if" you.[25]

There were many nuances, subtleties, and variations in the modes of lounge talk, however. In unpredictable ways, peer-group talk could shift from purely cycnical into more sincere, earnest expressions of meanings and feelings, even when it was not between close friends. In mid-September, while I was still getting to know the residents of Hasbrouck Fourth and while they were still sorting each other out, I touched off one of these talk sessions. In it, the student voices moved back and forth through a number of stances. Sometimes they were bullshitting. Sometimes they were simply being playful. Sometimes they were talking from the heart, evidently trying to present the "real me." Often they were trying to seize conversational control. And almost always, they were performing.

Louie had been hustling as usual, in an ironic mode he often used, simultaneously making fun of himself for hustling as he hustled: "Here I am, Mike, an unknown college sophomore, lost in the dorms at Rutgers. You're my big chance. You can make me famous. When are you gonna interview me? You *gotta* interview me!" So I decided to give him an interview I had been developing privately to elicit some simple cultural meanings. Except, as an experiment, I decided to give it to Louie around his peers rather than in private. We sat down with a tape recorder in a corner of the high-side lounge at about seven o'clock one evening early in the semester.

Fifteen feet away, Carrie was quietly reading a book and apparently minding her own business; two freshmen girls sat near her.

I led off with my standard opening question in this interview. I was a man from Mars, I told Louie. I understood about colleges educationally. Earthlings did not have preprogrammed knowledge like we did on Mars. But I did not understand about college "dorms" on Earth. Why did young Earthlings leave big comfortable homes a few miles away, where all their needs were provided for by their parents, and come to live in these crowded, noisy confines, packed together like sardines?

> Louie: Well, part of college is to grow, and not only to grow intellectually but to grow independentlywise. . . . When you come to college, it's not exactly the real world but it's one step towards it, it's kinda like a plateau. You become more independent. You have to do your own laundry. . . . And you feel a togetherness because there's sixty of you on the floor and all stuck in the same boat . . .[26]

Louie went on in this vein for five minutes, answering a few of my Martian's follow-up questions. Then, possibly aware that Carrie and the freshmen women were listening in, he paused and soliloquized: "How I bullshit! You want some real answers now? I don't know why anyone's here. They're all just getting ripped off!"

This gave Carrie her opening. "Do you really believe all that stuff you just said, Louie?" she asked. Louie moved over closer to Carrie, and I followed him, carrying my tape recorder in a visible position. Louie said that he really did not know what he believed, so Carrie offered her answer to the Martian's question:

College is a place where suburban brats come, to hang out for four years. . . . I think it's a step *away* from the real world. . . . I don't think a lot of people here *want* an education, whether from college itself or from interacting with other people. . . . And when they get out of here, they're just going into Mom and Dad's business, or Mom and Dad is going to pay for their apartment for three years until they get a real job. . . . Which is really fucked up.

Louie recognized the critique, but he did not consider himself a spoiled college kid. He answered Carrie by telling her that his father was divorced from his mother and was not putting him through Rutgers; he had to work hard at several jobs to stay in school. He talked about how hard he worked and how much money he made. A lot of other Rutgers undergraduates were serious, hardworking youths like him, he concluded. Carrie agreed that she was, but she was not sure about many others; and whatever the state of Louie's finances, she still thought his opinions were screwy: "I don't know, I see a lot of bullshit and a lot of bullshit people here. . . . And a lot of that stuff you were saying, I thought that was pretty *zorbo*. I said to myself, Louie man, if that's the way you think, I don't know . . ."

Louie challenged her to tell him what in the world was *not* bullshit? She made a case for the caring self, for "how you feel about yourself and how you feel about those closest to you. That's all that really matters." "*I'm* proud of myself," Louie replied, "so that's not bullshit, right? According to your definition?" Carrie agreed that it was good that Louie was proud of himself, but she thought Louie's pride was misplaced, since it was really just rooted in his ability to make money. And that, she said, still struck her as "zorbo bullshit."

At this point, one of the freshman listeners cut in. "What exactly is 'zorbo'?" she asked deferentially. "I've never heard the phrase." "Bullshit," Louie explained in a dismissive tone. "Nothing," Carrie added. Later I discovered that Louie had never heard the word either and was bluffing. Carrie had coined it the year before in an old clique on a different dorm floor. It was her synonym for "nerd." A real loser, she had decided for some private reason, a hopeless case, should have the name "Zorbo McBladeoff." Anything that such a character did was a "zorbo" thing to do. She was not able to sell the word to Hasbrouck Fourth in 1984, however; despite Louie's implication that it was a perfectly ordinary term in the talk of knowledgeable upperclassmen at Rutgers, I never heard it again.

Carrie and Louie went back to their argument. Carrie thought that the most important things in life had nothing to do with money. Finding something you really wanted to do was more important. So was helping and influencing others. "If you can do that for a friend, and one friend starts to think the way you do, that's two of you now, and if two of you can go out. . . . I want to be able to change the way America is. I'm serious! This place is so fucked up."

Louie replied that helping others often did you no good at all: "Like, if you believe in something, and every time you try to do it, nine times out of ten it gets pushed back in your face . . . Where does that get you? That and fifty cents and you can buy a cup of coffee." Right now, Louie decided, what *he* believed in was "*nothin'*." And he got bored easily, he said, so he liked to try lots of different jobs and he liked to date lots of different girls. In deference to Carrie, Louie did not refer to his erotic prey with his normal label for them, "chicks."

While Carrie and Louie were in the middle of this colloquy, Jay walked in and sat down. He had been working on a paper for an English course; "Does anyone here understand Isaac Babel?" he asked the group at large. "No," Carrie answered abruptly, and went back to her argument. Jay did not like being ignored; he listened for a minute and then tried to change the mood of the session: "Oh, *I* get it, we're being *cosmic!*" Carrie told him to shut up, so he began busting on her directly. She had been talking about personal satisfaction through an artistic vocation. "Carrie wants to be a really incredible actress," Jay declared to the group, now augmented by three more passing residents, "perhaps on the order of Bo Derek or Ursula Andress." Carrie did not look much like either of these two ridiculous Nordic icons. That ploy did not succeed either, however, and a few minutes later Jay walked away.

Carrie and Louie went on arguing, and after another ten minutes, an upperclassman strode confidently into the lounge from the elevators. He was a skinny, self-assured young man wearing a worn black sports jacket; I had never seen him before on the floor, and I never saw him again. Carrie stopped talking and gave him a big hello, without introducing him to anyone else, and they alluded briefly to unexplained old intimacies:

> *Carrie:* Heeey! It's you! It's the crazy man! What's up?
>
> *Stranger:* So good to see you alive, kid.
>
> *Carrie:* I know. I got through it.

Then Carrie went back to the meaning of life with Louie. The stranger listened for a few minutes, apparently felt he had caught the drift, and then stood up and actually danced around the lounge intoning the following paean to the self. He had a certain hypnotic charm, reinforced by the reiterative phrases he used, and a man-of-the-world authority reinforced by the density of his easy vulgarisms:

> If you want to go out and be a success, you're gonna have to go to school and do well, you're gonna go to college, and you're gonna find out you can live on your own [Louie: "You're 150 per cent right!"] And you're gonna find out it's

you! You know that song [croons]: "It is yoooooou, Oh yeah, Oh yeah"? [Back to normal voice] I can tell a person what's gone right for me, how I've gotten where I've gotten, how I've fucked up.

And that's all I can do. It's them, you know, it's got to come from them. . . . If they want to benefit, that's great. If they want to say, "You're an asshole," that's fine too. It hurts me to see them fuck up, but that's the way it's gonna be. And I don't get upset and say [tone of fake emotion], "You're fuckin' up, you're fuckin' up." I walk up calmly and say [calm tone], "You're fuckin' up." You know, "You could do it this way or you could do it that way." And it's gonna come from you. Nobody's gonna hand you anything.

That's the way I feel. You know, it's different for everyone, but that's the way I feel.

I was not sure what this tone poem had to do with the substance of Carrie and Louie's debate. But the stranger had captured everybody's attention, including my own. Everyone sat in rapt silence as he ended his spiel. Then, apparently deliberately, he punctured the mildly reverent mood he himself had created: "Yeah, and there's another thing. I don't like to *dog* anyone. I present myself, not *degrade* somebody else. And you know, it's rush week, everybody. And this is a lot of what my fraternity's all about . . ." The audience guffawed. The stranger laughed happily and made a quick exit. He had achieved what Jay had failed to do. He had popped the "cosmic" bubble. This little talk session was over, and the participants wandered off to other interests of the evening.[27]

PLOT COMPLICATIONS

Meanwhile, however, the cast of characters who lived on Hasbrouck Fourth in the fall of 1984 went on writing and acting out its particular annual drama.

Friends and Enemies

By late October, the residents of the floor had connected themselves together in the complex network of friendship shown in part in figure 3.[28] A number of the larger friendship groups or cliques[29] in this network have been introduced already: Dan and his friends; Carrie, Andrea et al.; Louie, Chris, and the girls next door; the DUK brothers; Gary and his two tough roommates. The remaining upperclassmen on the floor either belonged to smaller friendship dyads or triads with roommates or had their affiliations elsewhere.

Six of the twenty-one first-year students who had come onto the floor in September, including Howie and Leo, had formed their own friendship group. Most of the remaining freshmen floated between this clique and others on the floor. The three young women in the room next to my own, for instance, never did become close friends with one another, though they did get along all year long; each one made a separate set of friends of her own on Hasbrouck Fourth in 1984, however.

One of them, Judy, was a tall blond who considered herself a "jock" and who soon joined the women's varsity track team. Judy said her mother believed she needed to lighten up in college and was very happy that she was living on a coed floor. In the middle of the year, she found a boyfriend who lived elsewhere. She became friends with Howie on Hasbrouck Fourth, through studying together, and with Leo. (Howie and Leo, in turn, shared the problem of having sophomore roommates and a common dislike for the wedgie patrollers on the floor.) Judy also made friends with Carrie; the two of them were the most assertive women on Hasbrouck Fourth. It was not easy for women to stand up to men on most coed dorm floors, as Judy and Carrie almost always did. Many more women residents let the males bust on them without really trying to even things up in return. "What can I do?" one freshman woman on Hasbrouck Fourth complained. "They're all so much bigger than I am; they'll *always* get me back twice as bad."

Judy's roommate Lisa made friends with Ernie and Alvin, two apparently easygoing black sophomores who lived across from her. Lisa also had a black hometown boyfriend; she herself was white. Pete had impressed me with his liberal political opinions at the beginning of the year, so he surprised me when I asked him about a few difficulties that Lisa seemed to be having with some other residents of Hasbrouck Fourth in the middle of the winter. "Well, society doesn't approve of what she's doing, you know," he replied. I honestly didn't know what he was talking about. Drugs? Lesbian propositions? "Her boyfriend," Pete explained. "Haven't you seen him? He's *black.* Not that *I* have anything against it. But lots of people do."

And Fran, the third roommate, also white, established a quiet, yearlong romance with Tim, the Japanese-American male in Hank's group, one of the two stable erotic "re*lationships*" I knew of between opposite-sex residents of Hasbrouck Fourth in 1984–1985. Fran had struck me as un-

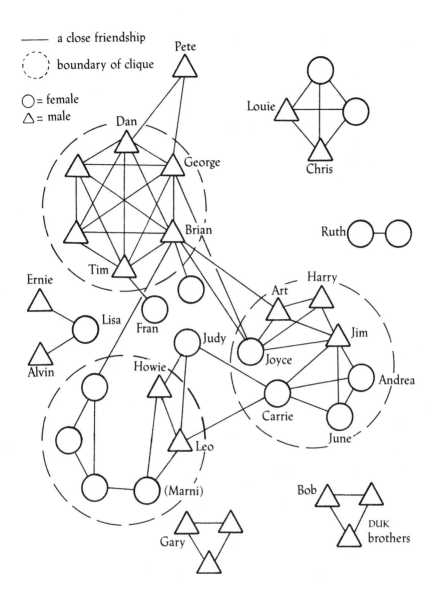

—— a close friendship

(⌒) boundary of clique

○ = female
△ = male

FIGURE 3 / Close Friendships, Hasbrouck Fourth, Fall 1984
(partial network)

usually conservative when I interviewed her at the beginning of the year; she herself admitted that she had a hard time with people who were "different" from herself. She seemed the least likely woman on the floor to have an Asian boyfriend, I told her at the end of the year. "Oh, but Tim," Fran proudly told me, "is more American than most Americans!"

The cliques on Hasbrouck Fourth did not determine all the friendships even of those students who belonged to them; virtually everyone had friends elsewhere at Rutgers. And, as figure 3 suggests, a number of clique members had friends in other friendship groups and outside the cliques on Hasbrouck Fourth as well. Dan's roommate Brian was a notable example. Brian was one of the more studious residents on Hasbrouck Fourth. He worked as hard as Jay, at communication and English. "Ask Brian if he wants to go out and shoot a few hoops," his friends quipped, "and he says, 'Sorry, guys, I'm working on this paper that's due next February.'" Though Brian was a charter member of the wedgie patrol, he did not spend much time defending its shenanigans; he had a quieter personal manner than Dan and most of his other friends—he was mellower, a "nice guy." And by late October, Brian had established more reciprocated close friendships with a wider range of other residents of Hasbrouck Fourth than anyone else on the floor (not all of them are shown on figure 3).

Figure 3 also underrepresents the stated individual friendship sentiments on Hasbrouck Fourth. It is only a partial map, and two people are linked on it if and only if each one named the other, confidentially and in private, as a close friend. By the end of October, Hasbrouck Fourth residents actually named an average of 5.3 other residents as close friends and another 12.5 floor members as friends. About 70 percent of the close friendship choices were reciprocated with close friendship choices; most of the rest were reciprocated with "friend." And the total "close friend" plus "friend" choices, an average of 17.8 per student, meant that about 35 percent of the total possible personal relationships on the floor were marked with some sort of sentiment of friendship beyond simple social "friendliness." When one subtracted the 16 floor members who were not around enough to be chosen as friends, the percentage rose to about 45 percent of the total possible relationships on the floor.[30]

But there were snakes in this Eden as well. By late October, certain students on Hasbrouck Fourth did not like one another very much, and they positively disliked one another in some cases. The dislikes were much fewer than the likes, an average of two per respondent, and they were much more asymmetrically distributed. Two-thirds of the students said that they did not dislike or have a hard time getting along with any of their peers on the floor; the other third, on the other hand, disliked anywhere from a few other residents to a dozen per person. Similarly, about two-thirds of the students on Hasbrouck Fourth received no dislikes from their peers, while about a third did, again in numbers ranging up to about a dozen mentions for the most disliked people on the floor. Finally, dislikes, unlike likes, were only occasionally reciprocated. Only 15 percent of them were returned to sender.

Sometimes the students disliked one another for simple characterological flaws as they perceived them, for flaws of interactive style ("obnoxious," "superior," "snotty," "condescending," "rude," "loud," "inconsiderate") or of essence ("baby," "extremely immature," "phoney," "shallow," "too old for his age," "thinks he's God's gift," "male chauvinist," "dick-tease," "bitch," "asshole," "scumbag," "flaming faggot," "all-American fraternity boy"). Many of the dislikes focused on three Hasbrouck Fourth residents whom I thought of as the "floor pariahs," social isolates without any or many close friends on the floor to compensate them for their local unpopularity among other residents. All three were aware in one way or another of these sentiments on the part of their fellow students. Two of them sought their closest personal relationships elsewhere; the third ignored floor feelings, but answered the "close friends" section of his questionnaire in late October with the names of four other residents of Hasbrouck Fourth—after which he poignantly wrote, "These are the people *I* consider my close friends, whatever they may think of me."

Other dislikes were aimed at better-connected students, at members of the bigger cliques on the floor. Some of these antagonisms had simple origins in the history of Hasbrouck Fourth to date. The three members of the wedgie patrol who had most loudly defended the patrol's right to practice its hazing, for instance, were all paid back with multiple dislikes on the part of other residents of Hasbrouck Fourth in late October.

The general norm of floor friendliness, however, meant that many of these dislikes had to be masked. And on the whole, as of late October, Hasbrouck Fourth was much friendlier than it was unfriendly. The residents knew that like most dorm living groups they had lots of cliques among themselves, but they also knew that a number of friendships on the floor cut across these cliques. The residents had also dealt with the one major internal conflict on the floor to date, with the wedgie patrol, by themselves, and Dan and his friends had not let themselves be entirely defined by these nocturnal missions. Four of them, for instance, had close friendships that reached outside their tight little men's group. Consequently, after two months of the academic year, most students on Hasbrouck Fourth rated it as "a friendly floor, where we all get along." But this collective rating was soon to change.

Preceptorial Problems

In late September, Pete organized one program for Hasbrouck Fourth, a bus trip to an ethnic fair in New York City. Subsequent accounts of the field trip focused more on the drinking the participants had managed to do in the clubs of the city than on the fair as a cultural event, however; and this program aside, Pete was true to his word as the fall semester progressed on Hasbrouck Fourth. He was very busy with his own affairs— with his lab research, with his student teaching, and with his girlfriend; he had very little time for his preceptorial duties.

The student teaching seemed to take the most out of him. Pete did it several afternoons a week all through the semester, dressing up more formally than the undergraduate norm, in a sports jacket and slacks. He apparently did not like his teenage pupils in the affluent nearby town to which he had been assigned; Pete himself was from a poorer urban background. He came back to the dorm with stories about how spoiled the high school students were, about how they all expected to go to fancy private colleges, about how many of them looked down on Rutgers. He sounded very old and sure of himself when he delivered these opinions, and a few students on Hasbrouck Fourth began to mutter among themselves that Pete was developing the same attitudes toward them that he had formed toward these high school students.

When he was around, that is. Much of the time he was not, and the Hasbrouck Fourth residents resented this as well. Preceptors have tough jobs, halfway between friendship and authority, and they manage them best by putting in many hours, by establishing relationships with members of all the different cliques on a floor, by knowing what is going on at any time, good or bad. Pete was not doing this on Hasbrouck Fourth in the fall of 1984.

In the middle of the fall semester, I became one of Pete's problems. Under most circumstances, I kept floor secrets to myself, but I slipped when it came to the wedgie patrol; I mentioned its existence to one of the asked by the deans to do something about a hazing practice that he himself had twice failed to suppress.

Cracks in a Clique

There were cliques and there were cliques on Hasbrouck Fourth in fall 1984. Some—Dan and his friends—were totally "tight"; everyone in them chose everyone else as a close friend. Others were much looser. Howie and Leo's freshman group, for instance, was linked together with some relationships of close friendship, but it was also missing many others. There was no reason for total closure, for among the residents of Hasbrouck Fourth as among other Americans, true friendships are fundamentally dyadic relationships. Someone else's choices should not determine your own; friendship is not transitive. If I am close friends with both Chris and Brian, that doesn't mean that Chris and Brian have to be close friends with one another. And there is no reason why people cannot hang around together without mutual close friendship among everyone involved. Cliques can tolerate a certain amount of personal indifference; what they cannot ordinarily tolerate is real hostility between two or more of their members. And in late October, I noticed that Carrie and Andrea's group contained one such two-way dislike.

Carrie and Andrea's clique was, in fact, almost two different groups. The clique held together only because everyone in it had a close friendship with Jim. But it also contained a tension, between Carrie and Art. Carrie could be a real toughie, that was clear. And Art, despite all the "outrageous" routines he enjoyed performing, clearly had his own limits as a white male. In late September, I watched him fail to amuse his friends with an impromptu skit in which he tried to make fun of all the TV shows with the theme, A woman makes it in a man's world. It could have been a good routine, but its audience couldn't quite follow Art's intent. "I don't get it," Jim asked. "Are you making fun of the shows or of the women?" On another occasion, Art succeeded in amusing a small, all-white group in the low-side lounge with his parody of a black student with a ghetto accent hustling whites in late-sixties language. As he performed this routine, Art looked around furtively, apparently to make sure none of the black residents of Hasbrouck Fourth was within earshot.

Carrie and Andrea's clique soon contained another complication as well. Andrea was a flirtatious young woman at the beginning of the year, given to scanty dress and a certain amount of erotic display around the deans. And, not surprisingly, Pete's supervisor soon suggested to Pete that he do something about it—ironically, a week or two after the other residents on Hasbrouck Fourth had really finished it off for themselves (though it was still occasionally operating downstairs). Pete was furious with me, as he had every right to be, but instead of talking to me directly about my faux pas, he cut me off. He simply stopped talking to me. He did nothing directly about the patrol, according to one of its leaders, but he did go around on the floor telling a number of residents that I was a spy for the deans and that they should stop talking to me as well.

For a few months, Pete succeeded in damaging my reputation on the high side of Hasbrouck Fourth, where the residents didn't know me so well on a daily basis. On the low side, on the other hand, some of my student friends told Pete that he was crazy, and I detected no change in their generally open, friendly attitudes toward me. When I realized what I had done, I talked to Pete about it, trying to apologize for embarrassing him. But it was clear that he no longer trusted me and that nothing I could say would reassure him.

Later, some of the sophomores who had been on Hasbrouck Fourth the year before, some of the nonadmirers of the patrol, gave me their own explanation for the implacability of Pete's anger. Pete himself had been one of the rowdiest students on the second floor of Hasbrouck Hall two years before, they said, close buddies with the seniors now known as the "Henry Street guys" back when all of them were carefree sophomores together. Last year, when Pete had first become preceptor on Hasbrouck Fourth, his old clique had moved up to the floor as juniors and helped him out by supporting his programs. (Preceptors often have an easier time when they can enlist the support of a group of influential upperclassmen on their floors.) Pete, in exchange, had winked at the activities of last year's wedgie patrol. He had remained close friends with many of the students involved, and he had also made friends with some of the new freshmen males who had enjoyed being wedgied by the patrol in 1983, with Dan and his friends as freshmen.

Last year, I was told by these sophomores, Pete had been very "one-sided" in his treatment of Hasbrouck Fourth. He had always gone along with his junior and freshman friends. He had also run an exceptionally relaxed floor: "No one ever got written up for *anything* on Hasbrouck Fourth last year," I was told. This year, 1984, Pete had continued with his laissez-faire policies, though he was becoming less interested in sophomoric juvenilities in their own right. Hence, perhaps, his anger at being

101

dorm floor. She and Carrie apparently enjoyed being mildly outrageous, and there were rumors that both of them were "wild" outside of Hasbrouck Hall. Sometime in October or early November, according to Art's account, Andrea and Art had a brief fling, a "one-nighter." But once was apparently enough as far as Andrea was concerned. She transferred her affections to Art's roommate Jim, and they actually began to develop a real romance. Art was furious. The affair would never last, he predicted. Andrea was much too wild. She was also much too good-looking, Art said; she could get almost any man she wanted, whereas Jim was just a pleasant, ordinary-looking guy. He was not in her league at all, Art maintained.

Art was not quite ready to break out of this clique on Hasbrouck Fourth at this point, though he did start making friends with Dan, whose theatricality he admired. But by the last month of the semester, Art was a human pressure cooker. He was quietly furious with Andrea; he had always had trouble with Carrie; and now one of his male buddies had betrayed him. Andrea, who was evidently really beginning to care for Jim, was also beginning to change her public personality on the floor. She dressed and acted more modestly; she stopped her open flirting. She and Jim spent more of their free time privately with one another and less with the clique as a whole. Carrie must have been bugged about the new relationship as well, although she claimed that she was not. But she and Andrea could no longer be partying buddies together.

CLIMAX

The degree of tension that existed on Hasbrouck Fourth by the late fall was not in fact especially abnormal by the standards of the Rutgers dorms. In the absence of further plot complications, the floor members might have gotten along relatively happily with one another for the rest of the academic year. But Hasbrouck Fourth in 1984–1985 was not to be so lucky.

Pete's Tantrum

In late November, Pete called the second floor-meeting of the fall semester on Hasbrouck Fourth, the first one he had scheduled since early September. He was fighting a bad cold and seemed to be in a nasty mood in general. The floor had to plan its annual Christmas party, Pete said, to be held at the end of the fall semester. Nobody was very interested in the party;

the residents were still skeptical about such affairs in the absence of alcohol. Someone suggested that its theme be Dead Rock-and-Roll Stars; you could dress up as your favorite and come. Pete rejected this macabre suggestion out of hand and decided that it would be a toga party, if anyone cared. He indicated that he was not pleased with the apathy on Hasbrouck Fourth, and he went on to his second piece of business. There was a strict new policy coming out of the deans' office about Secret Santa, he announced.

I had heard rumors about Secret Santa since my first yearlong stay in the dorms, on Erewhon Third in 1978. It sounded harmless—too innocent, in fact, for the enthusiasm it seemed to generate among the students; undergraduates went on talking about Secret Santa for months and even for years afterward. By random ballots, the women and the men on every coed dorm floor paired off in the last week before exams in early December. I might have a female Secret Santa on Hasbrouck Fourth whose identity I did not know, and be a Secret Santa to a separate female who did not know my identity. Then we all sneaked around all week long leaving amusing little presents for each other. And then, at the Christmas party, we revealed our identities and gave one another one more big gift.

It was Pete who clarified for me the real appeal of Secret Santa, back in September when we were still friends. To get each gift, he explained, you had to meet a challenge; you had to perform an embarrassing stunt, sometimes in public outside the dorm, more often in informal performance sessions held in front of your floor friends in one of the lounges two or three evenings during the Secret Santa week. Pete had made a scrapbook of his own photos of floor fun on Hasbrouck Fourth in 1983–1984. More than half the photos showed last year's Secret Santa performances. Transvestite males. Nearly nude females and males. Other outlandish costumes and carryings-on. Mardi Gras! Carnival!

But no longer, Pete informed the Hasbrouck Fourth residents in late November, for the deans' office had decided that Secret Santa had gotten out of hand. During the week of Secret Santa, students, faculty, staff, and adult guests of the college never knew when they would suddenly be exposed to shocking Secret Santa performances in public—stripteases, female impersonators, and other unsavory sights. Some students had also been psychologically damaged, the deans claimed, by the things they had been bullied into doing by the peer pressure of the dorm-floor group. There had been many complaints. It would all just have to stop, the deans declared. From now on, the emphasis was to return to the "nice, spirit-of-the-season" aspects of Secret Santa (the presents), one written announcement read. No students were to "humiliate themselves" in order to get gifts; no students were to act in "derogatory" ways or to say or sing "offensive" things; no "bizarre" clothing was allowed. Anyone ignoring these new edicts might be in violation of the university policies against hazing.

The residents of Hasbrouck Fourth booed when they heard this announcement. They hadn't liked the new antidrinking regulations in September, but at least that crackdown had been based on state law. What harm was anyone doing to anyone else with the fun of Secret Santa? And what business was it of the deans, anyway? The Secret Santa challenges were not really hazing, some students claimed. Hazing was a one-way practice between unequals—sophomores and freshmen, fraternity brothers and pledges—while Secret Santa challenges were perfectly egalitarian and reciprocal. All the participants in Secret Santa had to make fools of themselves. Nor did most of the residents of Hasbrouck Fourth believe that many of their peers had been damaged by their Secret Santa performances. Most people seemed to enjoy performing them; almost everyone loved cooking them up for others. And those who did not could always refuse to play the game on a particular floor. Or they could, and did, refuse and renegotiate particular challenges. Students who couldn't handle Secret Santa, one upperclassman said, were probably in trouble in their dorm-floor groups in any case. I tended to agree with him. The dynamics of Secret Santa, it seemed to me, were precisely identical to—were virtually a ritual map of—the dynamics of the student dorm-floor groups who practiced them.

Pete agreed that the new regulations were stupid. He also agreed that the deans' countersuggestions for "acceptable Secret Santa" activities were stupid:

> Secret Santa does one good deed a day for the elf. This involves everything from picking up their mail for the day to making their bed. . . . The most the Secret Santa does is send the elf on little treasure hunts to find the gift . . . [or request them to sing] a Christmas Carol.—Memorandum to staff, Office of Residence Life, November 15, 1984

But the deans were as serious about this as they had been about the new drinking regulations, Pete said, and therefore the residents of Hasbrouck Fourth would just have to *forget* about Secret Santa this year.

The residents at the meeting continued to complain about the inappropriateness of the deans' latest ukase, however, whereupon Pete threw a tantrum. Hasbrouck Fourth was *such* a bad floor. People tore down his signs. (Some early anti–Secret Santa announcements on the floor had been vandalized.) No one helped with anything. This was *it* as far as Pete was concerned! Next semester he was going to do the absolute minimum around Hasbrouck Fourth! After the meeting several residents sardonically wondered how this would differ from Pete's preceptorial policy toward the floor during most of the fall semester. And Pete brought the meeting to a close by angrily stomping back into his single room next to the lounge and slamming the door behind him.

Secret Santa

The next evening, about a dozen residents got together for what they later referred to as an "informal floor-meeting." The situation was really getting out of hand on Hasbrouck Fourth, they agreed, and Secret Santa *did* bring people together. If everyone participated in Secret Santa at the end of the fall semester, when tempers were thin and residents had stopped making the effort to get along with one another, its fun often rejuvenated a dorm-floor group. Secret Santa worked off tensions and revived the friendliness of a floor collectivity; people went home for the holidays, missed one another a little, and then got along much better when they returned to the dorms in late January. Listening to the students' reasoning, I thought to myself that they were spontaneously recreating most of the arguments that functionalist social scientists had applied to ritual in primitive tribes in the early twentieth century. Secret Santa apparently *was*, in anthropological terms, an orthodox, do-it-yourself ritual of integration for an intense face-to-face community.[31]

A little integration was just what Hasbrouck Fourth needed at the moment, the students decided among themselves. There were rumors on other floors that other preceptors had handled the new Secret Santa regulations more sensibly than Pete had. They had told their residents to go ahead and have their fun, but to restrict their performances *to* the floor and to talk about them only among themselves. One preceptor in Hasbrouck Hall had even instituted a little ad hoc Secret Santa committee—herself, a high-side person, and a low-side person—to which residents might come for the appeal of any challenges they did not like.

Therefore, since Pete had effectively abdicated his responsibilities to the floor, Carrie and Andrea volunteered to try to organize Secret Santa themselves on Hasbrouck Fourth in 1984. They went around with a sign-up list, and about thirty-five residents wanted to play. The next week when I arrived for my research, the floor had a buzz of collective excitement on it unlike the tired, slightly cranky mood that had become common by the end of November. Upperclassmen were telling stories to the freshmen of some of last year's wilder stunts.[32] Males and females were talking among themselves about how they would deal with the challenge they had just received and what they would stick their cross-sex partners with next. It was not hard to "get" anyone of the opposite sex on the floor if you wanted to, or at least to try to get them. Secret Santa identities were well-kept secrets between the sexes, but within each sex, everyone soon knew who everyone else had as their Secret Santa victim. If I was mad at Joyce, for instance, I could easily find out that Bob was her Secret Santa and suggest something especially diabolical to him.

Early in the evening on the first Wednesday in December, the Secret Santa performances began on Hasbrouck Fourth. A pretty freshman woman who had rebuffed the advances of some of the men in Dan's group early in the semester had to go around dressed as a little girl, sucking on a lollipop, knocking on doors and asking people, in a fake-innocent tone, "What is sex?" Lisa, known for her sloppiness, was required to dress up and clean the windows and empty the wastebaskets in every low-side room. Leo, who was good-looking and a little shy, had to parade while wearing a tight black leotard from the waist down and nothing from the waist up, in the manner of the sexy male waiters at Chippendale's, a popular local theme nightclub. And at 7:30, just when everyone was sitting in the lounges digesting their dinners, another shy freshman, Howie, had to take a shower in the women's room while loudly singing "I'm a Virgin."

On the evidence of the Secret Santa stunts, the students were bluffing in their common, worldly claim that there was nothing emotionally difficult about living in sexually-integrated dormitories; they were engaging in a certain amount of perhaps necessary denial. A few of the Secret Santa stunts contained no sexual references: Lisa's above; and the stunt of a white freshman male who loved black break-dancing music, who had to dress up as a "heavy metal freak" and talk about the pleasures of his new musical tastes.[33] But more than four out of five of all the Secret Santa stunts I saw or heard about were sexually embarrassing in one way or another. If the stunts were intended to work off the collective tensions that had developed after three months of close daily acquaintanceship on the coed dorm floor, sex was number one as the systematic source of these tensions.

Thus, students were required to say or sing or act out sexually inappropriate things in inappropriate places. They were required to administer sex questionnaires and bra surveys and jockstrap counts and kissing tests among their peers, and to report the results to everyone. Females *and* males had to appear in states of near-nudity. Secret Santa was sexually egalitarian in that it was not just the traditional male stare at the unclothed female body. Each sex got a chance to ogle the other. In perhaps a quarter of their stunts, men had to cross-dress. Male transvestism seemed to be funny to most of the students for its pure incongruity, not because it meant its victims were gay; real references to homosexuality were too insulting even for Secret Santa on most dorm floors. Female transvestism was rarely requested, on the other hand, perhaps because most women in the dorms tended to dress in a relatively masculine way most of the time: in jeans, pants, T-shirts, nonsexy blouses, and so on.

At ten o'clock that Wednesday evening, most of the Secret Santa participants congregated in the high-side lounge to watch and cheer and jeer one another's stunts. The main performance session had begun, with Pete conspicuously absent. Judy, the freshman jock, gave a weight-lifting demonstration in a very skimpy bikini, revealing a nice body and a well-developed set of muscles—which she made it clear she would use on anyone who gave her any crap. There was some male laughter, but it sounded like respectful laughter to me. Two of the DUK brothers had to have different parts of their bodies signed with each letter of "Secret Santa" according to the first letter of the body part in question (an *s* on their shins, for example) and then show each letter-and-body-part to the floor audience. Secret Santa ends in *a*. Everyone knew what was coming, the inevitable two-man moon. Joyce sunbathed in a tiny bikini, while Harry, dressed in an outlandish soft hat, a wild print shirt, and shorts, rubbed lotion on her back, making noises suggestive of near-orgasm.

Art knelt in front of a girl in the audience, looked soulfully into her eyes and recited the couplet:

> Could it be you're the girl of my dreams?
> Could you be the one to make me cream? [34]

Whereupon Joyce sneaked up on him and covered him with shaving cream. Art looked surprised and a little tense, and later he came to me to ask me if I thought he had lost his cool. I told him I didn't think he had. Other people in his clique had been razzing him about his reaction, he complained.

There were six or seven other performances in this vein. The two most memorable ones were those of Bob, the third of the DUK brothers, and Andrea. In a number of ways, Bob had evidently been vying to be the most outrageous sophomore male on Hasbrouck Fourth in 1984. His challengers were apparently attempting to neutralize him by telling him that he had to sing "The Twelve Days of Christmas" in the lounge wearing women's clothing. He did so, in a pretty pink dress, but he changed the words to the song just a little:

> On the twelfth day of Christmas, my true love gave to me,
> Twelve meals at Commons, eleven fake orgasms,
> Ten kegs of beer, nine nights with Lois,[35]
> Eight nymph preceptors, seven high school bimbos,
> Six girls alaying, five KUTs![36]
> Four circumcisions, three sloppy blowjobs,
> Two ribbed rubbers, and a bottle of Riunite!

And Andrea, perhaps due to her unusual sexuality on the floor earlier in the semester, was required to present a parody of the contraception workshops that college health professionals give in the dorms on a regular rotation. She did so with gusto. In preparation, she had gone to every male on Hasbrouck Fourth asking him to donate a sample condom. In her performance, she listed which males had given her which condoms, commenting on the sensuous properties of each one from a woman's point of view (what a ribbed rubber felt like, etc.); and then she led the women of the floor in a collective boo of all the males who did not have a condom, who "weren't prepared."

Then she asked her boyfriend, Jim, to come forward and stand in front of her, announcing that she was going to use him to demonstrate how to put a condom on. To increasingly nervous titters from the audience, she unbuckled his belt, unzipped his trousers, and unrolled the condom. Then she quickly pulled his underwear away from his waist and dropped the condom in, so that he was never *quite* exposed. Jim had been rehearsed; he said, mock-dumb, "Gee, is that how you put one of those things on?" End of performance, to relieved cheers.

Everyone sat around for some time after the performances laughing and talking and evaluating their peers' acts. Then I realized that other people besides Pete were missing. The rowdiest of the sophomores, Dan and his friends, had not appeared. I was told this was purely accidental: you could only play a decent Secret Santa with an equal number of females and males; a smallish number of women had signed up, so Dan and his friends had agreed to sit Secret Santa out this year. This explanation sounded fishy to me, however: Dan and his friends, especially Dan, seemed the least likely members of Hasbrouck Fourth to willingly forego a chance to exhibit themselves in this way. Later I was told something that sounded much closer to the truth. Pete had caught wind of Carrie and Andrea's plans, so he had gone to his only remaining friends on Hasbrouck Fourth, to Dan and George in particular, and asked them please—for old times' sake—not to participate, and they had agreed. The next night all of them did show up, singing Jacques Brel songs in unison; Jacques Brel was Pete's favorite sentimental singer. But it was very odd to watch other residents of Hasbrouck Fourth acting out their vivid adolescent vulgarities while the former members of Hasbrouck Fourth's wedgie patrol belted out the songs of a middle-aged French singer.

The next night, a Thursday evening, Pete was also present. For it was the evening of Hasbrouck Fourth's Christmas party. Somehow the high-side lounge had been fixed up: there was a tree, decorations, and a dozen and a half Christmas stockings hung in the corner. Certain rooms were rumored to contain alcohol. It was possible that a decent Christmas floor party *would* eventuate on the floor after all. But before the party started, many of the residents of Hasbrouck Fourth had one last round of Secret Santa performances to act out. Pete announced that he would be watching them closely, and the stunts began as they had on the preceding night. A beefy sophomore male in a dress and bra did a surprisingly graceful dance of the veils; a freshman female stood up in a tight body stocking and told everyone what she liked best physically in men; one of the DUK brothers danced as a ballerina. A quiet Cuban male, who was going to explain why Latins made better lovers, waited in the wings. But Bob had the stage first.

Once again, his challengers had apparently tried to neutralize him with a relatively innocent challenge. He had played baseball in high school, so they had asked him to put on his old uniform and come out and reminisce. He did so for a few minutes, but then he smoothly segued into baseball jokes. He said they were one of the real pleasures of the game; he would like to tell a few, but they would only be funny if he applied them to people whom the residents knew, to the students on Hasbrouck Fourth. Most of the jokes were very crude and scurrilous. But, surrounded by everyone else from the floor, it was difficult not to laugh at some of them. "A grand slam": four of the best-looking women on Hasbrouck Fourth (Bob named them) "in your room with you all night." "Leading scorers": four of the most erotically inept persons on the floor, plus "Mike Moffatt." "A pickoff play: what two lovers with herpes do to each other." "A hit batter: what happens to any guy who makes a move on Judy."

Pete became visibly angrier and angrier as he listened to this routine. Finally Bob came to a joke that involved Penny, one of the less-popular students on Hasbrouck Fourth, a returning sophomore. Pete had devoted some time to counseling her the year before, he had told me in September; she was easy to irritate, and Bob in particular enjoyed irritating her. "That's it!" Pete shouted. Background music had been playing. Pete whipped the needle off the record and threw his second tantrum. Secret Santa was now officially over, he said. He was going to report Bob to the authorities for his stunt, and he would report anyone else who continued with their performances; the students could do what they wanted with their party. Ten minutes later, Pete stalked out of the dorm and spent the night somewhere else. Everyone else looked disgusted and deflated, and the party, not surprisingly, was a flop.

And so, in this dispirited mood, the curtain came down on the fourth floor of Hasbrouck Hall in the fall of 1984.

ANTICLIMAX

When the students returned to the dorms after the Christmas vacation in late January, many of them were happy to see particular friends on Hasbrouck Fourth again, but most of them had given up on the floor as a whole. This was no big deal, they implied. So what if not everyone got along on Hasbrouck Fourth? Since when did everyone get along on a dorm floor, anyway? So that if the preceptor was mad at everybody? Preceptors were not central to the happiness of most students. Maybe Hasbrouck Fourth *wasn't* a friendly place this year. One could always find one's pleasures elsewhere. "We may not have a friendly floor," one male in Dan's group observed, "but we sure do have a friendly corner!"

There had also been some changes in the composition of Hasbrouck Fourth by the beginning of the second semester. Louie, whom Chris considered his best friend, had transferred to a business college in New York City without mentioning his intentions to Chris. Chris had also had to deal with the sudden death of his father in the middle of the fall semester. He said that this move was "just like Louie" and that he did not hold it against him, but he seemed mildly disoriented to me for a month or two.

The two girls next door to Chris and Louie had had a third roommate, Laura, who was majoring in political science. She had struck me as an interesting young woman with more social conscience than the average Rutgers undergraduate. But she had quarreled with her roommates and with Louie and Chris during the fall semester, and she was gone before Christmas. Ernie had moved out because he could not get along with his roommate Alvin, and a white freshman male from the other side who could not get along with *his* upperclass roommate had moved over and matched up with Alvin. And his old room, next door to Pete's, now had a new black freshman in it, Dwayne, a funny, verbose young man whom the other residents soon nicknamed "the Freshman Kid." Carrie was rumored to disapprove of the way Dwayne played the black hipster and what she considered other stereotypically black roles around the predominantly white residents of Hasbrouck Fourth. "This floor's *very* strange," Dwayne commented with a certain relish a few weeks after he moved onto it. "Some people really hate each other here. It's got *everything*. It's even got a nasty preceptor!"

Art Blows his Cool

Carrie and Andrea were upset and discouraged by their inability to bring the residents of Hasbrouck Fourth together through Secret Santa in spite of Pete, and in spite of the difficult regulations inflicted on the students by the deans during the fall semester. But when they discussed it with one another at the end of the Christmas break, they disagreed about what to do next. Carrie was in favor of writing the floor off entirely; Andrea felt that they would just have to try to get along better with everyone else.

Contrary to Art's predictions, however, Andrea's romance with Jim was flourishing. They were definitely in love with each other, they both said privately. Andrea and Carrie said they were still friends, but they seemed to be drifting apart. Carrie was around on the floor much less, and their room became a rorschach of their disintegrating relationship. Carrie took down her elaborate wall decorations, and the two of them shifted their beds and desks around so that the room now had two very distinct, separate studying-and-sleeping spaces in it. Andrea also continued to change her behavior on Hasbrouck Fourth; now she was just another nice, friendly, unassertive college girl. She and Jim might as well be married, Art observed darkly. Meanwhile, Art and Howie had decided that, as far as they were concerned, Jim was no longer their friend. This was news to Jim. And later in the spring, they quietly cut him out of their plans for the three of them to room together again the following year. Jim was hurt. "Well," Art said privately, "even friends get divorces occasionally."

But the hottest antagonism in their old clique continued to simmer between Art and Carrie. Late one night in early February, the two of them had an argument about the noise of Carrie's stereo, and Art complained to Pete. Carrie became very angry with Art for bringing the preceptor into the quarrel and told him, according to Art, that if he did not leave her alone, she "would get some friends of hers to take care of him." And the next afternoon, he heard her talking to her older sister on the phone in the corridor about her problems. "You can't let white folks push you around," Art said he had heard Carrie tell her sister. "You've got to kick their asses a few times to make them respect you." Art probably made a remark or two in return to Carrie and then, he said, he came out into the lounge to try to cool off.[37]

I happened to be sitting in the lounge at the time with Jim, Andrea, Gary, and a few other high-side residents. After a few minutes, Carrie walked angrily out of her room and confronted Art in front of all of us. This time her threat was more orthodox if equally unlikely: "Don't you *ever* complain to someone else about something I do again or I'll call the campus police!" Whereupon Art, who was a foot taller than Carrie, stood up and, towering over her, seemed to go impressively, quiveringly off his head. He screamed at her for what seemed like five minutes. The rest of us went into mild shock.

I sat there telling myself that anthropologists are not supposed to get involved; they are supposed to listen and watch as dispassionately as possible. Carrie held her ground. Gary, smaller than Art but well-muscled, stepped bravely between them and nudged Art away, gradually calming him down. Carrie retreated back to her room, and Pete burst out of his room and started yelling at everyone. And then, apparently realizing that this was more than the average foolishness in the lounge, he led Art into his room, asked Jim to join them, and kept them there for some time.

According to Jim later on, Pete did not want to know any details; he just lectured them both on how all this had to stop.

Out in the lounge, in the absence of the antagonists, the rest of us laughed nervously about the confrontation. "I've been reading this same sentence for ten minutes now," a freshman joked. Gary was congratulated for his heroics. He told Andrea that she and John had to talk to their roommates; she replied that they had very little influence over either of them any more. Over the course of the year so far, we had all watched Art work himself into some very convincing pseudoemotions during some of his comic performances, so we all speculated about how much of his rage was a put-on. One student thought that it was mostly acting—"some Springsteen, a little Scarface." I did not. But real or contrived, this uncharacteristically dramatic public display of intragroup hostility had been hard on all of us. When I tried to write up my notes an hour later, I discovered that my memory had not retained anything of what anyone had actually said, only the emotional tone and the moves the various actors had made.[38]

A week later, Art told me that he himself had been shaken by his explosion and had gone home for a talk with his father, who reminded him of why he was in college. He was going to "play more roles" from now on, Art had decided—not let people get to him so much. He had also decided that he could be real friends with other men but he could not really trust women. Carrie, for her part, had almost nothing to do with anyone else on Hasbrouck Fourth from this point on in the year, apart from a few close women friends. "I should have stuck with my first impression of Art," she meditated later in the semester. "When I first met him, I *thought* he was a psycho." Carrie had also decided that she had had enough of dorm life: "I mean, in high school, you were with people like this eight hours a day, but then you got to go home at night. Here, it's all the time!"

As a result of this antagonism and of other shifting relationships on the floor, the friendship network on Hasbrouck Fourth had changed significantly by early April (see figure 4). Some friendships had been stable since the fall. The old wedgie patrol males, Dan and his friends, were still tight, and so were most of the people in Leo and Howie's freshman clique. Likewise most of the roommate groups. But the fission of Carrie and Andrea's clique was almost total, and its disintegration had sent ripples out into other friendship relationships on the floor.

Art and Howie were on their own now, and Art was also good friends with Dan and Brian. Joyce and June had also gone their own ways. Joyce

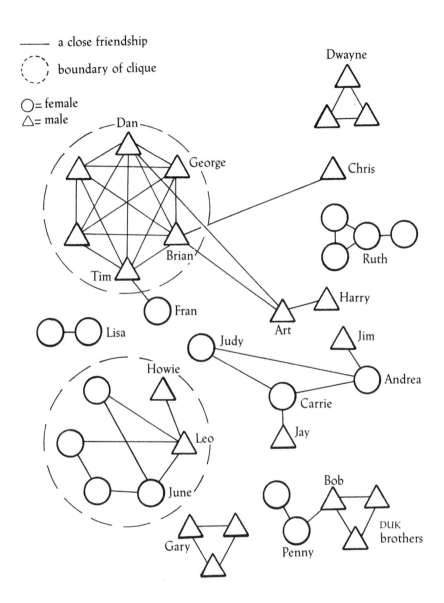

FIGURE 4 / Close Friendships, Hasbrouck Fourth, Spring 1985
(partial network)

was spending more time with her hometown boyfriend, and Harry was very angry with her for doing so—she had led him on, he felt. The freshman June had moved over and linked up with Howie and Leo's freshman clique (Marni, the girl she replaced in that clique, had moved out of Hasbrouck Fourth during Christmas break to live off-campus with her boyfriend). Jim had lost most of his old friends except for Andrea; and Andrea, Carrie, and Judy now had a small, three-woman clique of their own. Carrie had also extended to Jay the only reported close friendship that he was to have on Hasbrouck Fourth that year.

Elsewhere in the Hasbrouck Fourth network in the spring, Louie had disappeared and so had his little clique. Chris now had only one close friendship on the floor, with Brian. Brian in turn had become angry with the females he had considered his close friends in late October for considering him *"just* a nice guy." His close friends on Hasbrouck Fourth were now only men.[39] On the high side, Dwayne had linked up with two upperclassmen down the hall. Perhaps the most surprising new friendship on Hasbrouck Fourth as a whole in spring of 1985, however, was between the obstreperous sophomore Bob and his Secret Santa victim Penny. This was also Penny's first real friendship on Hasbrouck Fourth in 1984–1985, apart from one with her roommate.

Pete Throws in the Towel

Meanwhile, at the beginning of the spring semester, Pete had carried out his threat and written up Bob for his Secret Santa infraction; the residence counselor downstairs was investigating the incident. It could be serious for Bob, for he had been written up once before, in the fall, for noisiness. Two infractions in one year and you were automatically out of housing, or so Bob understood his position. Bob defended himself by circulating a petition giving his view of the incident and asking that he not be evicted from the dorms for a little harmless fun. Thirty-nine residents of Hasbrouck Fourth signed it, including Penny. Penny herself told me that Bob had come by her room before his performance in December and warned her what was coming; she said she had taken his act in good humor.

According to rumor, Pete had attempted to resign as preceptor early in the semester but had been talked out of it by his supervisor. But he grew even unhappier with the floor, and possibly with his own senior year, as the spring semester progressed. He had not done as well on his senior honors research project as he had hoped; it looked like he was going to be a high school teacher instead of going to graduate school the following year. His girlfriend also contributed to his alienation from the floor. She was "very snotty" toward the residents in her weekly visits, in the opinion of others on the high side. They struck back by writing little things on Pete's message board when she was staying with him, such as "Do not disturb. Having sex." Dwayne took special pleasure in irritating both of them. He went around saying that he was working on his own research paper that semester. Its subject was Pete's girlfriend; its title was "Studies in Bimbology."

Sometime in February, word went around the floor that the residence life authorities had decided that Bob's Secret Santa performance was not a serious enough infraction to warrant throwing him off Hasbrouck Fourth. Pete stewed over the decision for a few weeks, and then, around spring break in mid-March, the residents heard that he had finally quit. And for three weeks Hasbrouck Fourth had no preceptor at all.

Life Goes On

The residents of Hasbrouck Fourth breathed a collective sigh of relief when Pete finally resigned. By now the floor was used to taking care of itself in any case; in the opinion of most of its residents, it did not really need a preceptor. These were the days during which many of the students on the high side told me about all the nasty things Pete had said about me months earlier. "But he was wrong about you," Gary concluded. "You stuck with us. Pete didn't."

I had in fact got myself in trouble with some of the deans for siding with the undergraduates when it came to Secret Santa. It had not struck me as a very lofty ritual; I had thought the deans had every right to push its performances out of public areas in the college, back onto the dorm floors. But after that, I thought, the authorities ought to leave the students alone with this particular simple pleasure. Secret Santa was ultimately more innocent, in my opinion, than many of the other things that the students did more privately. It had its own set of rules and conventions monitored by the dorm peer group.[40] I had seen its positive functions within the dorm peer group. It had reminded me of some venerable western traditions of youth culture.[41] And Secret Santa was virtually the only collective event that the students inaugurated and carried out the way they wanted to in the dorms, other than parties, also restricted by

117

the deans in 1984. Aside from Secret Santa, purely student-initiated rituals no longer really existed in the individualistic undergraduate culture of late-twentieth-century Rutgers.

The deans were always saying that they wanted the students to develop initiative. They were therefore being hypocritical, I thought, in coming down so massively on *this* undergraduate initiative just because it violated their own sense of college seemliness. But the deans were not especially happy to have my opinion on this matter; like Pete, some of them became detectably less happy about me and about my presence in the dorms after I shared my views on Secret Santa with them, perhaps too frankly.

As spring blossomed all around Hasbrouck Hall, however, the thoughts of most of the young women and men in the residence halls turned to other things. Dan had taken a job as a night watchman for a month before the spring break, depressing his scanty studying time even further in order to save up money for a pilgrimage to the unofficial national student bacchanalia held every March in Fort Lauderdale. He flew down with one of his friends. Art and Harry scrounged the money to drive down, and they returned with stories of girls, endless parties, endless drinking, and their own "bizarrity." Art, however, had not been able to leave Hasbrouck Fourth entirely behind him even in Florida. He had spent St. Patrick's day in some bar, he remembered later, talking to some stranger about his crazy dorm floor at Rutgers.

Later in the spring, to coincide with the two-day Springfest held in the college, Dan and his friends organized their own "Zekefest" on Hasbrouck Fourth, another private beer party in their rooms. George had a girlfriend, and Tim had linked up with Fran, but the other members of the clique had not done very well erotically in 1984–1985; privately, they were very "frustrated." What was a poor sophomore male to do? They sent out printed invitations for Zekefest to all the women they knew or knew of. Hardly any women came, but they claimed to have a good time anyway.

In the middle of April, an interracial coalition of student activists at Rutgers led a university-wide demonstration to encourage the Rutgers Board of Governors to divest the stocks the university held in companies with South African investments. It was the biggest political movement on the campus in years, drawing hundreds of people to its rallies, and an estimated fifteen hundred to a visit to the campus by the Reverend Jesse Jackson. A hundred or so students also camped out on the threshold of the student center for two weeks, sleeping there overnight and more or less closing it down until exams started in early May. From Hasbrouck Fourth, Carrie was part of this demonstration. So, too, was Laura, the young woman who had been run off the floor by Louie and friends in the fall. Other residents of Hasbrouck Fourth visited the site of the demonstration sit-in from time to time, mostly to look and listen. Their opinions of the event varied widely. I did hear more political talk in the lounges than I had heard all year. Jay was a pragmatic liberal: the United States should support the freedom movement in South Africa, and it should get out of Central America, which was as bad, and as damaging to American national prestige, as Vietnam had been. Jim, who hoped to join the CIA after graduation, argued a more progovernment position. Some residents said that the leadership of the demonstration looked archaic to them: "Lots of late-sixties types, lots of graduate students, a few radical professors." And, speaking Undergraduate Cynical, many of them joked about the least idealistic motives for participating in the sleep-in. The spring weather was in a particularly beautiful phase; the sleep-in was a great way to meet girls or guys, many residents observed. As Judy put it, "A rally's an excuse for jumping up and down and hugging everyone you see and not feeling like a total dick for doing it."

Some people on Hasbrouck Fourth actually concentrated on their studies during the last month of the spring semester. Jay qualified for a summer program in England, where he hoped to study Shakespeare. Ruth continued to hit the books, and she graduated two years later as a Phi Beta Kappa. And Eric, the busy senior, continued to work as hard on his honors paper in economics as any graduate student I had ever seen during dissertation research. I spent over an hour with him one spring afternoon, listening to his woes and giving him what advice I could. He was doing impressive work for an undergraduate, and he soon heard that he had been accepted by the law schools of both Columbia and the University of Chicago for the following year, very good acceptances for a Rutgers graduate. He chose Chicago.

Almost everyone on Hasbrouck Fourth went through the one big trauma of the spring semester for most undergraduates: Where to Live Next Year. Even those residents who were lucky in the housing lottery would not have wanted to come back to Hasbrouck Fourth in the same numbers that they had done the previous spring. But Hasbrouck Fourth was not an option for the fall of 1985, for the dean of students, always trying to raise what he considered the deplorably low tenor of student life in dorms such as Hasbrouck, was reserving the floor for some new special-interest sections in the future.

In any case, many of the sophomores were ready for the greater challenges and freedoms of off-campus living. Dan would not be back at all. He had decided to pursue his real ambition in life; he was going to a drama school in New York City the following year. Most of his friends from Hasbrouck Fourth looked around for off-campus housing for the rest of the semester. I recommended a house I knew of on an "integrated" street in downtown New Brunswick. "Well, to tell you the truth, Mike," one of them told me, "most of us are 'mighty whities' and don't mix too well. Tim's *our* token." Eventually they settled, with a few other friends, two-to-a-room into a fancy new condominium a mile away. Art and Harry were also ready for an off-campus apartment and recruited the freshman Leo to join them.

Most Rutgers students who moved off-campus looked for single-sex housing. Apartments were a little too small and intimate for continued coed living. Andrea was not sure where she would live, nor was Jim. She had a chance to share with one other woman and two men, which she declined. According to Art, her mother did not want her to live with males—"which is ironic," Art added. Two years later, however, Jim and Andrea were still together, living in their own apartment in a neighboring town. My roommate Rich moved into his fraternity, and two of the DUK brothers moved into theirs. But Brian needed something cheaper than the dorms or off-campus housing, for his family, though straitened financially, did not quite qualify for financial aid. He might have to move back home and commute to Rutgers-Camden. With the help of the residence counselor in Hasbrouck Hall, however, he was chosen to be a preceptor—the job comes with a free single room and a small amount of money—and he went on to be a competent one in another dorm during his junior and senior years.

As the year drew to a close on Hasbrouck Fourth, some people on the floor grew nostalgic. Carrie and Andrea were looking at my photos from the fall one evening. "Oh, look at that one!" Carrie exclaimed. "Do you remember that evening, Andrea? That was the night we went off to hear Elton John in the city. Those were the days, weren't they?" Andrea agreed.

For the freshmen, Hasbrouck Fourth *had* been, as almost all dorm floors are for most freshmen, *the* central personal place for them at Rutgers.[42] I asked all of them at the end of the year what person they had met during their first year at Rutgers—student, faculty member, or other—had impressed them most. A third of them mentioned one or another outstanding professor. The other two-thirds named other undergraduates, most of them other residents of Hasbrouck Fourth.

Ironically, though most floor residents had agreed since Christmas that Hasbrouck Fourth was no longer a friendly place, the total number of individual friendship sentiments on Hasbrouck Fourth toward the end of the year, in early April, was higher than that reported back in late October. The average student named about twenty-one other floor members either as close friends or friends in the spring, versus about eighteen in the fall. And the dislikes on Hasbrouck Fourth were slightly down as well, from 2.0 per resident in the fall to 1.6 in the spring. But the friendliness or the unfriendliness of an undergraduate collectivity is not calculated by adding up all the individual sentiments in the group; it is a matter of visible collective behavior. And after Pete's two tantrums, the failure of Secret Santa, and Art and Carrie's ongoing public quarrel, the floor had become too demonstrably *un*friendly to reclaim its older, more harmonious self-evaluation.

In the middle of April, Ed, a junior from a lower floor of Hasbrouck Hall, moved up to Hasbrouck Fourth to finish out the year as its preceptor. Like Brian, Ed was also headed for a preceptorship the following year. Now he was getting a little emergency on-the-job training. Ed did not try to accomplish much on Hasbrouck Fourth in the last few weeks of the semester. He simply kept an eye on the floor for the residence counselor downstairs. His one official act was to conduct the last floor meeting in early May, featuring the annual Floor Awards Night, which took place on every dorm floor near the end of the year. Dorm residents seemed to enjoy this last little ceremony in the annual round of residence life. They voted for different floor members in the different categories on a mimeographed sheet circulated by the preceptor: "Best roommates," "Best looking," "Best dressed," "Studies hardest," and so on. What they enjoyed most, however, was dreaming up their own awards and writing them in on the ballots. The preceptor usually read out the write-ins and everyone had one last laugh together. The previous year on Hasbrouck Fourth, the write-ins had included "Most likely to blow off an hourly," "Floor airhead,"[43] "Most corrupted," "Most likely to break things—sinks, tables, speed limits, hearts"; "Most likely to get fucked up";[44] and "Most likely to survive nuclear holocaust."

But Ed was a newcomer, and he was not at all sure what was going on, on Hasbrouck Fourth. Before the meeting, he had opened the ballots and blanched. "Most likely to drink her own menstrual flow"?! Busting is only safe if you are sure the people involved are friends or at least friend*ly*, and Ed was taking no chances. He censored most of the write-ins, and awards night, the last collective event on Hasbrouck Fourth in 1984–1985, was accordingly a tepid event. At least it was not a disaster, like many of the group moments over which Pete had presided had been. My roommate Rich was "Floor Zombie" (he was never seen). I myself was "Most likely to pester people with questionnaires." And our year together on Hasbrouck Fourth had at last petered to an end.

THE REVIEWS

Hasbrouck Fourth was not a complete failure in 1984–1985. The students who lived on the floor seemed to have had their normal complements of college fun during the year—with one another, with smaller, more private friendship groups, and with their peers in other places. And some of the processes that took place on Hasbrouck Fourth were entirely normal as I knew them from other research in other dorms in the college. Friendliness and friendship making followed ordinary American adolescent protocols for the late twentieth century. As on other coed dorm floors, the students on Hasbrouck Fourth generally suppressed possible erotic emotions between female and male residents and settled friendly joking relationships. Lounge sociability followed ordinary undergraduate conventions, as did the modes of Undergraduate Cynical talk. And, as on other dorm floors where freshmen and upperclassmen lived together, the older students on Hasbrouck Fourth were the essential models for the first-year students when it came to the routine patterns of worldly undergraduate behavior in the college.[45]

Yet by wide agreement among the residents of the floor, both at the time and as they looked back on it several years later, Hasbrouck Fourth was unusually idiosyncratic in 1984–1985, a considerably more conflict-ridden place than the average Rutgers dorm floor.[46] It is often possible to learn more from situations of social stress than from normal ones, however. Fundamental cultural principles often rise to the surface in conflict and in agonistic behavior in ways that they do not during the flow of more ordinary social life. What were the probable reasons for the problems on Hasbrouck Fourth in 1984–1985?

The particular personality clashes on the floor might be dissected, but personal conflicts always existed among some of the sixty-odd residents of any dorm-floor group. And the residents of Hasbrouck Fourth had shown some real skill when it came to such things. Without any help from Pete, for instance, they had dealt with the wedgie patrol effectively, and some of them had tried to stitch the floor back together with their own Secret Santa around Christmas. Race might have played a small role in floor dissension: Carrie and Art. Sexism was not absent: Carrie and Judy were entirely too assertive for females according to the ordinarily male-biased norms of the coed dorm. There was also sexuality as a point of tension: Andrea and Jim and Art, for instance. Social class even reared its head. Jay might have felt superior to other residents of Hasbrouck Fourth, somewhat beneath himself at Rutgers. And Pete had apparently had his lower-middle-class buttons pushed during the fall by his experience in an affluent, upper-middle-class high school.

But there were much more specific reasons than these for the problems on Hasbrouck Fourth in 1984–1985. I may have been one of them. I had acted badly on two occasions—in letting news of the wedgie patrol leak to the deans and, conversely, in taking the students' side versus the deans over Secret Santa. On both issues I should have tried to be more neutral. When it came to Pete's hair-trigger temper about being preceptor, perhaps I was the last straw. And yet, in my opinion, Hasbrouck Fourth would have had much the same history in 1984–1985 if I had not been there at all.[47] The floor's problems, at least in retrospect, seemed almost overdetermined by the curves the deans kept throwing at the students in 1984–1985 and by Pete.

From a certain point of view, the new nationwide restrictions on adolescent drinking, which began to take effect in the Rutgers dorms in September of 1984, made sense. By the early 1980s, alcohol use appeared to be almost out of control in American college-age populations, and the adolescent drunk-driving death rate was very high. Yet the students definitely did not agree with the new laws; or, more precisely, some of them did agree that many of their peers drank too much, but very few of them felt it was fair or just to abridge their own freedom to drink. Drinking, of course, was not the only issue. Drinking was really about partying, and partying was really about sexuality. And sexuality was arguably at the heart of the pleasure-complex that was college life as the students understood it in the 1980s (see chapters 2, 5, and 6). Nevertheless, it is difficult to say what should have been done differently about the new liquor regulations in the dorms, other than to avoid the pretense that the residents of any dorm floor had any meaningful choices to make about local undergraduate standards for liquor use.

Secret Santa struck me as a more avoidable source of conflict. The cultural hiatus between the deans' and the students' sensibilities about having fun was so great, however, that the clash between them on this issue was less surprising than that so many students submitted to the deans' will so easily. For me, the deans' ability to suppress Secret Santa, for the most part, was a testament to the reality of their bureaucratized power when they chose to exercise it—and to a certain malleability on the part of the students. "Maybe some students *are* getting psychologically hurt by their Secret Santa performances," Andrea told me to my surprise a few months after the Secret Santa performances on Hasbrouck Fourth had become unglued. "After all, the deans say so, and *they* must know." Secret Santa, however, was not an issue any sensible modern undergraduate was ready to go to the barricades for. It was just one silly little pleasure of college life, most of the students seemed to feel. But if they could not play it the way they wanted to, they were not about to go back to the older, "innocent" form of the game that the deans recommended. They would just drop the whole thing. As most of them have done since.[48]

As for Pete, whatever his personal reasons for his actions, his ultimate sin as preceptor on Hasbrouck Fourth in 1984–1985 was withdrawal.[49] There were many ways to be an acceptable preceptor in the dorms. The preceptor on Erewhon Third in 1978–1979—the floor described in the next chapter for other reasons—was a real minimalist. And he did not exactly fit the dean's image of the ideal upperclass role model. He was very open about having taken the preceptorship for its benefits, for the free single room and the pay, and he worked at his duties as little as possible. During orientation, when a few freshmen once asked him whether or not to attend the official events of the week, he advised them: "You want the truth? It's a lot of bullshit. Use the time to catch up on your sleep."

He came in spectacularly drunk several times during the fall semester, acted foolishly, and became violently sick. ("There's the *ralph*," he ex-

plained to a freshman girl the next day, "and then there's the *power* ralph.")[50]
He played pranks on some of the freshmen on the floor, rather than vice versa; and he briefed the freshmen males in detail about college traditions of minor vandalism as he knew them. And it was an open secret on the floor that he smoked pot occasionally. Yet when push came to shove on Erewhon Third in 1978–1979, when there was conflict and dissension—when there were possible racial problems on the floor about which the whole college was being informed—he was in there, doing his best. Which made all the difference.

On Hasbrouck Fourth in 1984, after late November, Pete was really not there any longer. And how could a floor whose central undergraduate personage was demonstrably *un*friendly be a normal friendly place?

Further Comments

1 / One Italian exchange student at Rutgers told me that her college housing in Italy had been like this, just a place to live. And in her first month or two in the Rutgers dorm, she could not understand why everyone around her was always so "friendly." It all seemed very strange, she said.

2 / These deanly terms and quotes are all taken from the same pamphlet quoted in the epigraph to this chapter (Rutgers College n.d.), but they recur in many other written and oral sources.

3 / I do not mean to imply that the deans did not have their own more realistic perspectives as well; they weren't stupid. But American individualism is ideologically so coercive that they simply could not articulate them in official documents of the sort quoted here, or at least these particular deans felt they could not. The deans also became very proficient at talking this language much of the time. For some of the reasons identified by George Orwell in "Politics and the English Language" (1946), officialese did, through its vagueness, serve the useful purpose of keeping them out of unnecessary trouble. One often had to know them well, in fact, to realize that deanly officialese did not totally, naively, define everything about the way they thought. One dean I knew at Rutgers once signaled his shift out of this opaque language into 'what is *really* going on', for instance, by warning me that he was about to do a little "low talk"—"and I better not find what I'm about to tell you, Michael, in your book!"

he added. (I *have* left out what he then told me.)

4 / See Di Leonardo 1984:131–139 and Varenne 1986b for two other meditations by anthropologists on the ambiguous ideological meanings of *community* in contemporary American culture.

5 / Like many other ethnographers, I am indebted to anthropologist Victor Turner for his concept of the "social drama," which he first formulated in 1957. I would like to apply the drama metaphor a little more tentatively here than he did originally, however. Social life, Turner suggested, was not the smooth acting-out of a predetermined cultural script, but a constant struggle between self-interested actors, its outcome always unknown. So far so good. This struggle often fell into a particular dramatic form as well, Turner further proposed. He suggested five stages, rather like a five-act play: an initial state of relative normality; the introduction of dramatic tension (some violation of ordinary social norms, or "breach"); further dramatic complications ("mounting crisis"); climax and denouement ("redress"); and either a happy or a sad ending ("reintegration" or the "schism" of the social group that was together at the beginning of

the drama) (see Turner 1957: 91–93).

Real social life does not follow nearly so neat a dramatic form, however. There will be instances of crisis and of partial redress in the description that follows. But the drama these residents of Hasbrouck Fourth acted out in 1984–1985 resembles a much more experimental piece of theater than anything Turner proposed, a multiauthor play with unpredictable entrances and exits, unconventional patterns of climax and resolution, and a continually changing audience.

6 / As both of us knew, however, I was actually on Hasbrouck Fourth because that was where my roommate Rich had already been placed by the housing lottery. Rich had been a freshman in a small class I had taught the spring before. During the summer, when I had started thinking about returning to research in the dorms, I had contacted him and asked him if he would consider having a professor as a roommate for the following year. He had amiably agreed. We had one other roommate, a senior who was around so little that, to simplify description, I have left him out of this account. The room was a double; a top bunk had been moved into it for me. So I was not depriving any legitimate student of a room by my

presence on Hasbrouck Fourth (I had made similar space arrangements on Erewhon Third in 1978).

7 / Actually there were fifteen freshmen and three sophomore transfer students on the floor. But the transfers acted like—and tended to be treated like—freshmen, so I am combining them to simplify description.

Hasbrouck Fourth had many returning sophomore residents in 1984 because so many freshmen had enjoyed being on the floor in 1983, *and* because many of last year's freshmen had been lucky in the annual housing lottery. Once you got a low enough number to return to the dorms, you had preferential admission to your old floor, though not to any particular room in it. The returning sophomores were mostly males, twelve out of seventeen. Four of the nine juniors and seniors on Hasbrouck Fourth were also returning students, two males and two females.

There were also eighteen new sophomore residents, also skewed toward males; eleven were males. It is not clear why the housing authorities had put so many new upperclassmen on the floor. They could as easily have made freshmen a priority once the returning sophomores had been accommodated.

The average Rutgers dorm floor had declining proportions of freshmen, sophomores, juniors, and seniors living on it. Through all the residential facilities in the college, 35 percent of the occupants were freshmen, 25 percent were sophomores, 20 percent were juniors, and 20 percent were seniors. But many of the juniors and seniors were not living on dorm floors set up like Hasbrouck Fourth and Gates Third. Rather, they lived in more private apartments provided to upperclassmen by the university.

8 / I have labeled this clique and those that follow with the names of one or two of the more striking members for descriptive purposes only, not to imply any kind of formal leadership on the part of Dan or the other named individuals. Cliques have their more or less influential individuals; ideologically, however, they are purely democratic.

9 / There was in fact a seventh member of this clique living on Hasbrouck Fourth, Len, a sophomore with no dorm housing on campus, who spent two or three nights a week sleeping on the floor in George's triple room. As crowded as the dorms already were, they were so essential to college life as the students enjoyed it that extra floor members of this sort were common in the residence halls. One of the awards the residence

life staff placed on the floor awards ballot at the end of the year, for instance, was "honorary floor member."

10 / The argot of their all-male clique was also vividly sexist, full of male locker-room language. Ignoring its often deplorable contents, however, it was a linguistically impressive brew, rich in ellipsis, allusion, metonymy, metaphor, and irony. In the following example, members of Dan's clique also managed to make virtually the only spontaneous literary reference I heard in an entire year of dorm banter on Hasbrouck Fourth.

In the low-side lounge, in the hearing of several other floor residents, two members of Dan's clique were discussing a woman they had met at a party the night before. "Box is thinkin' Ahab," one of them commented cryptically about her. The other nodded his head in vigorous agreement. A male listener, half in the clique and half out, decoded all but one word. *Box* is an old male vulgarism referring to the female genitalia; here it meant "that girl as a sexual object." "Is thinkin'" was a very loose connective in their slang; here it meant "I think that [that girl as a sexual object] was . . ." But the listener didn't understand the rest of the predicate:

Listener: Wait a minute. *Ahab?* What is that? Is that a name or something?

Clique member: Ahab, as in *Moby Dick*, as in whale, dickbrain!

And therefore, via a double metonymy and a metaphor, the utterance meant "I think that that girl as a sexual object was fat and undesirable." ("Ahab" pointed indexically to Melville's literary classic, which pointed in turn to "whale," which stood metaphorically for a big, fat, unattractive person.)

11 / The major fields of study of the undergraduates on Hasbrouck Fourth amounted to the normal mix for American college students in the 1980s: lots of economics and "business"; moderate amounts of psychology, communication, and computer science; some of the larger "liberal arts" (English, political science); and the occasional oddball interest (art history). The hardest-working student scientists often chose to live across the river with the other "techies," in the dorms on the science campus of Rutgers College. See chapter 7 for more on the status of the majors among the undergraduates.

12 / Ordinary double rooms in dorms with Hasbrouck's layout

were twelve by twelve and a half feet on the floor, for about eighty-one square feet per resident. Ordinary triples were larger, with similar space per resident. "Voluntary" triples, on the other hand—increasingly common as the housing crunch on campus grew worse—divided ordinary doubles between three roommates, for an average of only a little over fifty square feet per resident.

13 / Many of these poor Latins were exceptionally tidy housekeepers in their own small apartments in the city, and in general considered mainstream American culture to be a much less hygienic one than their own. They needed a strong work ethic to put up with the Rutgers dorms. Their own teenagers tended to be much tidier than these privileged college students were.

14 / The job of the preceptors in September 1984 was not made any easier by the approach that university officials had decided to take, writing up the new regulations in a way that allegedly centered on undergraduate choice and responsibility. Every dorm floor was supposed to set its own collective standards for liquor use. It had to do so within limits set by the university, however. And these limits were so distant from any student consensus about drinking that they struck the average dorm resident as simply "more bullshit from the deans." For example, any legal party was required to have students in attendance who were of drinking age to make sure that no underage persons drank. But these monitors themselves couldn't drink while performing their duties. There had to be a minimum of one of them for every twenty party-goers. Did the students on a given dorm floor want to require more monitors? One for every ten party guests?

15 / Liquor and near-drunkenness were central to partying for white, mainstream American students at Rutgers in particular. European exchange students were often surprised at the social importance of alcohol for the average Rutgers undergraduate. And, it was widely agreed on the Hispanic special-interest floor in another dorm in September 1984, the new liquor regulations were no particular problem among Latin students; for the Latins, a party was about dancing. And what was the big problem if you couldn't have a large bowl of lethal punch sitting in the center of the lounge? You could always nip into your room for a drink if you wanted one.

16 / I did not just hear

about the wedgie, in fact. One afternoon, some of the patrollers demonstrated the wedgie in my presence by suddenly giving it to a nonresident youth who in their opinion had been hanging around on Hasbrouck Fourth too much. Four of them grabbed him and reached down through the tops of his trousers to the tops of his underwear, pulling them, and him, up. His feet were off the ground and his head literally against the roof of the dorm room before his underwear tore and its pieces could be pulled up and out by the patrollers. The victim laughed nervously and went off to the men's room to inspect the damage to his tender parts. And he took the hint and never returned to Hasbrouck Fourth. The patrollers threatened me with my very own wedgie on two occasions as well. Once they tried to suborn my roommate to leave our door unlocked one night. He didn't.

17 / George remembered trying to outfox the patrol in his freshman year by sleeping naked. It hadn't worked. They had "nudied" him instead, he said; that is, they had thrown him out of his room, naked, to run hunched over through the halls, hands in front of his privates, until someone took pity on him and threw him a bathrobe.

18 / The American college prank has a tradition all its own, of course. And by the standards of the past, these current stunts were penny-ante stuff. Given the size of Rutgers in the 1980s, it was also doubtful that any pranks stayed for long in the collective memory of anyone but the small groups who performed them; I never heard of one in the 1970s or 1980s that students in the entire college knew about, or one that was more than a year or two old.

In the past, on the other hand, undergraduate pranks in the much smaller student body were often told and retold for generations. One common prank at many American colleges had the transformation rule, Introduce a large, inconvenient object into an inappropriate interior space. In the agrarian nineteenth century, it was a cow on the podium of the campus chapel or in the campus bell tower; in the industrial twentieth century, it was a sports car in the dorm room of an unpopular student. Both stunts had been pulled off at Rutgers, probably more than once. In the mid-1930s, some undergraduates had tricked the president of Rutgers into coming down to the New Brunswick train station at three in the morning to shake the hand of presidential candidate Alf Landon; the Rutgers president was a vocal supporter of the Republicans against Roosevelt. Landon's campaign train then blew past the nonplussed college president and a few of his sleepy aides without slowing down, and the students involved were still bragging about the gag thirty years later (Lukac 1966: 160–161).

19 / *Moon:* to present someone with the sudden, unexpected vision of one's unclothed buttocks, round and shining like the white orb of the moon. In the presence of a victim, one turns around, bends over, and pulls one's trousers and underwear down about a foot. One's genitals usually remain politely covered by the trousers and underwear.

20 / Almost everyone on any dorm floor had friendships off the floor as well, of course.

21 / In a spoof of a freshman's first days at Rutgers written by a student in 1859, for example, the president of the college greeted the new freshman with a high-flown lecture about the student's duties and responsibilities in college:

> "I sincerely hope, my son, that you will do credit to our instructions. . . . These are golden opportunities, if you will only improve them aright, my dear boy. . . . Youth is the time to gain knowledge most easily and most

thoroughly [and] to serve God . . ."

The freshman then ran into an upperclassman he knew from home, who gave him a different kind of advice:

> "How are you, Herden, my boy? . . . What did you think of the Prex.? Fine old gentleman, isn't he? though he is getting a little touched about religion, you know. . . . Bet you ten to one that he couldn't, and didn't, let you off without telling you that 'youth was the time to serve the Lord.' Ha! ha! . . . Don't look so angry, now, it's no sort of use. I see that Prex. has inspired you with a great respect for him. . . . But then, you see, we look at these things differently, after a while. It's an American student's privilege to find fault with his professors. . . .
> Where will you board? At the charming Mrs. Donley's? . . . 'Dog-meat Hall'? Good! What! you told Prex. you had friends there? Did you tell him who they were? . . . It's well you didn't, or you would not have been half so graciously received the next time you happen to visit the old gentleman." (Rutgers College 1859: 182–184).

22 / An example of one of Art's briefer routines (Fall 1984):

> I was sittin' in class the other day, and there was this girl in front of

me? She was *so-ooo* beautiful! You know the kind of girl who just makes you "nerd out"? So she asked the time. And the guy next to her didn't have a watch. So instead of saying [affects nasal tone of nerd], "It's just five minutes till the end," I reached out my arm to show her my watch. [Makes suave gesture, leaning forward toward imaginary girl and pulling back sleeve from left wrist.] Only I leaned too far forward. You know those little desks they have? [Makes gesture of losing balance, flailing around, and tipping disastrously forward.] Crash! I'm all over the floor. Scrambling around, books everywhere. [Pauses.] I wonder if she still loves me?

23 / *Cake* (short for "piece of cake"): easy.

24 / *Argue points:* to question exact grading decisions on each individual answer in an effort to raise one's overall grade on an exam.

25 / A cynical peer-group speech code was not peculiar to American college students, of course. As a backstage language spoken out of the hearing of those in authority, codes like this undoubtedly characterized persons in passive, non-decision-making positions at the bottom of all kinds of modern complex organizations— factory workers, privates in the army, etc. High school students and other adolescents had their own ways of talking in this code. Collegiate Undergraduate Cynical might have had some distinctive features compared to the language of younger adolescents. It might have been more worldly-wise; it might have contained a wider range of things to be cynical about than high school codes did. I had the impression that new freshmen waited to see if older college students talked like this, and then slowly began practicing it themselves—being careful as freshmen, if they were smart, not to try to compete too quickly with the older and wiser sophomores.

Undergraduate Cynical was context-specific and age-specific as well. Student authorities who hadn't known me in the dorms, for instance, often looked surprised and shocked if I suddenly tried to drop into it with them. The students also abandoned Undergraduate Cynical surprisingly quickly when they moved into other roles. Student authorities, including some preceptors, often got very good at talking Deanly Officialese without showing any obvious stress about doing so. Though there were intermediate forms. For example:

Novice preceptor to residents of floor: You've gotta come to this dorm meeting tonight. It's really important. I know it sounds kinda stupid. But I'll really look bad if no one from this floor shows up. You don't want me to look bad, do you?

26 / This quote and subsequent quotes from this talk session have been transcribed from tape. Since I am not engaged in strict conversation analysis here, I have edited out some of the students' verbal hesitations and repairs. Otherwise, these words are exactly as the students spoke them.

27 / These talk sessions, which Rutgers students no longer called "bull sessions" or "rap sessions," often became more serious and "cosmic" the later at night they occurred and the fewer students there were around. At 7:00 P.M. the students were usually more flippant in their lounge talk (for more on the contemporary, unlabeled college bull session, see chapter 7).

Obviously, Louie and Carrie were performing for my tape recorder, though I think they were performing naturalistically. Jay and the mysterious stranger, on the other hand, were probably not especially aware of the tape, and the stranger did not even stay around long enough to discover that he was a subject of research.

28 / Figure 3 is based on a questionnaire I circulated in late October to all sixty-two residents of Hasbrouck Fourth, giving every-

one the names of every other resident of the floor and asking them to identify their close friends, their friends, and persons they disliked or had a hard time getting along with. Fifty-seven residents responded. Most of them followed instructions and filled out the questionnaires privately and confidentially, returning them to me in a sealed envelope. A few close friends filled them out after mutual consultations with one another. Figure 4 is based on a similar questionnaire, which was circulated in early April.

29 / As Varenne has pointed out, most Americans do not believe that they themselves belong to cliques. They tend to see themselves as friendly people whose friendships are not determined by any group affiliations. They *may* belong to a "friendly group of people." '*I* belong to a friendly group of people; *you* belong to a clique' (see Varenne 1982). Hasbrouck Fourth residents, however, sometimes *did* say that they belonged to cliques when their friendship groups were unusually tight and exclusive, though they tended to use the term egocentrically when in ironic or self-critical moods.

30 / Proximity and college class had a general influence on friendship making, but to different degrees according to the particular

histories of different dorm-floor groups. On most floors, most reciprocated close friendships did develop between people on the same side of a floor and in the same section. On two other floors where this same questionnaire was given out in 1978, close friendships across the sections comprised only 8 percent and 21 percent of the totals respectively. Hasbrouck Fourth had a relatively high incidence of cross-section close friendships, 23 percent. One reason was the number of returning sophomores with new room assignments; some of the previous year's intrasection friendships turned into cross-section friendships in 1984. Other cross-section friendships, on the other hand, were new to the floor in 1984. Since the freshman Judy, for example, did not get along with her roommates and did not like the wedgie patrollers who dominated her side of Hasbrouck Fourth, she went looking elsewhere for friends, and found Leo and Carrie on the high side.

Interclass friendships also varied widely by floor. Hasbrouck Fourth had fewer close friendships between students of different college classes than either of the 1978 floors, possibly because of the dominance of the already-bonded sophomores on the floor. Only 24 percent of all the reciprocated

close friendships on Hasbrouck Fourth in the fall of 1984 were between persons of different college classes. On the two floors in 1978, which had more normal freshman-sophomore distributions than Hasbrouck Fourth, the interclass percentages were significantly higher, 40 percent and 47 percent. On the topic of close friendships within or between the sexes, see chapter 2, and note 39.

31 / Secret Santa as it was practiced by the students had all the sociological characteristics of ritual as identified by Emile Durkheim in his classic text *Elementary Forms of the Religious Life* (1915), and as subsequently rediscovered by innumerable anthropologists in personal and tribal groups all over the world. It created a mood of what Durkheim called "social effervescence." It helped to release, or at least to express, certain key tensions—for Secret Santa, mostly sexual tensions. And it ultimately centered on an important collective value: the importance of floor friendliness.

What connection was there between the embarrassing stunts in Secret Santa and floor friendliness? The American cultural rule, You should be willing to make an idiot of yourself in front of your friends. If, under the ritual circumstances of Secret Santa, you make an idiot of yourself in front of your coresidents on a dorm floor, you are then reenacting all of them *as* friends. You are making them all back into friends—or at least into friendly acquaintances, whatever tensions and conflicts you may have had with one another over the previous three months. And this really happened among the students. Good rituals are transformative. See the changing relationship between Bob and Penny later in this chapter, for instance.

One irony of the deans' opposition to Secret Santa was that they themselves used exactly the same cultural premise ritualistically in their innumerable icebreakers during orientation. If you were encouraged to tell something personal to strangers, this made you feel more friendly toward them as a result (since friends tell one another personal things). In these terms, all that the deans were really arguing about was who got to set the ritual conditions, themselves or the students.

32 / Dan told one of the more riveting stories. During his freshman year, he explained, his Secret Santa challengers had wondered if they could come up with something too outrageous even for him, so they had dared him to perform a striptease in Commons. As he remembered it a year later, he had walked over around five thirty on an evening in early December,

when the dining hall tended to be most crowded. Dan had studied method acting, and he recalled concentrating and visualizing on the way over, getting himself in the proper actorish mood. Once at Commons, with a few friends as witnesses, he had jumped up on an empty table, turned on some music on the portable tape deck that he had brought with him, and begun to do a slow bump-and-grind. One by one, he had taken off his garments, twirling each one around and then throwing it out into the crowd. Hundreds of students had looked up from their meals in astonishment, Dan said, hooting, cheering, and clapping, and some of the adult cafeteria workers had come out to gawk. When he was down to a pair of purple underwear, a few students had run up and stuffed dollar bills into them in the manner of fans of barroom go-go dancers. For a climax, Dan had whipped around, bent over, and mooned the crowd.

And then, Dan said, "When the music stopped and I was down off the table dressed only in my purple 'wares, I suddenly popped out of my mood. And I couldn't *believe* how embarrassed I was!" He had thrown on another set of clothes and run back to Hasbrouck Fourth, where his Secret Santa stunt became the stuff of local legend for a year or two.

33 / The freshman student's mostly white peers may also have been commenting on the inappropriateness of a white liking "black" music. Though "heavy metal," a type of rock-and-roll involving very loud music, was virtually invented by black star Jimi Hendrix, it is stereotypically a white rather than a black musical taste. On musical taste and racial identity among the undergraduates, see chapter 4.

34 / *To cream* (for a male): to ejaculate sexually.

35 / Lois was an older female residence life authority.

36 / "KUT" is the name of a sorority.

37 / In the months in which this quarrel was brewing, Pete's aspersions on me had had an effect on Carrie, and I couldn't get her version of most of these events. When I did talk to her about the dispute months later when we were friends again, she was unwilling to talk about its possible racial aspects; she just wanted to forget the whole thing, she implied.

38 / To be fair to Art, I think I *would* have remembered it if he had said anything blatantly racist during his diatribe. His rantings, I think, had been more along the lines of "No one threatens me" and "You have no right to say the things you've said."

39 / As Brian put it, he was tired of girls thinking he was *just* a nice guy, coming to him with their problems about this guy and that guy, asking for advice, and never thinking about him "that way." As already indicated (chapter 2), cross-sex friendships among the students in the coed dorms were sometimes speculations on the part of one of the partners, relationships undertaken in the hope that something closer would develop.

The degree of gender segregation in the Hasbrouck Fourth friendship network by the spring of 1984 was probably atypical, however, a product of other idiosyncracies of the floor. In the fall, 24 percent of the close friendships on Hasbrouck Fourth had been cross-sex relationships, declining to 9 percent in the spring. On the two other dorm floors tested with this same questionnaire in 1978, on the other hand, almost half of all the reported reciprocated close friendships around the middle of the years were cross-sex friendships, 47 percent and 40 percent respectively.

40 / As I saw Secret Santa played on Hasbrouck Fourth, for instance, the student audience responded to particular performances with highly nuanced attention to the personality of the students performing. A shy student who ob-

viously had a very difficult time performing at all was generally encouraged and won praise even for standing up and trying. A self-confident extrovert, on the other hand, might be received with jeers and catcalls, which she or he apparently often enjoyed as much as the audience enjoyed giving them. Students clearly did try to get one another with some of the stunts. But there were many ways to get the challenger back. You could re-negotiate a challenge—"I'm not doing this one; try again" (challenges reached victims through intermediaries). Or you could win points by meeting the letter of the challenge while cleverly avoiding its intent. In another dorm, for instance, a shy girl was challenged to give a lecture on masturbation, and did so—in Italian. Or you could perform an embarrassing challenge with so much vigor and esprit that you triumphed over it: you as actor in the stunt could win credit for what they had made you as actor do in the stunt.

Another strict rule was that anything done in Secret Santa was specially framed in time and space. As the students put it, "The stunts don't mean anything." "They're just for fun." "No one should take anything personally that happens during Secret Santa." The Secret Santa stunts were folk theater. Like all good rituals, they were set apart; they were privileged, self-conscious performances.

41 / See, for instance, Davis 1971 and Gillis 1974:19−35.

42 / See chapter 2, note 17, for an indication of the centrality of the average college dorm floor to student friendship-making in the college.

43 / *Airhead* ("gasbag"): someone who talks all the time but has nothing intelligent to say.

44 / *To get fucked up:* to drink too much or to ingest too much of an illegal substance.

45 / One way the deans could try to interfere with this 'natural' process of student-to-student enculturation was by segregating the freshmen from upperclassmen residentially; over the years, the freshman dorm *has* been a recurrent strategy of deanly control at Rutgers. The deans first instituted freshman dorms in the early 1930s in order, they said, to foster "class spirit." But these dorms also clearly functioned to cut the average freshman off from the average upperclassman and perhaps from the Undergraduate Cynical frame of mind (assuming that the few upperclass preceptors who were allowed in these dorms did not introduce them to it).

In the late 1960s, Rutgers students themselves helped to bring about the demise of the original freshman dorms, on the grounds that it was "discriminatory" to make a freshman live in a certain place because of her or his college class. The deans at Rutgers College were quietly renovating them on a "pilot" basis in the 1980s, however, with preceptors and a few other upperclass "mentors." The freshmen in the revived freshman dorms often did say that they liked living in them, partly because everyone started off on an equal footing; there were no old-timers around with their preestablished cliques. But they also said that they had to go elsewhere to get essential upperclass wisdom about various aspects of the undergraduates' college, about beating the bureaucracy, about good and bad professors, and so on. Other students in the college sometimes stigmatized the revived freshman residence halls at Rutgers by calling them "diaper dorms."

46 / Five ex-residents of Hasbrouck Fourth (all ex-sophomores, all males) were enrolled as students in a large class I taught about my Rutgers research in 1987, so I invited them to come up and comment, as a panel of local experts, on my preliminary analysis of the floor. All of them agreed that Hasbrouck Fourth had been full of problems in 1984–1985, that it had not been a typical Rutgers dorm floor, though several of them also said that they had had very good times on the floor that year. Most of them said that Pete had been a lousy preceptor. One of the wedgie patrollers said he had grown up a lot since he engaged in those sophomoric activities. But he certainly did not regret them, and he thought I blamed the wedgie patrol too much in my analysis of the dynamics of Hasbrouck Fourth in the early fall, he said.

I had soft-pedaled Art and Carrie's fight during my classroom presentation, but Art, one of the commentators in 1987, brought it up again in all its vivid detail. He was still angry with Carrie; he apparently still felt that she had introduced racially based threats in an inappropriate way. But after he told the class his version of their fight—referring to Carrie with the phrase "let's call her *Grace Jones*" and giving her a stereotypic black accent, which she didn't have at all—I felt that I had to make some strong comments from the podium about undergraduate racism at Rutgers. I noted that Carrie might have told the whole thing very differently; that Art's own behavior had not been entirely impeccable; that black students, in my observations, had to work somewhat harder than the average white student to live amiably on the average "integrated" Rutgers dorm floor; and so on. See chapter 4.

47 / It is impossible to know for sure about a judgment like this, of course, or about other, more subtle control effects that my presence may have exerted on Hasbrouck Fourth in 1984–1985. One—always a potential influence in participant observation—was that by poking around all year long, I had made the residents of the floor more self-conscious about local culture and local social processes than they otherwise would have been. If so, that consciousness may have changed the culture and the processes themselves (the social scientist, or the "hard" scientist, always changes what she or he is studying by the act of studying it, as the Intro to Methodology lecture always goes).

At the end of the year, I circulated a short questionnaire, which I asked the residents to return without signing. "Are you aware of ways in which my presence has changed things on the floor this year?" I asked them. Some residents said that I had had no effect that they were aware of. Others said there had been certain goings-on from which the students had shielded me, some "partying" behavior, some sexual activities, the use of drugs, etc. And some respondents said that, though my presence had never changed their own behavior, they had noticed it had changed the behavior of other residents. Some people on the floor, they reported, had exaggerated everything they said and did when I was around. For example, when my tape recorder was on, the ordinarily boisterous members of the wedgie patrol clique had become even more boisterous than usual.

There is no reason why greater self-consciousness would necessarily have led to greater conflict on Hasbrouck Fourth in 1984–1985, however; it could as easily have had the opposite effect. And the other side of this reflexive coin was another common observation made by Hasbrouck Fourth residents on these questionnaires. At least half of them told me, politely or not so politely, that as a once-a-week resident, I was around so little on the floor that most of the time they had not even been aware that I was there.

48 / The crackdown on Secret Santa has continued at Rutgers; but two years later, rumors do occasionally reach my ears from reliable student sources that it continues to be played surreptitiously on occasion, complete with the challenges, in particularly secret nooks and crannies of the dorms.

And the alternatives, if anything, can be worse. One dorm

group in 1987 decided to replace Secret Santa with a drinking game centering on a collective viewing of "How the Grinch Stole Christmas." The Grinch reminded them of common childhood pleasures, and the drinking—keyed to certain events and words in the cartoon—got them all smashed, and bonded, even more reliably than Secret Santa had done, they felt.

49 / There was a resemblance, in fact, between what Pete did on Hasbrouck Fourth in 1984 and what the Robeson residents were thought to have done on Erewhon Third in 1978 (next chapter), though the motivations were very different. But both were perceived as unfriendly. And unfriendliness was the ultimate sin in the norms of ordinary dorm sociability, the one thing guaranteed to make everyone else almost irrationally angry.

50 / *To ralph:* to vomit (onomatopoeic).

FOUR / Race and Individualism

How did undergraduates in the "white" majority at Rutgers, about eighty percent of the student body in the mid-1980s, think about and act toward their black peers?[1] The students often said they liked or thought they benefited from the diversity of Rutgers, from the fact that, as a public institution, it attracted youths from all the different social groups in the state of New Jersey (see chapter 2). Yet many of them found real cultural differences distressing and intolerable when they actually had to live with them, and racial differences often made them even more uncomfortable.

The white students almost all knew that American blacks had been treated badly in the past. They almost all knew that they themselves should not be racists any longer, that, as sociologist Gunnar Myrdal has stated in *An American Dilemma*, traditional American racism was a violation of the American "value premise" of equal opportunity for all (1944: 23–25). But in ways that will become clearer below, I hope, the students' fundamental individualism was also simply too nonhistorical and nonsociological to allow them to grasp interracial situations of any real complexity. Some white students lived with the ensuing quandary as uneasy liberals. Others entertained the only apparent alternative given their individualistic ways of thinking about much more complicated human realities: the illiberal sentiments of racism.

Race was only incidentally important on Hasbrouck Fourth in 1984–1985. It was one possible subtext of Art and Carrie's fight, though Art was probably just as upset with Carrie as an assertive woman as he was with her as a black (see chapter 3). Otherwise the four blacks and the one Puerto Rican student on Hasbrouck Fourth—and the two Asian-Americans and the two or three Latins—lived reasonably amiably among their white peers all year long.[2] This was partly because they were swamped by the white majority on an "integrated" floor like Hasbrouck Fourth. It was also, unquestionably, because they lived on the floor on the terms of the white majority. None of them were "threatening." None of them made much of her or his black or Puerto Rican identity.

All five had close white friends on Hasbrouck Fourth. As far as I could tell, four out of five had about the same range of personal successes and setbacks as average white residents of the floor; one, Alvin, though charming, was a lost soul for reasons that did not seem to have much to do with his racial identity. As for Ernie, Alvin's sometime roommate, Ernie told me very emphatically early in the year that, in his opinion, the whole point of being a black student in a white college was to learn to get along with white people. He had no respect, he said, for black students who looked for all-black enclaves in which to live in college. And Ernie certainly did get along. He was a big, handsome, well-muscled young man who spent much of his sophomore year practicing with the varsity football team, which he had made as a walk-on. He belonged to a fraternity known for its athletic integration but dominated by whites. And whenever I visited him in his room, two or three pretty girls, almost always pretty white girls, stopped by to say hello.

With one exception, as far as I knew, none of these black students had to deal with openly racist remarks or challenges from their white peers on Hasbrouck Fourth in 1984–1985. The whites who did not like blacks for categorical reasons—there were six or eight residents who I knew or suspected held these sentiments—still usually said hi in the same friendly fashion that everyone else did. But then they carefully steered clear of closer relationships with the four black students and the one Puerto Rican on the floor. Danny, the Puerto Rican, believed he could spot these white racists, though he did not make a point of confronting them, he said, as long as they kept their feelings to themselves. And several of his suspects were students I heard being quietly intolerant among their close white friends.

One of them was not just a suspect, however. A sophomore male from the wedgie patrol clique, Danny told me two years later, used to confront him when drunk and say to him, non-jokingly he felt, "One thing we don't need on this floor is a dwarf spic!" (Danny was short.)

Other white students on Hasbrouck Fourth, however, were genuinely open and friendly across racial lines. At one time or another during the year, ten different white residents of Hasbrouck Fourth were partners in close friendships with black residents on the floor or with Danny, close friendships the minority partners also claimed on their own confidential questionnaires; and many more white residents were "friends" (as opposed to "close friends") with one or more of the black or Puerto Rican students on the floor.

Among the students on the other Rutgers dorm floor where I lived and did research for a year, on the other hand, among the residents of Erewhon Third in 1978–1979, race *was* the story. For Erewhon Third was where the college had located the Paul Robeson section, named for the early-twentieth-century Rutgers graduate who was perhaps the most illustrious alumnus in the history of the college, black or white.[3] The Robeson section was for students with a special interest in black culture. And on Erewhon Third, race and racism, overtly and covertly, were issues every day of the year.

RACE ON EREWHON THIRD

In response to the civil rights movement, black activism, and the college youth revolt of the late 1960s, Rutgers first began admitting significant numbers of black and Spanish-speaking minority students between 1968 and 1972.[4] Black student leaders soon called for separate dorms where black undergraduates could live together and support one another in the new, unfamiliar college environment. At first college authorities balked at what they saw as the self-segregative nature of such proposals, but eventually they came around. They compromised by redefining black living units as another type of special-interest group. Just as students whose particular interest in creative writing, for instance, might be encouraged by letting them reside together, so, too, a certain number of black students might be permitted to live together to enhance their interest in "black culture."

By 1978, the Robeson unit had been on the third floor of Erewhon Hall for two years, and it was still there nine years later. But it had not existed on Erewhon Third unproblematically, not at all. For in its fundamental organization—in terms of the situation into which any black or white student walked when she or he first took up residence on Erewhon Third—the floor embodied most of the dilemmas and contradictions of contemporary American individualism and race relations.

The Robeson group's very existence, to begin with, was an affront to many white undergraduates. Americans believe they should have the right to choose how they live and with whom they live; but inward-looking groups of any sort—status-conscious cliques, exclusive fraternities and sororities, self-interested political coalitions—are suspect according to these same individualistic American presuppositions. It did not matter to most white undergraduates I knew that blacks had not had any choice about their separate identity in the eyes of whites in the United States for hundreds of years. If blacks were good Americans, most white students felt, they should not want to live only among themselves any longer, because of an interest in black culture or for any other reason. Now that American society, and colleges like Rutgers, had decided to allow blacks to "integrate," *they* should want to do so too, or there was something wrong with them.

Second, Erewhon Third had been set up in such a way that the members of the Robeson group were automatically pulled in two different directions. Robeson members probably expected their special-interest group to be a unit unto itself; most of the other special-interest living units in the college were.[5] And in certain ways, the structure of Erewhon Third "said" that it was. The Robeson students all lived in their own bounded area, in their own section on the high side of the floor, with their own lounge (see figure 5 below). And the lounge itself was emblematically black, for in the early years of the section, Robeson residents had painted a mural depicting scenes from black history on one of its walls. The Robeson group did not take up the entire floor on Erewhon Third, however; black student demand on the College Avenue Campus had never been great enough, college authorities insisted, to justify assigning more than half the floor to the group, one section of fifteen rooms. On the low side of Erewhon Third was another set of rooms whose residents were mostly white. And the residence life deans in charge of the dorms apparently expected all of Erewhon Third to operate, just as any other dorm floor did, as a single collectivity—to build the usual deanly community under the direction of its single preceptor and through high-minded common programs.

College authorities may have made this implicit demand that Erewhon Third be a "normal" floor deliberately, in order to preserve official ideals of racial integration, or they may have set up the floor with no special forethought.[6] Whatever their motives, however, the average white student at Rutgers had strictly limited time and enthusiasm for "community" as the deans envisioned it (see chapter 3)—but the Robeson members were being asked by the structure of Erewhon Third to have twice as much.

In 1978–1979 at least, Erewhon Third had one further source of conflict built into it from the beginning of the year: the students who lived on the two sides of the floor had very different attitudes toward living there in the first place. The blacks in the Robeson section had, by definition, willingly chosen to live on Erewhon Third. Perhaps half the upperclassmen were returning residents, and many of the freshmen had been recruited from a special summer program for educationally disadvantaged students by Robeson veterans, who had promised them black friendships in a white college and a convenient central-campus location.[7] The whites on the low side of the floor, on the other hand, were there either because the housing computer had placed them there or through a combination of the housing lottery and much more reluctant choices than the Robeson members had made. The freshmen, like all freshmen in all the dorms, had been randomly assigned to their rooms. Most of the upperclassmen had chosen the floor, but they had chosen it *last.* For there had been rumors abroad among white students in the college of "problems" on Erewhon Third in previous years. Consequently, most of the white upperclassmen on the low side of the floor were students who had been unlucky in the annual housing lottery the previous spring; Erewhon Third was all that was left to them if they wanted a room anywhere at all on the preferred College Avenue Campus.

Given all these intrinsic problems and contradictions, and considering that many of the youths on Erewhon Third, black and white alike, had never really dealt with interracial relationships in their adolescent lives to date, the less-than-easy flow of daily sociability on Erewhon Third most years was less surprising than that things usually went as smoothly as they did on the floor. It has now been a decade since I did research on Erewhon Third, and the floor, like Hasbrouck Fourth and all other dorm groups at Rutgers, has undoubtedly acted out different collective stories every year since. But there is no reason to believe that the fundamental problems that the students had to cope with on Erewhon Third in 1978–1979 have disappeared from American or undergraduate culture in the last ten years. In the late years of Ronald Reagan's America, in fact, there is reason to wonder if things are as *good* interracially at present as they were back in the late 1970s.[8] Here, in any case, is Erewhon Third in 1978–1979 as I knew it, and my own opinion of why things worked out the way they did there.

Opening Moves

About fifteen white residents waited nervously for the first floor-meeting of the year to begin on Erewhon Third, on a Tuesday evening in early September. What would the Robeson members be like this year? The previous year, according to one vague white rumor, Erewhon Third had been an "armed camp." None of the whites knew about the floor for certain, however; not one of them had lived on Erewhon Third the year before, including the male preceptor. Many of the whites' minds were also filled, I realized later, with preconceptions about blacks drawn from the media and sometimes from their previous experiences in racially troubled hometowns and high schools: "Blacks like to threaten whites"; "Blacks are good hustlers"; "Blacks are tough, inner-city types"; "Blacks believe in black solidarity"; and so on. The new white residents of Erewhon Third were going to need a lot of reassurance from the black residents.

Then about ten young black women and men walked in together from the high side, most of them freshmen, led by Henry, a big sophomore. They didn't look so scary, but they did look a little tense themselves, and they all sat down in their own semicircle, facing the semicircle of whites.

The preceptor disposed of the usual beginning-of-the-year announcements and then broached what was to be the hot topic on Erewhon Third in 1978–1979, common programs for the floor as whole. First he asked for suggestions, and when none were forthcoming, he pulled out the one thing he had been able to think of himself: "We could have a coffeehouse. There's this student folk singer I know. He's really *good*. I've heard him. He plays James Taylor and other mellow stuff like that."

The blacks exchanged glances, and Henry laughed richly and gave what the whites took as the Robeson residents' collective response. "James *Taylor?!*" he said incredulously. There was another silence, and the anthropologist, unable to stand it, suggested his own hobby at the time: "What about a canoe trip for the whole floor?" More quick looks between the Robeson members, and then Henry once again: "Why don't you ask how many of us can *swim?!*" ("Yes, what a mistake, with *their* cultural backgrounds!" the preceptor said to me later in private.)[9] And that was about that for the first floor-meeting of the year on Erewhon Third in 1978. The blacks had made no suggestions at all, but neither, for that matter, had any of the whites other than myself and the preceptor. And the meeting broke up with no agreements other than an indefinite plan for a floor party later in the fall.

Henry, I found out later, had hoped to be a conciliator on Erewhon Third in 1978. The year before, Robeson residents, resisting what they saw as the ridiculous demand that they build two different types of community during their year on the floor, had not attended general floor meetings at all. Henry had hoped he could encourage students on both sides of Erewhon Third to at least be *friendly* toward one another this year. Which had not meant, however, that he wanted the Robeson members to go along with all-floor fun and games any more than they had done the year before. You lived in the Robeson section to enjoy your own particular black cultural pleasures, not to sit around pretending you liked to listen to James *Taylor!*

But the white residents of the low side of Erewhon Third were not impressed by the mere appearance of the blacks at the first floor-meeting in 1978. And although Henry's joking had actually not been nearly as rough as the razzing the white wedgie-patrol sophomores had given Pete in the first floor-meeting on Hasbrouck Fourth in 1984 (see chapter 3), the whites had not taken it as good clean fun. They were much too tense, it was clear, about living next to a large number of black students all year long. Only the most earnest, unaggressive friendliness from the Robeson residents would have made them happy; Undergraduate Cynical and ordinary busting were not what they wanted to hear from *black* students. If Henry thought he was being friendly just by showing up, most of the whites, on the contrary, thought he was being hostile.

And in private interviews in the next month and a half, most of the white freshmen told me that they thought there were, consequently, real problems on Erewhon Third already early in the fall semester, and they blamed them all on the Robeson section: "I try to be friendly, but it doesn't work." "I tried to be friendly, but I've stopped." "Most of them never say hi." Freshmen on the Robeson side saw the floor quite differently. Not all of them had attended the first meeting; not all of them knew what Henry had said. And those who did were puzzled by the suggestion that his remarks might have been considered unfriendly. Most of the black students on Erewhon Third, in fact, considered the floor to be a reasonably amiable place so far. If, for most of the white students on Erewhon Third, the only known blacks were the members of the Robeson section— and they were not as friendly as they might have been—for most of the Robeson residents, on the other hand, whites were the whole society, not just 'those people over there, who aren't bad.'

The blacks were thus judging the local white students comparatively, against backgrounds different from anything the whites were used to thinking about. The white students on the low side were preferable to nonstudents, some blacks said:

The problem isn't here, in the dorms, but over on Easton Avenue [in the Hungarian section of New Brunswick].—Freshman male, Robeson section

Or, for Robeson residents from inner-city backgrounds, the whites at Rutgers were definitely preferable to the whites back home:

> *Anthropologist:* What would you tell people at home that people at Rutgers are like?

> *Black student:* Well, I'd tell them at . . . Rutgers, there's a lot of Caucasians, there's a few blacks, but everyone here, you know, is here for one reason—to try to learn, to try to make something of himself. But everyone's . . . friendly, you know . . . they're not *hostile* up here. It's a break [from what it's like at home in Newark].[10]*

As *I* observed their behavior in the first few months of the fall semester, the black and the white residents of Erewhon Third were not entirely *un*-friendly to one another. Some of them exchanged the occasional nod and a hi or a how's it goin'? in passing. The biggest facilitator of these nodding acquaintanceships was the daily flow of women to the women's room on the Robeson side and of men to the men's room on the low side of the floor.[11] Some men from both sides occasionally watched baseball together on TV in the low-side lounge; one outgoing white freshman woman got to know a few students on the Robeson side on her own initiative, and there were rumors of a small integrated coterie of pot-smokers on the floor. But most of the black students and white students on Erewhon Third were not getting to know one another very well as individuals in the first few months of the year. Most of them did not even know first names across the sections; most of them did not feel comfortable sitting down casually in one another's lounges.

White Reactions

Meanwhile, without much personal knowledge to go on, the white residents of Erewhon Third were spending the early days of the fall semester whispering among themselves about what it all meant. Two young men and one young woman were the most outspoken white racists on the low side of the floor. One of the men, a sophomore, had obviously been brooding over his room assignment all summer, for he had brought a baseball bat with him in his personal effects when he moved into the dorm at the beginning of the semester. On it were carved the letters "NBC." They meant, he told me with a smirk, "Nigger Be Cool!" And in the first few months, he made incessant racist remarks when there were no black students around listening in. A typical "joke" (on seeing one of the larger black males emerge from the showers wearing only a towel):

> These guys could eat a poor little white boy like me for breakfast . . . honky on toast, cheese honky . . .

A typical "analysis":

> Don't you think they're overdoing the hostility business a little, Mike? I mean, it seems like they're trying to make up for two hundred years of slavery in two semesters. And they're *pushing* it.

Note the rare reference to the history of American race relations in the second remark, albeit a dismissive one.

Another man told a small group of white friends late one evening that he had been in the parking lot of a lonely dorm the night before, when five or six "niggers"—he looked over his shoulder when he said the word—had jumped out of a car and come toward him: "'Shit! This is it,' I said to my buddy. But they went right by us. They were just going to some party!"

To the private interview question, "Do you have any problems with blacks on the floor?" a freshman female gave an answer that is notable both for its racism and for its sense of the illegitimacy of same:

> *Student:* Yes! . . . I went to [high] school with them, and . . . the population was 30 [percent black and] 70 [percent white], and they're—how do I put it? They're always trying to do something. Like this morning [narrates an incident the same morning in the women's room on Erewhon Third, involving a misunderstanding with a black female over a bottle of shampoo]. . . . A couple of them are real nice. I say hello, I always say hello . . . but just some of them are real bastards! Yuck!*

> *Anthropologist:* Are the nice ones guys or girls?

> *Student:* That I can't even—see, I don't even really get close to them. . . . I try to be friendly, but then . . . I went to a [high] school and I guess I wasn't stuck with college people, and they were very uncivilized, very rowdy and gangy, and . . . you know, saying they—you say one thing wrong, and forget it! You had fifty of them on your back after school! So I came in with a very bad

149

attitude about them and it's just not getting any better. . . . [The ones at Rutgers] are a lot nicer than just regular ones, cause I guess they're smarter and they know a lot more.*

The terms in which blacks were condemned in this statement are consistent with those traditional to American white racism: "uncivilized," "rowdy," "gangy." Yet even this student, who along with the first white male above was the most openly racist student on the low side of Erewhon Third, and who described herself defiantly on another occasion as "prejudiced," had conflicting attitudes. Note the statement again. She could not stand to be near blacks, but some of them were "nice." They were all the same (first few lines), yet the ones at Rutgers were "nicer" and "smarter" than "regular ones." She even hedged on her personal responsibility for her own racism, indicating that she did not quite approve of it in herself. Bad experiences in high school had *caused* her to have a "bad attitude," which experiences in college were not altering, somehow without ever implicating the active, responsible "she" as an agent.

The statements of some other white students on the low side of Erewhon Third at the beginning of the year were equally ambivalent but less fearful:

> *Freshman female:* I don't really know anyone in the other section. Because, you know, you'll say hello to them, but they don't even say anything. I don't know, it's not that I'm an overfriendly person, but I think it's just snobbish when you walk past someone not to say hello . . . I just figure that color and race didn't make any difference, that people would still basically, you know, be the same. The only problem is, is just the music, like I don't like disco music at all.*

Two problems were mentioned here: lack of friendliness, closely linked to a disproof of the supposition that people were "basically" the same, and music. The salient cultural difference between blacks and whites cited most often by students from both racial backgrounds on Erewhon Third was musical taste.

One white transfer student had been placed in the Robeson section by housing, with a black roommate, but he immediately began to associate with white students on the low side of the floor most of the time.[12] Nevertheless, in the early weeks of the fall semester, he was the only white student on Erewhon Third with any daily knowledge of the Robeson residents. One day he was trying to reassure some of the more threatened white residents about the black students on the high side: "They're really nice. They're just different, totally different. They have different interests. They're totally into music—disco—they've never heard of the Grateful Dead! They have a different ethnic identity."

There is an affinity between this distinctive feature of the blacks in the minds of the whites and the classic white racist definition of blacks as "naturally musical," but no white student ever articulated this connection in my hearing. For it would have contradicted the whites' own fundamental self-definitions in the 1980s. In mainstream American white adolescent culture in the late twentieth century, one's musical tastes were at the core of one's personal identity, an expression of one's essence—a free choice, like friendship. Like friendship, music had to do with relaxation, with the real emotions and the "real self"—and, in the case of music, with the release of sexual feelings. For white students, musical tastes and the centrality of music tended to differentiate late-adolescents from adults, and the black youths on Erewhon Third apparently made similar assumptions.

Many students of both races said that they liked "all kinds of music," but against this claim was the disturbing percept that average musical tastes correlated closely with racial identity. For what one heard booming out of the rooms was not endlessly diverse. Disco *was* a common black taste in the late 1970s; rap had succeeded it by the mid-1980s. Heavy metal and more mellow rock-and-roll (James Taylor, for instance) were favorite white tastes, augmented by new wave and punk in the mid-1980s. Students tolerated the loud music of other students when it was within their own range of liking, but when it violated their own tastes, they heard it—as adults often hear adolescent music—as assertive noise.

The preceding quote also mentions "ethnic identity." And this explanation of racial difference was the one most commonly used by the white liberals on Erewhon Third, three of whom were especially vocal, two males and one female:

> *Freshman male:* Yeah, we got to do something about the conga section. They're not friendly. They're not interacting. I guess they have different cultural backgrounds.

"Culture" took the students to another level of analysis, to an apparently more relativistic one; except that, as the undergraduates understood culture, it only marginally modified their fundamental individualism. Positively construed, culture was something like individual choice at a collective level. Of course, just as any individual had a right to her or his own opinions, so, too, did any group. It was also consistent with a social-psychology corollary in the students' otherwise individualistic ideology: Our experiences *do* influence the way we think and feel, the students sometimes admitted. Thus the bad attitude of the reactionary white female quoted above resulted from her bad experiences in high school, and thus different cultural backgrounds might cause different groups of people to make systematically different choices in music and in other areas of personal taste.

Yet the realm within which most students allowed this relativistic assumption to operate was a very narrow one. People had the right to different opinions, most of the white students assumed; but in many everyday behaviors—those of friend*liness*, for instance—all normal human beings ought to act similarly, for many daily behaviors were "natural." A thoughtful white sophomore on Erewhon Third who had heard me lecture on symbolic anthropology the year before asked me one day in the dorms, "What are *you* doing here? There's nothing symbolic about *this*." I expressed my orthodox anthropological opinion: all human cultural realities are constructed or arbitrary to some extent. "But aren't some of them more natural than others?" she replied.

Given assumptions like this one, most students were very uneasy when a different culture was actually strongly manifested in behavior. On Erewhon Third in 1978, for instance, a white sophomore woman was defensive about her Lebanese boyfriend, apologizing for his Muslim name and saying that he was "really nice." He was an exception to other "Arabs" she had met; *they* were "*really* different," she said. Several young white men also told me, half-jokingly, about a south Asian who had behaved inexplicably in Commons the year before, eating alone, fastidiously, "with his hands." They had watched him with amusement all year, and since he was an "Indian" they had facetiously nicknamed him "Pow Wow." I was fairly certain from their descriptions that he was from the south of India, eating in traditional fashion, with his right hand. Silverware is considered unclean in traditional south Indian culture because it has been used by strangers. I explained this to my student friends one evening and gave them a demonstration of the eating style in question. They recognized it; they were polite and amused; but they were also apparently embarrassed by my cross-cultural display.

In other contexts, white students criticized "stereotypic" statements that implied that different cultures might have different behavioral entailments. A freshman male described one woman's hometown boyfriend, after his first visit to the dorm, as a "wimp" and as "typically Jewish." A non-Jewish listener protested against "typically Jewish" but not against "wimp." The teller responded that there was nothing wrong with such ethnic characterizations, that he himself would not mind being called "typically Catholic" or "typically Irish." An older student, listening in, told them both to shut up. On another occasion, this same older student said of a friend, "Joe gestures with his hands. He can't help it. He's Italian." Joe quickly shot back, "I'll breaka your legs. I can't help it. Ima Italian." [13]

Given these reservations, the students' working concept of culture, for use in an interracial context, was not especially deep or sophisticated. Notably missing from it was the idea that culture could fundamentally determine habitual modes of thought and deeply influence behavior, or that it was relativistic in any sense more profound than one person's having a taste for one leisure activity and another for a different activity.

> *Anthropologist:* What different types of people have you noticed here at Rutgers so far?

> *Freshman female* [September 1978]: Well, I've noticed a lot of people here are into Frisbee. Is that what you mean?

Nevertheless, the students were certainly better off in a racial context with even their diminished, American value-laden concept of culture than they would have been without it. For it did give some of them a semilegitimate explanation—a mediating explanation—of "difference" in a situation in which, otherwise, only overt racism might have been conceptually possible for them. [14]

Tensions

At Rutgers in the late 1970s and in the mid-1980s, black students had to put up with intermittent expressions of racism on the part of at least a few of the white undergraduates. White racism was nothing new to most black students at Rutgers, of course. For some of them, Rutgers may have been an improvement over their hometowns and high schools—Rutgers was not *nonracist*, but it was *less* racist than home. On the other hand, that any racism at all existed among college-educated youths may have been a surprise to some black students. In private discussions with Robeson residents in the fall of 1978, most of them suggested that they usually just shrugged off racist incidents.[15] They certainly did not walk around college in perpetual states of fear and trembling. Most of the incidents were verbal or semiotic ones: an epithet shouted out or read in passing, a little eloquent body language.[16] These things did not happen to them all the time; they happened sporadically. But they occurred often enough so that it would have been understandable if the average black student at Rutgers always had an edge of reserve in dealing with her or his white undergraduate peers, no matter how friendly any given white student appeared to be.

One freshman male on the Robeson side told his friends that a white girl had moved ostentatiously away from him, with a look of distaste on her face, when he had innocently sat down next to her in one of his first English composition classes in September. A carload of passing college boys shouted "Nigger!" at a few Robeson males on College Avenue late one night later in the month. And the same epithet appeared in one of the Erewhon elevators about the same time; the residence counselor for Erewhon Hall, a black graduate student, quickly had it expunged. "Things are going on here that I don't like, and I want them *stopped!*" the RC angrily told a private meeting of all her preceptors, with a particularly hard look at the preceptor from Erewhon Third. One evening later in the semester, when some Robeson residents had one of their stereos cranked up, unidentifiable voices from another floor of the dorm shouted out, "Will you Sambos keep it down!"

Only one incident I knew of took place between the black residents and the white residents of Erewhon Third in the fall semester of 1978, however. According to white accounts, a freshman on the low side was disturbed late one night by noise outside the dorm; he said later that he did not know at the time who was making it. "Shut the fuck up!" he yelled from his window. The noisemakers shouted back, angrily challenging him to give them his room number, which he did. Whereupon three angry black males barged into the low-side section, one from the high side of Erewhon Third, the other two from elsewhere. They hammered on the freshman's locked door and called him a "white bastard," white witnesses said. A white female from a nearby room, the reactionary woman quoted above, tried to intervene, probably in a nonconciliatory fashion, so the intruders verbally harassed her as well. Some low-side residents called the campus police, but before they could arrive, two other white males—liberals—intervened and convinced the intruders to leave. White residents on the low side of the floor talked about the incident for a day or two among themselves, agreed that the freshman had been stupid, and soon hushed it up.

The Robeson section had also had its own internal problems and cliques during the fall semester, I was told. As a white professor who lived on the low side of the floor, it was difficult for me to find out the details. One clique may have divided Henry and his admirers off from some other Robeson residents, who had no interest at all in being friendly to the white students on the floor. The black students were not all angels. They knew perfectly well about white fears of them, and just as white fraternity boys enjoyed the occasional act of intimidation, so, too, in all probability, did some of the black students. Even as an older white male, safely encased in my identity as a researcher, I sometimes felt intimidated on the Robeson side. Some of the Robeson residents were as amiable and open with me in private interviews as any of the white, low-side residents; others were only grudgingly helpful; and one or two of the older, tougher-looking males on the floor frankly scared me a little with their monosyllabic replies and what struck me as baleful stares.[17]

Another internal problem for the Robeson section apparently centered on a young man who had grown up in an all-black southern community. He had originally tried to live on an integrated floor in the Rutgers dorms, but had felt very alienated—by New Jersey or by whites, he was not sure which. So he had moved into the Robeson section in the middle of the fall, hoping that his problems would go away when he was among his "own kind." They had not, however, and he had apparently thrown some of them back at the section. The Robeson section also contained a black Jamaican male, new to the United States at the beginning of the year. When I first talked to him, he did not seem to feel any common identity with the other Robeson members. As far as he was concerned, he told me, almost all the blacks and whites on Erewhon Third were equally American and equally foreign to him. He certainly did not see significant cultural differences between the two groups. Within about two months, however—perhaps because he had experienced some of the white racism at Rutgers—he voiced these dissensual opinions much less readily.

All-floor activities continued to be nonstarters during the fall semester on Erewhon Third, and once again, in white opinion, the problem lay in the uncooperativeness of the Robeson students. Residents of both sides of the floor finally decided to try throwing a common floor-party in late October. In those simple days, before the resumption of the minimum twenty-one drinking age in the mid-1980s (see chapter 3), alcohol-soaked parties were the most popular way of "building floor community" among the undergraduates. The preceptor maneuvered the residents into voting to hold the party downstairs in the main lounge of the dorm. He was afraid that if it were held on Erewhon Third, arguments might break out about which side to locate the music and the liquor on, and that the side that won might then take over the party. But his strategy did not work. The Robeson members reportedly took over the party anyway, bringing in their own disc jockey and playing only "their" music; and all the white students left. "It was a reasonable move on the part of the Robeson people," the white preceptor observed defensively: "There had been three or four floor parties in Erewhon already during the fall, all white parties. The Robeson people were just having a party *they* could enjoy. But it wasn't a *floor* party."

In December, the preceptor and the white residents of Erewhon Third said, they offered to play an all-floor Secret Santa (see chapter 3), but the Robeson members didn't join in, the whites reported, and held their own Secret Santa among themselves instead. Shortly thereafter, a few Robeson freshmen engaged in a little late-night vandalism in the dorm, the sort of sophomoric activities that are ordinarily winked at in undergraduate student culture. But in this case, the white residents of the floor were very angry, for such carryings-on are only tolerated among friendly youths, and the Robeson residents had not been friendly.

Friendship questionnaires that I distributed in the middle of the year confirmed the lack of friendliness between blacks and whites on Erewhon Third. Only three of the thirty-three reciprocated close friendships on the floor were between persons of different races (see figure 5), and only 5 percent of the larger number of reciprocated friendships were interracial. Two of the three interracial close friendships involved the white preceptor, who *had* been successful in establishing personal connections with the Robeson residents. His style was a straightforward one that worked well with the blacks: he did not ordinarily seem threatened by them, nor did he appear to try too hard. "He's a *cool* white dude," one of the Robeson residents said to me. The other close interracial friendship was between the white transfer student who had accidentally been placed in the Robeson section and his black roommate. This white student had a chance to move out of the Robeson section in the middle of the year, but he declined to do so, out of loyalty to his roommate he said.

There *were* more than three close friendships between persons from opposite sections of the floor, between high-side and low-side residents. But

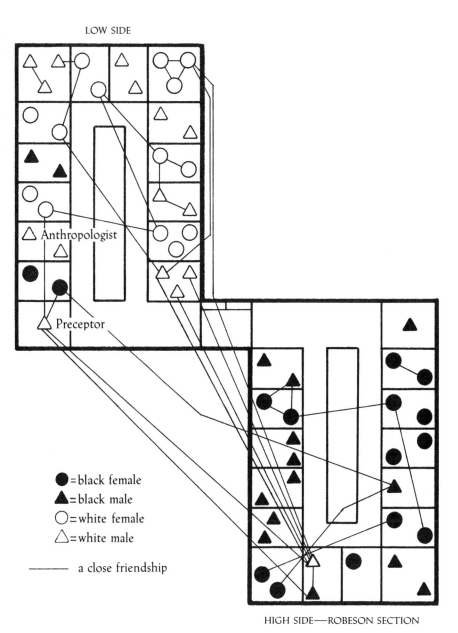

LOW SIDE

△ Anthropologist

△ Preceptor

● = black female
▲ = black male
○ = white female
△ = white male

———— a close friendship

HIGH SIDE—ROBESON SECTION

FIGURE 5 / Close Friendships, Erewhon Third, 1979 (not to scale)
(some architectural details changed)

the rest of them turned out to be monoracial friendships involving the few black students who had been placed on the low side, on the one hand, and the white male who had landed on the high side on the other. The section division and spatial closeness therefore did not entirely determine the friendship patterns on Erewhon Third by the middle of the 1978–1979 year. To a much greater extent, race apparently did.

In late January, the residence counselor insisted that the residents of the floor hold a meeting to talk about "floor tensions," and they unenthusiastically called one. Students from both sides muttered about how filthy both bathrooms were, but nothing else of importance was discussed; no progress was made. And so the situation stood after the middle of the year, in an uneasy ongoing truce. Erewhon Third had not been without its achievements to date, given the stresses and strains on the floor. There had been an absence of highly visible group conflict. The one possible incident had been contained. On Erewhon Third so far in 1978–1979, there had been nothing like Pete's tantrums or Art and Carrie's fight on Hasbrouck Fourth in 1984–1985 (see chapter 3). Residents talked quietly among themselves about the floor's problems. But their line to outsiders tended to be: We get along well enough under the circumstances. There's nothing here that we can't handle.

Agitation

In the middle of March, however, this posture became untenable, for the residents of Erewhon Third suddenly woke up one morning to find themselves splashed across the front page of the campus newspaper. "Sectional Tensions Plague Special Interest Dorm," the main headline ran. Names were named; students were quoted. The story described "lack of communication" and "limited interaction" between the black and the white students on the floor. Members of both sections felt shunned when they tried to sit down in the lounge of the opposite section, one white male resident had told the reporter. Females from the white side only visited the women's room on the Robeson side in groups of twos and threes, some black females had pointed out. "What do they think we were going to do? Attack them?" White residents had mentioned the failed floor party and Secret Santa, and the preceptor had capped it all off by observing that students on both sides of the floor were not making any real effort to understand one another, out of "ignorance and fear."

Though the newspaper story was fundamentally accurate—or perhaps *because* it was fundamentally accurate—it made students on both sides of Erewhon Third exceptionally angry. It was not a total surprise, of course. A few residents had mentioned to me that some guy had been poking around on the floor a couple of times the week before, asking a lot of questions. "He was a real political type," one of the white students had said. "You could tell right from the very beginning that he knew just what it was he wanted to find out when he came up here."

A week after the story was published, the reporter walked into my faculty office seeking me out. It was the first time I had laid eyes on him. I was amazed to discover that he was a young *black* man. Not one person on Erewhon Third—at least a dozen residents had discussed him in my hearing, usually in very unflattering terms—had mentioned his race to me. I should have figured it out, though. The Robeson residents had been particularly angry about him, and yet they had never called him a racist or any of the other terms by which they might have dismissed the opinions of a white commentator under similar circumstances. And in a much longer personal letter, which he had circulated to all the residents of the floor, the reporter had singled out the Robeson residents in a way that a white liberal might have found harder to do. They had a special duty, he had suggested, *not* to keep the old racial stereotypes alive. He had not been so hard on the white racism that existed on the low side of the floor, however, perhaps because he had not detected it.

The reporter proved to be an articulate, earnest liberal who had grown up in an "integrated" upper-middle-class New Jersey suburb, he told me. He simply did not believe that American blacks were culturally distinct from American whites in any important ways, and even if they were, he believed, they should act so as to reduce differences rather than reinforcing them. He was distressed about the amount of rancor his story had aroused on Erewhon Third. More than that: he said he had been approached by three males from the Robeson section in a student pub a few nights earlier and physically threatened for his "disloyalty."

Interracial Community

But his story *did* have an impact on the floor. It gave *all* the residents of Erewhon Third a common interest for the first time that year, a common enemy. And in doing so, it brought about the first genuinely cooperative activities that had occurred on Erewhon Third so far in 1978–1979. In the best-attended floor meeting of the year to date, white and black residents apologized to students from the other side for the things they had allegedly said, claiming that they had been misquoted or that their statements had been taken out of context. All personal apologies were acknowledged and accepted. Both sides also agreed that special-interest sections always tended to become self-absorbed, regardless of the ethnic or nonethnic character of their interests. (Not one single white resident of Erewhon Third had thought of this simple explanation for the unfriendliness of the Robeson residents in my hearing before this meeting.) Everyone also agreed that the reporter was the real villain, and a subcommittee with members from both sides of the floor was appointed to write a collective reply to the campus newspaper, which simply denied almost everything reported in the article. The anthropologist typed it up;[18] it was circulated and signed by most of the residents of the floor; and a week later it appeared in the paper.

Representatives of a campuswide black student organization attended a second meeting and told the floor members that Erewhon Third was being unfairly blamed simply for reflecting a racist society. Looking around at the impressive biracial attendance, these black visitors then observed: "*We* don't see any problem here. What *was* that story all about, anyway?"[19]

A few days later, the students held the first and only successful floor party of the year on Erewhon Third, a shaky ritual creation of something that had not existed before: floor friendliness. To overcome the greatest cultural divide between the black students and the white students on Erewhon Third, it was agreed that the two sections would alternate their music all night long and that another subcommittee—the RC, the preceptor, and one male from each side of the floor—would oversee this concordat during the party. The site of the party would be the low side of the floor, to encourage white guests from other floors of Erewhon Hall to attend; by this time, other dorm residents were afraid of the situation on Erewhon Third.

The party was not as big as most floor parties, but it did come off as planned. For most of the evening, members of both sections sat together in friendly interracial groups in the low-side lounge, but dancing was almost all black or all white. I watched one outgoing black freshman ask three or four white females in a row to dance; all of them turned him down, probably with the excuse that they did not know disco dancing. He did not seem upset, however, and he stayed all evening. When the music chosen by the Robeson section was played, usually disco, the blacks stood up and danced in an almost choreographed-looking group; when the music chosen by the white section was played, the blacks all sat down and the whites stood up and danced in diverse styles, in separate couples. Students sometimes drifted off into private rooms together (usually monoracially, once or twice interracially) for quieter talks, other music, drinks, or smokes. Half a dozen guests from other floors were present at any one time, watching rather than participating. To me at least, the party felt like a collective demonstration that was as much for the benefit of the floor residents as for outsiders, reassurance that things were not as bad as they had been reported in the paper. For a week or two afterward, students on both sides of Erewhon Third agreed that the party had been a success, but the party was not repeated during what remained of the academic year. (It was now late March.)

The collective energies the residents of the two sections of Erewhon Third had been able to generate in response to what they saw as an outside attack were now exhausted. Living on Erewhon Third in 1978–1979 had often been hard work, and in student assumptions, hard work should characterize the academic side of a college education, not private life in the dorms. The dorms should be places for friendly sociability and for choice, for the easy pleasures of college life as the students enjoyed it in the late twentieth century (see chapter 2). Though the early fears of some of the white students on Erewhon Third had declined throughout the year, though some interracial acquaintanceships and a few friendships *had* developed, and though many of the white students did say that they had learned something—that it had been a good experience to live on Erewhon Third for a year[20]—hardly any of them wished to try it again. Among the whites, only two sophomore males made plans to return to Erewhon Hall the following year.[21]

This was not just because of the tensions on the floor. The opportunities for a social life were also too restricted on Erewhon Third, several white students said; they could not meet as many "people" on Erewhon Third as on other floors. Though more black students were interested in returning for the sake of the Robeson section itself, they had similar complaints. Social life on the floor and on the College Avenue Campus was thin because there were so few of "us" in and around Erewhon Hall, they said.[22]

AFTERTHOUGHTS

Though the interracial events narrated so far took place a decade ago as I write, they were understood and interpreted by the students at the time according to notions that reached very deep into American middle-class culture—and which do not appear to have changed in radical ways in the last ten years. What were and are some of these racial notions, and how are they connected to other aspects of contemporary American culture?

General Attitudes

Most of the white students I knew well in the Rutgers dorms in the late 1970s and mid-1980s had one of three attitudes toward racial differences.[23] There were, first of all, the liberals, perhaps a third to a half of the white students. The liberals honestly wanted to believe that race made no difference; people were the same under the skin, or they ought to be, they believed. They often wanted to be real friends with their black peers, and they tended to be upset when, for any reason, interracial friendships did not work out for them. In my observations, racial liberals were most likely to come from middle-class and upper-middle-class family backgrounds.[24]

A large portion of the remaining white students, on the other hand, were uncommitted when it came to race. They clearly had their reservations about blacks. Many of them probably considered most blacks simply too strange to be known intimately as individuals; their backgrounds and their interests, they assumed, made them too different. Friendships are also supposed to be spontaneous, unpredictable relationships in American culture, however. If all of your friends are exactly like you, then you are not really exercising free choice; your friendships are not the authentic individualistic relationships that they are supposed to be. And there were regular instances of interracial friendships involving white students who were not racial liberals in other ways. These white students—and the white liberals, for that matter—almost always took particular pride in their interracial friendships when they did work out for them.

"Some of my best friends . . ." has been a racist cliché for many years, of course. Nevertheless, these interracial friendships apparently *were* considered real friendships by both partners. They were not just claimed rhetorically by the white partners; they were also verified by the blacks on confidential questionnaires in which they could easily have disclaimed them. American blacks are also individualists in their own way, and from a black point of view, a white nonliberal could perhaps be an easier friend than a liberal. Liberals could try too hard at friendship; you were never sure if they really liked you, or if they were more interested in fascinating *black* you. With nonliberals, on the other hand, you knew that it must be you that they liked. You could bust on each other about your racially distinct attitudes and identities, and then you could go on from there to enjoy one another as persons.[25]

And finally, undeniably, there *were* white racists among the undergraduates at Rutgers in the late 1970s and the mid-1980s. There had been at least three of them on Erewhon Third in 1978, and they were not peculiar to that floor. Undergraduate white racists "knew" that blacks were different, and they knew that they did not get along with them. They were scared of them, and they disliked them in return. And they had very little desire to know them or understand them better. The process of "understanding" for these students, in fact, usually consisted of scanning the behavior of black persons for anything that apparently verified their own implacable racism and focusing on it, ignoring everything else including their own possible effect on the blacks in question.

In 1987 I gave out brief, anonymous questionnaires about racial sentiments to a Rutgers class, in which I asked the students to try to answer with their real opinions (see note 26). One young man admitted to his racism as follows:

> When I say that I think I'm a racist I mean that generally I just can't get along with black people. There are some black people I like but I could never call them friends. There are a lot of white people I don't like but as a rule there aren't many black people I can get along with.—Rutgers senior, white male, 1987

Openly racist attitudes were usually illegitimate among the undergraduates, however:

> It's easy to say one is not a racist, but there are always outside influences passed on from all sides of society. . . . I may have racist feelings but I try to control them and not [let them] influence my actions.—Rutgers junior, white male, 1987

Therefore, real racism, when it existed, could only be ventilated with very close friends or in anonymous ways, in "incidents" or in the sorts of bathroom graffiti that one saw as pervasively in the mid-1980s at Rutgers as in the late 1970s. Due to the secrecy of real racism, it was almost impossible to estimate what percentage of the white students at Rutgers were racists in the late 1970s and mid-1980s. My own guess would be a deliberately imprecise one, between a tenth and a quarter of the white undergraduate student body.[26] Most of these white racists probably never acted on their attitudes, but it only took a few of them acting them out to generate the intermittent racist hassles that black students evidently took for granted in late-twentieth-century American white society.

Some white undergraduates who grew up in less-affluent communities were probably liberals. But racists and the uncommitted students tended to come disproportionately from working-class and lower-middle-class urban and suburban hometowns. In these communities, some sociologists have suggested, interethnic competition for jobs makes white racism—and perhaps black racism as well—more endemic and less apologetic than it is in the average upper-middle-class suburb.[27] Many of the racist students and the uncommitted students had the classic white-ethnic grievance about American blacks: My group of recent immigrants to the United States has had to make it through its own efforts; why do these blacks need all these special privileges?[28] Many of them also said that they had had bad experiences with blacks before they arrived at Rutgers. They tended to consider these experiences the exclusive fault of the blacks, and they usually felt that they proved the validity of their racism or their uncommitted attitudes toward black people.

Some white undergraduates indicated that these experiences had hardened into a racism that college was not about to change. (Two out of three of the white racist residents of Erewhon Third in 1978–1979 apparently were of this ilk.) But others thought that the generally greater liberalism of the college environment and the "better class" of blacks whom they believed Rutgers attracted had had a positive impact on their formerly negative attitudes:

> I live in a largely black hometown. I cannot walk in the downtown area in a skirt/heels without much verbal harassment, again, by black men. [I *am* prejudiced against] certain blacks—NONE of them my peers at [Rutgers]. Just the ones who speak the black vernacular and are socially abhorrent.—Rutgers junior, white female, 1987

> I used to be leery of [blacks], for [before I came to college], I was robbed at knife point. But since I've been going to Rutgers, this has changed. I am not so

quick to judge a group of blacks and classify them. Thank goodness, because they are humans, like myself. They hurt the same way. I hope someday we can all be equal.—Rutgers senior, white female, 1987

The Dilemmas of Individualism

The racial mentalities of the white undergraduates, and of many other white Americans in the late twentieth century, were also intricately linked to contemporary American individualism. Myrdal argues in *An American Dilemma* that racism is so antithetical to the individualistic value of equal opportunity that it should be regarded as a "caste-like" survival of something more primitive in an otherwise progressive democratic culture (Myrdal 1944). In a comparison of south Asian and modern western concepts of human inequality, on the other hand, anthropologist Louis Dumont makes a very different point. Indian caste is a particularly bad analogy for western racism, Dumont claims, because caste is in fact a consensual, infinitely graded notion of legitimate human inequality or of hierarchy, a premodern, holistic social sensibility.[29] Race and racism, on the other hand, are cultural corollaries of modern western individualistic ideologies. Modern American and Western European culture "valorizes" the individual, as Dumont puts it. Contemporary western culture largely ignores social causation and vigorously denies human hierarchy, refusing to locate perceived human inequalities in socially constructed, interindividual forces. It must therefore locate them in the individual, in sources that are ultimately physical, biological, or genetic. The inequality of allegedly lower races does not violate egalitarian values about humans, for racism specifically states that certain races are not quite human, or that they are not human in the same way as other, dominant races are (see Dumont 1960, 1982).[30]

If Dumont is correct, race and racism might be more difficult to eradicate from American culture than Myrdal's position would suggest. For racism, according to Dumont, is the dark side of the cultural assumptions that Americans and other westerners hold dear in most other circumstances. I never heard white students at Rutgers in the late 1970s or mid-1980s openly claim that they still believed the discredited notions of an older western "scientific racism," that blacks were unquestionably genetically inferior to whites, a truly distinct lower race.[31] Yet the students' individualism often pushed them in racist directions in ways that Dumont's argument would predict.

Consider friendliness, for example. Everyone *ought* to be friendly in the same way, most undergraduates assumed; a friendly, open personality was simply, unanalytically, the mark of a good person. And "friendly" in student assumptions was not subject to cultural variation; if you were not friendly in ways Americans take for granted, then there was something wrong with you—*inside* of you, as a person.[32] In the ordinary, almost preconceptual assumptions of the students, you must be characterologically flawed. You had an unacceptable interactive style: you were "obnoxious," or "snotty," or "rude," or "inconsiderate." Or you were unworthy of friendship because of your very essence: you were a "phony," an "asshole," a "wimp," a "bitch," a "scumbag," a "faggot."

Yet virtually all the students also knew that they had to block this common logic in interracial contexts. In response to a confidential question about personal dislikes, for instance, not one resident of Erewhon Third in 1978–1979 said a single nasty thing about anyone of another race on the floor, despite the known racial problems on Erewhon Third. On other floors, this same question reaped a rich harvest of personal invective, the normal negative pole of American friendship judgments. But on Erewhon Third, to utter such sentiments about persons of other races, even confidentially, was to sound like a racist. The most negative interracial emotion that anyone on Erewhon Third mentioned was "apathy."[33]

Given the students' pervasive individualism, however, no adequate alternative explanation for the failure of friendliness between persons of different races was readily available to them. "Different cultural values" worked for student liberals to a degree, perhaps because culture as the students understood it resembled individualism; culture was "group choice." Explanations rooting immediate racial problems in history, politics, or economic disparities, on the other hand, were rarely entertained by any of the white undergraduates.[34] Even a very simple sociological explanation for the problems on Erewhon Third, that the floor had been set up in a contradictory way from the beginning, that any special-interest group tended to turn inward, really did not occur to the white residents until they had been pushed into a common defense of themselves and the black students on Erewhon Third by an outside attack.

Thus, the students' individualism left them in a dilemma when it came to race. As a 'socio-logic,' their individualism was simply too impoverished to account for what was going on. Some white undergraduates lived with this dilemma, while others entertained racist sentiments of various shapes and sizes. Most of the white racists probably did not really care about the precise reasons for possible racial differences that exercise academic specialists most: biology versus culture, nature versus nurture. Most of them probably did not think about their racist sentiments this analytically. All they "knew" was that racial differences were there, that they were somehow the systematic fault of the other party, and that because of them, the best and safest strategy was to quietly exclude all or many persons with different colored skins from the circle of humanity toward whom they normally tried to act in personal, egalitarian ways.

What was the solution to white racism of this sort, given these individualistic values? Some of the more threatened white students proposed total cultural assimilation—so much for their commitment to the value of "diversity"![35] Students who had "problems" with blacks almost always protested that they had nothing at all against black people on physical grounds; different skin color really did not matter to them at all, they insisted. It was the way black people *acted* that bothered them. If only blacks were open and friendly and "just like us," then there would be no problems with them, these students claimed.

One white undergraduate who took my anonymous questionnaire in 1987, for example, identified herself as a racist on it. She did not agree that "everyone is really the same under the skin"; she did not believe that disadvantaged blacks deserved special assistance; she *was* prejudiced when it came to black people, she said. At the same time, she believed she had at least one close reciprocated friendship with a black person. It was the "majority outlook" of blacks that made her "somewhat prejudiced," she scribbled at the bottom of her questionnaire.

[Some of my best] friends *are* black. But they act like white persons. I don't see them as black at all.—Rutgers freshman, white female, 1987

For another image of the Good Black in the eyes of white American adolescents in the 1980s, consider the character played by black comedian Eddie Murphy in the *Beverly Hills Cop* movies and in films such as *Trading Places*. Murphy is an extremely funny comedian, a graduate of that undergraduate late-night TV favorite "Saturday Night Live"; his extraordinary popularity with white adolescent moviegoers is obviously partly due to his talent. But it also presumably has something to do with who he is in these movies. Who *is* he? For a start, he is always totally at ease; he is always open and friendly to anyone who gives him half a chance; he relates to everyone strictly as a person. On the one hand, he is apparently well embedded in his black identity. On the other hand, he treats his identity and almost everything else as a big joke. His movies also have no detectable political content. In the Beverly Hills films, he is a cop; ultimately, he works for the white establishment. In *Trading Places*, he uses Wall Street to ruin bad WASPs and to cash in for himself and for his white friends.

Whenever Murphy encounters old-fashioned racism or any other form of elitism in these movies, he immediately attacks and destroys it, excoriating the villains in the "naturally" vulgar language one ordinarily hears in adolescent busting around the dorms. Nothing in Murphy's real world is really very important, in fact; all that matters is wit, survival, the pleasures of the con in a good cause, and—above all—loyalty to one's friends. And Murphy is almost always portrayed in these movies as a black man who has very good white friends as well as very good black friends. Or, in *Trading Places*, he converts Bad Whites (inauthentic status-conscious racists) into Good Whites (authentic egalitarian Americans), who then become good friends of his during the course of the film.

If only *all* American blacks were such very perfect human beings, the white adolescent fans of these movies seem to be saying, then there would be no white racism left in American culture at all.

Further Comments

A different version of part of this chapter can be found in Moffatt 1986.

1 / You were "white" in the contemporary American understanding of race employed by most Rutgers students if your principal ethnic background was western, central, or eastern European, or if you were a light-skinned, assimilated Latin American or Caribbean without a strong Spanish accent. Otherwise you were black or some other "minority."

According to one college report, the 8,270 undergraduates enrolled at Rutgers College in 1984 were 79 percent "white," 7.3 percent black, 2 percent Puerto Rican, 3 percent "other Hispanic," 6 percent "Asian/Pacific Islander," and 3 percent "other/no information" (Rutgers College 1985).

2 / Most of the residents of Hasbrouck Fourth in 1984–1985 knew that Danny, the one Puerto Rican student on the floor, was a Puerto Rican; but the student racists, like other white Americans with other Puerto Ricans, tended to feel the same way about him that they did about the four blacks

on the floor. The other residents of Hasbrouck Fourth from Latin backgrounds were so light-skinned and/or unaccented in their speech that they didn't tend to fall into the same racially distinct category in the minds of the "white" students that Danny and the four blacks did.

The two Asian-Americans on Hasbrouck Fourth were east Asians. One is described in chapter 3—Tim, a second-generation Japanese male who was an apparently fully integrated member of the wedgie patrol clique. The other was a Japanese-American woman I knew nothing about; she was hardly ever around. Otherwise I don't know much about "white" attitudes toward students in this newer American minority (newer on the East Coast, at least), except that east Asians did do exceptionally well in education as a rule, especially in the sciences, and aroused a certain amount of jealousy among other students for this reason (though hostility was directed more at the east Asian teaching assistants who were beginning to proliferate in the sciences—many of them, the students maintained, with marginal English).

As for south Asians, on the anonymous racism questionnaire I circulated in 1987 (see note 26), which was about white prejudices toward American blacks only, three out of forty-five white respondents volunteered the information that, however they felt about blacks, they *were* definitely prejudiced against "Indians" and other south Asians.

3 / Paul Robeson, class of 1919, the third black student to attend Rutgers, was a debating champion, a Phi Beta Kappa, and a letterman in most varsity sports during his undergraduate days. During his junior year, when tiny Rutgers fielded an unusually strong team, he was widely considered to be the best college football player in the United States. He went on to a distinguished career as an actor, an operatic singer, and a political activist.

In the early 1950s, however, Robeson spoke out too forcefully too early against American racism and expressed unfashionably internationalist opinions during the McCarthy era. As a consequence, Robeson became a political outcast in the United States. And in the 1980s, Robeson's institutional remembrance on the New Brunswick campuses remains scanty at best, given his real historical stature.

4 / The new black student populations who moved into American higher education in the late sixties were soon experiencing white racism from supposedly educated Americans and finding them-

selves in institutions that seemed very alien to them. In February 1969, black protests swept across American campuses. Angry black students seized a building at the Newark campus of Rutgers University, and in late February, the dean of Rutgers College, against the opposition of some of his faculty, closed the college down for three days of collegewide discussions of black grievances: "convocations," discussion groups, sensitivity groups, and so on. Many faculty members were in sympathy with the moratorium, however, and the student newspaper supported it and urged everyone to go to its events. Twenty-five hundred "mostly white" students were reported to have attended one of the convocations.

Black student leaders asked for much higher institutional commitments to minority recruitment, for special programs to assist educationally disadvantaged students, for a separate "Afro-American Studies Program," for separate black deans, for more attention to black cultural programming, and for greater sensitivity on the part of the campus police to the possible collegiate status of the new black faces on the campus. Most of these initiatives were adopted by the college in one way or another and are still at least formally present in the institution in the mid-1980s. (See *Rutgers Daily Targum*, February 24, 1969, through March 5, 1969.)

Undergraduates from Spanish-speaking backgrounds had certain problems in common with black students at Rutgers in the 1970s and 1980s. They reported that students in the white mainstream generally disliked seeing or hearing them display their Latinness; they would praise a peer who was fluent in, say, French, but then get angry with Latins who spoke Spanish together in front of them. "White" students also often saw Latins as dark-skinned, resembling blacks. Most Latins, on the other hand, distinguished themselves very carefully from American blacks, and their own intraethnic diversity was so great that it was only an artifact of white American definitions of them that they were perceived as a single "Hispanic" ethnic group in the United States at all. For a study of these complex intraethnic relationships in the general Latin population of the city of New Brunswick, see Baldares 1987.

Spanish-speaking students have had their own special dorm living group at Rutgers for a number of years. In recent years, it has taken up an entire floor of one residence hall, so that section problems like those built into the relations of the Robeson section to the rest of Erewhon Third have not troubled it in the same way. Any internal problems, when the group has had them, have tended to originate in differences between students of the different "Hispanic" national-origin groups. It has also sometimes had to deal with racist attacks from outside the section, however. A resident of the Latin section told me in a paper written in 1987 that, for a week or two the previous year, unidentifiable male voices had shouted "Is *this* where the *spics* live?!" every time the dorm elevator passed the floor. And an outsider had sneaked onto the floor and urinated on the hall carpet, he also reported.

5 / Most other special-interest sections either took up an entire floor, like the Latin group, or shared floors with other special-interest sections, rather than having to get along with an opposite-side section made up of students assigned to the floor in the housing lottery, as the Robeson club had to do.

6 / The authorities I talked with all claimed that the setup of Erewhon Third was a simple artifact of the lack of demand for the section among black students; they would have opened it up to a whole floor if they could have. It had apparently never occurred to anyone to try to locate the Robeson section on one of the single-section floors on the cam-

pus, however, or to change the preceptorial system on the Robeson floor, or possibly to match it up with another special-interest section.

7 / College Avenue was attractive to all students because it was at the hub of the campus bus system and was the location of most of the biggest general classes, the main library, the biggest Commons, and the biggest student center on all the Rutgers-New Brunswick campuses (see appendix 2). It was also at the heart of the fun of college life for white undergraduates (fraternity row, etc.). Blacks, on the other hand, often felt much more comfortable socially in the dorm space that Rutgers College controlled on the Livingston College campus, whose student body was about 20 percent black. And this may have been one reason there was not more black demand for the Robeson section on the College Avenue Campus.

8 / On some known campus incidents elsewhere in the last two years, see White 1987 and Gold 1988.

9 / The white preceptor's assumption seems to have been that suburban middle-class status (swimming lessons, summer camp, etc.) was necessary for this skill. No one ever asked how many of the Robeson residents could swim, but I would bet that more than

half of them could, even if they were not crazy about canoeing. Perhaps two-thirds of the Robeson residents in 1978–1979 were from poor urban or poor rural backgrounds, but some of them were also from middle-class black suburban families.

10 / This student quote and others marked with an asterisk in this chapter are taken from tape recordings. As indicated in chapter 3, I have edited out some of the students' hesitations and repairs in these tape transcriptions, but have otherwise retained their vocabulary and their syntax.

11 / Some white women on the low side found this bathroom trip to the Robeson side so scary, however, that they started visiting the next dorm floor down to use its women's room.

12 / He was a transfer student from out-of-state who would not have received housing if he had not accepted this room. The other twenty-seven residents of the high side were all black members of the Robeson Club, to which he did not belong. On the low side, conversely, four of the thirty-three residents happened to be blacks. None of them were members of the Robeson Club either. (There was a technical distinction between Robeson Club, to which anyone could belong, and the Robeson Section, the high side of Erewhon Third.)

13 / The black students in the Robeson section were also apparently annoyed by stereotyping. They, however, had supposedly come together to become more aware of "black culture." But most of them would probably have had a difficult time identifying any specific things they habitually did in the present that were culturally distinctive, aside from a few food habits and a black holiday or two. For most of them, "black culture" seemed to gloss the distinctive historical experience of black people in the United States and some finer nuances in cultural style, which they could not analyze but which nevertheless undoubtedly—in my opinion, at least—existed. Like the whites, however, black students in the Robeson section would probably have objected to the notion that they were all "the same" in some way. One black woman on Erewhon Third said she became particularly irritated when one of the friendlier white liberals on the floor told her how fascinating she found her "customs" to be. "I brush my teeth a little differently, and she says to me, 'Oh, is that how you brush your teeth! That's really *interesting!*'"

14 / My thanks to Professor Roy D'Andrade for making this

point in a comment on an earlier draft of this essay at the meetings of the American Anthropological Association in November 1983.

15 / News of racist incidents seemed to spread rapidly among black undergraduates. They did talk them over and deplore them, but what could they do about most of them? One black freshman on the Robeson side, however, a young man with a tough, self-assured personal style, told me that "none of these things" had ever happened to *him*, and he made a point of never listening to such gossip from other black students.

16 / At least one set of incidents in the 1978–1979 academic year was more serious, however. During the spring semester, a black female student at Cook College, the old "ag school," was repeatedly harassed with racial threats. In the last and most serious incident, she found her car with its tires slashed and its front window smashed. These incidents were reported in the campus newspaper, and most black students in the university were outraged about them.

17 / White students sometimes excused their own racism on the grounds that, they claimed, blacks were reverse racists themselves. It would not be surprising if some of them were. Historically, however, white racism came first;

black racism, where it exists, unfortunately indicates that blacks *are* "Americans" at a certain level, that they are influenced by the same racist currents in the general culture the whites are; they simply turn them around. It may also indicate that they are caught in some of the same contradictions of race and individualism being highlighted here.

Second, their distrust of whites does reflect real social differences in which they continue to be the overall losers—persisting tokenism in certain central domains of American life (e.g., the small percentages of black business leaders, college and university professors, and major sports executives), the still-growing economic gap between poor blacks and the general white population in the 1980s, and so on. Third, it is a very different experience to fear a physically distinctive set of persons ("whites," "blacks") when you are in a minority, when your group makes up one-twentieth to one-tenth of the population (common black percentages in everyday settings at Rutgers College), than when you are in a much bigger majority.

18 / As these events unfolded, though I was aware of the basic accuracy of the story, I found myself almost as angry with the reporter as the rest of the floor

residents were. "Outside agitator!" I caught myself thinking. "He doesn't really understand. You have to *live* here to understand." And students from both sides of Erewhon Third also seemed to regard me as an insider during this period. I wasn't sure I would be welcome at the first big floor-meeting after the attack, so I asked some Robeson residents what they thought. "Of *course* you're welcome at the meeting!" they assured me. "*You've* lived on this floor all year. This guy comes up here once or twice and he thinks he knows everything!"

19 / The word "culture" came up with some frequency during this period of crisis, in ways that further indicated both its explanatory salience under the circumstances and its limited legitimacy in an individualistic culture. In the original article, a white resident of Erewhon Third was quoted as saying: "Some whites on the floor probably resent members of the [Robeson] section because they are so far into their own culture. I think culture may be a big part of the problem." And a black resident said: "Many blacks on the floor have personal preferences of being with their own kind, sharing their cultural heritage, and maintaining their identity."

Note that neither of these speakers took personal responsibility for the cultural attitudes in question. Similar ambivalence came out in a letter published in the campus newspaper later by the campuswide black student organization. The residents of Erewhon Third, the letter said, were being unfairly accused of "the unforgivable crime of preferring their own culture. . . . We're not saying that this situation is the most desirable, but preference is a God-given right, [and] who is [the reporter] to question it?"

20 / One of the liberal males observed, for instance, that "the way I feel when I'm in the Robeson section—that must be a little the way black students feel most of the time at Rutgers."

21 / These two youths were grinds who had not been active in student dynamics on the floor in 1978–1979 and probably would not be active the following year. They liked the convenience of the College Avenue location, and they knew that hardly any other white undergraduates would be competing with them for their rooms.

22 / Six years later I returned to Erewhon Third for two brief visits in an effort to discover how the floor, which was still set up in the same way, was working out another year. In February 1985, students living on both sides told me that there had been *no* problems on Erewhon Third that

year, and the floor did feel easier and more relaxed to me. It was, for instance, a less tense experience as a white to walk into the Robeson lounge for an idle chat. Students on both sides were relatively mature that year, I was told. The Robeson president was a black male who had grown up in an integrated suburb and had decided to live in the Robeson section for a year to experience living among his "own people" for the first time in his life. And some of the whites in the low-side section had actually chosen to live on the floor that year. They were so liberal that a gay male had come out among them without much grief, something that both straight and gay students at Rutgers agreed hardly ever happened in the Rutgers dorms. The preceptor that year was a black woman who lived on the low side. She did not threaten the white students in the same way a black man would have; she got to know them particularly well because she lived in among them; and she still had good relations with the Robeson students on the high side.

There was also some partying across the sections in 1984–1985, students from both sides told me. Black and white undergraduates still felt that they very much had their own musical tastes, but they had also discovered "crossover" music, which they could enjoy in common: Michael Jackson, Prince, and a few other black performers who were popular among white adolescents as well. Two white freshmen females had accidentally chosen to live in the Robeson section. "All we noticed in the catalogue description was that it emphasized academic achievement," one of them told me. One of them had actually joined the Robeson club and had taken part in a benefit that the club ran on behalf of a local mostly-black public school. There was even a quiet interracial romance on the floor that year.

This success, however, did not necessarily indicate that things were getting better and better at Rutgers, racially speaking. It probably only meant that Erewhon Third had been lucky in its particular cast of characters in 1984–1985. Two years later there were new problems again, problems between the Robeson Club and *everyone* else in Erewhon Hall. In 1986–1987, the Robeson Club threw an overly loud party of its own in the main lounge on the ground floor on a Wednesday night, a nonparty night for most white students. Suddenly there were packed meetings again, but this time there were arguments about the legal status of the club-as-a-section and angry remarks

175

from the Robeson residents about how the white dorm residents did not understand the club's special purposes.

23 / These are very rough judgments, of course. A number of students vacillated between two or more of these attitudes, and for all but the liberals, it was necessary to use a variety of behavioral clues and offhand remarks to estimate students' real attitudes beneath what most of them felt they *had* to say about race. Anthropologically speaking, it might be argued that I am committing an individualistic, psychologistic error here in attempting to make these assessments at all, that the only thing that matters culturally when it comes to race is the public attitude of the students because we all have our inner fluxes and ambivalence about such topics. Yet there *were* real differences between the students in how much they believed in the liberalism that they all knew was almost mandatory in public in the late-twentieth-century United States. And there were different levels of interpersonal discourse and behavior. Some students spouted liberalism around blacks but then said other, very illiberal things among their friends. And *someone* was producing the racist graffiti and the anonymous racist incidents on the campus.

24 / Which is not to say that people from the white middle- or upper-middle-class backgrounds were immune to racism, however. There is an unhappy potential for more middle-class white racism, in fact, as blacks begin to threaten economic prerogatives at higher class levels—medical school admissions, for instance. (On this theme, for instance, see the recent, exceptionally ambivalent movie *Soul Man*.)

25 / Or you could avoid racial topics entirely. One black student told me that he had been friends with his working-class, white-ethnic roommate ever since they had met two years earlier in a summer program. He considered him to be a very good friend. But there were certain things, he said, that they simply never talked about. Their friendship thus seemed to be based in part on their understanding *not* to talk about race. (The class-based trait they shared, on the other hand, both being poor enough to need the help of the financial assistance that went with the summer program, was a bond between them, this same student indicated.)

26 / After making these guesses in 1987 on the basis of my earlier dorm research, I wanted to check them. So I gave out an anonymous questionnaire in a small introductory anthropology class I was teaching at the time.

(All the 1987 quotes in this section of this chapter are also taken from these questionnaires.) I asked the white students in the class to try to give me their real opinions on the questions, however embarrassing they might be, rather than the polite ones that they usually felt they had to offer up in public. One yes-or-no question read, "I can honestly say that I'm not a racist in *any* way. I really believe, in every important way, that people are the same under the skin." Another read, "There's no question about it; I can't deny it; I'm prejudiced when it comes to black people."

Forty-five white students responded. Counting the students who answered yes to the first question and no to the second as liberals, those who made the opposite choice as racists, and students who gave mixed answers to these and to some other questions as uncommitted persons, the score was liberals 44 percent, uncommitteds 38 percent, racists 17 percent.

27 / Edna Bonacich's 1976 analysis of the racial politics of the American labor movement in the twentieth century, for instance, apparently predicts this sort of class difference in the overt expression of racism.

28 / Not all students from white-ethnic backgrounds were racists or uncommitted about race, perhaps because by the 1980s some of their families had been in the United States long enough to have made it safely into the upper middle class. And most of the "white" undergraduates at Rutgers in the late 1970s and early 1980s—liberals, uncommitteds, and racists alike—were of white-ethnic origin in any case.

Anthropologist [August 1978]: Look at this list. These are the last names of the kids on Erewhon Third, where I'm living in a month. There's supposed to be an all-black section on the floor. Do you think some of these names are black names?

Colleague: Yes, definitely. Look at the ones on this part of the list: "Gregorowitz," "Bartalowski," "Cohen," "Cyzminski," "Basantis," "Carrera," "Donovan." Typical undergraduate names. Now look at this part of the list: "Davenport," "Pearson," "Smith," "Brown," "Murray," "Hayes," "Davis." Good old English names. They've *got* to be blacks.

29 / Thus, Dumont suggests that the disparities between high castes and low castes do not resemble, in any culturally important way, those between whites and blacks in the United States, as the "caste school of race" has argued (see, for instance, Berreman 1960).

For the unequal relations between, say, high castes and Untouchables in India are not an *exception* to egalitarian principles that operate elsewhere in the social order. Quite the contrary: virtually every relationship in the classical Indian society is predicted on the notion of inequality—or, positively stated, on the value of hierarchy. (For an attempt to show that Dumont's interpretation of caste works even among Untouchables in India, see Moffatt 1979.)

30 / Also, according to McKim Marriott and Ronald Inden's 1977 "monistic" interpretation of Indian caste—a refinement, on this point at least, of Dumont—Indian caste is not racist in the early-twentieth-century American sense of the word because it is not strictly biologically determinist. For caste ideology does not rigorously distinguish between the natural order and the social order. It is true that what you *do* socioculturally is believed to be a product of what you *are* biophysically; your "code for conduct" is implicit in your physical "substance," as Marriott and Inden state it. But the reverse is also true, they suggest; your code for conduct can, reciprocally, change your biophysical essence. Thus, for example, if your whole caste group stops eating meat, in a few generations you will be biologically pure enough to rise in the caste hierarchy.

If this last feature of caste resembles anything in Western thought, then, it most closely resembles a "liberal" Lamarckian racism. Some late-nineteenth-century American liberal racists, for example, believed that if American blacks became educated, their very biological nature would change within a few generations (see Fredrickson 1971:283–319; Stocking 1968).

31 / John came close to suggesting he believed this, however; see chapter 1. And the average undergraduate seemed to be unaware of how epiphenomenonal most modern physical anthropologists and populations geneticists considered phenotypical "race" to be. (Also, one undergraduate told me in 1987 after reading a version of this chapter, he had heard an all-knowing freshman assuring some friends the year before that "blacks definitely have smaller brains." "Science has proved it," the freshman had confidently claimed.)

32 / In 1985, I checked this conclusion, which was based on much other evidence, with two undergraduates. First I asked a white sophomore male on Hasbrouck Fourth the suppositional question, "Imagine someone from a different

culture lived on this floor and acted 'friendly' in a different way than Americans do. Would she or he get along?" He answered that since this hypothetical outsider was in "our" country, he or she would have to learn American patterns of friendliness in any case. Otherwise the person would not deserve to be part of American sociability. Then I asked him, "So does that mean that if you went to India you'd be willing to demonstrate friendship with another male by holding his hand in public? That's one way they show friendship there." He replied in a shocked tone, "Oh, no, I'd never do that!"

Second, I asked a black sophomore male back on Erewhon Third if it was possible that American blacks and American whites had different ways of signaling "friendly." Though he was living in a black culture section, he declined to agree that American blacks and whites were different in any fundamental cultural ways. Even if they were, he continued, he could not see how that would affect the manner in which they were friendly to one another. This particular black male had had a very close white male friend on the other side of the floor the year before, by the way, a friendship that residents of both sides of the floor

in 1984–1985 had commented on favorably.

33 / Interestingly, the racial tensions on Erewhon Third in 1978–1979 seemed to block this normal process intraracially on the floor as well. No one said anything personally nasty about another member of their own race either. This kind of blocking probably contributed to the feeling that it was "hard work" to live on Erewhon Third.

34 / Ethnographically, it might be more accurate to suspect that the undergraduates occasionally did argue out such positions in private, in their long talk sessions—after all, I did not hear everything that the white students said on Erewhon Third in 1978–1979. But such theoretical understandings, even if they did exist, had little impact on the students' daily behavior or on what they said on the spur of the moment about race. At this level, only individualism made much sense to the students. This in turn may have been a function of the undergraduates' assumption that the dorms were places for easy sociability; you should not *have* to think too much about ordinary friendly relations in the dorms. They should come "naturally," that is, individualistically.

35 / Similarly, I was told in

1987 by student leaders connected to one of the minority residential sections, some staff members in the college's residence life program had asked them why they continued to insist on having separate living sections. Such units just stirred up needless animosity among whites, they were told; whites were threatened when they saw more than two or three dark-skinned students at one time (social scientists refer to this genre of argument as "blaming the victim"). Diversity was apparently only acceptable to certain parts of the official mind at Rutgers when it was a matter of personal life-style, not when it was rooted in any of the real differences that exist and have existed in American society.

FIVE / Sex

I AM A 21 YEAR-OLD MALE, SLIGHTLY PAST HIS PRIME, AND I GUESS
I WOULD HAVE TO ADMIT THAT SEX IS VERY MUCH ON MY MIND. . . .
IF I STUDIED IN MY CLASSES IN HALF THE TIME THAT I SPEND DAY-
DREAMING, FANTASIZING, REMINISCING ABOUT THAT STUFF CALLED
SEX, I WOULD UNDOUBTEDLY BE ON THE DEAN'S LIST. —Senior male,
anonymous paper, 1986

SEXUAL DISCRETION

If friendliness was the first thing I noticed when I began my research in the Rutgers dorms in 1977, then the new college relationships of sex and gender were the second.[1] I had also spent a
great deal of my time thinking about sex in late adolescence, but I
had not lived with persons of the opposite sex during my years in
college. Since I had started teaching at Rutgers, I had sometimes
wondered what really went on in these new institutions, the coed dorms—
officially undreamed of in the early 1960s, virtually unstudied in the
student-life literature almost two decades later.[2] Now I was apparently in a
position to find out. And yet the finding out was not to prove so easy to do.

An inevitable middle-aged fantasy about the coed dorms was that they
were ongoing sex orgies. For here were young women and men, unrelated
by blood or other family ties, living side by side at just that time in their
lives when, according to American popular psychology, the sex hormones
coursed most insistently through their bodies. They were heirs to the second great sexual revolution of the twentieth century, the one that took
place in the late 1960s and the early 1970s.[3] They had access to modern
biotechnologies that effectively divorced sex from pregnancy and childbirth. They were free from the moral supervision of their elders. And, considering the eroticized nature of contemporary American popular culture,
they were fish swimming in a sexual sea.[4]

I thought of anthropological parallels for what American college sexual
customs might have become by the late 1970s. The adolescent youths of

181

Verrier Elwin's tribal India, whose young women and men lived together in special communal sleeping huts, in many different premarital sexual permutations and combinations, before settling into conjugal sex with other partners (see Elwin 1968). The sexual courtiers of Polynesian cultures, who creep into their lovers' sleeping huts at night and then creep back home again before dawn (see Marshall 1971).

And yet the actual erotic realities on the coed dorm floors, as I observed them during my years of live-in research, were quite different from fantasy. Despite the apparent potential, despite the new cultural ingredients, the undergraduates maintained a set of conventions among themselves, with no detectable adult influence, in which sexual expression and sexual behavior were restrained—if not actually repressed. The sexual ambience of the coed dorm floors—the conventions of the mixed-sex friendship groups in the lounges—was in curious ways more like older American erotic sensibilities than one had any reason to expect.[5]

Women and men, for example, did not usually walk around in front of one another in their underwear, let alone naked. The near-nudity of many of the Secret Santa performances was funny because it broke tacit student conventions about how one should ordinarily, decently, present one's body to other residents of one's floor collectivity (see chapter 3). On most floors most of the time, a resident who paraded past a lounge toward a bathroom draped only in a towel was likely to be busted on by other students who saw her or him in passing: "Woo-woo-woo!" "Goin' to the beach?!" "Hey, everyone, look at Joe's *muscles!*"

Daily informal dress in the dorms was relatively sex-neutral, a loosely unisex style tending toward the masculine. Men wore jeans, T-shirts, and sneakers, substituting shorts for jeans in hot weather or "sweats" for jeans and T-shirt at any time. Women wore the same, perhaps substituting designer jeans, a prettier T-shirt or a blouse, pants or a neat preppie skirt. In the mid-1980s, the new "GQ look" and the "Miami Vice look" among the undergraduates—oversized, layered clothes—were also popular styles at Rutgers for both women and men. If, on the average floor in the middle of the day, a woman came out of her room wearing obvious makeup and a sexy dress featuring bosom and legs, other residents almost invariably made kidding or disparaging remarks about her apparel. In the evening, on the other hand, on her way to a date or a party, a woman was allowed or even expected to look this "hot."[6]

The mixed-sex language of sexuality among the undergraduates was also notably indirect, unerotic, and sometimes oddly archaic in its usages. Females and males were not generally "women" and "men" to one another; they were "girls" and "guys." (The terms marked age, but they also marked a kind of sexual innocence or immaturity. To "make a woman" of a female, for instance, was to take away her virginity.) Female students themselves were no longer "coeds," but the mixed-sex floor was a "coed floor." People went on "dates." If a "relationship" became "serious" and turned into a "*re*lationship,"[7] then the partners had a "romance" or they were "seeing" one another; then they were "boyfriend" and "girlfriend."

If a student speaker suddenly introduced a vulgarism into ordinary dorm talk, especially in the hearing of mixed-sex audiences, student listeners usually commented on the word. A speaker trying to come across as tough and worldly-wise might persist, but the use of impolite sexual language was linguistically marked; its effect was dramatic. Undergraduates were often much more vulgar or direct in their language in the sexual backstage of the dorm floor, in single-sex groups. Or at least the men were; I was not allowed to listen in on woman-to-woman sex talk. Among the men, there was "locker-room" language, the traditional bragging vernacular of the American male peer-group. In the 1980s as in past generations, men's locker-room was characterized by its vulgar Anglo-Saxon vocabulary, by its focus on the starkest physicalities of sex itself, stripped of any stereotypically feminine sensibilities such as romance, and by its objectifying, often predatory attitudes toward women. On Hasbrouck Fourth in 1984, perhaps a third of the men apparently enjoyed talking this talk and spoke among themselves with only a modicum of irony about "chicks" and "broads" and "sluts."

More privately, among close friends, men would sometimes discuss their own sexualities in a different language, speaking ordinary words in apparently frank tones. Honest sex talk[8] was one of the personal disclosures that defined close friendship for most Americans in the 1980s, but the students, like other Americans, did not hear it from very many of their peers. It was evidently too dangerous. Both women and men suffered if it spread too far. Men might have their allegedly wide sexual experiences deflated; women could suffer from opposite disclosures, from the knowledge that they were more active than a discreet woman. Therefore, most students clearly made an effort to limit the distribution of such sexual confidences. In the course of two years of research in the dorms, I heard a little of this franker talk, in private, from the males I knew best. It tended to be confessional; it tended to be the opposite of what males felt they had to say in the locker-room argot of the male peer-group:

I'm making out this birth control questionnaire [administered by the university]? And they have all these questions about "Do you do this?" and "Do you use that?" It's embarrassing. To tell you the truth, my only sex partner right now is my hand.—Sophomore male, 1978

Yeah, I have some friends who are girls, but I don't know. They're always telling me what a nice guy I am, and they're always coming to me for advice about this guy or that guy. But they're never there when *I* need *them*. And how come I'm so unthreatening to them. How come they never think about *me* that way? —Sophomore male, 1985

It's really threatening, you know? All these girls have that Calvin Klein° guy hanging on their walls? How is an ordinary-looking guy like me supposed to meet their fantasies? I hate it. And another thing. I don't know why it is, but I just can't ask a girl out. If I like her, I'm too intimidated. If she likes me, I wonder why. I wonder what's wrong with her. Am I fucked up or am I fucked up? —Sophomore male, 1985

If I heard only a little honest sex talk in my research in the dorms, I saw even less direct evidence of undergraduate sexual behavior. Some student acquaintances told me that this was because I made most of my weekly visits on weeknights, Mondays through Wednesdays, while most student sex took place on the more relaxed "social" days of the seven-day cycle, during the long three-day weekends, Thursday nights through Sunday afternoons. But it was also because the students could be as discreet among themselves about their sexual behavior as they could be about their sexual language, even in the crowded, gossip-laden coed dorm-floor community. Steve, from Hasbrouck Fourth, made this point in a formal comment on my research in one of my anthropology classes in 1986: "There was a lot Mike Moffatt didn't find out about Hasbrouck Fourth last year. But there was also a lot we didn't know about each other. For instance, I only found out this year that my own roommate was sleeping with a girl on the floor last year, all year long. My own *roommate!*"

From what I did see and hear, however, it seemed that women and men in the same dorm collectivities did try for the most part to keep their closest personal relationships with one another within the relatively sex-neutral code of friendship. Except in the occasional rhetoric of student preceptors, coed floors were not "families"; as student groups, they were not metaphorically so close. Most women and men explicitly denied seeing cross-sex floor mates as "brothers" and "sisters"; coed sexuality was therefore not blocked by something like a floor-specific "incest taboo." And some sexual liaisons did develop between the coresident women and men on most dorm floors. Entirely secret affairs were safest, but they were probably very rare on a long-term basis.[10] Quiet, stable "romances" could also work out, especially if they were either independent of the complex social networks constituted by the larger friendship group, or if they developed early in the history of a particular group and then did not change. Tim and Fran's relationship on Hasbrouck Fourth in 1984 was apparently a good example of this.

But most dorm residents also felt that intrafloor sexuality had a higher potential for conflict than for collective harmony. Most floor groups contained at least a few instances of strong dislikes between floor members, or even of major, public clique fragmentations, resulting from erotic relations or unrequited erotic overtures between floor members—Andrea and Jim's romance on Hasbrouck Fourth, for example. On-floor sexuality could lead to jealousy among one's friends. It could also lead to personal embarrassment in the future. "What if you break up? How are you going to stand bumping into each other every day for the rest of the year?" As a result, most Rutgers dorm residents apparently believed that daily life was much easier if one's erotic partners lived somewhere else, anywhere else but in the same floor collectivity as one's self.[11]

Nevertheless, there could be no doubt about the salience of sexuality and eroticism among the undergraduates in the dorms. The iconography on the students' walls—the lyrics and the body language of their favorite singers—spoke volumes. Since the 1920s, "social life" has been the college euphemism for erotic activities with members of the opposite sex (or with the same sex, for homosexuals). And today, "social life" and "college life" are often virtually synonymous: "I have two goals in college, to do well in my classes and to have a good social life" (common freshman sentiment). And partying, the way in which contemporary young Americans met cute guys and cute girls, was something that most of the students did a great deal of (see chapter 2).

185

But to how much "real" sex did all this social life and partying actually lead? There was no way of knowing from the evidence at hand. One outcome, however, was known. About fifteen hundred pregnancy tests had been given per year at the biggest student health center at Rutgers-New Brunswick, the College Avenue center, in the mid-1980s.[12] This represented between 10 and 20 percent of the females on all the New Brunswick campuses in a given year. One-third of these tests had been positive. And virtually all of the pregnancies, on other evidence, had been dealt with through abortion. Clearly *something* very heterosexual was going on among the students.

But it was very hard ethnographic work indeed to find out much more about it. If my research methods had consisted only of local-level interviewing and observation, this is all I would have had to report about undergraduate sex: that the undergraduates who lived on the mixed-sex coed dorm floors managed their own peer-group sexualities with remarkable secrecy and restraint; that no one knew a great deal about anyone else's sexual practices or sexual beliefs; and that quite a lot of real sex evidently did go on, but there was no easy way of knowing what or how much, especially since the students themselves did not know for sure. They had their guesses, but they only knew for certain about themselves and perhaps about their closest friends.[13]

If I wanted to find out more about undergraduate sex, about student sexual mentalities as well as about possible sexual behaviors, I needed to find a way to ask my subjects about these things in different, safer ways than those provided by the social gossip and by the occasional confidences of dorm ethnography. I also needed a wider range of informants than a few dorm friends. Half by accident, half by design, I discovered another research method, which was exceptionally productive. In a large course on the anthropology of sexuality, which I taught at Rutgers College in 1986, a year after ending my field research on Hasbrouck Fourth, I invited the undergraduate students to write voluntary, anonymous self-reports about their own sexualities. Two hundred and thirty-seven Rutgers undergraduates chose to do so. As a collection, these papers offered up a whole new universe of sexual discourse, provided by a large, diverse, evidently willing sample of undergraduates from the college and the wider university.[14] What do they tell us about how some Rutgers students thought about sexuality in the mid-1980s? And what do they tell us about some of their possible sexual practices?

TEXTUALITY AND TRUTH IN THE
SEXUAL SELF-REPORTS

The undergraduates enrolled in the course received my optional assignment after they had studied patterns of sexuality and eroticism in selected non-western cultures for four weeks. They had a choice about writing this paper. They could write anonymous sexual self-reports; they could, after four weeks of 'thinking *out*' about human sexual diversity in other cultures, 'think *in*' about themselves. Or they could write a conventional compare-and-contrast essay on two of the exotic cultures we had studied in class. Every single student in the class in 1986 chose to write the sexual self-report.[15]

Anonymity was ensured. The students were not to put their names on their papers; they were only to indicate their sex, their college class, and their marital status. The papers would be graded on a credit/no-credit basis, I told them; when they handed in their papers, my teaching assistant would check off their names for completion of the assignment, shuffle the papers, and pass them on to me. A few students wrote into their papers the opinion that they would not have minded signing them:

> I'd look at it, kind of, as though—you're a doctor, sort of—and well, I'd like to talk about some of these things.—Junior female

Many more of them indicated that they liked and trusted the confidentiality of the procedure:

> The only reason I can write this is that Im pretty sure that this paper is untraceable, and so I dont have to worry about my typing either.—Senior female

(In order to retain a sense of the students' written "voices," I am not correcting these quotes from their papers in any way.)[16]

The assignment was not highly directive. The students were encouraged to be as explicit as they felt comfortable being and to be honest. They could write sexual fantasy if they chose to, but they were asked to identify fantasy *as* fantasy. They were also asked to avoid the sexual conventions of their gender—women were to try to avoid undue discretion, and men were asked to avoid braggadocio. In class, I had discussed what I considered the current American English "languages" of sexuality with rough genre-labels of my own devising: sex-manual technical, romantic, psychobabble, *Penthouse*, and locker-room. The students were told they could choose their languages and their narrative forms, and they were given nine or ten suggestions as to what to write about (e.g., pleasures and pains of sexuality, best and worst sex ever experienced, sexual development, emotions of sex, sexual techniques).[17]

Finally, the students were told that the information in their papers might, in a general, summarized fashion, contribute to my research on student culture at Rutgers. Then, immediately before they handed their papers in, they were asked to think carefully about what they had written and to write across the top of their paper whether or not I had permission to quote directly from them in my own published research. One hundred women and forty-four men, 61 percent of the students in the class, gave me this permission; these are the only papers I am citing here. Two-thirds of the class happened to be women; 85 percent of the class were older undergraduates, juniors and seniors.[18]

There is no precise way to evaluate either the smaller sample of 144 quotable papers or the larger sample of 237 for representativeness. But there was no obvious sexual bias in either set of papers. Every contemporary American sexual orientation was reported, from "neotraditional" to lesbian/gay. Some students indicated that they were very shy about sex, that they hardly ever talked about it with anyone; others were normal sexually obsessed adolescents. Most types of sexual practice celebrated in modern mass-market erotica were also described in these papers, at least occasionally. And many levels of sexual activity were reported, from self-confessed female and male virgins to maximum performers and "scorers" of both sexes.[19]

There is also no way of being certain about the honesty of these papers, though there are some clues in the way they were written. On the one hand, many of them were extraordinarily textual, following models in contemporary published writing. These undergraduate papers clearly could not have been written without the currency in contemporary American mass culture of such genres as Kinseyesque sexual life histories as popularized by *Playboy*, *Cosmopolitan*, and other men's and women's magazines; contemporary women's romances, especially Harlequins; sex manuals; contemporary erotic novels; and hardcore pornography. Young Americans could not have written about their own sexualities in the way these undergraduates did—and arguably could not even have *thought* about their own sexualities in the same way—a generation or two ago.

Yet, in my opinion, most of these reports were not straight fiction. Most of them sounded true, or they appeared to be *fictional* in the constructive sense of the term: they employed well-known writing genres to construct and to comprehend experiences that their writers themselves considered to have been real. Many of these reports had earnest, anxious tones or apparently conflicted tones, tones that somehow seemed appropriate to the complexity of actual contemporary American sexuality rather than to fantasy. Sometimes the details of a text pulled against the overall narrative frame—the writer's fictional inexperience showed—and when this happened, in my opinion, facticity was leaking through. In an occasional female pattern, for instance, the writer alleged during her formal textual evaluations that she had experienced or was now experiencing the pleasure-filled, experienced, meaningful sex that is the modern American ideal, while her narrative details suggested precisely the opposite.

Some of the writers, especially the younger women, were also textually self-aware, thinking *in* their papers about how to write such papers honestly. They sometimes declared that it was difficult to be frank, but implied, I think, that they had given it their best effort:

> Since I usually don't talk about things like this . . . it's going to be hard coming up with the right words to describe everything.—Sophomore female

> The hardest part about writing this paper is organizing it, because there's so many different topics that can be covered. . . . Being frank with the description is hard . . . writing it down and having a permanent record that can fall out of your backpack into the hands of a stranger, or worse—someone you know, is a scary thing to do.—Sophomore female

Other students began or ended their papers by expressing a wish to help me with my research, implicitly by being truthful; and perhaps 10 percent of the students spontaneously thanked me for the assignment:

> Incidentally, this assignment has given me the chance to vent a lot of frustration and generally get a lot of things off my mind . . . I appreciate it.—Senior male[20]

Certain themes, practices, and problems also came up so consistently across the papers that we either have to assume they were "out there" objectively, in shared belief and possibly in practice, or we must somehow posit that over two hundred undergraduates, writing in private, were accidentally concocting the same or similar things. And the identified fantasies, perhaps 15 percent of the papers, tended to be predictably generic. A typical female fantasy of good heterosexual sex, for instance, featured a romantic setting (a beach, a beautiful old hotel); a tall, dark, handsome male; inspired foreplay; fantastic oral sex; ecstatic mutual coital orgasms; and no subsequent emotional complexities. Here is one example, a woman's fantasy seduction of a sexy young French professor. It is worth quoting at length as an introduction to the extraordinary explicitness of many of these papers on the part of both female and male writers, as well as for its apparently unintended academic comedy.

As I left my french 101 Class that first day, I could still hear his voice ringing in my ears. Although I've never been to Paris I could imagine strolling down the Chames de Lie Sei with this tall dark man. As I sat on the bus on the way back to [my dorm] I began to realize that I had to have this man before the end of the semester. . . .

. . . After [the next] class had ended I slowly made my way up to the front of the room, careful to let every one filter out before I had reached my destination. "Professor X, I am having such trouble with this French, I just cant tell the difference between the words amie and amor, do you think you could help?" Well that got my an appointment at 5:00 at his office. This guy would have to do better than that. "Sorry Prof. I eat dinner at that time do you think we could make it a little latter this evening?" As 8:00 sliped from his sensuous lips I felt a chill go down my spine. . . .

. . . I spent at least a half an hour going through my draws to find the sexiest black teddie I owned and planed to wear my favorite black silk dress. This prof. was not going to know what hit him. . . . To add a final touch I splashed on some Obsession. . . .

At exectly 8:00 I knocked on the door. When this guy saw what I was wearing I though his eyes were doing to pop out. Calmly he asked me to come in and sit down so we could begin our French lesson, I had other things in mind. "Proffesor X, do you think you could get me a class of wine, I am very thirsty."

"Please call me Jim." Now I was getting somewhere . . . I slipped out of my shoes and loosend my dress. When Jim returned I was ready and waiting. He sat next to me on the couch and opened up my French book. As fast as he opened it I shut it and looked deeply into his eyes. Well the man finally got the hint, he reach around and unzipped my dress. While I was slowly undoing his zipper, he buried his head between my breasts. As his mouth slowly desended down my body I could feel the heat rising from between my legs. . . . To add to my desire he started speaking french to me. You didnt have to be fluent to understand this. As his mouth continued to nible away, his tongue zeroed in on my clit and sent me to a mind boggling orgasm. As my pleasure subsided I began to return the favor. I slowly kissed my way down his body, stoping periodicly to taste his flesh a little more deeply. As I neared his manhood, I could once again hear him speaking french under his breath. As I removed the final piece of clothing left on either of us, his underwear, I let out a murmur of disbelief. He had to the most endowed man I had ever been with. The chances of me taking all of him in my mouth were slim so I proceeded to nibble and lick like a demon. This didnt seem to bother him because he was moaning like a mad man. As he was about to orgasm he pulled away and shot his cum all over my belly and chest. To my amazement and shear delight he then licked me clean. . . .[21] Although I had enjoyed several orgasms by now the night was far from over. Jim then got on top of me and made love to me for what seemed like an eternity. As I dressed to leave, I knew I would have no problems with French that semester (or with the prof.). AS I turned and saw James Lying in his bed looking sexier than he ever looked before I could only think of one thing to say to him, "jusqu'a ce qu'on se recontre encore, ma cherie."—Senior female[22]

In the equivalent men's fantasies, the opposite number might have been blond; *she* might have picked *him* up and then done "everything" to and for him, insatiably. And similarly, no later emotional entanglements.

"Actual sex" tended to be written quite differently. Consider the following example, a sophomore woman's description of her "first time":

About eleven months ago, I met my present boyfriend. From the start, I felt differently towards him than I had with any other guy. . . . I fell in love with him before I would admit it to him. I think that I had to wait to hear him say he loved me first. Then, I felt mor secure. . . .

I guess that I knew all along he would be the first person that I would sleep with. . . . I don't think I will ever forget the night that I did lose my virginity. It was this past September (September 7th to be exact). My boyfriend and I had been going out for six months. I met him at a party late that night but, by the time I had gotten there, he was extremely drunk. We came back to my room because my roommate was not going to be there. We always slept together without making love so, it wasn't like we had had those intentions on that night. Well, my boyfriend was very drunk and very amorous to say the least.

Once we got into bed, I knew exactly what he had in mind, he was all hands and lips. I figured that we might as well have sex. . . . So, I made the decision to let him do whatever he wanted.

For the actual act of sex itself, I hated it the first time. Not only was it painful but, it made a mess on my comforter. I hated my boyfriend at that time. I actually kicked him out of my room and sent him home. I was upset for a lot of reasons: My boyfriend was too drunk to remember the night so, I had made the wrong decision in letting him do whatever he wanted; There had been no feelings involved; I hadn't enjoyed it in the slightest; My comforter had to be washed at three O'clock in the morning; I had lost my virginity and betrayed my parents. I was upset for just a couple of days.

After that first night, the sex between my boyfriend and myself has been great.

Half the women who wrote about their actual sex lives described the central drama "loss of virginity" in detail, and many such descriptions resembled this one. The careful specifications of boyfriend rather than casual partner, of length of time together, and of exact time and circumstances for the "first time." The complex negotiations of love and sex. The textual ambivalence between the female themes "I decided when it was going to happen" and "I let him bully me into it." The latent assumptions about what good sex ought to be—intentional, feeling-laden, meaningful, mutual, and pleasure-giving. The partial excuse for not-so-good sex: alcohol. And the canonical plot: pain or ordeal followed by, if lucky, subsequent pleasure and fulfillment.[23]

Men did not describe their first times as often in their papers, perhaps because they were more reluctant to admit exactly when they had first experienced sex. But when they did, their equivalent admissions about actual sex included being clumsy and inexperienced, being stupid about the woman's problems and feelings, and being too anxious to "get it up." Both women and men commonly used comedy and farce to deal with the disappointments of actual sex. Comedy and farce, at least as deliberate stylistic devices, were somewhat less common in the identified fantasies.

What convinces me of the basic truthfulness of most of these descriptions of actual sex is the way in which they were written against fantasy. I am also generally convinced by the way in which their homey details were not the details of fantasy. It is possible that the undergraduate writer who described her loss of virginity above, for instance, was an accomplished fictionalist who knew how to garnish her writing with realistic, concrete dailiness. But the otherwise careless quality of her writing suggests that she was not. I am particularly convinced by that soiled comforter at three o'clock in the morning.

Of the roughly eighty-five female self-reports that claimed to be about real sexual experiences, only a few rang obviously false—they sounded like unalloyed generic fantasy.[24] A higher proportion of male papers were in this gray area, perhaps 10 percent. (In a common pattern, a male would report the details of fantastic pickup sex with an unknown, beautiful female and then comment, "I know you're not going to believe this, but it really *did* happen.") It is possible that other parts of other narratives improved on actuality in their details, or that close friends' sexual experiences were sometimes borrowed and reported as one's own, or that pure fictive skill *was* sometimes involved.[25] On the other hand, even these fantasies-as-fact were useful evidence about the sexual mentalities of their writers.

In what follows, I will indicate my own judgments about the factuality of various papers as I deal with them. I am aware that such judgments are likely to be debatable, but as an anthropologist interested in attempting to go beyond purely textual, hermeneutic approaches to this material—in attempting estimates, however approximate, of actual behavior—I am unwilling to abandon these judgments entirely. I am also aware that, no matter how much I try to control for my own identity as a white, middle-aged, academic male, my reading of materials of this sort is likely to be influenced by my background. Likewise, of course, what the students themselves reported to me was likely to be influenced by my identity, by my attitudes, and by the way I taught the course in which these papers were assigned.[26] In any case, because of considerations of this sort—and because of the undeniable interest of the self-reports, intellectual and not-so-intellectual—I am including lengthy quotes throughout, so that readers can make up their own minds about my interpretations and readings wherever possible.

Taking these papers, then, as unavoidably honest at the level of values, attitudes, and sexual ideation and as relatively honest at the level of behavior, what do they tell us about sex among the late-adolescent American undergraduates who attended Rutgers in the mid-1980s?

THE NEW SEXUAL ORTHODOXY

I am a twenty-one year old male with a Roman Catholic up-bringing. Sex in our household was a four letter word. My parents did everything they could to protect their innocent children from the sexual deviants of the real world. This might have made any other childhood dull but, I feel it made mine more curious. . . . I've always admired the female anatomy. . . . The curves and bumps; the cleavage and the shape of their butt, "It's wonderful!" A portrait or a photo of a nude woman can give the most naive boy the biggest hard-on. . . . As a child, these thoughts and emotions were nothing more than fantacies that came to life on a television screen or in the movies.—Senior male

[When I was eleven and twelve], I found Playboy and other magazines under my brothers mattress and when he wasn't around I'd go into his room and read them. . . . I loved to read the letters and forum sections. I would masturbate while reading a really sexy story. Once I found and actual "dirty book" in that library between the mattress. It was called something like Insatiable Sara. The woman in the story did every possible sexual act with every possible partner in every possible position. I loved that book. My imagination ran went wild. Sara loved her vibrator and I was determined to find out what one felt like. I took apart the motor from my electric waterpic and made my own vibrator. It was a little bulky but it did the job. The main problem was it was too loud and I'd have to wait for everyone to be out of the house or take chances when the family was asleep.—Senior female

The first thing these papers tell us is that, sexually speaking, their undergraduate writers were the products of many influences besides college, let alone of Rutgers in particular. Perhaps one-third of the student writers mentioned the distinctive impact of college and college friends on their sexual developments. And about a third mentioned parental values and religious upbringing. But, on the evidence of these papers, *the* major influence on the sexualities of these undergraduates was contemporary American popular culture. The direct sources of the students' sexual ideas were located almost entirely in mass consumer culture: the late-adolescent/young-adult exemplars displayed in movies, popular music, advertising, and on TV; Dr. Ruth and sex manuals; *Playboy, Penthouse, Cosmopolitan, Playgirl,* etc.; Harlequins and other pulp romances (females only); the occasional piece of real literature (one Catholic boy mentioned *Catcher in the Rye* with erotic gratitude); sex education and popular psychology as it had filtered through these sources, as well as through public schools, and as it continued to filter through the student-life infrastructure of the college; classic soft-core and hard-core pornographic movies, books, and (recently) home video cassettes. *Deep Throat* was the paradigmatic college hard-core film at Rutgers in the late 1970s. ("Can a guy really last that long?" one of my sophomore roommates asked me as we returned from the annual student ritual viewing in 1978.) *Bad Girls* and *Debbie Does Dallas* were coming on strong in the mid-1980s.[27]

In *The Sexual Fix*, a recent political and literary analysis of "western capitalist" popular culture, the British critic Stephen Heath suggests the existence of a "new sexual orthodoxy," one that is in some ways as coercive as older, rejected western sexual codes. If pre-Victorians associated sex with sin and guilt but nevertheless often enjoyed it quietly as a private pleasure, Heath argues, and if the Victorians discovered sexuality and then repressed it, contemporary Anglo-Americans almost *must* celebrate it. Sexuality almost *must* be central to one's sense of self. And the essence of sexuality itself, in currently established conventions, is a technique-centered act of intercourse to orgasm—Heath calls it "the big O." If the archetypal Victorian novel ended in the good marriage, Heath quips, the archetypal contemporary romance ends in the explicitly described perfect orgasm (Heath 1982).[28]

Much in these student sexual self-reports was consistent with Heath's somewhat polemic interpretation of the contemporary mass culture of sex. It was virtually impossible, for instance, for any writer of these papers, woman or man, to say, Sex is incidental, or I'm too young to think about such things, or To tell you the truth, I don't like sex very much. Sex *had* to be important, even for the sexually inactive:

> I have never had sexual contact of any kind: no intercourse, no petting, no kissing, no anything. And I am not proud of this fact. You see, I am shy . . . [but] I am not a prude; I'm not content with my lifestyle. I believe in premarital sex; I just haven't been fortunate enough to have any. I consider sex a basic need in life, comparable to food and shelter.—Junior male

And those few students who tried to move away from the orthodoxy, who tried to say something idiosyncratic, were in the end "controlled by the discourse." In the end, pace Foucault, they virtually had to cop out for the centrality of sex and for sexual pleasure as an ideal:

I personally prefer sex not too often. My boyfriend is just the opposite. . . . I think my disinterest might be from the idea that I am not ready to handle being sexually active. (Don't get me wrong. I do enjoy sex and I do need it.) —Sophomore female)[29]

The new sexual orthodoxy, as it was written in many of these papers, posited the normality and importance of sex for any postpubertal individual, female or male, unmarried or married. Among these college students, the value of premarital chastity was thus almost as dead as the dodo. Some of the student writers, about one in five of both the women and the men, did admit to being virgins. But almost all these virgins, like the young man above, suggested that their virginity was an embarrassment to them:

By the time I turned 20 I was growing anxious about my virginity. I was ready to get rid of it but nobody wanted the damn thing.—Junior female

Only 3 of 144 student writers suggested that they were intentional virgins. All 3 were women; all 3 were Catholics; and all 3 were clearly defensive about their archaic sexual stances:

I don't consider myself a prude, but I strongly believe that *for me* sex without commitment (marriage) is wrong. I stress "for me" because although I feel that my morals are right, I generally don't judge other people.—Senior female

And even the intentional virgins believed in their right to sexual pleasure as unmarried persons, another tenet of the new orthodoxy:

I have strong sexual desires and would definately consider myself an extremely sexually-oriented person. . . . I truly believe that I have had good sexual experiences with my past boyfriends. My experiences go from kissing to "everything but" intercourse. I don't think that my relationships have left my partners sexually frustrated because I take much pleasure in giving and receiving oral sex. —Senior female [30]

Perhaps two-thirds of the women and half the men overtly or tacitly promoted some version of the Playboy ethic, the obvious goodness of sexual pleasure for all persons. Only a few, perhaps 10 percent, were unambiguously sure that they experienced it or had experienced it on a regular basis:

I've always been told that sex is like candy: once you're introduced to it, you can never get enough. And boy, is that the truth!!—Sophomore female

Sex is an awesome sport and I have to admit if I had to stop it, I couldn't wouldn't and won't!"—Senior male

Another 5 percent of the writers considered themselves, all-in-all, unsuccessful at sexual pleasure, and they tended to sound depressed about themselves in general for this reason: they were abnormal in their drives; they were being cheated out of their rights.

I don't enjoy sex. . . . Actually, I think I'm afraid of sex. I have performance anxiety which is based on my lack of experience, my not very strong sex drive and the fear that my body might not match up with my partners. I don't have a very masculine physique.—Senior male

I have a boyfriend and I do feel genuine affection for him, but I never feel arousal. Sexually he is only in a slightly better position than I am . . . but at least he has an orgasm once in a while. I never do. So I guess I'm frigid.—Senior female[31]

The rest of these writers gave their varying experiences with actual sexual pleasure as many different mixed reviews as there were sexual autobiographies. (About two-thirds of these students chose to write sexual life histories.)

Women explicitly promoted the value of sexual pleasure more than men in these papers. This might have been partly due to the history of twentieth-century American sexual discourse regarding females; these women writers often seemed to be making a deliberate or scripted late-twentieth-century denial of an outmoded early-twentieth-century belief, of the stereotype, Nice girls don't (or shouldn't) like to do it. Some women simply said, as above, that sex was fun. Other women, especially the younger ones, came closer to older female ambivalences.

I guess I can't explain how I feel because my sexuality is too intricate and varies in every situation depending upon the male. I am basically afraid of what people might think of me if they knew about my sexual experiences.—Sophomore female

Women also discussed sexual pleasure in the negative more often than men, noting their difficulties achieving it in required form under the new orthodoxy—orgasm through intercourse. About one-third of the sexually experienced women described their problems reaching orgasm:

> The first orgasm I had was about a year ago. I was nineteen year old. I did it myself with the jet stream of water from the shower massage fixture in our shower. . . . My tub in my apartment now doesn't have such a fixture and I miss it.
>
> My present boyfriend is the first and only guy with whom I've had an orgasm. This took place last spring. At first I could only relax enough to come when he'd bring me off with his hand. I feel vulnerable when I have an orgasm because it causes such bizarre movements and noises which I can't really control. Soon I was at ease enough to allow him to make me come by oral sex. . . . I still have never had an orgasm just from fucking and sometimes this turns me off to anything but oral sex done on me. I feel like what's the point.—Junior female

About half of these women said they were still "failing." The other half reported qualified success resulting from more experience, a change of lovers, the greater trust of sex with love, or the greater thrill of experimental sex.

Six women also described the physical pleasures of orgasm in varying metaphoric detail:

> [I] had so many great sexual experiences [with my second boyfriend]. . . . [Once] we pretended he was a t.v. repair man and he was fixing my t. v. I came on to him and we slowly peeoled each other's clothes off. . . . We finally make love and both came at the same time. This was the first time I had ever had an orgasm. It was FANTASTICC!—Junior female

> The climax I like best is the kind that comes over me slowly and last a while. First my stomach will bottom out—it's kind of like the feeling of an elevator going down too fast—and then all the muscles in my body will tense up, even my toes curl up, my back arches and then everything releases.—Senior female

> The explosion. It [feels] like a million geese [have] just taken off in the pit of my stomach.—Senior female

Men discussed sexual pleasure less often than women did, either as an actuality or as a problem. The male subtext on sexual pleasure was, in all probability, Of *course* I enjoy sex. I'm a normal guy. It goes without saying! And the distinctive feature of sex, orgasm, evidently came easier to young American men than it did to young American women. Only two men in the sample talked about problems relating to orgasm. Neither was talking about intercourse; both had had problems having any orgasms at all, apparently because of sexual guilt. The following account was also the only detailed male description of orgasmic pleasure in these papers:

> For several years before losing my virginity, I had been looking at nudie magazines like CLUB, PENTHOUSE, and PLAYBOY, for sexual thrills. I would sit in my room late at night with a flashlight and look at all the pictures, get a raging hard-on, and not be able to relieve myself of the pressure. I was so uptight sexually that I couldn't come when I masturbated. This caused me to get the dreaded "blue balls" which occurs when you have a stiff dick for at least 5 to ten minutes and don't relieve the pressure by coming. Let me tell you, It feels like someone punched you in the abdomen or squeezed a testicle. (well, not quite that bad). . . . Anyway, the summer after [I first had intercourse with a woman] I discovered how to masturbate or "jerk-off." I had matured a lot in my own sexuality in that I felt comfortable with the fact that I lost my virginity at 18.
> The relationship with my left hand and my dick began one night when I was reading the FORUM section of a PENTHOUSE. . . . [I] found I had gotten very hard. So I began to slowly feel and stroke my dick which sent an extremely good feeling shooting up my back. I got up and grabbed some Vaseline and liberally applied some onto the head of my dick and to the inside of my left thumb and forefinger. Again, I began stroking my dick paying particular attention to the head and reading the magazine at the same time. Soon I was stroking furiously and had forgotten the book. After about 10 more seconds, I felt this incredibly good feeling almost like a cescendoing tingle starting at my toes and ripping up my entire body. Afterwards, I was so weak that I had to stay still for 5 minutes. "So this is masturbation," I said to myself.—Senior male [32]

As has been suggested, another tenet of the new sexual orthodoxy as it was written or assumed in most of these papers was the contemporary meaning of "real sex":

> I was very sexually active with [a high-school girlfriend] but, I never actually had sex with her. In the beginning we made out a lot and even masturbated each other frequently. . . . Eventually we started having oral sex, she performing fellatio on me more often than I performed cunnilingus on her. . . . We also had a great deal of pseudo-sex through the pants. She had the nicest

breasts I've ever seen, they weren't very large but, they were by no means small either. I really liked to put my penis between them, I think that is very exciting. Once we almost had sex, we had all our clothes off and I was wearing a condom, we just started to do it and my mother called me to feed the damn dog. I could have screamed. Ah well, we never did have sex but I gained a lot of experience.—Sophomore male

There was "sex," in other words, and there was "real sex." "Real sex," as Heath and many others have noted, was genital-to-genital heterosexual intercourse, preferably to orgasm—the standard definition of mid-twentieth-century American sexological research. And, as in the classic sex research of Kinsey and his followers, as popularized by Hugh Hefner and *his* followers, your sexual success, in the implicit logic of most of these papers, is determined by your frequency, by your variety, by your technique, and by your emotional mastery of sexual experience.

Not every student writer was, in fact, in search of all of these sexual goodies at the moment of writing; but those who were not almost always sound a little apologetic:

I'm not exactly well stocked in the technique department. I'm basically a traditional missionary girl.[33] I've never tried it with me on top. I'm still a little inhibited about that. "Doggy-style" isn't bad, except there's no one in front of you to hug or kiss when you do it that way.—Sophomore female

If intercourse was the most "real" and the most "meaningful" sex, however, oral sex was not far behind. Loss of virginity was the event described most often in these papers as a whole. The techniques and experiences of subsequent heterosexual intercourse were the next favorite topics. And the third favorite was oral sex. When saying what they liked best for pure erotic pleasure, men cited oral sex much more often than intercourse. Women also regularly noted its pleasures, though not with quite the unflagging enthusiasm of the men.

According to both female and male accounts, in fact, oral sex had become a multipurpose solution to a variety of problems associated with "real sex"—it was the new sexual fix-it in the new sexual orthodoxy.[34] In many descriptions of loss of virginity, for instance, oral sex was the last "base" before "going all the way," part of the getting-to-know-you process that preceded intercourse, or the most erotic practice tolerated by the modern technical virgin quoted above. Two out of three of the intentional virgins said they practiced it; the third did not date at all. For most couples, oral sex was the central hors d'oeuvre in the foreplay before "real sex," the practice most likely to assure that the woman, like the man, got her "big O." According to half a dozen female and male accounts of established couples in which the writer also mentioned very strong mutual fears of accidental pregnancy, elaborate oral sex was the chosen heterosexual substitute for intercourse. And oral sex was the most common sexual practice reported, often with especially detailed relish, by the student writers who defined themselves as homosexuals.

Different writers reported different rates of getting used to oral sex, but with remarkable consistency across both the women's and men's accounts, oral sex was said to be an egalitarian, mutual practice for established couples. Perhaps because it was not quite "real" sex, oral sex did not seem to touch off the alarm bells of guilt in either female or male practitioners as often as did "going all the way." Its dilemmas were more often those of hygiene. Men and women worried about learning how to do it and about whether or not their partner enjoyed doing it to them. Men complained occasionally about vaginal cleanliness. Women commented on male cleanliness as well; but for women, the key issue in the practice of oral sex was whether or not to swallow. Almost everyone said the men were for it. Women writers' policies varied widely, as did their opinions of the aesthetics of the process ("You can't taste it if you love him, it's disgusting if you don't"; "It's o.k.—I've read it's full of protein").

Despite the AIDS epidemic and the developing fear of its threat to heterosexuals, sexual danger was a minor theme in these papers, one that seemed to be almost intentionally ignored by both female and male writers. Only 5 to 10 percent of the student writers of both sexes discussed sex and disease—herpes, VD, fear of getting AIDS from bisexual male partners.

AIDS was equally absent from similar papers written in early spring 1987. But by late spring that year, the threat of AIDS to heterosexuals was being discussed everywhere; one graduating senior even mentioned it in a commencement address in May. It was widely assumed in the popular press that AIDS was going to reverse the sexual revolution among late-adolescent Americans.[35] Is this likely? If there were major outbreaks of AIDS in heterosexual American college-age populations, something like this might take place.[36] Without such visible danger, however, given the pervasiveness of sexuality in late-adolescent culture and in wider American culture and the unlikelihood that old-fashioned adult supervision could be reestablished over late-adolescents in the late twentieth century, the more likely outcome is a somewhat higher reported use of condoms, a possible decrease in the practice of casual sex, but relatively little effect on other attitudes or behaviors of the sort reported here.

Just as they ignored sexual disease, most of the students, women included, also soft-pedaled the realities of contemporary American sexual violence in their sexual self-reports. Ten out of the one hundred women writers described at least one incident of abuse, rape, or incest being inflicted on them by males during their sexual comings-of-age, for instance, but then deemphasized the significance of these attacks in their subsequent accounts.[37] They assessed the psychological impact of these events on themselves, and then usually went on to assert and to describe their sexual normality in spite of these acts of abuse.

The final tenet of the new American sexual orthodoxy, undergraduate version, was the importance of sex with affection. Almost all the student writers of these papers said or implied that there was a difference between sex with someone you love and casual sex. Different writers had different ethics and opinions about whether or not they themselves could or should enjoy both; and different writers had different opinions about how others should act with respect to these two kinds of sex. But almost all these adolescent Americans—females and males, sexual gourmets and gourmands, conventional heterosexuals and sexual radicals—agreed that the preferable or superior sexual practice was sex with affection (with "love," with "caring," with "commitment," with "strong feelings," and so on). To adapt a concept from Louis Dumont, sex with affection was the "encompassing value" in nearly all these undergraduate sexual self-reports.[38]

MORALITIES AND PRACTICES

> I do not believe [good sex can happen] without love. Having intercourse with anyone, although fun to think about sometimes, doesn't have the same fulfillment as when it is with someone you really love.—Senior male

All but a few of these undergraduate writers took ethical or moral stances on sex. Sometimes they stated them as philosophies, usually in personal terms: This is what *I* believe. Sometimes they embedded them in running evaluations, in the adjectivals they often attached to specific individuals and incidents in their sexual life-histories: Then I met this sleazy girl; Rutgers guys only have *one* thing on their minds.

Perhaps a fifth of the writers, female and male alike, alluded to guilt, almost always in relation to heterosexual intercourse only. Guilt was something that interfered with their sexual development, or that they had overcome, or that they had learned to live with. Almost everyone who mentioned guilt also said they were from a Roman Catholic background:

> All in all I feel my sexual experiences were very enjoyable. I have had a fair amount of "fooling around on the side" along with a couple of intense relationships. Sometimes I feel a little guilty about sex—caused by my up-bringing and my religious beliefs. I sometimes have the urge to confess about my "pre-marital sexual experiences" to a priest and give up these experiences until married, but I realize that I am too tempted to ever commit myself against indulging in such activities.—Senior female

A few of these undergraduate writers sounded confused or ambivalent in their sexual ethics. They argued two incompatible philosophies, or they articulated different moral stances in different contexts without noticing the shift. And other, more centered writers also indicated at least the occasional ambivalence. A woman, for instance, might say that she felt free to do anything sexually, without self-judgment, but might then tell a sexual adventure with unconscious self-disgust.

Nevertheless, it was possible to classify the average moral stance of most of these writers into one of a number of rough types. As general orientations, these moral categories of sexual behavior will not come as a surprise to anyone who pays attention to the themes in current mass-market erotic and romantic writing, to the messages in popular music, or to the sexual role models on television or in the movies. The specific constructions of these moral stances among these contemporary adolescents, on the other hand—their rough distributions, their subtle variations, their adolescent trade-offs between sexual ideals and sexual pragmatics—are worth examining in some detail.

Neotraditionalists and the New Double Standard

The new sexual orthodoxy is, at a certain obvious level, an ethic of gender equality. Its enemy is apparently the older American sexual double standard. No one should feel guilty about sex, man or woman; women have as much right to sexual pleasure as men; it is not necessarily bad for women to initiate or lead in sex. And there were indications in these papers that a generation of sex education in the public schools has not been entirely in vain; some of these liberal notions were apparently effective contemporary values among many of these students. All the female or male writers who commented on sexual pleasure felt that they, personally, had a right to it. And with great consistency in both the women's and men's accounts of sex within established girlfriend-boyfriend pairs, the undergraduate writers reported sexual mutuality. Long-term partners in affectionate sex evidently worried about their sexual responsibilities, about birth control and pregnancy, together.[39] Both women and men said that their partners paid attention to the narrator's own sexual pleasure ("Sometimes my boyfriend worries more about my orgasm than I do."—Junior female).

However, a modern variant of the older double standard was also articulated in many of these undergraduate self-reports. Over half the women writers and about half the men argued or assumed that women and men should follow different sexual moralities. We can call these students the neotraditionalists.[40] Sexually, they were, due to their numbers and their continuities with older western sexual sensibilities, something of a moral mainstream among the students. And undergraduates who took other stances on sexual morality sometimes specifically contrasted themselves to these "typical women" or "typical men."

The neotraditionalist women and men differed systematically from one another in their moralities, along some old western gender-linked lines. And, like many older Americans, they formed a matched set. Both imagined sex as a battle or a bargain or a game, as a trade-off of physical sex for love, as a contest between necessarily reluctant women and inevitably aggressive men. Both agreed that, sexually, women came in two types, "good women" and "sluts"; neither commonly made an analogous division of men. And neotraditional women and men both struggled to adjust these older moral distinctions to the new sexual orthodoxy.

Neotraditional Neanderthals and Other Men. All the male neotraditionalists said or implied, assertively or quietly or, occasionally, apologetically: I am a man and I need sex. Most women want it more than they admit. Men have the right to experiment sexually for a few years. There are a lot of female sluts out there with whom to so experiment. And once I have gotten this out of my system, I will then look for a good woman for a long-term relationship (or for a wife).

The most primitive of the male neotraditionalists I chose to call the Neanderthals.[41] There were eight specimens in the sample of forty-four male writers; five of them were members of fraternities. The Neanderthals only described casual sexual adventures, either pickup sex or "orgies" of various kinds. Two who belonged to fraternities mentioned "shows," male group voyeurism of a "brother" with a woman, always with a "pickup" partner. The Neanderthals described the "two-on-one" (the ménage-à-trois, or "being double-teamed"). And they occasionally even gave accounts of "gang bangs," one female being fornicated with by many males in rapid succession while all of them watched. It is possible that the neo-traditional Neanderthals had not taken part in these activities as often as their narratives suggested, though they often described them only as "a thing that happened to me once." But they described them so consistently that we have to assume they were central to their manly sexual identities.

The Neanderthals often suggested that they were not especially experienced in sex. It is possible that they would evolve into slightly less extreme forms of male neotraditionalists in a few years, when they had gotten these things "out of their systems." But at present, their attitudes toward sex itself were loaded with disgust; their papers celebrated their own bravado for daring to dive into such sleaziness; and they saw women almost entirely as sexual prey. They depersonalized them in description, they exploited them in reported behavior, and then they judged them as sluts, with no corresponding judgment of their own male selves:

> When my friends pick up chicks and bring them back to the fraternity house Everyone else runs to the window to look at somebody else domineer a girl and I tell you what you almost get the same satisfaction. Some of the guys like to put on a show by doing grosser things each time. We were watching one time and the girl caught us and invited us in (no lie). It turned into 12 on 1 She fucked four of us and blew 9 of us. All she kept asking us for was a beer because she was thirsty. She got dressed aftrwards and acted like nothing happened. AS she was leaving she told us it wasn't her first time doing this so everyone from that point was afraid of catching VD but nothing came of it . . .
>
> Watching my friends have sex with other girls is as almost as satisfying as doing it myself. . . . By the same token I enjoy conquering girls and having people watch. The thing that baffles me is that girls know whats going on at fraternity houses but still insist on returning. What could be the reason for this type of person unless they enjoy it as much as the guy who is doing it. Don't laugh it may have happened to your sister once.—Senior male

A step away in crudeness from the Neanderthals were the more experienced Don Juans. There were only a few reported cases among the male writers (the assignment *did* ask the males to avoid bragging). One, a senior, wrote a genre classic entitled "The List," in which he unknowingly laid claim to being the maximum sexual achiever among all these undergraduate writers. Sex itself did not come through in his paper with the loathing or distaste that it carried for the extreme Neanderthals, but, like most of the neotraditionalist men, he never really described sexual pleasure either. What apparently interested him most was the man-to-man competitive thrill of his sex-life list.

He first had sexual intercourse in eighth grade, he tells us, and began keeping score in high school. He remembered his nineteenth birthday fondly.

> On my 4th night [at Rutgers during my sophomore year], after a couple boring . . . dance parties, I picked up a chick at some rush parties. A few night later I registered "number 20," I was psyched about this cause I was only 19 yrs. and it was the first time my numbers exceeded my years. That first chick slowed me for a semester, but second semester I moved into a frat and started picking up where I had left off. . . .

As a fraternity brother he pushed his numbers up even faster. He said that he had been in love once or twice, but not for long; he confessed to "abusing" a few women who "really loved me"; but mostly his account was a dispassionate record of one-nighters or "girls I would do just two or three times." The previous weekend, he said, he had made a sexual mistake: "One a big fat bitch that climbed in my bed after the frat party and fucked me when I was so drunk that I had to ask my friends what I did the night before." So he solaced himself as follows, and set his claimed mark at the moment of writing:

> The next night after a harrowing experience like that I decided to redeem myself and picked up a pretty nice chick at a bar to get #60. To this day I can remember all of them by name and chronologically, So any time I get in an argument with a frat brother or a little bragging match, I've got them all beat so I say "Let me consult the list."—Senior male

Good Women and Sluts. Not all the neotraditionalist men were so extreme and misogynistic in their sexual sensibilities. One junior provided an apologetic but ultimately unrepentant example of a more moderate variant of the species. His often unintentionally funny account of his sexual odyssey in and out of Neanderthal has a certain naive charm. Unlike the Neanderthals and the Don Juan quoted above, he hints at real sexual pleasure. He describes his "good" and "bad" female partners in human terms. And when judgmental, he includes himself in his judgments. In the end, however, he still adheres to the double standard as a fundamental ideal, and he provides a fine-tuned statement of the revised contemporary distinction between good women and sluts—an unwitting answer to the implicit modern problem, how do you find a virtuous woman when everyone agrees that premarital chastity is out-of-date?

He had his first extended experiences with heterosexual intercourse with a high school girlfriend, he begins by telling us. Though he felt a certain affection for her, he also attempted to break up with her regularly, to try "experimenting with many types of girls." But every time he tried to break up, he says, "she would lead me into her room, strip to her bare skin, and lie 'spread eagle' on her bed. Now, I was just seventeen and her strategy was quite effective even until our first semester at the banks of the Old Raritan." They came to Rutgers together, where he finally did manage to end their relationship. He still runs into her, and thinks fondly of their past good times together, but he also feels embarrassed, he says, whenever they meet.

> After finally breaking up my high school fling I went crazy in a sense. I pledged a fraternity and experienced my sexuality at the same time. No longer was there one girl to always have sex with, but there was many. Any night the boys and I went out we were looking to find Miss Wrong in a sense. She didn't have to be beautiful, just willing to do it. I quickly got the hang of the game and ended up sleeping with many different girls. Seldom do I take a class at [this campus] without a past bed partner in it. Your class happens to have two.

Like the other male neotraditionalists, he sees casual sex, and the "Miss Wrongs" who are part of it, as "sleazy." But unlike the more hardened neotraditionalists, he directs his retrospective judgments at himself more than at the women:

> The sex . . . had no real chance of being good. First, I was usually so drunk that even if I could get it up I could never come. Second, the girl who I might have just met once or twice or have seen in class and who I have never "felt" out, lead to awkward sex. Usually with these things in mind I would try to get as far as I could and if she let me stick my long hard blow pop inside of her I would just try to explode as soon as possible and try to pay a little attention to her needs.

> During this period of my life . . . I was known for being a "male whore,"[42] "a real asshole to girls," and a "typical fraternity brother."

But he quickly excuses himself in retrospect by arguing that boys will be boys: "I think this is what all young men try to accomplish during this time of their lives." And though that phase of his life had had unexpected academic benefits, he says, he soon felt he needed a better kind of sex and a better class of woman: "This sexual life style was good for a while, it helped me relax while taking Organic Chemistry (I got [straight As] that semester), but I knew I had to change. I liked when sex could be with someone special, and someone Jewish like myself. . . ."

Though he does not strongly stigmatize the "Miss Wrongs" of the fraternity scene, he also clearly does not expect to find the better class of women he now desires among these females. Or rather, he has a behavioral test that allows him to separate good women out from the possible sluts:

> Finally, I found a girl that was amazingly beautiful, shorter than me, intelligent, and Jewish. That night, I was still in my taking home and fucking mood so when I offered to take her home, she said yes. This made my expectations of a long lasting relationship deflate. A girl that will do it to me in one night will do it to anyone. . . .
>
> We went back to her room and I went home with only a succulent good night kiss. My faith was still alive because I thought that this might be the girl to pull me out of the sewer.

For an unspecified period his dream woman held him off: "We continued to date and had a lot of fun together without having sex. This is the kind of girl guys are really looking for in college."

And then at last she let him have her. Was she a virgin? She might have been; there was an incidence of virgins among Rutgers females, particularly among the freshmen and sophomores. Had she been a virgin, however, she probably could not have handled him. And, from his account, he evidently did not expect her to be.[43]

> Finally, we made love and in my eyes it was a horror show; but to me that was good because I was nervous and it meant that I really cared. What happened was that I wanted to make her enjoy the sex so much that we engaged in intense foreplay. She was so moist with cum that when I penetrated her I could only last a few strokes. We hadn't talked about contraception until I was ready

to explode, unprotected in her depths. Thank god she was on the pill from a previous relationship.

With out first time behind us, it was straight up from there.

The modern good woman, then, should not immediately have sexual intercourse with someone she likes. If she has been sexually active in the past, she should have been so in the context of "a relationship," not—to the male's knowledge, at any rate—out on the fraternity "meat market." But the modern good woman is not necessarily any less experienced than the slut:

There's a fine line between a girl who enjoys sex and a slut. *I don't care what a girl does. But a girl should at least be discreet about it.*—Sophomore male, Hasbrouck Fourth, private talk, 1985

Neotraditionalist Women.

The first time I made love was with my second boyfriend . . . [a] guy I started seeing when I was 15. We'd been hoing out for 1½ years we first made love and when we did it really meant something special. . . . Before we made love, we had an extensive sex life, but not kinky. We engaged in manual and oral sex and always enjoyed it. I'd say the most exciting or shall I say different thing we did was make love in a bubble bath. Even though we haven't been going out for 4 yrs., he's still very special to me. . . . After this relationship was over I went through a year of dating and it was this period of time I realized that dating wasn't for me. The sexual experiences I had had with my boyfriend could not happen anymore without great feelings of guilt and emotional attachment. . . . At a bar one night, I ran into a guy who I knew of and we talked and danced and drank and then he drove me home. In front of my house in a small Prelude we had sex in the driver's seat. . . . Needless to say, I now felt emotionally attached to this guy and wanted to get to know him better. Needless to say like many other young men he was in it just for the sex. . . . One lesson I've learned is that if you wnnt a relationship to last and develop to its fullest potential, I feel that sexual intercourse must wait until mutual trust, respect, and love is present.—Junior female

The neotraditionalist woman (slightly more than half the women writers of these papers) is the perfect complement to the neotraditionalist man; she is the other side of his coin. The only good sex, she says, is sex with love (or sex with caring). I myself have tried casual sex once or twice but I hated it; or, alternatively, I would never consider trying it. Most guys only want one thing. A girl has to wait, either for the right guy or for a guy she likes to change his views on sex ("Sometimes I think most guys almost have to be retrained about caring, loving sex."—Junior female). Just as neotraditionalist men can no longer expect a virgin, so, too, the women can no longer expect to wait, or no longer need to wait, for marriage; but wait they must: for "love," or "commitment," or "caring," or "strong feelings."

The neotraditionalist women in these papers, like the men, held their positions with differing levels of certitude. They also differed among themselves in their views on the opposite sex and on sexual pleasure itself. A few, generally the inexperienced, were the opposite numbers to the Neanderthal misogynists; they focused on their fears or their suspicions of the other sex:

> Living in a college dorm is the ultimate social experience anyone will ever encounter. There is no one to supervise anything or watch over what you choose to do. The opportunities to become sexually active are greater than ever before. The majority of guys coming into this situation are determined to take full advantage of the situation.—Senior female

A certain number of neotraditionalist women, perhaps half a dozen, stated new versions of the older female lament, Sexual pleasure is really only for men. They now stated it as a subclause to the new sexual orthodoxy, under which they now also had to claim that they did like sex:

> Sex is a big part of my relationship right now. It gives me a way or an outlet to show my boyfriend how much I care about him and love him.—Junior female

> I do enjoy sex and I enjoy satisfying someone else. I think I find greater pleasure in satisfying my sex partner than in myself being satisfied.—Junior female

Others described their own sexual pleasures with more enthusiasm. Some wrote ethereally and euphemistically. Others wrote with more physicality. Here is one woman's account of the erotic gestalt of good sex with someone she loved. Within the writing limits of these undergraduate authors, it is a particularly pretty evocation:

> [Last summer with my boyfriend in an off-campus apartment] I was a very sexual and sensual individual. I loved walking around the apartment naked. I loved sitting naked in an armchair in the living room with my legs spread teas-

ing my boyfriend. . . . My favorite spot to make love was the front room at early evening. The sun hadn't yet gone down and sunlight would stream through the white eyelet cotton curtains. I would sit on the edge of the bed or the couch propped up with my elbows with my feet touching the floor my knees bent and my thighs spread. My boyfriend would kneel on the floor between my legs. He would move slowly, then quickly, then slowly. He would cover my breasts with his hands. I knew he loved me. He loved making me feel good. I loved having him inside me. My body would quiver all over. He says I wear this expression on my face when I'm sexually aroused. I always wished it could last forever because it felt so wonderful and so beautiful.—Senior female

Sometimes the neotraditional women also described casual sex, but always with disapproval. And they agreed with the men about whom they should disapprove of—of their own female selves. If the neotraditional men threw the blame for casual sex on the women, the neotraditional women accepted this blame and incorporated it in their own moralities. The following young woman was typical for the negative self-judgment with which she framed this description of her participation in an episode of pickup sex, but she was also somewhat atypical among the female neotraditionalists for the way in which she allowed sexual pleasure to thread throughout her account as a subtheme:

The worst sex I've ever had happened recently. A friend and I met two guys and we went back to their place to hang out; we had a few beers and the guys started to get pretty "friendly." We decided that if we tried to cool them down at that point, we would look like teases, so we realized we'd have no choice but to screw them. The sex itself wasn't so bad. It was actually kind of neat because he had mirrors over his bed and they were driving me wild. The guy was nice-looking, and he had an amazing body; he really turned me on. However, I was extremely drunk and tired, and generally when I'm drunk I get lifeless, like a rag doll. I wasn't very aggressive and couldn't move with him very much; he was doing all the work. Some parts of the night I can't even remember! The next morning I felt like crap!! He seemed like such a nice guy, and it was so nice sleeping in his big, strong arms; if only I had not had sex with him. My friend and I felt like sluts, meeting two guys, getting trashed, and then fucking them! It's just not our style. It is an experience I choose to forget.—Sophomore female

Gender Simplicities, Gender Complexities

If we could somehow read the papers of the neotraditionalists for their professed sexual moralities alone, without paying attention to anatomical details and without noticing the often characteristic feminine and masculine turns in the writing, we could still predict the sex of all the authors without fail. For in these papers, the match between gender and espoused morality was simple. Neotraditional women always wrote one personal morality and neotraditional men always wrote its complementary opposite. But we could not be so accurate about the rest of the papers. The remaining undergraduates, less than half the women and about half the men, wrote alternative sexual moralities, which were not so easily gender typed. For there were romantic men who agreed with the neotraditionalist women: The only good sex is sex with love. And there were experimentalist women who agreed with the neotraditionalist men: One has the right to enjoy casual sex for a few years. There were also liberal women and men who agreed with each other: Both loving sex and casual sex are fun, but loving sex is best. And, finally, there were a very small number of sexual radicals of both sexes—feminists, bisexuals, and homosexuals—who combined sexual liberalism in uneasy mixes with more fundamental questions about gender, sexual culture, and sexual politics.

Romantic Men. Historically it can be said that romance has not been purely or intrinsically a women's erotic perspective. For men have been troubadours and romantic poets and novelists and musicians. Still, in American popular culture in the mid-1980s, the romance was an overwhelmingly female genre. Young American men did not read Harlequins.[44] Nevertheless, about one-third of the forty-four male writers of these papers did take sexual stances that could be called romantic, sometimes in opposition to what they themselves saw as the more powerful men's mainstream:

> In reasoning with myself, I always come to conclude that I do not fit stereotyped typical male, the man who is always sex-seeking, and dominant, love em and leave em kind of guy that never gets too attached or hurt. (Please excuse hyped-up definition of the typical male but this is the impression of what men intend or pretend to be and also what women blame men to be).—Senior male

Like the neotraditionalist women, the romantic men maintained with varying degrees of conviction that the only good sex was sex with love:

> I could not imagine having sex with someone you did not love. Something very important would be missing and it would bring a wonderfull thing like sex down to some very menial hip exercises.—Sophomore male

Cheap sex I might find good and fun. . . . I won't deny that it must be great if it is wanted and no one gets hurt. Moreover and mostly I must confess that, for me, sex without love is an empty feeling and a totally meaningless experience.—Senior male

Like the neotraditionalist women, the romantic men suggested that they had never tried casual sex, or that if they had, they had disliked it. They did not believe in the man's one-way right to sexual experimentation. They did not divide women into good women and sluts.

As males by ascribed biocultural identity, the romantic men did not write as if they had been the objects of serious sexual aggression. It did not sound as if, like the neotraditionalist women, they had been systematically pressured or bullied into sex. And they had not had to make the women's hard choice, nor to worry that they might be thought to be sluts if they partook of casual sex, for there were no real male sluts in American erotic culture. But like the traditional women, they indicated that they occasionally had been the reluctant partners in sex. Like traditional women, they had sometimes wanted to wait until they were ready for mature sex with love or until the right kind of person came along:

I do enjoy sexual play with women about my age. . . . My one big problem is I am a recovering shy person. . . . My first sexual encounter occurred when I was almost 17 years old. I took my date out to dinner and then we went back to my place for some heavy petting. I told her as soon as we were undressed that I didn't want to have sexual intercourse (I feel that the first time for *me* should be with some one whom I really care for.) We went as far as mutual masturbation. . . .

As far as sex with my [present] girlfriend we both feel that we should wait a little longer until we feel ready (This my seem ethnocentristic, I believe it is but who cares!). . . . Although we performed oral sex a couple of times, neither of us really enjoys it and therefore we have abstained.—Sophomore male

I think I can say I'm fairly attractive. I'm certainly not a Mr. Universe, but I've had plenty of opportunities that I didn't "take advantage" of. I just want to find someone that has the same feelings about sex that I do (I wonder if that's possible). When I do find her, I will not have only found the perfect lover, I guarantee that I will have found my wife.—Senior male

The romantic men wrote both in locker-room language and in romance, but their proportions of romance were higher than other men's.

And in either language they were more likely to focus on mutuality or on their partner's pleasure, rather than on their own manly triumphs in sex.[45]

> I enjoy giving head as well as getting it. A vital part of making love is getting your partner aroused with your mouth and tongue. What is most enjoyable is to see the reaction from a girl when here clitoris is stimulated by the flick of a tongue. They squirm like little children getting their feet tickled.—Junior male

When they did write romance, the romantic males sometimes sounded very "feminine." In this account of an evening of pleasure with his girl-friend, in a family house with parents away, this young male hits all the right notes of "women's erotic romance." Setting. Extended, sensitive sexual technique. Delight in her pleasure. Delight in his pleasure. And *love*:

> One of the best parts about an evening alone with my girlfriend is the anticipation. Everything must be perfect. Its very rare that we get to be alone together for a whole night, so we really take advantage of it.
>
> . . . We like to go shopping together. . . . Scented candles, a bottle of wine and a "dirty movie" are some of the things we might get. By the time we are done shopping, Im already excited.
>
> . . . We both help make dinner which is usually simple and the dishes are left till later. My girlfriend then gos into the bedroom and changes into her blue (my favorite color) silk nightgown. While she is doing this I start a fire and set the movie up to watch. I then quickly change into a pair of shorts with nothing else on. My girlfriend then enters the room and we both sit on the couch pulling a blanket around us. After spending the whole day waiting for this moment, were both incredibly turned on. I turn the movie on and both our hands are beneath the blanket as we start to tease each other. I love to tease my girlfriend and watch her face light up as I do it. I take care not to move to fast as I circle her breasts with my fingers getting closer and closer to her nipples. Sometimes its too much for her and she pushes my hand down below her waist where shes already very wet. . . . She starts to breath heavily with little gasps of pleasure and then tells me to use my mouth on her. I slowly work my way down her body, stopping at her breast, making each nipple hard. By this time, she cant take the teasing anymore and she tells me to please make her come. This I do with pleasure, as I start to tease her with my tongue. I try to keep from getting too excited while Im making her come because afterward its my turn. Soon she starts to cry my name out as she climaxes, and I hold her tightly telling her how much I love her. Next I start to enter her slowly so as not to hurt her and when Im finally in, we both smile with pleasure. I start pumping slowly getting faster with time but after a while I pull out and lie on

my back as she gets on top of me. This is my favorite position. She starts moving up and down as fast as she can while I lie back enjoying every second. Sometimes I think to myself "life cant be better than this." I try to last as long as possible but with each thrust it get harder + harder. Finally, I give in to the pleasure and come, as I clutch my girlfriend to me. I stay in her for a while longer and she rests her head on my chest smiling at me with what I know is true love. We both love to talk after we make love. . . . I feel so close to her at theese times. . . . After talking for a while we fall asleep in each others arms . . . In the morning we awake and welcome the day in with some more lovemaking. life is good, I think to myself at times like this.—Sophomore male

Experimentalist Women and Women's Locker-room. If the romantic men adopted moralities and sexual sensibilities resembling those of the neo-traditionalist women, there were also some women among the female writers of these papers who shifted toward traditional men's sexual styles. They alluded to "guy-watching." Some of them said they did so socially with women friends and with a good deal of enjoyable woman-to-woman talk and banter. They called it "scoping," as in "telescope," and they often noted campus locations known for particularly good scoping. They also often noted their tastes when they looked over males as sexual objects: "a cute butt," "muscles," "a fantastic body," "a good crotch," "sexy legs," "a 'Bruce' kind of guy" (someone who resembled rock star Bruce Springsteen).

About half the women writers also apparently felt they had as much right as men to use the erotic language once thought to be "unladylike" ("'from the gutter,' as my grannie used to say"—Senior female), the physically explicit, Anglo-Saxon-laden words of the locker-room. They generally confined the use of these words to safe contexts: they used them among close women friends; they used them in these anonymous papers. They employed them in various densities, in various mixes with other female erotic vocabularies. Sometimes women wrote almost exclusively in locker-room—and not always to describe sexual fantasy or casual sex. Women could write in this earthy language even about romantic, loving sex with boyfriends. They almost always added distinctively feminine turns to their locker-room prose, however—"we cuddled," "it felt wonderful," "a perfect ending . . ."—as in the following example:

[My boyfriend] began to lick my cunt in an up and down motion which drove me crazy. Then he sucked my clit which drove me absolutely wild. My body became very hot and sweaty, my hips were thrashing about, and moans were escaping from my lips. Then he plunged his tongue into my cunt, in and out it went. . . . He lay me back to where his legs had been and covered my body with his. My legs opened and he slipped his cock into my cunt. His cock felt so good. . . . He got off of me and positioned himself so his body faced my head . . . my head . . . my mouth opened and was filled with his cock. I sucked him until he was ready to come. He pulled his cock from my mouth and came all over my tits. He rubbed his cum over them. It was warm and slicky and felt wonderful. . . . We laid down together, body against body, and just cuddled together. It was the perfect ending to a perfect loving moment.—Senior female

If half the women felt free to experiment with sexual language, a smaller number, perhaps one in five, described experiments with sexual behavior that went beyond the occasional flings of the neotraditionalist women. They wrote about sexual experimentation in widely differing tones of self-confidence and self-assurance. Some sounded ambivalent or worse. Here is the apologetic account of an experimentalist woman who probably feared that she was, or had been, a slut. Her powers of denial are striking, and they are characteristic of a number of these female writers, at least episodically. Note how this writer in particular resists defining two different episodes of apparently coercive sex as "real rape."

I went sort-of wild when I was a freshman. Lots of frat parties. . . . When I get drunk I get myself into these spots like you would not believe. . . . [One time] I met a guy at [name of fraternity] and when he went to drive me home, he decided to kidnap me to his apartment in Woodbridge (at the time I had no idea where I was). I was scared, but ever DRUNK and after an hour he still wouldn't take me home, so I slept with him to get out of there, and got back at 4:30 a. m. It could have been a very bad experience. I was lucky.

Not much later I was at the same frat and met a guy and somehow ended up in his room, I can't really remember how, but I'd say that this was the closest I've ever been to being raped. The guy was very strong and holding me down. We didn't ever really have sex because he was too drunk and was limp. *Then*, his room-mates came in from another door somewhere & were yelling & screaming & drunk & some of them pulled down their pants & were saying stuff like "when's it my turn?," etc. I ran out of there & home to [my] dorm and I've only been back once. I learned my lesson.—Senior female

Most of the experimentalist women, however, sounded calmer and more deliberate about their sexual practices; they sounded as if they had consciously chosen to try enjoying sex without guilt, and without the traditional women's commitment to and from males. One senior, who narrated one of the longest and most diverse sexual curricula vitae in all these female papers, for example, writes in a unique, peculiarly impressive, almost totally flat tone. She does not interpret. She does not defend. She does not apologize. For the most part, she simply chronicles:

> I first had sex when I was about thirteen, at the end of eighth grade, The boy was about 18 or 19, and I had met him that same day. A group of my friends and I were cutting school and we were in an abandoned house drinking beer. . . . I really didn't know what he was up to. I can remember that he asked to put his hand down my pants nad I asked him, "What for?" After this first encounter, I had quite a few different partners, and no steady boyfriends until I was sixteen.
>
> At this time Imet and began dating a guy from the Air Force Base near my house. . . . Joe was my first serious, ongoing relationship with a man . . . I tried alot of things for the first time with Joe, such as fellatio, anal sex, dildos and alternate positions, Joe was fun to experiment with because he never pushed me into doing anything that I didn't want to do.
>
> . . . When I went on my [high school] senior class trip to Atlantic City, a classmate and I were picked up by a thirty-six year old man who was staying in our hotel. . . . My girlfriend and I went to his suite and had a menage-a-trois. I'm not sure what more to say about this except that it was fun. . . . [Now in college] I have about fifteen different men that I have sex with on a regular basis. (About once or twice a month each) These are all guys that I have gotten to know, and although I would like to have sex with more guys than this, one never knows what someone has. I have also wanted to try sex with another woman, but I really haven't had the opportunity.—Senior female

Another experimentalist tells of a woman's scoring game analogous to the activities of the male Don Juan quoted above, in cheery, girlish tones of "what fun!"

> [After two college relationships] I decided that I did not want to have any more commitments. I wanted to go out with as many men as possible. This summer started it all. Since I was not living at home and had my own place, my plan could go into action. To make the summer fun-filled, my girlfriends and I devised a point system . . . : 1 Point—Kissing[;] 2 points—Petting [;] 3 Points—Oral Sex[;] 4 Points—Intercourse; 5 Points—Anything out of the ordinary. Well, the four of us racked in those points and we had a helluva time doing it. (To say the least). Even though I did not win, my experiences were great. I think it was the excitement of it all that turned me on. Fooling around

in the same room as another couple, having sex on the stairs, and in the bathroom were just some of my new-found adventures.

. . . One night I went to this club where I always hang out at. I saw this really hot guy standing at one end of the bar. Right there and then I decided that I wanted him. . . . I started staring at him. He returned my advances. Soon enough he came over to me, bought me a drink, and eventually we left together. . . . We went to a nearby park, took out a blanket and went at it. . . . Any guy who goes down on me is God. And boy did he. When he finally did put himself inside I me, I was a bit surprise. His dick was the biggest thing that I have ever had. It was great.—Senior female

And a senior woman discusses both casual sex and sex with affection in perhaps the easiest, funniest, and most relaxed voice found in any of these papers, female or male—and, in the process, articulates female sexual liberalism:

Variations on a theme: My First—What a dick! Figuratively speaking, that is. He was only concerned with his own pleasure, never mine. His goal was to teach me how to give the perfect blowjob. I think this has contributed to . . . compliments I've gotten [since] . . .

The T. A.—I experienced my first orgasm my freshman year of college with my biology lab [Teaching Assistant]. Least you get the wrong idea, we were dating, an "item" so to speak. He taught me alot and how I could derive the most pleasure from it. He was slow and gentle, savoring every minute of it.

The Bartender—I met him at a local college hangout, where he works. We've been friends for about two years, and I've gone home with him twice. . . . He is a real talker, saying things like "Come with me girl," in the middle of intercourse. That personally does nothing for me except make me laugh. . . . Nice of him to care though.

The Booze Wang—I met him on a blind date. We tried on three separate occasions to have sex, and each time he failed to get it up due to alcohol intake. Hence the name "Booze Wang," which has brought much mirth [to myself and my women friends] . . .

[My present boyfriend] has reminded me of just how much better it is when it's with someone you love. All the arousal and stimulation in the world can't replace the look in the eyes of a person whom you care for deeply. The fact that he also happens to be a terrific lover doesn't hurt! . . .

I feel sex, on the whole, is pretty terrific! I can get enjoyment from it even when I am not seriously involved with my partner. I can get more pleasure when I am. . . . I am comfortable with my own sexuality and can talk about it openly. I don't know if I represent the typical female college student, but I sure fit in with my roommates!

In response to a classroom query on my part, many women writers discussed how they talked about sex among themselves. The younger women, especially the neotraditionalists, often said that they simply did not engage in sex talk:

> In my experience, I don't think there is such a talk. Most girls like to be discrete about their sexual experiences. Also when girls speak in private they talk nice.—Sophomore female

Some older women said that they did, but distinguished their sex talk from male locker-room:

> My girlfriends and I frequently talk openly about our own bodies and our sexual experiences with our boyfriends. It is not competitive or in vulgar terms— it is more like sitting around giggling—I guess the stereotypical female "pajama party."—Senior female

And other older women, usually women experimentalists, apparently talked fully explicit women's locker-room among their female friends with considerable gusto:

> In my apartment, terms such as banged and fucked his brains out are commonplace. We would think nothing of saying, "He made me wet," or "Did you make him hard?" There's an air of kidding accompanying these phrases, but they are said and sometimes are more appropriate when discussing a casual encounter.—Senior female

A few women suggested that these woman-to-woman sex talks became competitive. A few mentioned comparing their total male conquests, or the numbers of male virgins they had each "had," or their "grossest" sexual experiences. My most naturalistic sample of women's locker-room talk, taken from an anonymously donated tape recording rather than from a written paper,[46] sounds particularly masculine in the conventions of its turn taking: I'll listen to one of your crude funny stories and then I'll tell you one of mine. A, B, and C are close women friends.

A: I got caught fucking by a policemen in a churchyard once. . . . Me and this guy Bob in a *Volkswagen,* no less. He had this fuckin' little *Volkswagen.*

B: You must have had feet out every window!

A: Trying to maneuver ourselves, like we couldn't even fuck and stay up, barely, let alone lay there and spread our legs. So what we did was, he sat in the passenger seat? With his pants like half down? And I sat, like, on top of him, like facing him? With my pants all the way off, cause there's just no way, like I tried . . . So we're goin' at it, he's goin' at it, my head's like fuckin' hittin' the roof. I'm screaming half out of pleasure, half out of pain. And this car pulls up, with this big fuckin' spotlight!

B: When I was [at the beach], I fucked Jim in an old boathouse. It was really disgusting. The [beach patrol] would have killed us if they had found us in there. We used to go there to get stoned. There was this couch, and it was *really gross.* I wondered how many times it had been fucked on before. We were making out, and he was, like, "I want you to suck my dick!" "Suck my dick!" he said. "Suck my dick!" So all right, I sucked his dick.

A and C: All right! All right!

B: And he was really getting up on it. And then he like fucked my brains, and it wasn't anything spectacular.[47]

Experimentalist women may have resembled traditional men in their interest in casual, uninvolved sex; and a larger number of women may have resembled traditional men in their use of "dirty" language. But male-type women's stances in these papers differed from traditional male sexual sensibilities in one systematic way. The women who followed these countertraditional female sexual orientations did not try to turn the double standard around on the men. Unlike neotraditional Neanderthals, experimentalist women directed no moral disapproval and no detectable disgust at their male partners in casual sex. Their accounts suggest that they sometimes used feminine wiles on their male sex objects; but angry aggression against the opposite sex, even at the level of fantasy, was not a significant theme in the sexual narratives of these women.

The experimentalist women usually sounded pleasure-seeking and pleasure-taking toward their male sex partners. Compared to the Neanderthals, they sounded almost innocent and almost childlike in their sexual tones. Neanderthals were misogynists; experimentalist women were androphiles. Neanderthals proved their manhood through sleazy sex with sleazy females; experimentalist women looked for sexual fun wherever they could find it. Neanderthals picked up sluts and pigs; experimentalist women picked up cute guys.

Liberals.

I found a girlfriend whom I care very much about and whom I have sex with. I also, by agreement with my girlfriend have sexual relations, including intercourse, with other people. As of now I am sexually involved with 4 different women; all of whom know the situation. . . .
   My sex life has been fairly liberal and multiple. I treat all my partners with care and affection. Sex is not worth it just for the orgasm. I like variety and am not biased against any sexual practice except anal intercourse. I feel sex combined with love is one of the ultimate pleasures.—Senior male

Sexual liberals were the apparently unconflicted offspring of the new sexual orthodoxy. They attempted the higher synthesis: casual sex without guilt *and* the deeper pleasures of romance; the meaning of sex with commitment *and* the thrill of the quick sexual encounter. To be an authentic liberal, a male had to stop believing that the women he fooled around with were sluts, or he had to modify the male-romantic stance so that he himself could enjoy casual sex. The youth above was the only young man among forty-one heterosexual male writers who said that he had done both, but another five or six men sounded like possible liberals in their narratives. They described pleasurable sex without mentioning either neotraditional or male-romantic values. Their female partners were not sluts or prey. Their male selves were not emotion-laden lovers.
   The following three male narrators all said or implied that they were describing actual sexual encounters. There may in fact be high proportions of fantasy in their accounts, but truth or fancy, in their narratives they apparently thought about pickup sex with hedonistic enthusiasm and without apparent disgust either for the act itself or for the women with whom they enjoyed it.
   An episode of a limousine driver in Atlantic City:

[Two summers ago] I had the "pleasure" of chauffering two beautiful women around town for the evening. I took them to a few clubs and was invited to attend a party back at their hotel room at the end of the evening. What I didn't know was that the party was very small; just the two girls and myself. I had the wildest, the most erotic evening I've ever experienced. These girls fuck me in more ways than I thought could be done. . . . This is something I've only read about, I didn't think it would actually happen.—Junior male

An episode in a lonely classroom at Rutgers late at night:

After a solid hours of studying. . . . SHE walked in. It was her, the girl I made goo-goo eyes at all last year in Microtheory. . . . [After more studying] she informed me she needed a break. I agreed and we both took off for the grease trucks.[48] We returned [but] . . . before I could open my books, she planted a wet kiss on my lips and said "thanks for treating me to a Coke, now its my turn to treat you!" . . . She started kissing me and rubbing my ass. Soon enough she was down my pants jerking off my rock hard cock. My pants were off in no time and she proceeded to give me the best blowjob I ever had or dreamed of. . . . —Senior male

An episode at the Jersey shore, on a motorcycle:

She then positioned herself on my [parked] bike in front of me and, locking her legs behind my waist, began to kiss me and run her fingers down my back, giving me chills. She attacked me with her tongue, pulling me to her.

I then began to untie her [bikini] top and her gorgeous tits sprang out. I couldn't believe how fine this babe was. She had a body worthy of Pet of the Year. . . . I moved her forward so I could pull off her [bikini] bottoms, but not before I stopped to gaze at her beautiful form. . . . I couldn't wait to get inside her. She couldn't either, as she pulled me to her, kissed me, and wrapping her feet around me, guided my dick to her wet pussy. . . . She let out an "ohhhh" and began to move her hips back and forth . . . and came all over my seat and my still-pounding prick.

. . . She wrapped her arms around me and tenderly kissed my shoulders and then my lips, sucking on my tongue. She looked at me and told me I was wonderful.—Senior male

To be an authentic sexual liberal, a woman, correspondingly, had to stop believing that if she fooled around she was a slut. Also, like a male romantic, she had to modify the neotraditional woman's stance so that she herself could enjoy casual sex without commitment. In this sense, the experimentalist women quoted above could also be thought of as sexual liberals-in-the-making; not all of them commented on sex with love, but those who did comment always said it was still best.

Sexual Radicals. If, in this pluralistic democracy of undergraduate sex, the neotraditionalists were the Conservatives, the repositories of older sexual meanings in contemporary form, then the romantics, the experimentalists, and the liberals were the Moderate Reform parties. Each worked within the established current consensus, within the same new sexual orthodoxy of romance and sexual pleasure. Each tried, with a slightly different party platform, to legislate in favor of gender equality, to deny the double standard, which the Conservatives believed to be inevitable or even "natural" ("Guys *do* have a stronger sex drive than girls."—Sophomore female). Let women and men be equal in both renouncing casual sex (the Romantic Sentimentalists). Let women and men be equal in both enjoying casual sex (the Experimental Hedonists). Let women and men be equal in both rising to a higher, modern synthesis of the two (the Liberal Hegelians).

From outside the walls of this hypothetical sexual parliament, however, we can still hear one or two other voices, voices shouting in loud disagreement in these papers. There were a few remaining undergraduate writers who made more-radical criticisms of neotraditionalist morality and of the new sexual orthodoxy itself, who brought political and cultural analysis to bear on contemporary sexual meanings. There were very few of them, however; and the very scarcity of these sexual radicals might be as significant as the fact that they existed at all.

Feminists. References to feminism were conspicuous by their absence in the sexual self-reports of almost all these men and women writers. None of the women who apparently considered themselves unproblematically heterosexual, nineteen out of twenty of all the women writers, referred to feminism directly except once or twice in dismissive or trivial ways. Of the ten women writers who described experiencing sexual abuse, not one drew a conclusion about contemporary sexual politics from that experience. One heterosexual woman did discuss sexuality and female autonomy without mentioning feminism. She was unusual among these student writers for the way in which she thought ahead, however, beyond her current erotic life toward her realistic ambitions in the adult world. She also described herself as sexually unhappy, as a "late bloomer" with an off-and-on boyfriend who sounded exploitative. Her overall tone was humorous but somewhat cranky:

> I'm really looking forward to having my own career and living on my own. The last thing I want is a responsibility. Even if I ever find a "true-love-of-my-life," and get married, I don't ever want children. I would have an abortion immediately. I particularly find the idea of marriage distasteful, maybe living through my parents' divorce had something to do about it. I know I'm very stubborn and hard to get along with, and *if* I get married, I'd probably get a divorce anyway—I figure I'll live in sin—in my apartment + when time's up—out he goes!—Senior female

The single strong woman's feminist voice in these papers came from one of the two self-identified lesbians among the women writers:

> As I grew older . . . I began learning how disgusting some pornography was, and how offensive it was to women. I learned that when I started learning what real feminism was. It wasn't just ERA, but many other things, which I think you have to have the sensitivity to understand. . . . Being a lesbian makes one more aware of sexual politics and also more aware of the minority situation, and dealing with descrimination.—Junior female

Two of the forty-one heterosexual male writers referred to feminist ideas or to related cultural criticism at least in passing. One was an earnest senior who said that he was terrified of getting any woman pregnant: "The reason that I refuse intercourse sometimes is because I don't think I could deal with the thought of an abortion. I would never try to prevent a woman from doing whatever she wanted to do with her body. I would feel very guilty that I was responsible for the baby being aborted. Intercourse is a very ambiguous issue for me." So, he said, he avoided intercourse and enjoyed the mutual heterosexual pleasures of oral sex instead.

The second man, a more consistently political analyst, was also the least sex-positive writer of any of these papers, male or female: "Personally, I have not been involved even in a non-sexual relationship, partly because I have somewhat less confidence in myself than I probably should have, but also partly because I am skeptical of relationships in general. . . ." In thoughtful, detached prose, he proceeded to make a systematic critique of the new sexual orthodoxy as it was expressed in current mass culture:

> Our everyday popular culture . . . encourages exploitation of females ("chicks," "babes," etc.) and males ("hunks"). Advertisements do this mostly to intimidate less-than-perfect consumers (which 99% of us are) into buying products for which there is no need . . .

And, in general, he came closest of any undergraduate writer to unashamedly rejecting his "need" for sex as the new orthodoxy defined it and to rejecting the sorts of sexual expressiveness found in contemporary mass culture.

A different assignment, or a different course or instructor, might have elicited more feminism from these undergraduate writers.[49] In the coed dorms in the mid-1980s, everyday countersexism was more common on nonerotic topics, though it also had its limits nonsexually (see chapter 2). When it came to eroticism, in any case, contemporary feminism might have cut too close to the bone, at least for these suburban-born, mostly nonminority undergraduates. It might have violated the fundamental assumptions of the new sexual orthodoxy too deliberately, as most of these late-adolescent Americans evidently believed in them. For feminism did not accept the basic presupposition of the new orthodoxy—that "sex life" could be carved off as an independent, ahistorical, technique-centered, psychology-driven human need. Feminism did not invariably celebrate sexual pleasure; it tended to criticize the mainstream definition of women as sex objects. Nor did feminism celebrate romance; it tended to reinterpret it as an artifact of ideological false consciousness whereby women bound themselves to men.

Such radical critiques were evidently threatening to most of these students. Many heterosexual women and men probably regarded feminists as spoilsports when it came to heterosexual pleasure. And this alienation in turn might have contributed to a well-known stereotype among the undergraduate population: If you're a feminist, you may well be a lesbian. Thus, even a young woman who routinely thought feminist about other aspects of her identity, about her right to a gender-unrestricted occupation in the "real world," for instance, might have felt intimidated about talking feminist—or even blocked about thinking feminist—in heteroerotic contexts.

Nonheterosexuals

> I am not a homosexual myself but I find nothing wrong with being attracted to the same sex. I have never attempted or experienced a homosexual relationship and I don't believe I will ever want to, but I can see how it is possible to one man to love another man. I do not find it amusing when somebody uses the terms "homosexual," "Fag" or "gay" in a derogatory fashion.—Freshman male

Like half a dozen other heterosexual males, this young man wrote the standard liberal-male sentiment about homosexuals. I myself am not one. Lots of other men are very nasty to homosexuals. But I disagree; everyone has the right to follow her or his own sexual preference. Most undergraduate males, however, found homosexuality much harder to tolerate. In 1978, a sophomore on Erewhon Third stated what might be considered the middle-of-the-road position among male students at Rutgers during an idle talk about sex in the lounge: "I don't care if somebody wants to be gay, as long as they don't do it around *me!*"[50] And the conservative male position could be summed up only in epithets such as "faggot!" On a questionnaire completed by 151 students in 1987, 7 out of 8 heterosexual men reported that they had never experienced homoerotic desires of any sort. Over half of these deniers believed they were innately so masculine that they could never have such feelings; another quarter said they would be very upset if they did have them; less than a quarter said that the gay twinge or two would not unduly upset them.

More undergraduate women, on the other hand, knew what Freud had taught, that it was "natural" to experience homosexual desires, whether one acted on them or not. Two out of five admitted to having such feelings occasionally or regularly. They were probably able to do so because historically constituted homophobia in the United States has not been as powerful for women as it has been for men (see Weeks 1977).

On the 1986 sexual self-reports, two nonhomosexual women said that they had fantasized about "trying it with a woman." A third said she had tried once, very timidly, but was rebuffed, and a fourth described what she considered an attempted lesbian seduction, which scared her into her first heterosexual experience. Two men also mentioned homosexual fantasies, which they thought might mean something, but neither had acted upon them to date.

Four of the remaining 144 student writers, two women and two men, considered themselves to be homosexuals. Three said they were very active sexually and outlined long, diverse bisexual pasts. Two out of three said that they did not dislike sex with the opposite sex; they simply liked it better with their own sex. And a fifth writer, a man, wrote a paper whose title stated his sexual sensibility and felt identity with some eloquence— "The Confessions of a Single, Bisexual White Male, from First Sexual Encounter to Last: A Slow Progression toward Craziness."

One of the two lesbians was the feminist quoted above. Her feminism aside, the distinctive sexual opinions of these nonheterosexual students were those of their particular chosen genders. Most of them complained about the stereotypes and myths that heterosexual people had about gay sex, and they contrasted these stereotypes to the actualities of nonexclusively-heterosexual practice:

> I'd love to get rid of some of the ridiculous myths that exist. One—I am not a lesbian because I wish I had been born a man. . . . I am a woman who appreciates and enjoys my female body and who appreciates and enjoys other women and their bodies. 2—I do not hate men nor have I turned to women because I have had a traumatic experience with a man. I enjoy sex with men . . . [but] I do hold the opinion that women are better lovers. Three—The majority of lesbians do not engage in Butch/Femme sex roles. . . . If I'm in the mood to initiate sex and be aggressive thats fine, tomorrow maybe I'll feel the opposite and the same with my lover. We don't have rules and we express ourselves however we feel like whenever we want.—Senior female

Though the nonheterosexual student writers sounded as if they had tried harder to free themselves from certain aspects of the new sexual orthodoxy than most of the heterosexuals had, they were, on the evidence of these few papers, nevertheless still controlled by it in many ways. One of their basic sexual choices, "which way do I swing?" evidently had to be as monolithic for them as it did for heterosexuals. One of the two lesbian women was not yet "out," and she deplored not only the stereotypes of the straight world; she also complained about "the reverse discrimination from lesbians who do not know I'm gay." Some nonwestern erotic cultures allow persons to do what they like sexually with whomever they like, regardless of apparent biological sex, without having to declare themselves either heterosexual or homosexual. These cultures define gender and public sex-role identity in other ways; the mechanics of sexual practice are simply not very significant in them (see Whitehead 1981 for some impressive native American examples). Modern American erotic culture apparently does not give its members the same freedom. As the bisexual male wrote:

> It's tough to impossible to be a bisexual; you really have to decide on one or the other, and it's not only because very few women will sleep with a guy who sleeps with men (for more reasons than the fear of AIDS), but because it's a terrible drain on the psyche. . . . I see bisexuality as a sort of tight-rope walk with the only safe footing at the ends (forward to homosexuality and back to heterosexuality), and a pit of dispair below.

And there were other suggestions in these papers that these nonheterosexuals, perhaps not surprisingly, measured their physical practices and pleasures according to minor transformations of the same orthodoxy observed by most of the heterosexuals. The two lesbian women both described lubricious sex lives centered on the pleasures of solitary and mutual masturbation, the use of dildos and vibrators, and the most elaborated oral sex narrated in any of these papers:

> I love [giving oral sex to a woman] . . . I like to wake my lover up by going down on her. I'll use my tongue with quick flicks around the clitorus and move down to the vagina and taste and probe and lick. I use my lips and chin for variation. . . . Women have a very earthy smell, the closest my friends and I have can compare it to is brocoli and mushrooms. . . . I'll usually always be in the mood to receive oral sex. I have found women to be better at giving oral sex than men. One man I know is a master, he's an exception to the rule. My experience is that men pay too much attention to the vagina rather than the clitorus. . . . I love totally relaxing, lying back and enjoying a good tongue on my clitorus. . . .—Senior female

The active homosexual man, and the one bisexual man as well, described homosexual oral and manual sex with the same pleasure; but, for the active homosexual at any rate, anal sex had the same privileged role that "real intercourse" had in the sexual meanings of heterosexual romantics: "I've experimented with anal sex, somewhat, but it has always been a source of tension with me. I've been made to feel like my ass has been tagged as a rare commodity to be bargained for. Silly but I also wanted to save it for some one 'special.'"

Both homosexual men also complained about the existence in their sexual worlds of males who replicated the Neanderthals among the heterosexual men:

Since this first guy [my freshman year in college], however, I have only had a very limited number of sexual experiences and boyfriends and it has been nearly four years already. . . . I was always quite put off by my sexual experiences because they weren't based on much love and could be classified as "one night stands" or the simple release of tension. I was beginning to think that the small number of homosexuals I knew were solely interesting in getting it on and had no intention of combining love with sex.—Senior male

Two of the nonheterosexual student writers enjoyed liberal sexual experimentalism, two were bonded to lovers, and one was looking for such a bond. But all five of them, like most of the students in the heterosexual mainstream, considered romance or sex with love to be the transcendent sexual value:

My lover is a twenty-one year old woman. . . . We are very much in love. We have an extremely healthy sex life which I think is a direct result from being extremely psycologically healthy.—Senior female

I love my man very much and I think beleive that this love is mutual. . . . If I had to live my life over agian, and be faced with the same decisions, I would definitely do it the way I have done it, except that I would have tried to have met [him] earlier in my life.—Junior male

MEANINGS OF SEXUAL FREEDOM

For many of the young Americans who wrote these papers, then, sexual fun and sexual satisfaction were at the heart of contemporary adolescent notions of fun—and hence, because these same adolescents were in college, sex was at the heart of contemporary notions of college life. Undergraduates in the 1980s, not surprisingly for anyone in touch with the wider culture, had more real freedom to be physically sexual than college students had had in earlier American generations; and many of them apparently exercised this freedom with some enthusiasm, or at least they tried to do so.

This held true for undergraduate women about as much as it did for men. Although neotraditionalism limited women more than men, female alternatives to neotraditionalism also existed among the students. And the pure size and anonymity of undergraduate Rutgers provided women with some sexual compensations (see chapter 6). The notion "good girls

229

don't do it" was nearly extinct in late-adolescent culture in the 1980s. Generally in student assumptions, sexual pleasure, mutual sexual pleasure, was a right that belonged to everyone, even to intentional virgins.

As was true with other American individualistic notions, however— friendliness, for instance, or diversity—with sexuality there were also some strong tacit understandings among the undergraduates about the limits of choice, about what kinds of sexual choices could be exercised.[51] The further from neotraditional, the more difficult; and all forms of homosexuality were still largely unacceptable to students in the heterosexual mainstream. In terms of the larger culture it was exceptionally difficult for any of these students to choose *not* to consider sexuality to be at the core of their beings and their identities. This was a cultural dictate that the students shared with their elders, of course. A post-Freudian middle-class American in the 1980s was free to say, Yes, I have to eat, but I really don't care much about food. She or he was not free to hold the same sort of nondiscriminating opinion about sex, on the other hand—not without a built-in apology for it, at any rate.

Similarly, despite the confidentiality of these papers and their emphasis on choice and variation, the degree of cultural consensus in almost all of them was remarkable. Some beliefs were virtually uniform across them, explicitly or implicitly (e.g., Romance or Everyone has a right to sexual pleasure). There was more dissensus in other opinions, but it was a repetitive, and eventually predictable, dissensus. Sex can be fun without emotional commitment versus Sex is an empty experience unless you care for your partner. Or Some girls are really sluts versus Some girls are admirable sexual experimentalists. Anthropologist Hervé Varenne has argued that a culture should not necessarily be thought of as a shared set of common, discrete beliefs. Instead, it can often be regarded more fruitfully as a shared set of structured oppositions; as a common language of dialogue, argument, and dispute; as an implicit agreement about what the local terms for *dis*agreement are (see Varenne 1984). A good part of the students' working consensus about sexuality consisted of this sort of agreement; a consensus on a limited number of disagreements when it came to sex.[52]

And finally, although there was no clear evidence that the students saw it in this way, undergraduate sexuality under the assumptions of the new orthodoxy was arguably a freedom with a male bias, just as life in the coed dorms tended to be (see chapters 2 and 3). The new sexual orthodoxy was not unproblematic for young men, of course. It told them that it was right and proper that they should have what their hormones seemed to be calling for—sex. But emotionally satisfying sexual pleasure did not always come easily to them. They might be sexually inept; they might not be good-looking or suave; they might not be able to manage the intricate negotiations of modern sex. Or they might have entirely too many sexual choices for their own youthful good.

As many commentators have noted, however, the dilemmas of the new sexual orthodoxy for women went well beyond these male psychic problems. Women had to work harder than men to ignore certain realities that the orthodoxy itself did not account for. One was that they were far more often the objects of sexual abuse and violence than men were. Another was that early intercourse was more painful for them than it was for men—and that, in intercourse, real sexual pleasure often came more slowly. And a third was that pregnancy and abortion were experiences that belonged to *their* bodies, not to men's and the traumas that were part of these experiences were almost always more severe for women. Finally, women who were no longer adolescents might discover in their thirties and forties that, as an ethic of personal choice rather than of necessity and commitment, the new sexual orthodoxy had left them with dependent children and an absent spouse, with drastically reduced sexual prospects of their own, and with inferior occupations and much higher poverty levels than those of equivalently educated men of the same age (see Ehrenreich 1983).

The young women who wrote these papers were not in this real world of sexual adulthood yet, however. Nor did they spend much time trying to think ahead toward it. By and large, like their mostly male sexual partners, they lived in the present. And for the most part, like the men, they found the sexual present to be good and fun and exciting and, ideally, laced with pleasure.

Further Comments

1 / The most common question about this part of my research has been, What impact is AIDS having on the adolescent sexual mentalities and behaviors outlined in this chapter and the next? Curiously, according to my research, not much. As indicated below, most heterosexual Rutgers students were not thinking about this issue with any intensity in 1986 and early 1987, when this research was conducted. Not that the AIDS threat was unknown dur-

ing these years. But just as these youths seemed to block on other kinds of sexual danger because the possibility of sexual danger threatened the principles of pleasure, freedom, and experimentalism at the heart of their contemporary sexual ethics, so, too, with AIDS.

Suddenly in the late spring of 1987, however, everyone *was* discussing AIDS, probably because the U.S. Secretary of Health and Human Services had just issued a stern warning that a heterosexual AIDS epidemic "worse than the black plague" might be in the offing. Despite many stories in the popular press that AIDS was going to reverse the sexual revolution, however, there is little evidence of major attitudinal or behavioral changes among these students or other heterosexual American youths as a result. The "new sexual orthodoxy" seems too powerfully, multiply determined—even over-determined—to be so easily turned around in the absence of an actual heterosexual epidemic, which happily has not occurred as of 1988 (the homosexual epidemic, on the other hand, has simply reinforced a preexisting pervasive homophobia in the American adolescent mainstream).

Moreover, a year after his warnings of disaster, the same U.S. official had reevaluated more recent research and was now predicting that no heterosexual epidemic was likely to occur (see Boffey 1988).

For more on AIDS and the "new sexual orthodoxy," see below.

2 / In the early sixties, a dorm was "coed"—the institution existed on a few liberal American campuses—if one wing of it was for women and the other was for men, with many doors and many restrictions in between. Robert Rimmer, a countercultural psychologist, imagined something much more intimate in an earnest tract published in the late 1960s, *The Harrad Experiment:* females and males living together in the same rooms in his imaginary dorms, making personal contracts with one another, having sex, and keeping diaries about this new liberalized collegiate "learning experience" (Rimmer 1968).

Real coed dorms began to develop widely on American campuses shortly after this. *Life* magazine published a cover story in 1970 about the new, experimental dorms at Oberlin College. Women and men lived on every other floor of the same dorm, but had unlimited hours of intervisitation with one another. The article claimed that there was not an undue amount of sexual activity in these new college living units, but the photos subverted the message. The cover, for instance, showed a long-haired male and a female sitting together in an easy chair in a conjugal posture, holding hands and gazing affectionately into each other's eyes ("Co-Ed Dorms: An Intimate Revolution on Campus," *Life*, November 20, 1970).

Coed dorms grew more and more common in American colleges and universities in the early and late seventies, until in many places they became the norm rather than the exception. And the separation between females and males in them declined progressively until it reached the current limit, alternating rooms. In the early 1970s, the new coed dorms were the subject of a few tentative articles in the *Journal of College Life Personnel*, the professional organ of college deans of students and related residence life specialists. Since then, nothing. They are also virtually unmentioned in such standard student-life tomes as Chickering et al. 1981.

3 / The first big jump in the reported rate of premarital intercourse among middle-class Americans in the twentieth century occurred in the 1920s. This rate then leveled off between the 1930s and the early 1960s. The second jump occurred between the late 1960s and the early 1970s.

Current evidence suggests another plateau since the late 1970s. See Hildebrand and Abramowitz 1984.

4 / One recent quantitative study of the actual incidence of sexual messages on American prime afternoon and evening television, for instance, calculates that viewers receive an average of twenty-seven messages every hour, including nine kisses, five hugs, ten sexual innuendos, and two to four references to sexual intercourse and other sexual practices (see Blau 1988).

5 / Undergraduates will sometimes suggest, rather allusively, that coed dorm life is considerably more sexually unbuttoned than my characterization will indicate. In my opinion, however, what they are really saying is that they take the ordinary sexual norms described here entirely for granted and don't pay attention to how pervasively these norms govern their lives most of the time. When they allude to sexually "wild and crazy" occurrences, they are focusing on the exceptions—nonconforming females or males, backstage or late night or drunken incidents, and so on. For instance, the youth who narrates his amazing sexual introduction to Rutgers in the section "Going Away to College" (chapter 6) is certainly not claiming that incidents of this

sort took place every day in the dorms. He remembers this one so vividly because it was so unusual.

6 / Men also often had their party clothes, more erotic apparel than 'dorm casual.' It might be their tightest jeans and a special shirt, unbuttoned at the top to reveal their manly chests, or some GQ or Miami Vice fashions. Punks tended to dress punk all the time. Preppie, on the other hand, was a distinctly antierotic style.

7 / Anthropologist Hervé Varenne once collected the following piece of contemporary American psychobabble from some adolescents:

> [Girl talking]: "I had a nice relationship with this guy, but then we got into a *re*lationship and it completely wrecked our relationship!" (Varenne, personal communication)

"Friend" with a special stress could also be used to carry a sexual load, as in [young woman addressing her liberal mother], "Mother, I'd like you to meet my *friend* Dick."

8 / Among themselves, as well as between themselves and older or younger persons, the students had different discourse styles in different social contexts. The peer-group styles of Rutgers undergraduates included Undergraduate Cynical (see chapter 3), typically spoken in the dorm lounges;

Locker-room, typically spoken in all-male groups (and to an increasing extent, in all-female groups); and Private-Sincere, typically spoken in rooms or in other private contexts to friends. This third code for friends was supposed to be frank and honest—which didn't mean, of course, that it *was* always true in any simple literal sense, especially when it came to sex. Lying was always possible in this talk as well; and any discourse style was a construction of reality more than it was any simple reflection of it. I am assuming, however, that frank, honest personal talk was more likely to represent what the subjects thought was true than the other discourse styles were.

9 / A favorite piece of beefcake for female delectation in the mid-1980s, a narrow-hipped male model who posed with marginally clad females, with the photographic emphasis on the top of his tightly filled designer jeans.

10 / Some sophomore males who listened to some of this material in a class in 1987 couldn't believe what Steve had said in 1986, that he had missed a long-term affair right under his nose: "It *couldn't* have happened on our floor. No way. We've got the whole floor taped. *Every*one's being watched."

11 / Women probably believed this more than men did.

For in the case of local sex, the woman's reputation would suffer, while the man's would likely be enhanced. Moreover, most dorm residents were freshmen and sophomores, and heterosexual relationships in American culture are 'age-hypergamous': women tend to date men of their own ages or older while men tend to date women of their own ages or younger. The freshmen and sophomore men in the dorms thus had access to far fewer heterosexual partners in college than did the women, so the women in the dorms could afford to be more choosy. This imbalance inverted in the junior and senior years, by which time most students lived elsewhere.

The moral shift that some women made from sexual neo-traditionalist to experimentalist or liberal during their college years, incidentally, might have been partially a response to this changing market situation for heterosexual partners in college. Such a shift was far from being inevitable, however. Some women did not make it, and others shifted in the opposite direction, trying experimentalism as freshmen and sophomores and then moving back to "romance" as juniors and seniors.

12 / My thanks to Dr. Robert H. Bierman, Medical Director, the Hurtado Health Center, for reading chapters 5 and 6 and giving me his opinion that the material in them was consistent with what he and his medical staff knew about this subject.

13 / Similarly, even if I had broken my professional and personal code and participated sexually with some of the students—which I did not do—I would not have found out most of what I needed to know. Like any given student, I would then have only known about the sexualities of a very limited number of students. Like them, the rest of my opinions about undergraduate sexuality would have been based on rumor and surmise.

14 / Undergraduates in the different affiliated colleges of Rutgers-New Brunswick may take courses in any of the colleges. About half of these papers were written by women and men from Rutgers College. About one-third were written by females from Douglass, the all-women's college in the New Brunswick system. And the rest were written by smaller numbers of students from the other undergraduate units (Livingston, Cook, University College, Mason Gross, and the rest—see appendix 2).

15 / In an even-larger class in 1987, a single male, from an east Asian background, was the only undergraduate out of about

six hundred students over two years who chose the more impersonal assignment.

16 / For readers unfamiliar with the shaky literacy of some contemporary American students, the spelling, punctuation, grammar, and writing facility visible in these papers were well within the range of what hardened Rutgers faculty members had come to expect at the undergraduate level. These papers were slightly sloppier than average because they were graded on a pass-fail basis. In certain ways, however, they were better as writing, or at least more vivid, than average undergraduate papers. This assignment apparently interested the student writers as no other assignment that I gave in thirteen years of college teaching had.

17 / The assignment as the students received it in January 1986 in the course *Anthropology of Sexuality and Eroticism*, 070:292, 01 (Rutgers-New Brunswick, Faculty of Arts and Sciences):

> I'd like you to write a *confidential* paper about your own sexuality. You may write about any aspect of it, in any linguistic style you choose: feelings, behavior, fantasies; best sex you've ever had; worst sex; no sex; frequency of sex; development of your own sexuality through time; pleasures and pains; sex and love; sex and other emotions; anxieties; techniques.

If you're not especially active sexually, don't be intimidated by this assignment; try to write about your eroticism in any way you can. If you *are* sexually active, frank descriptions would be of use to my own research—but I leave such descriptions up to your own choice.

I leave the form of this assignment to you, but I do ask you to be as truthful as possible. For most males, this means avoiding braggadocio; for most females, this means avoiding undue discretion. If you choose to write about fantasies, let me know they're fantasies.

Please do not put your name anywhere on this assignment, but please *do* indicate at the top: *your sex; your age; your college class; and whether you're unmarried (i.e. never married), married, or formerly married.* When you hand the TA a 3 to 7 page paper on this topic, she will check it briefly to make sure it's long enough, and she will check your name off as having completed the paper; and you will then receive "credit" for the assignment. If you don't hand it in, you'll get "no credit" for the assignment and it *will* affect your overall course grade.

The TA will not *read* any of these papers. She'll shuffle them and hand them over to me. I'll be the only one who sees them.

I may report back to the class on the general results of these papers, though only so generally that no single person's paper can be identified. I may also use data from these papers (in the same confidential way) in my own research on Rutgers student culture.

I'd like to receive all these papers in class at the end of the 4th week: Weds., February 12th.

Remember:

1. 3–7 pages.

2. Don't sign the paper or put your name anywhere on it.

3. *Do* indicate at the top: your sex; your age; your college class; your marital status.

(For anyone who finds this assignment too personal or too excruciating, please write 3 to 5 pages on the following topic: "Compare and contrast the sexual practices of *two* of the *four* cultures on whom we've read ethnography to date: Messenger's Irish, Marshall's Polynesians, Shostak's Bushmen, and Berndt's Australian Aborigines." Hand it in, unsigned, at the same time, for the same ungraded credit.

18 / Only a small number of students actually asked me *not* to quote from their papers. Due apparently to confusion in the classroom on the day in which this assignment was collected, the remaining students did not answer my question one way or another.

Virtually all these students were age-graded by college class. Almost all the freshmen were eighteen to nineteen years old, almost all the sophomores were nineteen to twenty, and so on. Only one of the

eighteen to twenty-two year olds was married.

19 / When I taught this same course again in the spring of 1987, the enrollment was even higher, 383 students, far and away the biggest anthropology course I know of at Rutgers in the last decade. And in 1987 I checked the demographic typicality of the class more carefully. Though the sample of enrolled students was biased in the same way by sex and by age— 66 percent women and 71 percent juniors and seniors—otherwise it appeared to be representative. The mean cumulative grade point average, for instance, was one-tenth of a point above the undergraduate average for the college as a whole. Only three in ten of them had taken other minicourses like the one I was teaching, and those who had done so had taken an average of only two each. ("Minis," correctly or incorrectly, are perceived as "guts," or easy courses, by many students. I therefore apparently did not have an unusual number of students who habitually looked for easy courses.) The range of majors was normal. And about a quarter of the class members were fraternity or sorority members, also close to the average for the college.

Finally, although the answers to the following question are not easy to interpret, I could think of no other way of asking it:

237

Compared to other students I know well, sexually I am:

1. much less active [9% chose this]

2. less active [17%]
3. about as active [43%]

4. more active [25%]
5. much more active [5%]

The curve of these answers tilts slightly toward higher perceived sexual activity for one's self than for one's peers. But the responses also tend to suggest that the class was not disproportionately loaded either with sexual superstars or with sexual novices.

20 / There was another kind of thank you in two or three of the papers:

I had a date with [my boyfriend] last week and he asked me to read this paper. He read it, and when he came to the part [in which I described] his inability to have oral sex with me, he told me that he thought I didn't like it. He then finished reading the paper and displayed the hard-on that it had given him. I immediately began to suck on it and then he began to lick and kiss my cunt "with reckless abandon" . . . until I came. . . . Not only has this assignment taught me

that writing erotica is fun, it improved my sex life. Thanks.—Junior female

21 / There are a number of indices of fantasy in this account beyond the genre clues. One is the improbability that a Rutgers faculty member—one who was not planning to be seduced, at any rate—would give a student an appointment on the evening of the same day she asked for it, rather than at two in the afternoon on a day the following week. Another is this particular erotic detail. A pervasive female dilemma during oral sex, as we will see later, is whether or not to swallow. This exemplary male sex partner is like none reported by any woman in the world of actual sex; the guy actually cleaned up after himself!

22 / One or two other women discussed sexual fantasies about men on the Rutgers faculty, fantasies on which they apparently had not acted. No student reported an actual sex act with a faculty member in these papers. (In one of the 1987 papers, a male claimed to have had an exciting affair with a female "professor." She was about six years older than him, and the paper suggested that she was actually a teaching assistant or a temporary instructor in a writing course.) According to college therapists, deans and others in a

position to know, however, student-faculty sexual seductions did occur at Rutgers in the mid-1980s. Clearly there was a market for them in some student sensibilities; some female undergraduates apparently saw a sexual liaison with a "cultured professor" as part of the college experience. But clearly there were also faculty members quite willing to provide such services and to advertise their availability.

The names of a few male faculty members at Rutgers continually recurred in reports of these incidents (affairs between male students and female faculty members were also rumored to occur, but much less often). It was not difficult for an intellectually adroit faculty member to manipulate the emotions of a late-adolescent, and these affairs often had unhappy effects on the adolescent psyches involved. They were also in intrinsic violation of the supposedly disinterested, impartial attitude a professor was supposed to adopt toward students, especially toward students whose work he or she is grading. On this problem nationwide, see *The Lecherous Professor* (Dziech and Weiner 1984).

23 / Using data gathered from two hundred women in a course taught at Douglass College (the women's college at Rutgers-New Brunswick) in 1980, sex-ologist David Weis argues against the "cultural mythology" that a woman's first time is always intensely painful. His data do show what the present self-reports also indicate: a great deal of precoital sexual activity on the part of many young women, making first intercourse a less-traumatic initial experience than it perhaps once was. Even in Weis's sample, however, almost three-quarters of the sexually experienced young women remembered moderate to severe pain their first times (Weis 1985).

24 / In one, for example, a woman said she lost her virginity to a tall, dark, and handsome Princeton boy who belonged to one of the best eating clubs at Princeton, had flawless technique, caused her no pain, brought her to an "ecstatic" orgasm the first time, *and* drove the expensive red sports car of her dreams.

25 / Generally I have assumed that if the papers looked sloppily written, as many of these ungraded papers did, then anything in them was quite spontaneous, quite off the top of the head. One counterhypothesis, however, at least for some of these stories, is that they had been liberally polished as oral narratives told to close friends, that they had existed textually long before they were first written down. And this oral

polish, where it occurred, might have made more fantasy possible in parts of these reports than I am ordinarily taking into account.

26 / I tried to present the students with a wide range of erotic cultures, some apparently more open and relaxed about sex than our own, and some equally restrictive or more restrictive, but often in quite different ways. (Readings included selections from Messenger 1971, Marshall 1971, Shostak 1981, Berndt 1976, Gregor 1985, Daniel 1984, and Herdt 1981.) I placed a certain emphasis on sexual pleasure and on sexual fun, and though I offered a serious analysis of everything we studied, I attempted to keep the mood in the classroom light. I did talk about the politics of sex, about the impressive correlation between advanced forms of social organization and intensive control of sexuality, for instance, especially of women's sexuality. But I did not stress the politics of sex in modern western society or some of the more problematic aspects of sex for the individual. Nor did I emphasize the theme of sexual danger.

In 1987, I made a greater effort to emphasize the politics of sex, sexual danger, and that, regardless of culture, females and males always have very different existential relationships to sexuality. Chang-

ing the message from the podium had no discernible effect on the sexual self-reports I received in response to a similar optional assignment, however.

27 / The audiences for these movies at Rutgers tended to be about two-thirds men and one-third women. A few couples attended, but more often women and men came to these films in little single-sex gangs.

28 / Heath's argument draws on, or is consistent with, much of the new social history of western sexuality written in the past twenty years. Notable works include Smith-Rosenberg 1975, Stone 1977, Foucault 1980, Weeks 1977, and Walkowitz 1986.

29 / It might be argued that my assignment encouraged the students to write according to the assumptions of the new sexual orthodoxy. In lectures in the course in which this assignment was given, I did try to show that sexuality was often constituted quite differently in other cultures, however: that sex was rarely, as in contemporary American culture, a thing in itself; that it was much more often an integral part of wider human or cosmological meanings. Even if my assignment was culturally biased, however, what was striking in the papers was the ease and gusto with which the students wrote within the orthodoxy. On

the evidence of these papers, I was certainly not asking them to do something that came hard to them or that did not make a great deal of cultural sense, even if it was an unusual classroom assignment.

30 / On a sex questionnaire that 151 students made out in this class in the following year, the reported virginity rate was slightly lower, and it was somewhat more differentiated by sex. Again, about 1 in 5 females said they were virgins, 18 in all, 2 of them intentionally. Only 1 in 8 males owned up to the same unhappy state, on the other hand, none of them by intention.

About 25 percent of the women in Weis's sample reported engaging in fellatio when they were still virgins, and 30 percent reported receiving cunnilingus (1985:432).

31 / Two of the forty-four male writers of these papers sounded worse than depressed; they sounded sexually disturbed. One wrote a series of sexual fantasies, which all turned scatological at the end. The other said he had mentally transformed all his classes into private erotic fantasies since grade school, often with female teachers in dominant roles. At Rutgers, he said, he once exposed himself in front of a female faculty member in her office. And he reported that he sometimes followed his younger female teachers

around the campus, fantasizing about them.

32 / Apart from male virgins for whom masturbation was the most sexual practice performed, neither women nor men worried a great deal about masturbation in these papers. This late-bloomer and one or two others aside, men usually said they started around puberty. Women mentioned both early and late starts.

33 / *Missionary* ("missionary position"): the standard western man-on-top prone position for sexual intercourse. This term and *oceanic position* were among the few terms from my course lectures that turned up in these papers.

34 / The rising acceptability of oral sex, like that of premarital sex, was probably also part of a recent nationwide trend. For a California college sample, Hildebrand and Abramowitz (1984) say that in 1971, 77 percent of all the sexually active students in their sample reported practicing oral sex; in 1977, 85 percent; and in 1981, 88 percent.

Newcomer and Udry (1985) also report the generally high acceptability of oral sex among contemporary adolescents as a way around some of the dilemmas of "real" sex.

35 / See, for instance, Brown 1988. Quoting a freshman from Rice University, the subhead-

ing to this article read, "The sexual revolution is a term that will go into the time capsules." (The substance of the article itself only suggested that students were becoming somewhat more careful about casual sex, however.)

36 / But see note 1 above.

37 / Three said they had been manually or genitally abused as children or as young adolescents by older males—two by relatives (an uncle and an older brother). Three said they had suffered acquaintance rape, two at Rutgers. One reported being forced to fellate a date in high school. And two indicated tolerating long-term physical abuse from boyfriends. No male mentioned sexual abuse in the 1986 papers.

The reported abuse rate was somewhat higher on the sex questionnaire returned in the same course in 1987. Sixteen percent of the women reported abuse of one kind or another, and 4 percent of the men (two cases: one by an incestuous mother who handled the subject much too familiarly after puberty, and the other by a homosexual neighbor when the subject was eight to ten years old).

38 / In *Homo Hierarchicus* (1982) and in other theoretical works on south Asian culture, Dumont uses the concept of "encompassment" to suggest how hierarchy, a positively constructed concept of the value of social rank, dominates south Asian collective values, even those that seem to cut against it.

39 / Perhaps one-quarter of the sexually active writers discussed birth control. The diaphragm was the preferred method, and the pill (for spontaneity) was second, though a significant number of women also avoided the pill for fear of its side effects. About two-thirds of the women in stable relationships who discussed the matter said that they arrived at birth-control methods by mutual consultations with their boyfriends (or, in some cases, said that they made mistakes mutually). A smaller number suggested that their boyfriends left birth control up to them or bullied them into methods that the male liked better than the female (e.g., the pill).

Four women in the sample of one hundred female writers mentioned accidental pregnancies followed by abortions, one in high school and three at Rutgers. Two of the women who had become pregnant at Rutgers reported severe depressions after the abortion. One said she had made a suicide attempt. The other was the only woman of the four who said her boyfriend had gone through the whole thing with her. She seemed surprised and grateful that he had. She said, with perhaps a hint of qualification, that he was "very very patient, kind and loving for someone who is 21 years old."

40 / By "traditional," I don't mean to suggest that these patterns are somehow timeless, for all traditions are historically formed. I am using the term only as a convenience to refer to a familiar set of older American sexual standards, built on Victorian foundations and widely followed by middle-class women and men in the United States prior to the sexual revolution of the 1960s.

In similar papers written in 1987, the proportion of students assuming this and the other moral stances was somewhat different. There were fewer neotraditionalists—perhaps a third of both the female and the male writers fit clearly into this category—and somewhat more romantics, experimentalists, and liberals. There were almost precisely the same number of homosexuals; and radicals and feminists were still conspicuous in their near-total absence.

41 / This label draws on the common connotations of "Neanderthal" in American popular culture. As an anthropologist, however, I feel bound to note that there is no particular reason to believe that actual Neanderthal Man was as uncivilized and unevolved in his sexual ethics as the American male undergraduates being described here.

42 / This was the only instance in all these papers of a writer using a term that stigmatized males in the same way that "slut" stigmatized females. It is impossible to know how seriously it was meant.

43 / Only one woman in all these papers said that it was important to a male sex partner of hers that she was a virgin, her first time. He was reportedly Italian.

44 / Harlequin Romances are short, formulaic women's romances, which have achieved phenomenal mass-market success in the United States in recent years. They are also the subject of considerable interpretative literature. See Radway 1984 and Snitow 1982.

45 / Male neotraditionalists who had moved on to affectionate sex with "good women," such as the neotraditional apologist quoted above, sometimes also wrote men's romance, focusing on erotic pleasure and on mutuality rather than on male bravado.

46 / In response to a general request for samples of women's locker-room talk in the very large sexuality class I taught in 1986, a young woman I did not know

came up to me after class one day and handed me a tape recording. She said she had made it surreptitiously one day when she and two of her girlfriends were talking about sex. The other two women had not known the tape recorder was on. After they had finished their conversation, she explained, she had told them what she had done and why, and they had all agreed they were willing to donate the tape to "Professor Moffatt's research on student sex." I would like to thank the three of them here, anonymously, for their helpfulness.

47 / Given the different neotraditional background assumptions about women's and men's sexuality, there was one major difference between this female locker-room talk and its male form. A man who told a story "grosser" than another man's scored over him—he won. A woman who did the same might have been doing just the opposite. She might have been demonstrating that she trusted her close female friends enough to let them know the worst things that there were to be known about her. Women sometimes said they only used this talk among women who were just as "bad" as they were, who would not dare to judge them for the things they described. And in this sample the women listeners'

chorus on the subject of fellatio ("All right! All right!") sounds much more like traditional female peer-group verbal support than anything commonly heard in men's locker-room talk (see Maltz and Borker 1982).

Other sections of this same tape, by the way, though still consistent with the vividly explicit overall tone, sounded more "feminine." For instance:

> You know what the neatest thing was, though? The neatest thing that a guy ever did to me? It wasn't just the sex. I mean, I already told you we had spectacular sex, but, uuum, I remember, he was the only guy that I ever slept over with that . . . his breath in the morning, it was just so sweet. I'd never smelled anything like it. He had *sweet* breath in the morning. And we used to fuck like beasts in the morning . . .

48 / *Grease trucks:* panel trucks and food wagons from which private entrepreneurs sold various kinds of fast food to the students at all hours of the day or night. Usually parked on the side of one block of a street near the biggest classroom buildings on the College Avenue Campus.

49 / I experimented with a few changes in the same course in 1987 to see if I could elicit more feminist or more politically critical

student opinions about sexuality. I spent half of one lecture on the different micropolitical relationships of women and men to sexuality in almost all societies (regardless of culture, women are more likely to be objects of sexual aggression than men, women are more likely to be sexually controlled than men, and so on) and another half on the politics of sex in western culture. And I added the following lines to the optional assignment for the anonymous sexual self-report: "Women (and men): Do you ever think 'feminist' about your sexual experiences? If so, how? Examples?" The feminist silence continued to be deafening, however.

50 / Note that the notion of homosexuality as somehow polluting by proximity or contact was well established among heterosexuals well before the outbreak of AIDS.

51 / See Carole Vance's "Gender Systems, Ideology, and Sex Research" (1982) for a splendid, ironic analysis of how the practice of contemporary American sexology subverts its apparently liberal message, how sexologists can say "anything goes" while transmitting stronger implicit messages about which things are acceptable or preferable or normal and which are beyond the pale.

52 / Varenne's point, which is influenced by Lévi-Strauss's notion of culture as well as by a range of modern dialogic approaches to culture, helps us to understand one way in which culture and ideology can channel and influence thought. Most Americans have demystified certain alleged cultural choices: a hamburger versus a hotdog, a middle-of-the-road Republican versus a middle-of-the-road Democrat. Other choices seem to be so genuine and all-embracing, on the other hand, that the fact that the structure of choice itself rules out a universe of other possibilities and alternatives is rendered opaque. Compare, for example, contemporary American notions of homosexuality to those of the native Americans outlined in Whitehead 1981.

SIX / Sex in College

[COLLEGE] SEEMS TO BE SUCH A DECADENT PLACE . . . IT SEEMS THAT EVERYONE HERE IS ALWAYS TALKING ABOUT SEX OR THE PERSON THEY'VE BEEN HAVING SEX WITH. —Sophomore female, anonymous paper, 1986

College was the place, or so the dean had proposed back in orientation, where the students should try to broaden themselves by seeking out new and different experiences. This was the meaning of a liberal education. And college authorities as well as undergraduates often took pride in the diversity of Rutgers, in the wide range of choices available to those students who wanted the broadening experiences of college. On the evidence of the students' anonymous sexual self-reports,[1] Rutgers as a sexual institution—presumably without its policymakers exactly thinking of it this way—did indeed give its undergraduates an opportunity to realize these institutional values. Not all the students did so, however. Not every student enrolled in the whole sexual extracurriculum, and there were even some nonmatriculators. What were the crude Kinseyian facts of undergraduate sexual behavior in the college as they were reported in these papers? How might a numbers-oriented sexologist, reading these papers, have summarized these Rutgers students sexually?

WHO WAS DOING WHAT TO WHOM, AND HOW OFTEN . . . ?

The simplest statistical generalization from the sexual self-reports is that there was no typical Rutgers woman or typical Rutgers man in terms of sexual behavior. Sexual meanings might have been largely uniform and consensual among the students (see chapter 5). Sexual actions, on the other hand, were distinctly idiosyncratic. Morally, the students came in or moved through the ethical varieties outlined in chapter 5: neotraditional, romantic, experimentalist, liberal, radical, and nonheterosexual. Behaviorally, the students reported as many different levels and patterns of sexual activity as there were undergraduate writers of these papers. Some women and men described years of sexual experience before arriving at Rutgers; others said they were still virgins in their last year in college. Some started early and then went through long dry spells, even up to the present; others started late and made up for lost time; and still others started late and progressed slowly. The majority of these self-reporters said they had restricted themselves, by and large, to sex with commitment and to conventional heterosexual practices. A minority, on the other hand, suggested that they had sampled from virtually every sexual elective in the modern erotic curriculum.

Some enthusiasts in casual sex sounded as if they were out every night, or at least every weekend night; others said they took their tastes of casual sex only every now and then. Some boyfriend-girlfriend pairs reported having intercourse on a daily basis; others said that it was difficult to make love more than three or four times a month because of different academic schedules, roommates, off-campus jobs, and so on. A few heterosexual couples hardly ever had intercourse for fear of unwanted pregnancy. No student writer of these papers said she or he was ready, even hypothetically, to deal with pregnancy or childbirth.

As noted in chapter 5, about one in five of both the women and men who wrote these papers said that they were still virgins. Of those who were not, most of the women and about half the men indicated when they had lost their virginity, and the various years in which persons of both sexes said they had first had "real" sex fell on a near-perfect bell-shaped curve. The left tail of the curve was on eighth grade, in the junior high school years. The right tail was on the senior year in college. And the apex, the period at which about half the sexually experienced students had already "lost it," was at the life juncture "going away to college": the senior year of high school and the freshman year of college. If these figures were at all representative, then, we can guess from them that almost half the freshmen (women and men) at Rutgers were still virgins, and that the collegiate virginity rate then declined for both sexes until it was somewhat less than one in five for Rutgers seniors (the one-in-five virgins in the overall sample included some lowerclassmen).[2]

The women's papers were more comprehensive and more honest-sounding than the men's about frequencies and types of sexual engagement. Two-fifths of fifty-five sexually experienced women who gave the precise details of their sexual ontogenies said that—independent of their reported practice of casual sex—they had had only one long-term boyfriend or lover since loss of virginity. Slightly less than two-fifths mentioned two such boyfriends; slightly less than one-fifth mentioned three or more long-term partners. Only 8 percent (or three) of these women described sex lives that had occurred with casual partners only.[3] One of these women later decided that she was a lesbian.

As for casual sex, one-third of the fifty-five women who evidently told all said that they had never tried it; they stated or implied that they had been involved only in long-term, "caring" sexual relationships. Two-thirds of these fifty-five women, on the other hand, did mention what they referred to variously as "mistakes," "pickups," "experiments," "flings," or "affairs." Thirty percent mentioned one of them; 22 percent mentioned two to four; 38 percent indicated an indefinite number ("a few friends, a few friends of friends," "more than I should have," "a series of pickups," "quite a few," "many"). And 8 percent once again described, undefensively or with some relish, ten to thirty casual sexual liaisons to date.[4] Most of these women were juniors and seniors, and they suggested that they had practiced perhaps three-quarters of this casual sex during their years in college.

However, according to these student self-reports, to be sexually experienced was not necessarily to be in a happy or satisfying sexual relationship or set of relationships at present. Sixty-five percent of the sexually experienced women indicated that they were involved in ongoing relationships or other erotic networks at the moment of writing. Only 40 percent of the sexually experienced men suggested the same—once again, mostly juniors and seniors.

The majority of undergraduate writers who described their current sexual practices discussed the themes and variations of conventional one-on-one, privately conducted heterosexual intercourse. Reported frequencies ranged widely, from "6 or 7 times a week" to "any time we have a chance." "Conventional" sex (my category, implicit in the students' accounts) meant, under the new orthodoxy: mutual oral sex as foreplay followed by heterosexual intercourse, preferably to mutual orgasm (alternatively, orgasm during foreplay could substitute for orgasm during intercourse, especially for females). Most undergraduates reported that they liked to experiment with different positions during intercourse: "missionary," "woman-on-top," "doggy style," "Oceanic";[5] and so on. Some otherwise conventional students said that they considered heterosexual anal sex just one more variant of nonkinky sex; others said that it was "disgusting" or "unthinkable."

Conventional couples also said they enjoyed different settings for sex—in a bubble bath, in a rented hot-tub, at a motel for a thrill. More than a dozen wrote with delight of the occasional lovemaking out-of-doors or almost-in-public, with the added spice of possibly being caught in the act. One could draw from these descriptions a Woody Allenesque map of the sexual campus. In wooded glades or under bridges or on the university golf course. Under the official gates of the university. On campus buses following lightly traveled routes. In lonely classrooms reserved for study, late at night. In dorm basement corridors and stairwells and bathrooms and laundry rooms, also late at night. Fellatio by a girlfriend while sitting in a study carrel in a campus library. Two different students even bragged about stealing into the private dining room of the president of the university after hours and fornicating on his carpet. (This room, though often locked, might have been accessible to student workers in Dining Services.)

Advanced sexual practices were those techniques that most students classified as "kinky," even if they engaged in them themselves. ("With Sue I experienced the whole spectrum of kink."—Senior male) Some combined sex and food ("Hagen-daus and cunnilingus"—cf. Canaan 1986). A few alluded to costumes and role-playing: Milkman, Hitchhiker, Sorority Girl Losing It to Fraternity Jock, High School English Teacher, Hooker, and so on. A half dozen mentioned "light" B and D; a few referred in passing to S and M. (Seven or eight students mentioned using drugs, or "illegal substances," to enhance sexual pleasure; two specified crack.) Seven women and eight men said in their sexual chronologies that they had experimented with different kinds of group sex once or more, two-thirds of the time in college. Most of these incidents, fraternity gang bangs aside, were two-on-ones of either variety. And three homosexual students mentioned enjoying the occasional homosexual or bisexual "group grope."

Any readers whose sensibilities are offended by these advanced sexual practices can possibly comfort themselves by concentrating on what the great majority of the students' sexual self-reports were in fact reporting: either no "real" sex at all (those one-in-five virgins) or (most sex for most undergraduates most of the time) sex that was one-on-one, heterosexual, in private, conventional in technique and caring in emotional style. In other words, for the most part, modern American suburban sex in its adolescent variant.

SEX AND OTHER COLLEGIATE VALUES

According to the new orthodoxy, sexuality, perhaps the central private fact of modern personal identity as it is thought of in American culture, was an *autonomous* zone of physical, psychological, and emotional sensibility. It did not necessarily refer outside of itself; there was no reason why sexual development should be directly relevant to anything else in one's personal ontogeny. And, in these sexual self-reports, very few student writers spontaneously referred to more formal collegiate values—to the relation of sex to studying, or to academic success, or to the life of the mind. Sexual development and intellectual development in college, these papers implied, ought to be parallel but independent processes. They both ought to occur during the same years, but there was no need for any systematic connections between the two of them.

As a physical versus an intellectual behavior, as an "animalistic" versus a "higher human" activity, sexuality *was* mildly opposed to life of the mind in student ideation. Thus, a favorite undergraduate locker-room expression for vigorous fornication, used symmetrically by females and males, was "I fucked his/her brains out" (short form: "I fucked his/her brains"). But there was no indication in these papers that these contemporary young Americans thought that sexual and intellectual activities conflicted with one another in any way. There was no suggestion that chastity or abstinence might enhance the higher processes of collegiate cerebration. Sexuality and mental hard work, on the contrary, were seen as values, which, like "college life" and "academics," should be balanced during one's college years. All work and no play . . . Women and men implied that happy, fulfilling sex lives made them happier and more successful students. Men such as the neotraditionalist quoted in chapter 5 sometimes said that any sex at all, loving or casual, relaxed them so that they did better in the classroom. No one said that an active sex life interfered with academic success or achievement.[6]

By the implication of these papers, then, these undergraduates, like students in earlier American college generations, ascribed to the old college value mens sana in corpore sano. But they had a rather different idea than did the vigorous student athletes of yore about the particular activities that would insure the health and happiness of their bodies.[7]

251

COLLEGE AS A SEXUAL NONCOMMUNITY

After high school . . . I met Judy. Now Judy was one of my younger sisters friends: she was beautiful: she was infamous: she was a sex machine . . . and I was ripe and ready for the challenge. We did it everywhere; on the road behind Kilmer Campus, outside one of the churches in town, but most often on my fathers motorboat. . . . But now, Judy is in college, and when I last spoke with her, she was happily seeing one guy, (Oh, how college can change a person). She was, so far the best sex partner I have had, and I was deeply saddened by her switch to a monogamous relationship.—Senior male

I enjoy being at a large university where one is not subjected to constant scrutiny by the entire student body.—Senior female

Though intellect and sexuality were autonomous, separate, complementary cultural domains in the implicit conceptions of most of these undergraduates, "college" nevertheless did occur all the time in their sexual self-reports as the institutional context or setting for the student writers' sexualities. Rutgers in particular had two opposite meanings as a sexual environment in these papers. In one of its meanings, interestingly, the conventional values of American "community" were inverted. When the subject was the human side of college, Rutgers was often excoriated by undergraduates for being a large, anonymous institution in which hardly anyone really knew anyone else "as a person." When the subject was sexuality, on the other hand, Rutgers as these undergraduates described it in the sexual self-reports was often admired and appreciated for precisely these same institutional properties.

For sexually, many students pointed out, hardly anyone knew what you were up to at so vast an institution. No adults supervised your behavior. There were eight thousand potential players in the game of undergraduate sex in Rutgers College alone, and many more thousands on the other undergraduate campuses of Rutgers-New Brunswick; you would never know all these undergraduates and they would never all know you. Moreover, after four years you yourself would move on to other sexual environments. You did not need to be labeled indefinitely as having any one sexual reputation at Rutgers. If you were embarrassed in the eyes of old friends by a change in your sexual style, then you could always find a new set of friends.

Thus, impersonal Rutgers provided the undergraduates with an open, flexible sexual environment through which individual women and men could maneuver with some freedom. Neotraditional women could try being "sluts" and then retreat to the comfort of romantic commitment to one male, or they could decide that they are guilt-free experimentalists and evolve in other ways. Romantic men could change their stripes and become liberals; conceivably, liberal men could decide they are not really liberals and fall back into romance. Heterosexuals, if so inclined, could quietly check themselves out against bisexuality and homosexuality. Even Neanderthals could experience conversion—to pure romantics, to liberals, conceivably even to radicals.

THE SEXUAL ORGANIZATION OF THE UNDERGRADUATE COLLEGE

Actual Rutgers, on the other hand, was not an entirely anonymous social environment. It did have its undergraduate collectivities, its networks of personal acquaintanceship and knowledge. Since Rutgers abandoned its older in loco parentis responsibilities for the sexual moralities of its undergraduates in the 1960s, college authorities were no longer personally significant in influencing or controlling student sexuality on a daily basis. But as in the sixteenth- and seventeenth-century French villages analyzed by social historian Natalie Zeemon Davis, youthful peer groups were significant (cf. Davis 1971). Student collectivities could encourage some types and rates of sexual activity and discourage others. What sorts of regular influences did the different forms of undergraduate society have on student sexuality as it was described in these papers?

Going Away to College

Boy oh boy was [Rutgers] an eye opening experience after a lifetime of Catholic school education!!!—Senior female

Before I came to college, my views on sexual relationships were very old-fashioned, prudent ones. Although I had urges, I refused to let myself act on them. I felt that sexual intercourse was for married couples only and that girls who slept with their boyfriends were cheap. . . . However, [in my freshman year] I looked around and realized that *most* of the girls my age were sexually active. I began to look at sex differently; I realized that feeling horny was normal, and that it wasn't something bad.—Sophomore woman

The erotic values of Rutgers students were constructed almost entirely from sources in American mass culture, and many incoming freshmen were already familiar with these values when they first arrived at Rutgers. But some were not; some came from politer or more sexually restricted backgrounds. And in the reports of these undergraduate writers, going away to college was sometimes remembered as a moment of sexual shock. Even those youths who were familiar with contemporary sexuality in theory occasionally remembered their first contact with the actualities of collegiate sex with a sense of surprise, whether unhappily or happily:

I remember the shock an disgust I felt [freshman] year when I mentioned one of my friends to someone and he said, "Oh is she the one who's fucking Fred?" . . . I think if someone said it this year I wouldn't think twice.—Sophomore female

My third night of school, as a freshman, I met a girl and within 15 minutes I was in bed with [her] treating her like a piece of meat. I was [in a dorm corridor] at about 3 A. m. and a drunk blond stumbled out of the elevator. I smiled but did nothing. She came over said hi and stole my hat. She started running around the lounge saying come and get me, so I did. I caught up to her and grapped her belt loop to stop her. She said "wooooo" so you wanna get in my pants. Iwas shocked and blushing. She ran down the hallway and into her room, I followed. In no time we were fucking like lunatics, well she was anyway. I said I have to come and asked if I could blow it in her. She pushed me off, grabbed my cock and started sucking until I erupted my love juice into her hot steamy mouth. It was then I knew college was for me.—Senior male

One woman recalled allowing an upperclassman to pick her up on her second night at college as a freshman and take her back to his room on another campus, where she let him to teach her how to give a "blowjob." Then, she wrote with surprise, he maintained his one-way oral-sex relationship with her for several more weeks: "Strangely he didn't dump me" right away.[8] Another woman told of going to the fraternity in which she was to be a "little sister" the third night of her freshman year, when she was still a virgin. A male friend introduced her to a friend of his; she got very drunk; and the next morning she decided, from pains in places where she had never hurt before, that this new acquaintance had raped her.

These student memories were in the great minority among all the writers of these self-reports, however. They came from perhaps a dozen of the 144 sample papers. In many more reports, going away to college was not recalled as a particularly sexually marked event. Most Rutgers undergraduates came from hometowns within fifty miles of college. Some students confined their sexual relations to a hometown girlfriend or boyfriend for their first months or even years in college. As one sophomore male wrote, "I haven't cheated on my [hometown] girlfriend (yet)."

Others stayed with a hometown partner for a certain period *while* cautiously sampling from the movable feast of Rutgers sex. Some women who came to Rutgers as virgins let the new collegiate sexual ambience work on them slowly and changed their sexual styles only when they felt ready to do so. ("By the end of my freshman year, I decided I had had enough of my virginity."—Sophomore female) And many undergraduates simply saw college as the next stage in their steady sexual development:

> For me, highschool served as a trial and error period where I learned what was the right thing to do and what was wrong. The first weekend of college, I met my boyfriend and we began getting serious. The college atmosphere allows one to get to know another fairly easily because there is no adult supervision or restrictions. One is basically on his/her own and can do whatever he/she chose to do. The relationship between my boyfriend and I grew strong and stable. Sexually, we took it slow. . . . Eventually (six months later) we had sex for the first time together (the first time for me but not him).—Sophomore female

Dorm Fantasies, Dorm Realities. The coed dorm floor, the basic personal collectivity for most students in their freshman and sophomore years at Rutgers, was described sexually in these papers much as I saw it in my two years of participant observation in the dorms (see chapter 5). "This place is gossip-city," one woman resident observed of Hasbrouck Fourth in 1984. Most women did not want their sexual practices widely discussed among the various floor friends and acquaintances with whom they had to live for a year; most of them said they tried to find their erotic partners elsewhere. Younger men did not necessarily make the same effort; they had less to lose by local sex, or so they felt. But the women were still the no-sayers in sex, especially between floor friends.

Which is not to say that such no-saying always came easily between female and male coresidents or that coresidence always produced reliably nonerotic, brotherly-sisterly sensibilities between opposite-sex neighbors. Consider the following woman's account of an apparent sexual adventure with the boy next door on her coed dorm floor. Following a common pattern, she and her female roommate had been friends with the two males in the next room—but that was all they had been in public definition, "just friends." And the woman narrator had a boyfriend of her own who presumably lived elsewhere. But friendship was not in fact quite the only thing that had gone on between her and the boy next door. Other emotions simmered:

> I went to bed early that night because I had early class the next morning. I wasn't tired so I just lay there thinking. I kept thinking about the time he kissed me when I was in his room. I was talking to his roommate and mine when suddenly he came behind me, pulled me into his arms and kissed me hard. I was taken aback and just left the room without a word. I've been avoiding him since but I kept thinking of him instead of my boyfriend.
>
> Hours had gone by and I wasn't getting any tired just horny.

She had a problem, however. A known sexual relationship with a local male would be very complicated. Discretion was necessary. Any liaison had to be carefully hidden from everyone else on the floor, including the closest associates (and, presumably, friends) of the two principals, her roommate and his roommate. Not only that; she had to figure out a way to seduce the male in question. It was very late now. Everyone else on the floor had gone to bed. She figured out her gambit and made her opening move:

> I had concocted a great but "innocent" way to feel his touch on my body. I quietly—very quietly—so as not to wake my roommate, got out of bed. I took off my heavy pajamas and my underwear and excitedly slipped on my thin red velour bathrobe that accented my nakedness underneath especially my shapely bottom. . . . I snook out of my room and walked over to the hall phone. I had the operator call me back. After the phone had rung three times, I answered it.
>
> I went to his door and knocked quietly but firmly. . . . Well what seemed like hours, he finally came to the door—in just his underwear.
>
> Although I had seen him dressed or undressed as it may be, I looked at him through new eyes. His shoulders were wide, muscular and tan, and his stomach was pretty tight . . . and the bulge in his shorts was "very nice." I had never felt that way the other times I saw him undressed. . . .

Once his roommate could not hear I said, "I need a favor. Will you come with me, please?" He nodded and went back into his room and came out with his robe and slippers on. He still looked sexy.

Note how the participants in this account were following the correct sartorial etiquette of the dorm. The young woman wore a proper bathrobe over her nakedness; the young man, even when faced with a well-known female standing all alone on his doorstep late at night, went back into his room and politely dressed to a point of minimum decency. She apparently had glimpsed him in his underwear before ("undressed" in this context probably did not mean entirely nude); such glimpses were not uncommon between friends in the familiarity of the dorm. But the glimpse had probably been accidental, not the result of a deliberate display on the male's part. And now her look was being transformed by her new intentions; now, atypically between dorm coresidents, the glimpse was becoming sexual, for her at any rate.

The narrator had a moment of doubt, but she concentrated and heroically carried on. She had chosen one of the commoner, more trustworthy female ploys: The Massage. But where? She had this worked out as well:

I started feeling silly for doing this but when I closed my eyes for a second I remembered my plan. So I took his hand and led him down the hall and up three flights of stairs to the laundry room. I said, "I'm sorry to bother you but I can't sleep. I need a massage and you are the only one I could think of that could give me a good one . . . and besides you owe me!" He didn't look happy but he didn't protest. He asked me what to do and shyly I suggested that I lie down across the washing machines so it would be easier to massage my whole back.

From this point on, as the male got the idea and rapidly became much more enthusiastic about their nocturnal exercise together, the text narrated a standard seduction, well within the limits of sexual explicitness found in many of the other female and male undergraduate sexual self-reports. This particular account was unusually well plotted, however. Its moments of possible awkwardness and embarrassment were well imagined, realities such as birth control were kept firmly in mind, and the female narrator always remained in control of the action, calling virtually every shot. Consistently, in the tones of a guiltless female experimentalist, she as protagonist was the agent. Her male partner was only the tool of her sexual pleasure:

Well I layed down and he started massaging my shoulders. I could feel his eyes on my bottom. He started rubbing lower. . . . It felt good and I started opening my legs a little. He then murmured "now what?" I knew he had weakened but I was enjoying the teasing too much so I said "now my legs." He started with my feet and then went onto my calfs. I was really starting to get wet and even started moving slowly back and forth. . . . I pulled my robe up to just where he could glimpse my cheeks and my red lips. . . . he started rubbing my thighs higher and even "accidentally" touched my lips. I couldn't take anymore and wipped around onto my back. Doing so one of my breasts and my mound became exposed. I quickly covered them up but barely and I said, "now my arms and . . . my chest." He wouldn't look me in the eye but said, "I should get up there 'coz I can't do your right arm right." I said, "Whatever you say" and closed my eyes.

He got on me and boy was he hard! . . . My breasts were dying to be licked, sucked and squeezed and my pussy was aching to be penetrated—hard, real hard! He started tracing my breast through my robe and then he put his hand through my robe and started playing with my lips.

I started calling his name, slightly groaning, and arched my back so that my lips were rubbing the rod in his underwear. He jumped off me and took off his underwear and started to climb back up but I said "No!" and sat up exposing both breasts. I jumped off the washers and stood close to him facing him. I started kissing his neck, rubbing his chest and just above his hard cock. . . .

. . . He picked me up and started to put me on the washer. I said, "No, I can't that way I haven't been taking my pill." . . . He kept trying to shove his cock into my pussy but I kept him at bay until he knelt down and started licking and sucking my pussy.

Oh that got me really going. I wanted to feel something hard in there so I said, "Your finger—oh please! put your fingers in me!" He obliged and oh he knew where to rub. While he was slowly going in and out with two fingers his pinky kept touching my other whole and wetting it, through I know it wasn't intentional. That really made me want to be fucked so I pulled away from his fingers and slowly pulled him up so that he was standing with his cock pointing straight for my pussy. I smiled and turned around. I walked over to the washer and pulled him close.

I leaned over the washer and quietly said, "Fuck me." He didn't understand so I pulled his cock and started rubbing it between my cheeks. Then I said, "Come on I know you'd love to fuck me there and I want to feel you there. I want you to ram me." I seperated my cheeks and I said, "Fuck me." He smiled shyly and made his way into my whole. I said, "Fuck me hard!" He grabbed my waist and started pumping hard. I said, "Harder!" I felt my insides starting to vibrate and tingle and then I felt his cock surge and come in me. I yelled and . . ."

And now, in the last sentence, we discover that the conventional sexual restraints of the coed dorm floor had in fact ruled even this account. Not only had its female narrator told this adventure in an anonymous paper, possibly as a fantasy; not only had she safeguarded herself as protagonist within the narrative by keeping the encounter a secret from everyone else on her floor. But the tale was, it turned out, only a dream. And her sole remaining anxiety in the text was the fear that she would disturb her roommate when she woke up:

> . . . I woke up disappointed and hoping I hadn't woke my roommate.—Senior female [9]

To say that most undergraduates tended to avoid actual sexual relations with floor coresidents is not to say that college residence halls—or, more precisely, the private rooms in college residence halls—were chaste, asexual places. There were not too many other places to "do it" with your off-floor erotic partner if you were a freshman or sophomore dorm resident. In this sense, the fundamental sexual constraint imposed by the overcrowded undergraduate dorms was, Where and when can one find a little sexual privacy?:

> I mean I absolutely hated it when my boyfriend and I would be in the middle of sex and my roommate walked in and nearly ripped the door off its hinges because we chained the door shut.—Senior female

> [My] dorm was so overcrowded that sexual activities seldom got a chance. But when everyone went home for the weekend the place would go quiet except for the squeaking of bed frames. It was always so obvious because everyone would have tossled hair when they went for Sunday brunch and the doors always have strange messages on them like "Your aunt from Florida called" or Smiley faces . . . or flowers . . .—Junior female

Different roommates had different arrangements. Most roommates had private codes among themselves, apparently innocent message-board scribblings that really meant, Would you please go away for awhile? I've got someone in here. Some roommates worked around one another's daily schedules and grabbed their opportunities when they could. Sometimes an amiable roommate agreed to spend an occasional night in another room, camping out on the floor of a neighbor or using a spare bed left vacant by other nocturnal peregrinations. A few students reported that their roommates sometimes stayed in the rooms in which they were sleeping with a sex partner. Sometimes this was literally all the narrator was doing: sleeping with a sex partner simply for closeness and convenience, without intercourse.[10] Other times, writers said, they waited until it sounded as if their roommates were asleep, and then went at it as quietly as possible.

Virtually all coed dorm floors at Rutgers, by all indications, were aggressively heterosexual in their erotic ambiences. Both heterosexual and homosexual subjects widely agreed that gay, lesbian, and bisexual dorm residents either had to remain entirely in-the-closet on the average coed dorm floor, or risk having to live with real social ostracism all year long.[11] Most heterosexual men said they would find it very hard to handle the revelation from a new roommate-friend that he was gay, even if he made it very clear that his erotic interests were directed elsewhere. Many heterosexual women, on the other hand, thought they could deal with the same revelation from a lesbian roommate more calmly. Almost all heterosexual women and men said they would worry, however, about what other people on the floor would think about *them* if they discovered their roommates were homosexuals. One or two gay students did report in other contexts, however, that they had first decided they were homosexuals when gay roommates, other years, initially turned them on—very quietly, without the knowledge of anyone else on their floors.

Fraternities and Sororities

Some people believe that fraternal social events are just orgies where guys + girls get real drunk and fuck each others brains out. This is so far from the truth that it makes me laugh. . . . I've met a great deal of very nice girls through my association with the house and feel these girls would no more like to be termed sluts as I would a playboy. Please don't misunderstand, we do have our share of "wild adventures." . . . I think a lot of these so called sexual adventures are because of our reputations as sex animals. I'm not familiar with the proper psychological term but to describe it—*we become in peoples' minds what they expect us to be.* This is where the fun part begins.

There are alot of undersexed liberal women who want to meet men, have a good time etc. . . . but not get involved in long-term relationships. Alot of guys from the house get involved in these types of affairs—Including myself. But you know, even us fraternity boys have feeling and I know I've been hurt afew times by such relationships—this kind of shoots down the idea that were sex animals. . . .—Senior male

Seven identified fraternity members wrote about sex and the fraternities in their sexual self-reports, and many other students described them in passing. Three of the fraternity members have already been quoted in chapter 5—one on thirteen-on-one gang fornication, the second on his "list," and the third on the new distinction between good women and sluts. A fourth narrated the pleasures of pickup sex; a fifth wrote a possible fantasy or put-on about "abusing" a "young voluptuous, erotic, CHERRY, blond starlet" whom he had picked up at a party in his fraternity one night and taken up to his room (he also described her as a "frat rat," a "slut," a "cunt," and a "horbag"); and a sixth celebrated "doing a nigger" while his friends in the next room played "Back to Black" on their stereos (and one "stuck his head under my door and watched").

The earnest apologist quoted above was the only writer who attempted to deny or to give nuance to the salient sexual connotation of the fraternity in contemporary undergraduate erotic culture. And in trying to do so, even he reaffirmed it. In virtually all these reports, by brothers and by nonmembers alike, the fraternities, and the wild parties on Thursday and Friday nights that characterized them, were uniformly described—simply and without qualification in most cases—as the biggest and most available sexual "meat markets" on the campus.

Which is not to say that every young woman or man who went to such parties was looking for sleazy sex or for guilt-free experimental sex, depending on the subject's moral stance. Nor is it to say that everyone who was looking for these erotic delights necessarily succeeded in finding them. As the fraternity apologist quoted above added, "Believe me, more guys go home with 'blue balls' so to speak than picking up girls." But it was clear that if you were a male or female undergraduate and pickup sex was what you wanted, then the many parties in the many nearby fraternities were the most likely places to go to look for it.[12]

The same sort of generalization could be made about the sexual moralities of those male students who belonged to the fraternities, on the evidence of these papers. There were neotraditionalist men outside the fraternity system; and there may have been male liberals and perhaps a few pure romantics—but certainly very few known gays—within it. It was not absolutely necessary to be a brother in order to be a sexual Neanderthal at Rutgers. But if you wanted to be a Neanderthal with good peer-group support, if you wanted to be surrounded by other men who also thought that sleazy sex with sluts was the way to prove your manhood, then the fraternities, or some of them at any rate, were the places for you. In them, by all evidence in these papers, you could escape the complicated and relatively more egalitarian contemporary gender relations of the coed dorm floors. You could escape the tensions of dealing with female next-door neighbors as friends. Once again, as in the good old days, only other men needed to be your friends. Women were once more at a safe distance. Some fraternity members may indeed have had real woman friends, but if they did so, they had them very much on their own time. As far as fraternity values went, at least as they came through almost without exception in these papers, women once again came in two types: good women (present or future girlfriends and/or wives) and sluts.

Sororities were newer and less developed at Rutgers than fraternities, with only one or two residential houses in the mid-1980s. One senior woman's paper described the erotic policies of a sorority in detail. Her sorority sounded well-matched to the fraternities, and her paper provided a handy woman's guide to the subtleties of being a good woman under the neotraditional version of the new sexual orthodoxy (compare to the male account in chapter 5):

> At the time that I was a [sorority] pledge . . . morality played a large role in my chapters' pledge program. This was do to the fact that my chapter was attempting to change its image after a sister had been a willing participant in a "gang bang" incident with a fraternity. Consequently, we as pledges were under the watchful ey our elder and seemingly musch wiser sisters. . . .
>
> This did not mean tat the members of the sisterhood became celibate. Far from it, we now had to be discreet about our comings and goings. An unofficial list of rules and regulations became the key to successful sorority sex.
>
> 1. No prolonged making out on the dance floor, porch or other public area. Take it upstairs.
>
> 2. No public display of affection with anyone other than one's boyfriend while wearing one's pin, letters, or crest.
>
> 3. When staying at a fraternity be discrete. Do not make a scene for the entire party as you go upstairs Do not roam the halls half naked or in a state of undress covered up only by a brother's. Mostimportantly, do not stay for brealfast with the brothers. If you can smell the bacon you've obviously overstayed your welcome.

4. Never participate in group sex. It will make you as well as everyone else in the house extremely famous.

5. Attempt to avoid riding on campus transportation the morning after your fraternal slumber party. No noe wants to haves dogs follow thame or fellow greeks yell "Hey Bimbo!" at them. . . .

6. Most importantly, use some reliable method of birth control. One's collegiate years are no time to be creating legacies.

OFF-CAMPUS LIFE: PREFIGURATIONS OF ADULT SEXUALITY

In their first years in college, most undergraduates traded the sexual supervision of parents and other adults for the gossipy peer-group controls of the coed dorm floor. After their sophomore years, however, they almost invariably decided that they had had enough of the dorms. Some of the males then moved into the fraternities with their sexually curious, and differently coercive, male cohorts. Other males and females, most of the upperclassmen, moved into off-campus housing. And here for the first time they began to escape the strong influence of their age-mates upon their sexual behavior. For the first time since they had left home to go away to college, they were sexually on their own to act as they wished, with something like the autonomy of adults in the real world.

Undergraduates did live with some of their peers in off-campus residences. Because of the high rents in housing-poor New Brunswick, students often had to share houses, apartments, and even rooms with varying numbers of roommates. But now their roommates were much more likely to be their chosen friends, youths who were sexually similar to themselves. One's off-campus roommates were not as likely to gossip with others about one's own sexuality; and there were not so many others around all the time with whom to gossip. Women who enjoyed themselves with sexual experimentalism or with sexual liberalism and women who reported fairly easy, frank woman-to-woman sex talk were usually older undergraduates who lived in off-campus housing or possibly in the apartments the university made available to older students. And lesbian, gay, and bisexual students, in these papers and in other research, universally said that off-campus housing was the only reasonable residential setting for their particular sexualities.

Most off-campus housing, three-quarters of it or more, was a single-sex arrangement. Students said this was because of the wishes of New Brunswick landlords. They also said it was due to the greater intimacy of off-campus living arrangements. It was not the same to share a small apartment with a single bathroom with opposite-sex roommates as it was to share a large dorm floor with separate bathrooms. But some women and men did live together in off-campus housing as friends, or as acquaintances, who were simply sharing space. And some lived together as "boyfriend and girlfriend," enjoying their new erotic freedom, living *almost* like married couples:

> This summer I lived with my boyfriend [in an off-campus apartment]. Before living together, sex was fairly regular, but often there were times when we both wanted to, but often couldn't for various reasons—his parents were home, my roommate was there, too much homework, exams, pressure, tensions, interruptions etc. But this summer changed everything.
> . . . anytime either of us felt the urge, we merely had to wander into our room and have sex. . . . Now I know what old-fashioned people mean when they say; "They're just itching to hop into bed" . . .—Senior female

Almost all Rutgers undergraduates eventually did intend to marry, according to other interviews. But in these papers, only a few of the writers alluded to marriage, and then only in indefinite, romantic terms for the most part:

> I never thought that a relationship with sex could be as comfortable as the one I'm in now . . . and will be in forever.—Junior female

The undergraduates' lack of planning was an accurate projection of their immediate sexual futures. Like most middle-class Americans in the 1980s, most of them would defer marriage into their mid-twenties or later, until they had finished further schooling or until they were settled into the work world.[13]

Some of them sounded as if they would be happy to stay pair-bonded to their present lovers until they were finally ready to start thinking seriously about marriage. Others sounded as if they felt they were just getting started sexually, or, in the case of the unintentional virgins, as if they were still waiting to get started. They were just beginning to enjoy themselves; the last thing they wanted to do was to become tied down prematurely. Most of these writers seemed to assume that, when married, they would be sexually faithful to one partner. But however much they were looking forward to marriage for other resaons, they were not especially looking forward to marriage for the sex. It got boring pretty fast, many of them imagined:

> Where else [but in college] can you have sex with 14 different girls in six months, when you are married?—Junior male

Only one student in these 144 sample papers, a woman, wrote a specific fantasy about sex in later years. Here it is, in conclusion, one young woman's version of the sorts of carryings-on she apparently thought would be necessary in order to ward off the inevitable monotony of sex in the adult world—the erotic future under the new sexual orthodoxy, adolescent point of view:

He lay there naked upon my bed. Arms and legs tied to the bed posts. My whip cracked loudly—powerfully. He started as I crossed the room. The blazing fire threw an interesting glow out to my leather pants and halter.
    . . . I stroked his chest lightly for several moments and then in a swift motion broke through his skin with my sharpened nails, leaving long red trails. . . . My tongue, drawn to the deep rich red of the blood, lowered to his flesh. Slowly, enjoying every drop, I licked and teased—my hands clutching his chest. A chill of excitement, like electricity, shot through me.
    . . . I leaned forward so that my breasts smothered his face. He licked wildly at my cleavage. . . . My halter fell open. He rubbed his face on my naked breasts. I lifted my shoulders and arched my back so that my nipples dangled just above his mouth. His tongue darted out and his neck strained forward as he tried desperately to reach them. A smile crossed my lips then; I threw my head back in laughter. Beg for it, motherfucker, beg for it!
    . . . My hand slid to his public hair and began to play as I licked his balls. That familiar musky scent filled my nostrils and I began to get excited. My tongue followed the length of his dick—up and down, up and down . . . Then, in one motion, my mouth engulfed him. I then withdrew and repeated once more before I got up.
    . . . I looked up ans reached to the night table where the switch blade sat waiting. . . . Quickly, I slashed the ropes that held his left hand and then his right. . . . After a short while he lifted his body and I saw the flash of the switch blade as it fell upon the ropes that tied his feet. He threw the blade across the room and fell upon me. . . . Our bodies pressed and rubbed against each other. My nails dug into the flesh on his back as his hands kneaded my buttocks. My back arches towards him. I grasped the back of his head with my hands and my

lips found his. He entered me as we kissed. He held me tightly against him, his chest pressing against mine. We fucked wildly. His hips pumped madly between my own legs. We then climaxed together.

There we lay, our arms and legs intertwined, my face buried in his chest. He lifted my chin and told me how much he loved me. After twelve years of marriage, we could still have a great sex life.—Senior female

Further Comments

1 / See chapter 5 for an explanation of these papers. As in chapter 5, they are quoted without correction of spelling, punctuation, or grammar.

2 / These figures were based on what the students chose to say in their papers in 1986. As indicated in chapter 5, in 1987 I circulated a more conventional, more directive sex questionnaire through an undergraduate class taking the same course, and the curve of reported ages for first times showed a slightly different distribution. Both for women and for men it peaked earlier, in the eleventh- and twelfth-grade years of high school, with males reporting earlier sexual comings-of-age than females. Of the reporting nonvirgins, 70 percent of the men and 62 percent of the women said they had lost their virginity before arriving at college. And, as noted in chapter 5, among students with about the same college-age distributions as those in the 1986 class,

the reported virginity rate at the time the papers were written was the same for women on the 1987 questionnaire as in the 1986 papers (one in five) but lower for men (one in eight). Ninety-six women and fifty-five men returned these questionnaires in 1987, less than half the students enrolled in the course.

In his 1980 data from Douglass, Weis had a reported women's virginity rate of 35 percent, higher than in my sample. But he does not indicate the ages or college classes of his respondents (Weis 1985). If they were mostly freshmen and sophomores, his figures would be comparable to those suggested here.

Working with a 1981 collegiate data set from almost eight hundred female and male subjects in northern California, most of them freshmen and sophomores, Hildebrand and Abramowitz (1984) found that 40 percent of the females reported they were virgins and 30 percent of the males made the same admission.

3 / Data on this sexual variable were similar on the 1987 questionnaire, though the spread was a little wider. Forty percent of the women who were sexually active reported one boyfriend only since loss of virginity; 15 percent reported two; 14 percent reported three; 18 percent reported four; 10 pecent reported five or more; and 3 percent indicated that they had had all their sexual relationships with casual partners only.

4 / Female figures for 1987: 27 percent of the sexually active women reported never having tried casual sex; 43 percent reported trying it with one to three different partners; 15 percent reported four to six partners; 12 percent reported seven to twelve partners; and 4 percent reported more than twelve (twelve, twenty-five, and twenty-nine). Male figures from 1987: of nonvirgins, 16 percent said they had never tried casual sex; 24 percent had tried it with one to three partners; 20 percent with four to six partners; 16 percent with seven to twelve partners; and 22 percent reported sexual encounters with over a dozen different partners (with highs up into the fifties).

5 / *Oceanic:* a native sexual position reported by anthropolo-gists from the south Pacific, one requiring good thigh muscles. The male squats or kneels between the legs of the half-supine female, and both of them move freely during intercourse. One young woman told me proudly in her report in 1986 that she and her boyfriend had discovered this position on their own, six months before learning about it in my class.

6 / The emotions of an unhappy sexual relationship *could* throw you off your academic stride, of course, but the culprit in this case was not sex itself, but bad sex.

7 / This comparison is not an idle one. Late-nineteenth-century ideologues of collegiate "manliness" were very worried about the impure and enervating activities to which adolescent males might apply their "animal spirits" if they did not exhaust themselves through vigorous athletics: loose women, homosexuality, or, worst of all, masturbation!

8 / The generalization was offered in chapter 5 that oral sex rarely aroused guilt among these student writers. This woman was an exception. She evidently thought that the male who taught her to perform fellatio on him should then have thrown her over for being a slut.

9 / It seems very unlikely that this text actually had been a

dream, at least the way the narrator told it here; it was entirely too carefully and conventionally plotted. Rather, it seems to belong to a common set of American colloquial stories and jokes with a particularly elementary twist at the end—an unbelievable event told in the first-person singular, ending with "and then I woke up!"

10 / With some regularity, particularly before their "first time," women reported that they slept with boyfriends without intercourse for weeks or even months— partly to get used to the whole idea, partly to see if the boyfriend "really cared."

11 / An exception, at least one year, was Erewhon Third (see chapter 4, note 22). Another exception was Nelson Hall, a special-interest dorm set up for students at Rutgers who, for various reasons, wanted to live in a different ambience than that found on the average coed dorm floor. In this dorm, at least in 1984–1985, lesbian and gay students tended to report more tolerance for their sexualities than on the average dorm floor. This tolerance was well known on other dorm floors, however, so much so that Nelson had a minor reputation among the students for being the "fag dorm" (and nonhomosexual students who lived in Nelson sometimes felt they had to protest that they were not "guilty" by association).

As for the atmosphere on the average coed dorm floor, one of Pete's old sophomoric friends burst into his room on Hasbrouck Fourth one day in early September 1984 and greeted him excitedly: "Hey, dickhead, I've been lookin' all over for you!" Before Pete could introduce him to me, he burst out with the story he had come to tell. He now lived in Gates Hall. He and a few friends had been in an adjacent high-rise dorm the night before, he said, and one of the residents had had a pair of binoculars, so they started using them voyeuristically, to peep into the windows of the private student rooms in Gates.

> And we see this guy in one room, with about five other guys, curtains wide open, and they're all dickin' each other up the ass! I couldn't *believe* it. Then I counted the floors, and this guy lives on *my* floor! So I call up on the hall phone and ask for him. I say to tell him his mother's calling. But he won't come to the phone.
>
> But I couldn't *believe* it. What's this place turning into? *My* dorm's turning into another Nelson!

Whereupon Pete replied, in a very even tone, "X, have I introduced you to *Professor* Moffatt?"

Then, later in the semester, when I was doing research with some students who belonged to the Lesbian/Gay Alliance at Rutgers, I heard their version of the same story and met the protagonist:

> I'd just met this guy, and we went back to my room. And we started to make out. We were just taking off our clothes. I *had* left my curtains open. Well, apparently some people were watching from [the adjacent dorm] and they saw us. And I guess they called some people on the phone. I'd already decided I wasn't going to answer the phone if it rang. So when I didn't respond to the door, they hammered on it and someone yelled, "Hey, put your pants on!" I couldn't *believe* it. Then someone went downstairs and hollered up at me in a effeminate voice. After that, I had some nasty stuff put on my door, and once a guy walking past my room said, "I can't stand *fags!*"
>
> I couldn't believe they'd do that, look into my room. . . . If I'd seen the guys who did it, I'd have given their names to the deans and tried to have them thrown out of housing.

By the end of the semester, *he* had moved out of Gates, however, into an off-campus apartment.

12 / In theory, these parties were open only to other members of the fraternity-sorority system and to invited guests. In practice, however, virtually any roving male who tried a few houses on a Thursday and Friday night could crash such a party. Or he could find a friend or acquaintance who would invite him in as a guest. High school students from neighboring towns commonly got in. Women, collegiate or otherwise, were generally given a quiet pulchritude test at the door of a fraternity, and any of them who met that house's particular standards or needs were readily admitted as instant invited guests.

13 / For about twenty years following World War II, the ages for marriage and initial parenthood declined into the late teens and early twenties among middle-class Americans, atypically youthful years in recent American and British demographic history. These ages had returned to historical Anglo-American levels by the 1970s and 1980s, however: marriage and parenthood in the mid to late twenties and early thirties (see Gillis 1974; Kett 1977; Stone 1977). In past centuries, delayed marriage in middle-class western culture also often meant delayed sexuality, but obviously no longer. It has been the case once again, however, that delayed marriage means youths wait a number of years past their early twenties for

full economic adulthood; most of them defer marriage until they acquire the additional schooling to become established in the professional occupations they dream of, and many of them plan a few more free years after that to enjoy modern affluent young adulthood. (To be strictly correct, then, the title of this book ought to be *Coming Partly Of Age in New Jersey.*)

SEVEN / The Life of the Mind

THE OPPORTUNITY TO WRITE ABOUT MY INTELLECTUAL LIFE I FIND EVEN MORE GRATIFYING THAN AN INVITATION TO ANONYMOUSLY DISCUSS MY SEXUALITY. . . . I'VE BEEN READING SINCE I WAS 3 AND ONLY STARTED HAVING SEX SINCE I TURNED 20, [SO] MY "LIFE OF THE MIND" IS ALSO MORE CENTRAL TO MY PERSONALITY.—Junior female

ONE'S STUDY HABITS [ARE] JUST AS TOUCHY A SUBJECT AS ONE'S SEXU-ALITY AND MAYBE MORE SO. SEXUALITY IS SOMETHING, AT LEAST FOR ME, WHICH JUST HAPPENS OR DOES NOT HAPPEN. IT REALLY HAS NO BEARING ON ONE'S LIFE LIKE ONE'S ACADEMIC SUCCESS AT COL-LEGE. . . .—Junior male

College for the students was not just about autonomy and friendship and fun and sex and the extracurricular development of the individualistic self. It was also a place to get an education, a surprisingly satisfactory one in the opinion of most of the undergraduates. Why surprisingly? Because, if we are to believe a number of recent critics and commentators, almost all the news about American colleges and American students in the 1980s is bad. Precollege students are culturally ignorant, these critics say (Hirsch 1987); they know the correct answers to less than 60 percent of a set of basic questions about western history and literature (Ravitch and Finn 1987:1). The colleges themselves have lost their sense of mission (Boyer 1987:2); they are, along with the professoriat and the educational liberalizations of the 1960s, responsible for the decline or the demise of literate culture in the United States in the late twentieth century (Bloom 1987; Bennett 1984). College students are lost in meaningless worlds of relativism and pop culture, in which intellectual and moral values cannot be formulated, in which Truth cannot be realized (Bloom 1987). Or, alternatively, the liberal critique: modern students are gray vocationalists who do not take the intellectual and political chances that undergraduates were taking back in the good old 1960s. They no longer challenge authority; they no longer argue back (Levine 1980; Horowitz 1987).

It was impossible to live in the Rutgers dorms as a college professor and not to agree with some parts of these critiques, if not with the causes or the solutions they often proposed. But if the critiques were all true, then the students would have had to have been in hopeless states of delusion in their belief that they were learning anything of importance in college at all—and this, in my opinion, was not the case.[1] Or they would have had to have given up on the academic side of college altogether, to have only been really satisfied with college as a place for adolescent fun and games. And this, in my opinion and in their opinions, was also not the case.

According to one recent official survey, for instance, about 90 percent of the students at Rutgers were generally satisfied with their college education (Rutgers University 1986). And forty-two students who wrote intellectual self-reports for me in a class in 1986[2] indicated similar levels of approval:

I have found that college has a much more intellectual atmosphere than high school. One can usually find a demonstration or a lecture . . .—Freshman female

Since I've been at Rutgers, I've had many more chances to develop my mind than I ever had in high school. In high school, there is an unwritten but widely accepted set of standards that govern the ways in which one should act, dress, socialize, etc. I was glad to break away from those standards so I could begin to develop my own individual character.—Sophomore female

Although I am critical of many of my classes I feel I have learned a large amount since I began college. Now most of my interests stem from my class material . . . and some of my classes have profoundly changed my view of the world.—Sophomore female

In the four years I have spent at Rutgers, both my intelligence and my perceptiveness have grown, motivating me to be more intellectually active.—Senior male

Undergraduate satisfaction nationwide in the mid-1980s was comparable to that at Rutgers.[3] How could this be? Obviously the students' definitions of the situation were fundamentally different from those of virtually all adult commentators on contemporary American higher education.

And this certainly was true for Rutgers students, for at least two reasons. First of all, when college elders thought about college, they tended to think only about those narrow parts of it they knew best: about the classroom, the curriculum, and their own role as teachers. When the undergraduates thought about it, on the other hand, they tended to consider (as the earlier chapters of this book have tried to suggest) a much wider range of "learning experiences." And even when they were asked to evaluate their classroom educations narrowly construed, they were likely to be influenced by these wider meanings. At Rutgers in the 1980s, most of the students felt that they were challenged by classroom and extracurricular learning, that they did learn a lot from living autonomously in the residential undergraduate student body, and that they did change and develop in their four years in New Brunswick.

For most of the students, then, the sum total of all the pluses and minuses of college was a positive one. And for those rarer students for whom it was not, the fault, in their own opinions, lay partially with themselves, not just with college or with Rutgers. This young man, for instance, gave academic Rutgers one of the few negative evaluations in the 1986 self-reports, a not-inaccurate description of the underside of Rutgers as a place for autonomy:

> Coming to Rutgers was like walking into the world of a mirror in that the social and academic life I had in high school had suddenly become backwards and upside down compared to Rutgers. In high school I lived in the comfort and security of a middle class family . . . [High school] teachers gave out encouragement and showed concern over not only what they were teaching, but concern for the student's academic welfare. They also gave me the feeling that they acknowledged me as a person and not just as a student.
>
> At Rutgers I have felt and still feel very confused. For the first time I am essentially on my own. If there is any supervision it often seems very vague or token. For example, Preceptors or R.C.s in dorms who try to keep order but aren't a good source for guidance, and faculty advisors who seem more concerned with their advisees accommodating a program than with trying to shape an ideal and truly meaningful education. . . . It is rare to find a professor, from my experience, who has office hours for more than one or two

hours a week, and even more rare to feel welcome to come talk with them. . . . The phrase "once out of college and on your own in the real world" is absurd. I already feel as if I am "on my own" and in the "real world." . . . Isn't college supposed to prepare its students for the "real world," not thrust them into it? . . .

But, good moralist and American individualist that he was, he then went on to amend his criticism of modern mass education with some self-criticism:

[But I also realize that] I lack motivation . . . I have realized that to get a really good education at Rutgers I have to look for it on my own. There are excellent and interesting professors at this school, but they have to be sought out. —Sophomore male

The second reason the students saw the academic college through rosier lenses than most adult critics did was that, unlike them, they did not usually compare it to archaic, idealized, or even imaginary alternatives. Instead, they thought about what they had known before they came to college; they thought about their families, their suburban hometowns, their high schools, and intellect as it was presented to them in American popular culture. Undergraduate Rutgers, in their perception of it, was by no means perfect. The learning was often passive and mechanistic; the teaching, indifferent; and the professors, anonymous figures glimpsed distantly across the podium. Nevertheless, in contrast to the life of the mind as most of the undergraduates had known it in their young lives to date, Rutgers often looked very good.

How, then, did the students interpret the meaning of the education that, in their opinions, college was more or less adequately providing? What were the purposes of a college education in their understanding? Like adult ideologues of higher education, most of them believed or hoped, one way or another, that a college education would be a civilizing experience. College should broaden their intellectual horizons, they believed; it should make them into better, more liberal, more generally knowledgeable human beings. At the same time, however, college should have a useful vocational outcome for them. However much it contributed to their personal enlightenment, a college education should definitely lead to good grades in a good major, and eventually to a good career in one of the professions or in business.

And this second, vocational meaning of college was—unmistakably— its much more important purpose for most Rutgers students in the late twentieth century. Many adult critics have been saying the same thing about the predominant educational values of American undergraduates on a nationwide basis since the idealism of the students of the 1960s suddenly wore off, about the time the draft was discontinued and the American economy went into decline, in the early and mid-1970s.[4] If the adults who call contemporary students "vocationalists" mean to imply that they themselves are innocent of such impure drives, however, then they are either being stupid or hypocritical. American college professors officially renounced their own interest in the "whole student" and in general education as their most fundamental function almost a century ago, when they professionalized as academic specialists.[5] To be a professional is to be interested in a narrow segment of expert knowledge; and, to ever-increasing degrees, this is what most college American professors are in the late twentieth century. And this is also what most college students are trying to become. The only difference between them and their college elders is that most of the students are not aiming themselves at academic professions.[6]

Let us look more closely, then, at the shape of undergraduate vocationalism at Rutgers in the late 1970s and the mid-1980s. What were its manifestations? How did it affect the students' ordinary academic and intellectual routines? And to what extent did it coexist with other, presumably purer and more admirable "intellectual" meanings of a college education among these modern American adolescents? A good place to begin is with the students' attitudes toward the basic stuff of a formal education: the curriculum.

VOCATIONALISM AND
THE CURRICULUM

On paper, the curriculum of a large liberal-arts-based college such as Rutgers is a pluralistic universe of knowledge, a cornucopia of possible learning for the intellectually adventuresome student. Rutgers College students could study with about 950 faculty members in the wider university in the mid-1980s, organized into 52 different departments and programs whose majors were accepted by the college.[7] All this choice might not be altogether a good thing, educational authorities sometimes worried. What guided the students through it? What general or unifying principles were they likely to discover in their college educations?

The Hierarchy of the Majors

For most of the students, however, the curriculum was organized in a very simple way. There were useful subjects, subjects that presumably led to good careers, and there were useless ones. Some of the useless subjects were "interesting," the students conceded. You might study one or two of them on the side in college, or if you could not stand any of the useful majors, you might actually major in something more eccentric:

> *Dorm Resident* (Hasbrouck Fourth lounge, September 1984): What did you say your name was again?
>
> *Anthropologist:* Mike.
>
> *Student:* Someone told me you're in anthropology?
>
> *Anthropologist:* Yup.
>
> *Student:* That seems like kind of a strange thing to be majoring in. I mean, what will you ever *do* with anthropology?
>
> *Anthropologist:* I'm not majoring in it. I *am* an anthropologist. And what I'm doing with it right now is studying *you.*
>
> *Student:* Oh, *you're* the guy . . . I've got to stop sitting around out here without my glasses on.

Oddballs aside, however, your bread-and-butter choice, your main field of study, ought to be something "practical," most of the students agreed.

Thus, in one recent year, almost three-quarters of the upperclassmen at Rutgers College were majoring in just ten departments (see table 7.1), while the remaining forty-two departments and programs divided up the other 28 percent of the undergraduates among themselves, in much smaller numbers.[8] As most undergraduates understood them, eight of the ten top majors were sensible vocational choices. Economics presumably led to business, psychology to psychotherapy or to counseling, political sci-

TABLE 7.1 / Top Ten Majors, Rutgers College (Juniors and Seniors, Spring 1986)

Major	Number choosing	Percentage of top ten majors	Percentage of total majors
Economics	836	32	23
English	333	13	9
Psychology	306	12	8
Political Science	252	9	7
Biological Science	213	8	6
Communication	173	7	5
History	164	6	4
Computer Science	156	6	4
Mathematics	106	4	3
Accounting	101	4	3

Note: In 1986, Rutgers College students could major in one of fifty-two departments or programs. The top ten majors listed represent the actual choices of all juniors and seniors who had declared their majors.

ence to law school, biological sciences to medical school, communication to work in the media, and mathematics to the sciences or to teaching. Accounting and computer science require no explanation. Only English and history were apparently pure liberal arts choices. But many of the students majoring in English had in fact double majors, and their other choice was usually a more useful one. Moreover, it was widely believed, the ability to write well made a difference in the business and professional world after college.

These top ten majors and all the rest then fell into a gradient of status in general student opinion, one that was based on three criteria.[9] First, how good was the occupation to which a given subject presumably led? Second, and closely related, how difficult was that subject at Rutgers? And third, much less important, how much social good did the occupation or profession in question accomplish? By all three measures, biological sciences was number one. What real world profession, after all, was more prestigious than doctor? Doctors also made a lot of money and, conveniently, helped people. Premed was a very difficult major as well, the students agreed, known for its early "weeding courses," for its difficult prerequisites such as organic chemistry, believed by the students to be expressly designed to weed out underqualified undergraduates. Some of the other hard sciences were almost equally tough in undergraduate opinion, though they were taken far less often, perhaps because their target occupations were not as well known. And then came two very popular, respected choices: engineering and computer science.

Majors in the social and behavioral sciences ranked below most of those in the hard sciences. These subjects were definitely easier, the students believed, but they did still point you toward known professions or semiprofessions. And they were often about relevant, human things as well: psychology and psychotherapy, sociology and social work, and so on. Economics had a special position in the social sciences. Like the rest of them, it was considered to be only moderately difficult. This meant that many students could handle it, however; bio-sci was simply too tough for the average undergraduate. And, though the students did not see business as a socially beneficial occupation, they did see it as one of the surer routes to personal benefit, to a middle-class or an upper-middle-class income. Economics was thus the most popular single choice by a factor of three over the next favorite major at Rutgers in the 1980s, and it had the same popularity nationwide in the 1980s.[10]

Finally, bringing up the rear, behind the hard sciences and the bigger and the better-connected of the social and behavioral sciences, came the poor old humanities. The students often equated the humanities with all of the liberal arts; and every one of them, the students usually agreed, was a "gut"[11] major that prepared you for nothing at all in life. Sometimes capable, hardworking students did choose to major in these subjects out of pure interest in them. But to do so, they had to swim upstream against student opinion; they had to be forever excusing themselves to their friends for their peculiar choice. "He's a throat personality in a gut major," an acquaintance of one such misplaced student joked about him in 1978.[12]

What made most students think that some majors were more difficult than others? First of all, like many of their elders, the students firmly believed that mathematical and scientific knowledge was intrinsically harder to attain, more cumulative, and more precise than the knowledge typical of the social sciences and the humanities. You could not fake a knowledge of mathematics, they believed, whereas reading and writing, the cognitive skills that counted most outside the sciences, were much more "subjective." Reading as most students thought of it was actually entirely unproblematic; who, after all, could not read by the time they got to college? [13] Writing, on the other hand, could be difficult. Writing was obviously not a talent everyone possessed. There was some difference of opinion among the students as to whether it could be learned or not. But if you could write, then you could "bullshit" your way through almost any course in the humanities or the social sciences, the students believed. For who could say why one paper received an A and another a B?

> Most engineers [believe] that their discipline is far more demanding in terms of time, brainpower and competition than any others, except Pharmacy or the other sciences. . . . Non-engineering majors . . . have the easiest life in college. To study their material requires only reading whereas engineering requires reading, comprehension, and problem-solving. . . . However, I do respect [nonengineers] for the amount of papers they must write.—Senior male, engineering major

Non–science majors sometimes tried to argue back against these collective put-downs of their chosen fields, but they also often accepted them as well:

> Sociology, sometimes known as the "articulation of the obvious," is an example of a discipline lacking esteem. People . . . more readily accept mathematical science because [it] represents concrete knowledge. Whereas Human Communication, Philosophy, Anthropology, and Sociology, some of the many liberal arts, are based more on abstract thinking and abstract principles. —Sociology major, undergraduate paper [14]

> The most serious and intellectual of all students seem to be those in engineering and pre-medicine. . . . Unfortunately psychology majors are not seen as very intellectual or challenged academically. When a person is a psychologist, it is respectable, but before they get there they are seen as having a gut major and an easy course load. . . . For some it is a major to take when you don't know what else to major in.—Junior male, psychology major

The students had another, even more convincing reason for ranking the majors according to difficulty, however: their own correct sense that the various academic departments and programs in the college gave widely differing grades for widely differing amounts of required work. And the difficulty of a given subject did tend to correlate with its perceived vocational desirability, for a very simple reason. Administratively, the college and the larger university had been set up to operate as an academic marketplace. Under guidelines from the state of New Jersey, the resources the academic deans gave to the various departments—faculty positions, secretaries, budgets—were partially "enrollment driven." The more students your department taught, the more resources you could demand and the larger and more influential your department could potentially become within the university. The fewer, the smaller you were likely to shrink.

Therefore, professors in student-poor departments were often encouraged by their chairmen to "up their enrollments" by making their classes more attractive. Better teaching was one way to do so. Easier grading was another obvious technique. Faculty members in the student-rich departments, on the other hand, often felt overburdened. The deans never increased their resources fast enough, they complained, and therefore they had too many distracting undergraduates around; how would they ever get their research done? They could thus afford to be much tougher in their grading. They could afford to "maintain standards." They could afford to "resist grade inflation." They could even institute weeding courses!

The degree to which this economy of supply and demand actually determined grading and the perceived difficulty of different majors was indicated by a list that the dean's office of the Faculty of Arts and Sciences, the biggest faculty unit serving Rutgers College, quietly circulated to all its departments once a year, probably in an effort to shame its easier departments into shaping up. In these lists, the departments and programs were ranked according to the percentage of A's, B pluses, and B's that each one had given across all its undergraduate courses during the previous year. The 1986 list (table 7.2) had the easiest departments at the top, the most difficult at the bottom. The range was striking, as were the distributions. The department at the top was over two times easier than the department at the bottom. It had given 72 percent A's, B pluses, and B's, while the department at the bottom had given 30 percent. Also note the degree to which the humanities really were easiest according to this evidence, the social sciences somewhat harder, and the hard sciences hardest. Finally, note the generally direct correlation between the majors in highest

TABLE 7.2 / Departments and Programs, Easiest to Toughest Grading (FAS Departments and Programs at Rutgers College). Capital Letters represent those in the top ten in Table 7.1

1	/	American Studies
2	/	Italian
3	/	German
4	/	Hebraic Studies
5	/	Spanish and Portuguese
6	/	Chinese, Comparative Literature, and Slavic Languages and Literature
7	/	Women's Studies
8	/	Linguistics
9	/	Puerto Rican Studies
10	/	Labor Studies
11	/	Africana Studies
12	/	Classics and Archaeology
13	/	POLITICAL SCIENCE
14	/	French
15	/	Biochemistry
16	/	Anthropology
17	/	Religion
18	/	Sociology
19	/	Philosophy
20	/	ENGLISH
21	/	Geology
22	/	HISTORY
23	/	Art History
24	/	Statistics
25	/	PSYCHOLOGY
26	/	Physics and Astronomy
27	/	BIOLOGICAL SCIENCES
28	/	COMPUTER SCIENCE
29	/	Medieval Studies
30	/	ECONOMICS
31	/	Chemistry
32	/	Interdisciplinary Studies
33	/	MATHEMATICS

demand in table 7.1 and some of the tougher subjects (in capitals) in table 7.2.[15]

Most students did not know about the existence of this list, but they did have a working sense of what it reported. At the easier end of the scale, for instance:

> I've made the dangerous discovery that I can do a various amount and even quality of work and maintain good grades. Thus it has become a matter of how little work I can get away with and keep my [B average] or better. The nature of my major (English) aids in maintaining my lax study habits. Since exams are totally subjective and paper topics are chosen by the students, one doesn't need to read all of the books and attend all of the lectures. This year I have become amazed at just how little work is necessary.—Junior female

Liberal Arts Ideals

As suggested above, the students' vocationalism actually matched them up very well with their professors; it made them into fellow specialists. Just as the most important piece of information two faculty members usually exchanged when they first met was their department affiliations, so, too, What's your major? was often an early question between two new student acquaintances. And most of the faculty had even less interest in general education than their students did. The small number who cared about general education were almost always in the humanities or in the less-popular social sciences, and, among other possible motivations, they probably saw in resurrected liberal arts requirements a shot in the arm for the enrollments of their beleaguered disciplines. The vast majority of Rutgers professors, on the other hand, were perfectly happy to go on being what they had been since graduate school: experts in narrow academic subjects. If you trained the undergraduates to think intensely and pre-cisely about some special problem, they sometimes argued, then you were doing most of your pedagogical duty by them.

Most undergraduates claimed to be interested in the intellectual sub-stance of their majors. Those who were not were usually in the presumably more useful majors and did not dare to drop out of them (or sometimes their parents would not allow them to). Their majors aside, however, the students I knew best on Erewhon Third and Hasbrouck Fourth tended to regard most of the rest of the curriculum as a necessary evil, as something they had to sit through in order to get a college degree. Occasionally they

found an interesting course or professor outside their major, or a second- ·
ary interest, as a result of all the other things they wound up taking in
college. And this was good, they usually believed; college should be an intellectually broadening experience. But very few Rutgers undergraduates
went out of their way for liberal arts values, and none of them had anything like the old liberal arts ideal for comprehensive breadth as educational authorities sometimes daydreamed about reviving it at Rutgers in
the mid-1980s: science, social science, English and other humanities, a foreign language, mathematics, the arts, other cultures. The average student's
spontaneous liberal arts motivation amounted to something like, I'll major
in this because I want to be a thus-and-such, and maybe I'll also study a
little of that on the side because it's good to learn new things in college.
One's major was like a job; one's other academic interest was like a hobby.

Sometimes the students' hobbies could be quite engrossing. Three of
the students on Hasbrouck Fourth in 1984 were obsessed with theater
and with acting. One (Carrie) was majoring in it, however; a second (Dan)
went into theater by dropping out and going off to drama school in New
York. Only the third, Art, stayed with his more "practical" poli-sci major.
Three or four other residents of the floor daydreamed about making a
living at creative writing, majoring in something allegedly more practical
and minoring in English to hone their artistic skills. As mentioned earlier,
art history was also a popular way to pick up a little culture. Sometimes
initial motivations for the pursuit of culture seemed to be trivial ones:

> Hey, man, I enrolled in Art History this semester? And it's really *interesting*.
> Can't you see me at 48 or something, walkin' down the street with my wife, and
> we walk into some art museum, and I say to her, "Look at the shape of this
> line. Look at the naturalistic posture of that statue." I'll blow her mind!
> —Sophomore male, Hasbrouck Fourth, 1985

Initially trivial motivations could lead to real changes in direction, however. One sophomore on Hasbrouck Fourth started the year as a bored
and mediocre economics major, then took art history, and by the end of
the year had switched into it. "Economics majors are a dime a dozen," he
accurately observed. He was not going to get a job right out of Rutgers on
the strength of such a specialization. "I might as well study something that
really interests me in college," he decided. Practical considerations might
have influenced him even in this choice, however, for an older student in
the fraternity he had joined had found a lucrative part-time job in a local

art gallery that year, selling "corporate art." (At the end of the year, this older student gratified the deans by throwing a small art show in his fraternity, an almost unheard-of act of culture in the Rutgers Greek community in the 1980s.)

The hardest-working student on Hasbrouck Fourth in 1984, a senior who lived two doors down from me (Eric, chapter 3), came to me with the following unsolicited confidence during the first week of the fall semester when he heard I was a professor:

> When I came here, all I wanted to do was major in business and become an accountant, and I just took the courses I had to. Then, in my sophomore year, I started to get dissatisfied. I realized I was cheating myself. College should do more than just get you ready for a job in life. It might be the last time you have in life to try new things, to experiment, to really broaden yourself.

So he had applied to the General Honors Program as a late admit and had taken three of the best undergraduate courses he had had at Rutgers, he said. Now he was writing what turned out to be an impressive senior research paper in economics. The following summer, he celebrated his graduation with high honors by going on a cultural tour of Europe. And the following fall he reaped his reward: law school at the University of Chicago.

Choosing Courses

Rutgers undergraduates usually began to wend their way through the vast curriculum by the choice of a major, ten to twelve courses tightly or loosely structured according to the department. The students' remaining general college requirements were then exceptionally flexible ones. In its most recent curriculum revision in the mid-1970s, Rutgers had divided all its departments into one of three curricular divisions: Humanities/ Languages, Social Studies, and Science/Mathematics. You had to take a six-course minor in a department under one of the two divisions that your major was not in and a two-course "mini" under the other. You might thus decide on an old-fashioned liberal arts combination—English, history, and physics, for example. But you could also graduate from Rutgers in the 1980s with a major in dance; a minor in health, physical education, and sport studies; and a mini in meteorology.[16] Everyone had to take an expository writing course in her or his freshman year. Then you simply needed a minimum cumulative grade point average (a "cum") of 1.8, a little less than a C, and a total of 120 credits to graduate. This might mean another nineteen courses, the choices strictly up to you.

How did the students make these choices? Educational planners sometimes assumed that they did so on purely pedagogical grounds, but the students' decisions were actually based on intricate calculations and trade-offs of necessity, interest, convenience, availability, and difficulty. First you took care of requirements in your major. In some of the bigger, more popular subjects (economics or computer science) basic courses might "close" early; they might fill up with students. You might need several semesters to get yourself into one of them. Then you started thinking about your minor and your mini; what did you find interesting? Alternatively, what possibly complemented your major and made you vocationally even more attractive? Economics and English, for instance. Then, what fit your preferred hours and days for classes? What, on the other hand, was impossible? Did you have to make a campus bus connection between back-to-back classes on different campuses of the sprawling New Brunswick system? (On the spread-out Rutgers-New Brunswick campuses, see appendix 2). Forget it. Eliminate one of those two classes, this semester at least.

You also wanted a balanced schedule—one that was not too difficult in any particular semester and that perhaps combined boring requirements with more interesting electives. Some students signed up for their electives blind, but more experienced undergraduates asked around, and they often checked with a number of other students; a single opinion could be misleading. They also knew that it was the professor, not the subject, that they needed to find out about most carefully. Was she or he interesting? Fair? A hard grader? One tactic for finding out for yourself was to over-enroll: sign up for more courses than you intended to take in a given semester, attend all of them for a week or so, and then drop one or two that you found boring or badly taught or too difficult.

You were willing to put up with tough grading in a course you had to have, in microeconomics for you economics major, for instance. You were less likely to do so for Introduction to Anthropology. There was a difference between a liberal arts course of average acceptable difficulty and a "real gut," however. An average introductory course in the liberal arts might give mostly A's, B's, and C's, with the middle of the curve in the B's. A gut, on the other hand, most students agreed, was a guaranteed A or B in exchange for almost no work.

The biggest guts were usually widely known among the students. In the mid-1980s, according to the sophomores on Hasbrouck Fourth, they included Theater Appreciation, Italian Cinema, Word Power, Literary Experience, "Cowboys and Indians" (History of the Wild West), Baby Bio, and the very popular Drugs and Plant Hallucinogens. These last two courses had, apparently, been thoughtfully provided by the biological sciences department in order to help non–science majors locate a handy two-course mini in one of the sciences. It did not hurt to take the occasional gut, most students agreed, but you should not take too many of them if you were serious about your academic career. Bio-sci majors should avoid them entirely, in fact, several students told me. Medical schools could spot them by their titles alone, premed advisers had warned them; they weakened your record. A common tactic for students who did take such courses was to claim around their friends that "this course *used* to be a gut, but this year they've started to make it tougher."

Almost all the students believed that the general advisers available in one of the deans' offices knew very little of the real nitty-gritty of the curriculum; they believed they could learn of it much more reliably from their peers. You might go to these advisers to make sure you were straight on college rules and regulations, but many of the students never did so. And the separate faculty advisers in the departments only knew about your major; *you* knew more about the rest of the curriculum than they did.[17]

ACADEMIC PRACTICES

The academic routines of Rutgers students in all relevant time frames— daily, weekly, semester-long, and over their four-year college careers— were determined by their basic vocationalism, by their weaker desires to improve themselves by studying some subjects for their own sake, and by two other contextual factors. The first was that (as discussed in earlier chapters) college in undergraduate assumptions should be a sensible balance of work and play, of academics and college life (see chapter 2). There was a time and a place for academic work and for intellectual endeavors, most students believed. But the rational undergraduate should also devote at least as much time to pleasure and relaxation.

The other fundamental determinant was the simple fact that the one thing college gave you back in return for your tuition payments and all your academic hard work was grades. Three sociologists have written an excellent ethnography of the grading process at the University of Kansas based on research in the late 1950s that proves that the pragmatics of "making the grade" came first for almost all the students and that substantive intellectual understandings of the material they were learning came a distant, optional second (Becker, Geer, and Hughes 1968). The mentality is undeniably a general one among American college students, as central to undergraduate academic routines at Rutgers in the 1980s as it was at the University of Kansas twenty-five years ago. The only puzzle is why three otherwise intelligent sociologists should have expected—given the institutional structure of modern American higher education, especially in its mass, state-college version—that any other socially conditioned mentality might have dominated among the students.

Freshmen Adjustments

The undergraduates usually entered Rutgers as vocationalists, with career goals and intended majors linked to them. If their majors proved too difficult for them, they traded down into something easier and, they generally then discovered, more interesting. In discussions at the beginning of the year about their reasons for being in college, freshmen rarely referred to an interest in pure learning, but they often talked earnestly about their hopes to succeed in class. They had typically been good but not outstanding scholars in high school—"not the cream but the top of the milk," as an admissions official once quipped.

Admissions standards had slowly climbed in the 1980s as Rutgers upgraded its faculty and improved its general reputation and as a decent state-college education became a better bargain in the inflationary market of American higher education. By 1985, average combined SATs[18] for incoming freshmen were a little less than 1100, ranging from 600 for some educationally disadvantaged students to as high as 1500 for specially recruited students in the general honors program. These academically advanced undergraduates had been attracted to Rutgers by the promise of small classes, good teachers, and intellectual equals in a public institution that cost about a third as much as Harvard or Princeton. Given their presence, plus that of average students and of marginally qualified undergraduates, the Rutgers student body was thus as diverse academically as it was in almost every other way:

> Rutgers, in my opinion, is not considered a school for the intellectual elite. However, Rutgers is anything a student wants to make of it. If a person chooses to travel in cerebral circles, the opportunity is there to do so. . . . If a student wants only to party and clown around, there's plenty of opportunity for that as well.—Freshman male

Most incoming students expected college to be more difficult than high school, where they had often gotten by on charm, intelligence, and perhaps an hour of homework a day at the most. Now they were going to have to learn to work harder, without parents or guidance counselors around to prod them. And the competition was more intense—even, perhaps especially, for the bright honors students:

> At first, [my honors] seminars were very intimidating. Most of the references flew right over my head and everyone seemed to be speaking with such authority. My notebook margins are filled with notes to myself: "Camus? Who is this?" Or "Read *Das Kapital*" (an effort since abandoned).—Senior female

> After hearing some worldly-wise sophomores express interest in surrealism (?), op art (??) and composer John Cage (???), I felt like enrolling in my local community college. My first assignment in [one course] was to read fifty pages from *The Locke Reader.* "Locke who?" My knowledge of history didn't extend past America, and I had never read anything written earlier than 1850, except Shakespeare.—Junior female

Non–honors students had to learn how to *really* study for their big classes. The crunch often came after first midterms. C's and D's??!! So, sitting around in the lounge with a book open was not really studying. Reading something through quickly did not make it stick. Listening to lectures without taking good notes was not enough. Most freshmen made adjustments. Sometimes friends helped, but more often the novices figured out new study routines for themselves. With the exception of some of the disadvantaged students,[19] however, hardly any of the freshmen sought or received guidance from professors or from other adult advisers about how to cope with the new academic challenges of college.

An important adjustment for almost all the students was finding a quiet place to study, away from the noise and hedonistic distractions of undergraduate society in the dorms. Not even your room was sacrosanct, for you could not shut out your roommates. Here is an academically serious senior giving a bemused chronicle of what his two sophomore roommates had put him through in one three-day period at the end of the spring semester in 1986:

> Monday night Ed and Mike distracted me from typing by talking to me and starting a pillow fight. Tuesday and Wednesday night they "interviewed" prospective roommates to replace me after graduation. Tuesday afternoon Mike listened to albums on headphones loud enough that I could hear the music, which I knew well. Tuesday evening (twice) and Wednesday afternoon and evening, Mike complained to me about his having four papers due in two days after his band's first date. Wednesday afternoon and evening Mike and later Ed and I discussed the two poems I had just written for my creative writing class. Wednesday night and Thursday afternoon Mike and I listened to albums. All in all, about ten hours of distraction . . .

On the College Avenue Campus, favorite hidey-holes for studying included the main library, the pretty old Sage Library at the Theological Seminary, and "the Tombs," underground classrooms left open late at night in three of the dorms. But not "The Roost," an all-night study hall—not if you were serious about your work, at least. For The Roost, most students agreed, was really for "scoping" and for picking up girls and guys.

Classroom Realities

The freshmen also had to learn to cope with the anonymity of the big classes and with the uneven quality of undergraduate instruction. The distance between the faculty and the students had been steadily increasing at Rutgers for at least eighty years; the trend was a national one in American higher education. In the early twentieth century, American professors had given over their older function of in loco parentis to the new deans of students and had organized themselves into purely academic professions. But as late as the 1930s, faculty members at Rutgers had still taught four classes a semester, three class meetings a week, Saturdays included. Most classes had had less than thirty students in them. And one alumnus remembers that virtually all his professors had known him personally and that some had taken a long-term avuncular interest in him.[20]

In the 1980s, on the other hand, Rutgers faculty members with ordinary release time for research taught something closer to an average of two undergraduate courses a semester at the most.[21] Classes met twice a week, everyone avoided Fridays, and Saturday classes were gone out of memory.[22] Professors rarely had students more than once, and, especially in the larger classes, they hardly ever knew them by name. The professors were almost as anonymous to the students as the students were to the professors. There was the occasional faculty "superstar"; and that was exactly the way one or two best professors were known by their student admirers, like celebrities in popular culture—known about, but not known. But the great majority of the professors, perhaps 99 percent of them, were virtually faceless. I had some version of the following conversation several dozen times in my two years in the Rutgers dorms:

> *Student:* I had a good [or bad] course [sometime in the past] in [such-and-such a department] on [such-and-such a topic].

> *Anthropologist:* Oh yeah? What was the professor's name?

> *Student:* What *was* [her or his] name?

State-supported research-and-teaching universities like Rutgers commonly adopted this form of mass education in the United States in the late twentieth century in an attempt, their leaders said, to provide the average undergraduate with at least some access to scholars of national and international reputation, while also giving these professors the time to do the research necessary to be significant figures in their specialized fields, and while also keeping student tuition down. From the point of view of the faculty, however, research and teaching were certainly not in an even balance. Career success at Rutgers in the 1980s depended so predominantly on research that it is not surprising there was a considerable amount of indifferent teaching in the undergraduate college. What is more surprising is that there was any good teaching around at all.[23]

And there was some, the students usually testified. In one classroom poll I took in 1987, the undergraduates were asked to imagine that they were looking back at Rutgers twenty years after graduation. Did they think they would remember a particular professor or professors as persons who had really influenced them, who had really made a difference in what they were today? To my considerable surprise, 82 percent of them said yes. (This same poll was also cited in chapter 2.)

The average was not nearly so good, however. The *Survey of Student Satisfaction* released by the Office of Institutional Research at Rutgers in 1986 claimed in its early pages that the majority of the undergraduates at Rutgers considered at least half their professors to be "superior teachers" who were "genuinely interested" in their students.[24] The meaning of this generalization was unclear, however, and the data had been treated in an irregular way that served to make mixed results look better than they were. Reanalyzed, data from the report suggest at least as much unhappiness as happiness with their teaching on the part of the students; average opinions were closer to those expressed in narrative form on many of my student papers in 1986 and 1987.[25]

[In my first year at Rutgers] I have had several bad professors. One mumbled his lectures in a monotone, while another was as confused and disorganized as his students were. . . . Occasionally one finds a teacher who can keep his class alive and eager to learn.—Freshman male

Most of the classes that I am currently taking are very boring. My friends and I feel that it's virtually impossible to get to know our professors on a one-to-one basis, and to spend some time discussing various things with them after class. I get jealous when my friends from other colleges tell me that their professor took them on a field trip on his own time or simply invited them for a barbecue to his house. . . .—Sophomore female

If forced to evaluate [my college teachers], I would be hard pressed to find many who would merit a grade higher than a "C".—Junior male

I have had a wide variety of classes and even a more, let's say, diverse array of teachers. Some have made the class extremely interesting while others have disillusioned me with flimsy concepts [and] irrelevant data and statistics. —Junior female

In my four years at Rutgers, I have had very few teachers that have stood out as above average.—Senior male

I am a senior . . . and until this year I have never had a teacher that has left an impression on my mind.—Senior female

When I first came to Rutgers, I was ambitious and excited. While many of my peers felt overwhelmed by the sheer size of the university, I saw a great challenge lying ahead of me. There was no end to the opportunities that lay waiting. Unfortunately, somewhere along the line, I became alienated. With the majority of my classes being 100–200 people (one this year is even 400 people), it is easy to become lost in the shuffle. It was a hard adjustment to make from high school, where I had close ties with many of my teachers. —Senior male[26]

How big were the classes at Rutgers in the 1980s? The information was sunk somewhere in the university's computers; it was almost impossible to dig it out, I was told. In a brief classroom questionnaire made out by 149 randomly chosen students in 1987, however, the average estimated class size in the courses these students were taking at the moment was 110 students. Classes of 300 and 400 were quite common. Less than two-thirds of the students had even one class, out of the four to six they were carrying, with 25 or fewer students in it. Sophomores reported the largest average class sizes, 144 students per class; the small writing course required of most first-year students may have kept the freshman average down to 108 students per class. Juniors dropped back to an average of 101 per class, and seniors, perhaps because they were involved in more specialized work in smaller advanced subjects in their majors, reported the lowest average, though it was still 86 students per class.

When thinking about formal learning, the students clearly disliked the herd approach to higher education.[27] In other ways, however, this aspect of academia contributed to the students' freedom and autonomy in college. Mandatory attendance—rules about "cuts"—had been abandoned in the late 1960s. Grading in the larger classes was usually done solely on the basis of two or three "objective" tests announced well in advance. Only in some of the tougher subjects did some of the tougher professors call on the students by name. In the smaller discussion sections for some of the larger classes, perhaps 10 percent of the students spoke up on a regular basis.[28] The majors differed widely in difficulty, and there was always an attractive sampler of gut courses available in any given semester. You could, in other words, take it very easy indeed in the Rutgers classroom in the 1980s if you so desired. Or you could pace yourself exactly as you liked. And so the students did.[29]

Styles of Studying

Even though up-to-the-minute preparation was not really necessary in most Rutgers classes, some students did study steadily and hard all through the semester for reasons of their own. On hundreds of daily time reports, perhaps a sixth of the undergraduates indicated that they studied four to five hours a day, five days a week (or more), and casual observation in the dorms supported these claims. Some of these grinds were in the sciences and had to work this hard. Others were not.[30] Some studied hard out of anxiety and the desire to succeed:

> Speaking only for myself, I can say that grades are important!! My grades illustrate my effort, enthusiasm, determination, intellectual ability and understanding, dedication and discipline. . . . For me, grades seem to be linked with confidence level and level of self-esteem. I've always lacked in the confidence department. I think a good grade helps me out in that sense.—Senior female

And some apparently did so, amazingly enough, for reasons of curiosity, intellectual drive, and the pure love for learning.

A larger minority of the students, perhaps about a quarter of them, took the opposite tack. They took advantage of the latitude built into formal education at Rutgers in the 1980s to slide through college on as little academic work as possible:

> The best way to describe the attitude around my apartment (all seniors) is, "sit and wait to graduate." . . . I've come to the conclusion that it is possible to do virtually nothing at college and still manage to pull Cs.—Senior male

Some of these "blow-it-offs"[31] had marginal grades. Others were doing better by, as one of them put it, "living on the edge," by loafing all semester and then compensating with intense cramming and sometimes with "all-nighters"[32] around exams:

> I . . . am the type of person who works best under pressure; or shall I say, who works, only, when under pressure. Even when I am aware that an exam will be

given in a couple of weeks, or even days, I am unable to bring myself to study in advance . . .—Sophomore female

When I finally crack open the book before the exam, I often get this enlightened experience and think: "Ahh, this is what the Professor has been talking about all these weeks."—Senior female

The rest of the students, about half of them, chose the middle path, the golden mean of modern college life (see chapter 2). Like the blow-it-offs, they alternated between ease and hard work, but they did so less drastically. They enjoyed extracurricular play ten or eleven weeks out of the average fourteen-week semester, but they still studied during these periods of low intensity from one to three hours a day, three to four days a week. (With an ordinary five-course load, this worked out to between twenty minutes and an hour and a quarter of study time for every eighty-minute class meeting.)[33] They then worked much harder around exams, but not in the states of near-panic (not in extremis) as the blow-it-offs sometimes had to do.

Many students studied this way at Rutgers without thinking about it much. For others, however, this was a well-reasoned pace for learning, which, they argued, was the most sensible adaptation to the nature of teaching and testing at Rutgers in the 1980s. Their arguments were persuasive. And they explained why, from a professor's point of view, the average student in the average Rutgers classroom did not seem to have done the reading on any given day. This student theoretician of learning came from a family that was unusually centered on education. He defined himself as an intellectual, and he was a nearly straight-A student in his first year at college:

As a general rule, as I go through the daily course of events in class, I do the minimum amount of studying. . . . At any time during this period, if I were given a pop quiz, I would probably fail it. . . .

Three or four days before an exam, I have some idea of what is going on in the class but by no means a full understanding of the material. I very rarely miss a class. I pay careful attention in class and take very thorough notes all semester. It is during the few days before an exam that real learning takes place for me. I devote full time to studying for a specfic exam to the exclusion of all other subjects. . . . At this point, I am motivated purely by the overwhelming thought of the need to succeed. I begin to feel guilty about not putting forth enough effort up to this point. I'll begin to think of the long-range consequences—a failure will keep me out of law school or grad school and I have only myself to blame. I will spend this time reading and rereading every assignment. . . . If I do not understand a concept, I will track down someone on my floor who can help me. . . . I have learned from experience that the night before an exam is best devoted to narrowing in on a specific trouble area. By then, I have become comfortable with the test material.

I feel that with my method of studying (total emersion for two or three days before an exam), I have reached a fuller understanding of the subject by the night before the exam than those students might have who had been doing the reading regularly and who spent the last night reviewing—those same students who just a week earlier were probably ahead of me. . . .—Freshman male

Some students remained faithful to whatever style of studying they entered Rutgers with, freshman through senior year: grind, blow-it-off, or middle-of-the-road. More of them changed, however, in different directions. Some of them changed radically. A few did so every year:

I have been three different students in the three years that I have been at Rutgers: the unfriendly, study-holic, 4.0-is-my-life nerd; the overly-committed-outside-of-class journalist/student; and the average study-a-little, let's-have-as-much-fun-as-possible-before-we-have-to-join-the-real-world college guy. —Junior male

No simple trend or trends in these changes applied to all the students, however. An underachieving high school student might be intimidated by college academics at Rutgers and begin to work harder than she or he had ever done before. A serious student, on the other hand, surprised and delighted by the adolescent carnival of modern American college life, might go crazy for a few years and turn into what one female called herself, a "quasi-derelict." Many upperclassmen suggested that they had matured academically in college; they had "gotten certain things out of their systems" in their freshman and sophomore years, settled down, and were now taking their studies more seriously. Others, on the other hand, indicated that they had wised up. They had learned how to get by on much less work, or they had become cynical or "burnt out" due to their dislike for mass education Rutgers-style. In any case, there were no major differences in study times in the self-reports by college class. The same wide variations and the same averages were reported by younger students and older students alike.

Among the students on the whole, however, most undergraduates were behind in their academic work most of the time. This meant that the workaholics among them were, effectively, rate-busters. And their peers busted on them regularly for their deviant behavior:

> What's more difficult—to get Jane Doe to stop flirting or [name of student being busted on] to stop studying?—Ad in the personals, student newspaper, 1985

> Ask Brian if he wants to go out and shoot a few hoops and he says, "Sorry, guys, I'm working on this paper that's due next February."—Sophomore males, Hasbrouck Fourth, fall 1984

But on the dorm floors I knew best, the mockery of serious students was mild and sometimes even affectionate in tone. For in a mass university, if a few other students worked so hard that they got very good grades, they were not going to affect your grade point average in any discernible way. This would only occur if you were in a small class with them in which the professor graded on a curve. Moreover, given the vocational meaning of college among most Rutgers students in the 1980s, almost everyone knew that they themselves should be working harder. They knew that the rate-busters really ought to be their exemplars.

Nor was there anything wrong, in student opinion, with helping one another out in the quest for good grades. On many dorm floors, informal study groups existed for some of the bigger, more popular courses—friends or friends of friends who were taking the same course at the same time. Someone who had had the course the year before might sit in before exams, with notes or old exams or advice on what the "prof was likely to ask." And, if you lived in the dorms, you could almost always find someone through personal connections who had taken any course you were taking, big or small, general or specialized, for one-to-one help if you needed it.

Cheating to get good grades also undoubtedly went on at Rutgers, but there was no way of knowing how frequently.[34] It was inevitable. For grades often mattered more to the students than the substance taught in courses, at least in some of the courses. So you were not really "cheating yourself" when you cheated; you were getting exactly what you wanted. And, of course, big anonymous classrooms meant enhanced opportunities to cheat. In moods of bravado, some students openly fantasized around their friends about cheating without recrimination:

> My biggest ambition before I graduate from this place is to get a hold of at least one big exam I have to take 24 hours in advance.—Junior male, preceptor, Erewhon Hall, 1979

> They're giving my poli sci exam twice, on two different days, to two different classes. I *know* they're not going to change it that much. So I wonder if I can sneak into the first exam, take it, sneak out with it at the end and then come back and take it for credit the second day?—Sophomore male, Hasbrouck Fourth, 1984

When they actually cheated, however, the students usually did so discreetly, for many of their peers disapproved of it in practice, especially in classes they themselves were taking. They disapproved of it in other students, and they disapproved of the professors for not catching it:

> A major problem [at Rutgers] is student cheating and professors' apathy. *Many* students cheat, and professors fail to monitor them. I am told that the cheater's cheating will catch up with him some day, but that does not console me. The students' cheating directly effects my grades (because of "bell curves") and my esteem . . .[35]

When they were caught, most students claimed that it had all just been a big misunderstanding:

> I did a stupid thing last week, Mike. In an English paper for Professor X, I didn't listen really closely to the instructions. She said not to use the library, to use our own ideas only. I went to the library and copied a few of those things into my paper. I guess it was plagiarism. Only it's funny, I didn't really think of it that way. . . . I really felt like they were my own words after I'd written them down! But she spotted it and asked me about it. Then she gave me a break. She gave me a B. Shit, I was relieved! But she *did* say I would have gotten an A otherwise.—Sophomore male, Hasbrouck Fourth, 1985

HIGHER MINDEDNESS

Were vocationalism and the cold-blooded pragmatics of making the grade all there was to the undergraduates' life of the mind at Rutgers in the late seventies and the eighties, then? Not entirely.

Intellectual Intimacies

There were some classic, old-fashioned American anti-intellectuals among the undergraduates at Rutgers, youths who found any kind of extracurricular thinking on the part of their peers threatening and unegalitarian. To use your mind was to feel superior to other people, they asserted. It was also to be abnormal; it was, prima facie, evidence that you were a nerd.[36] This anti-intellectual specimen—almost too good to be true—lived in a fraternity:

> As far as people who consider themselves highly intellectual and therefore better than other people I have to laugh. . . . [They're] socially inept. It seems to be one of these intellectualities you must wear some kind of button damning one thing or another. . . . They call me stupid, lets see them make 25,000 dollars and a company car to start their first year out of college. . . . Another reason I seem to picture those intellectualities as wimps because they are so busy studying they have no time to work out. . . . Me personally when I'm not going to class, studying or working out I still seem to find dead spots during the day. I like to call these dead spots M-time where I immensely enjoy watching MTV (moron tv).—Senior male

But most Rutgers undergraduates considered themselves much friendlier to intellectual enterprise. Most of them claimed that they did have a higher life of the mind in college. Their modest versions of the liberal arts ideal were one instance of their purer educational values, they felt. Another was their claim that the now-unlabeled college "bull session" was still in fact alive and well at Rutgers in the late twentieth century.

I had not heard much evidence of these spontaneous student-to-student intellectual talks during my two years in the dorms, but my very presence might have inhibited them. However easy and friendly I had tried to act, my undergraduate friends had probably not wanted a known professor listening in on their private intellectual forays. In any case, most of the writers of the self-reports in 1986 asserted, they talked this talk all the time among themselves, about all sorts of fascinating things: the meaning of life, the existence of God, the nature of the cosmos, current national and international political events, the arts, personal ethics and morality, even some subjects they were studying in class. But, they also said, they usually did this talk quietly and intimately, with one or two friends. It was not surprising that I had missed it.

There was, in fact, a certain analogy between sex and mind in the assumptions of the students. The expression of your real, honest mentality, like that of your real sexuality, could make you vulnerable among your peers. It was not that mind was unimportant to the students; it was that it was too important. What if you were not really smart enough to keep up in college?:

> I was very intimidated when I began at Rutgers because all the students I was meeting seemed very intellectual. . . . I found myself with intelligent thoughts behind a very weak vocabulary.—Sophomore female

> I would like to be viewed as someone who is thought to be intelligent. . . . I have talent to fool the average person to believe that I am intelligent but I am not as well informed as many of my friends in such areas as literature or philosophy.—Junior male

What, on the other hand, if you were too smart? You might intimidate those around you, or you might think too differently for the comfort of the average undergraduate; you might really be weird.

In any case, the display of intellect had to be carefully stage-managed in the average dorm. You could be witty and clever among your peers in the low-minded, joking code of Undergraduate Cynical in the dorm lounges, and many students were. I often heard livelier, funnier talk during my day-a-week visits to the dorms than I did among my colleagues in the university for the rest of the week. But to moot serious subjects in the lounges was to risk getting busted upon (see chapter 3).[37] As with sex talk, so, too, with mind talk: the safest place to do it was outside the hearing of the dorm peer-group—very late at night in the lounge with just a few friends, or in your room or a friend's room, or elsewhere. Nevertheless, many students said, such talk was one of the more valuable things that went on for them in college.

[Though I have a hard time with my academic motivation], I enjoy holding intellectual conversations with several people. My roommate is a good companion for this. He and I understand each other very well. . . . A topic that comes up a lot between us, while sitting in our room, is space. We both enjoy thinking about what other planets are like, other galaxies, and in general, what is "out there" beyond it all. Where does it all end? How small are we (humans and earth) in comparison to it all? . . . Is there a God who did it all? . . . How long is forever? How everything is relative. . . . These are some of the questions we try to provide answers to. We often drive ourselves crazy trying, but enjoy it very much.—Sophomore male

Love for Learning

Not all the youths who represented themselves as friendly toward the life of the mind in papers like these were real student intellectuals or highly motivated scholars, however. Only a small number of them, somewhere between 10 and 20 percent of the undergraduate student body as a whole, fell into this imprecise category.[38] About nine of the forty-two students who wrote intellectual self-reports for me in 1986 came across, intentionally or unintentionally, as serious students, as "known brains" or simply as young women or men with a certain passion for learning. How did they get along in a college like Rutgers? On the evidence of their papers, not badly at all.

Aside from them all liking to study, or think, they were a very diverse group. All nine were doing well in their classes. Their average cum was 3.6, or A−; none had less than a B+. Most of them showed evidence of the literate interests in their papers, some of which were written with real flair. Six were women and three were men. Two were majoring in economics; seven were in less-vocational majors, including anthropology, art history, English, history, linguistics, and philosophy. Nonvocationalism, however, did not unfailingly distinguish them from other students. An inherent fascination with what they were learning did. Charlotte, for instance, described below, was as apparently pure in her intellectual drives as any student at Rutgers. But by graduation she was parlaying her abilities into an academic career. She was, in other words, making a vocational choice about what she was good at intellectually.

Lisa, on the other hand, was obviously aimed at a possibly lucrative career: "Upon graduation this Spring, I would like to gain an entry level position on the Stock Market, or in Financial Analysis." But she approached her economics major with an intensity unlike that of the average student and quite like Charlotte's attitude toward anthropology, sociology, political science, and history. Lisa described herself as a cute blond who had done well in public school but who had never been allowed by anyone, including other intelligent students, to present herself as anything but the all-American cheerleader. She had started down this same road at Rutgers, she wrote, with a boyfriend in a fraternity and the attitude, "party when you can, study when you have to." But then, she said, for unexplained reasons, lightning had struck. She had realized that "college is not a playground, but a preparation for the future." She had started to work extremely hard; she had found that she could get good grades, and she had developed a real fascination for what she was concentrating on, economics:

> When I study, it is traditionally done seriously. I am usually up-to-date in my class readings. . . . As I am reading, I take a comprehensive set of notes on the material. These references provide the basic framework for exam studying. I try to liken college with a full time occupation, and devote at least eight hours of my day to classes and studying. . . . I tend to question many of the nation-wide activities which occur. Who has decided on what? How do they know what they're doing—how can they be so sure? I also actively follow the financial news: residential housing outlooks, prime rate, loans, and GNP.

Lisa credited what she considered the challenging, competitive nature of Rutgers with helping her "fight for my rights—specifically, my right to be intelligent." She also gave Rutgers credit for providing her with at least the occasional peer who encouraged her in such tendencies:

> I was introduced [at a recent party] to a 23 year old guy who allowed me to take pride in my gesthalt being. We started talking about Marketing and Finance. This was one of the most stimulation conversations. I would venture to say we talked "business" for a good four hours. We were completely in tune . . . [and] I greatly respected this man's inputs and logic. At the end of the night, he told me he had never had such a conversation on such a wave-length. He had admired my thinking and my mode of rationality. He confessed that the initial reason he was introduced to me was because of my looks. "You are a very special person, not because of the way you look, but rather because of your brain," [he told me].

Workaholism did not unfailingly distinguish the nine student intellectuals from the rest of their peers either, however. Five or six of them did describe themselves as moderately hard-working to very hard-working scholars. As Lisa further characterized her work habits, for instance:

> On the average, I study between four and five hours a day . . . [and] around 17–18 hours per day during finals. . . . I am also prone to crying jags, violent fits, (i.e. throwing things at walls), and breaking up with my boyfriend [during finals]. Luckily, people realize that this is only temporary.

The other three, on the other hand, were guilt-ridden, last-minute workers ("I have spent the last four years honing my procrastination skills," as a senior female among them wrote), though they did do enough studying to maintain decent grades. But like many of the hard workers, they also applied their minds to extracurricular reading, lectures, art, politics, and so on:

> With my feminist friend . . . [I] discuss sexual inequality, the peculiarities of male-female behavior, the kind of men we like, and how much we dislike the repressive and conservative attitudes of mainstream Americans. With my friend from New York . . . I discuss sexual topics, the injustices of life, anthropological articles I have read and found interesting, political situations and foreign films. With my friend, who is interested in Art History, I discuss travel, being in Europe, the behavior of Europeans, the trendy scene in New York and London . . . and what little I know about art.—Junior male[39]

> My friends and I usually don't go to parties during school. Instead, when we get together, we'd more likely go to a movie or go to a musical event. When I have discussions with my friends, the flow of the conversation always seems to drift toward an intellectual topic.—Freshman male[40]

Most of these student intellectuals considered themselves part of an intellectual minority in college:

> I realize that my pursuit of knowledge may not be normal by Rutgers standards, indeed it seems strange amongst most of my friends.—Senior female

One of the nine felt embattled and lonely in this minority status. As Jane, a junior, wrote of her freshman year:

One thing surprised me very much, everyone was unintellectual. I discovered I couldn't find anyone to have an intellectual conversation with, I had thought that was what college was all about. The most intellectual my [sophomore dorm at Douglass College] ever got was during a game of Trivial Pursuit. I spent most of my time [that year] in Hasbrouck Hall with my friend Ruth who had transferred to Rutgers College.[41] I noticed there that people studied [even] less and I watched in amazement at the lengths Ruth went to hide her intelligence and her near perfect cum.

By my junior year . . . I felt I was beginning to learn only for exams and then forgetting everything (except for art, which stays with me always). My social life at Rutgers is minimal at best. Ruth now lives at [the science campus], too far to drop in for a few hours. . . .

It doesn't bother me as much as it used to that most Rutgers people are anti-intellectual. I'm learning many things that I can use later when I do meet people who share my interests . . .

Most of the rest of them, on the other hand, were much happier at Rutgers. Their experiences as reported in these papers suggest that, whatever its imperfections as judged against Harvard or Reed or the University of Chicago—or against Allan Bloom's never-never land of great books and great men and no corrupting ideas or cultural influences originating after about 1850—a big state university like Rutgers managed to be as satisfying a place for these bright late-adolescents as anywhere *they* had ever known.

They had adapted to Rutgers, they suggested, in two opposite ways. Two or three of them had sought out and (unlike Jane) found like-minded friends in college, all through the general honors program, though not unproblematically. Charlotte, for instance—academically, the highest flier of the lot—had really felt that she needed peer-group support in college. For as a female who liked to use her mind, she remembered being even more miserable in her elementary and high school years than Lisa had been:

When I was a small child my parents sent me to an alternative nursery school where I learned to read, add, subtract and multiply before I could tie my shoes. That was the last place where I felt completely free intellectually. When I entered the real world known as public school . . . I soon learned that unadulterated intellectual zeal was a real social liability as I was labelled "a real weirdo" and was summarily ostracized by my peers.

Charlotte had been planning to attend an expensive "little Ivy" college when, she wrote,

> the Rutgers Honors Program decided to woo me . . . [depicting] itself as an elite bastion of true learning dedicated to protecting those few individuals with combined SAT's of 1300 or more from the harsh anti-intellectual world know as Rutgers . . .

But though she had made her first college friends through honors and through living in a special-interest dorm during her first two years at Rutgers, honors had not been a panacea for Charlotte, and the other honors students said similar things. For the undergraduate honors elite also contained its frauds and its charlatans:

> Honors seminars became something of a letdown. In the typical seminar half the class was apathetic, two or three students were really interested in learning, and two or three were interested in hearing themselves talk. I was soon able to spot these "pseudo-intellectuals," who knew a great deal about esoteric subjects about which most people knew nothing. They could avoid doing the work that was assigned by bullshitting about their preferred tangential topics.

Thus, by her junior year, Charlotte discovered that she was friends with intelligent academic dropouts rather than with classroom achievers like herself. And they were not entirely comfortable with her classroom abilities, she felt—"I finally feel comfortable with myself as an intellectual," she wrote in her paper that year, adding the marginal qualification "most of the time":

> Sometimes I still have reservations about fully participating in class, especially if a friend of mine is in it. Few of my friends actually see me in the classroom but when they do I think that they respect me overall. . . .

Whatever her doubts about her peers, however, the heart of her mental life in college by her third year, in Charlotte's opinion, was what went on between herself and her professors:

> I have encountered some truly outstanding professors at this University from a variety of departments. I regard a few of them as friends and can go to them with either intellectual or personal problems. A good professor also brings out

the best in me. If a faculty member really impresses me I will overextend myself in order to earn his or her respect.

And she was not kidding. For Charlotte had a real talent for ferreting out capable faculty members in the subjects of interest to her throughout the university, and then figuring out ways of studying with them in small classes or, preferably, on a one-to-one basis.

Pedagogy of this sort is what the leaders of mass institutions like Rutgers hope can go on for undergraduates, at least occasionally. Charlotte was very unusual, however. It is difficult to say how representative she was of even the most academically engaged students in the college. Very few other students were so self-confident, for example. In her self-report, she hinted at a personal self-doubt or two, but she did not seem to have any doubts at all about her intellectual abilities, or any reluctance in demanding personal attention from busy, invariably research-productive professors.[42] Moreover, from a teacher's point of view, Charlotte was very easy to like. Her intelligence and her ability were difficult to miss.

The description she wrote in her self-report of both the appeal and the limitations of anthropology as it is often presented at an elementary level in college, for instance, is as insightful, and made me feel as uncomfortable, as any I have read:

> Anthropology first appealed to me because it offered the fantasy of fitting into another culture when I couldn't fit into my own. Many ethnographies read like fairy tales: timeless and faraway with problems rarely more significant than family squabbles. Reading an ethnography about women's trading societies in West Africa conjured up an image of proud, black women striking through the forest earning the respect of men. A year later I learned that this culture area had been fucked over by the colonialist powers, that their land had been sacrificed to a monocrop economy, that they lacked skilled people to combat hunger, illiteracy and population problems.[43]

Accordingly, though she had completed the requirements for her anthropology major, Charlotte had also moved toward a more comprehensive education in her junior and senior years through an interdisciplinary mix of courses of her own choosing in sociology, political science, and history. By the time she graduated, with highest honors, headed for an excellent graduate school in history, five or six of the best professors in three or four different departments in the university reciprocated her regard.

The rest of these nine bright students had led much quieter academic and intellectual lives among their peers in college. Judging from their self-reports, in fact, it is doubtful that many of their professors even knew they were out there at all. Yet they had apparently been just as happy at Rutgers as Charlotte had been, but in more private ways. Some of them wrote heartfelt eulogies to the pleasures of thinking and learning in college:

> Many of my intellectual interests are now fostered in the classroom. I tend to apply what I learn in class to other aspects of my life. . . . My main outside interest is studying people. . . . I prefer to remain personally anonymous; Rutgers can be a good place to do this.—Sophomore female

> I really enjoy learning; it gives me a feeling of self-control, because no matter what a teacher says or does in front of me, only I can determine what is accepted by my mind and what is rejected.—Junior female

> I love reading good literature and writing short papers on what I have read. To pull apart a novel in my mind and find associations and links within the story, and to organize my thoughts into a paper is the most stimulating intellectual activity I know. I like to being writing the papers around eight o'clock at night. I sit in front of my typewriter, writing and revising sometimes until dawn. Then I crawl into my bed totally exhausted, but satisfied with the work I have just created.—Senior female

Otherwise they described amiable existences in college among academically more average undergraduate friends and acquaintances.

It seems fitting, in the end, to bring the curtain down on this chapter—and on all seven of these essays—with the stories of two of these easy-going student intellectuals, both of them seniors, a male and a female, looking back untraumatically on what they recalled as four happy academic years at Rutgers. The first of them, Joe, an English major who hoped to go into publishing after graduation, wrote easily and fluently about himself as a reformed nerd:

> Throughout my elementary school years, I was occasionally referred to as a "brain," and even through high school it was generally assumed that I spent most of my time studying—apparently because I was small and quiet, wore glasses, got good grades . . . and was rarely involved in any extracurricular activities at school. Even through college that stigma has remained with me to some extent, but rarely has it really been accurate.

For Rutgers had opened him up as a human being, he believed:

> At Rutgers . . . [I have] been more exposed to other points of view and ways of thinking which have contributed to my own intellectual development. . . . I am a friendlier person now. . . . I rarely turn down the chance to "party," but I also pay attention to what goes on around me at an intellectual level.

But Joe had also led an unconflicted cerebral existence in the college, as he described it. In his earlier schooling, he said, he was "mostly spoon-fed 'general knowledge' with little motivation to pursue other intellectual avenues"; but Rutgers had challenged him and broadened him pedagogically. He had enjoyed reading "a large number of novels from all periods of English and American literature" in his major, and he found the intellectual substance of his minor, history, equally fascinating. He approached his studies rationally and carefully:

> [This week I finished all my work except for] my assignment of reading Robert Burton's *The Anatomy of Melancholy.* . . . The twelve-page paper I typed Monday was the result of one night of preparatory note-taking, three nights in the library and one afternoon at home writing, and about four hours of typing, not to mention a few hours of reading (I received an A) . . .

In his spare time, he wrote, he enjoyed talking to his two younger roommates and listening to music with them (one of them was in a rock-and-roll band), watching "M*A*S*H" and "Star Trek" on TV, doing a little light reading, writing songs and poems, and even attending the occasional poetry reading on campus.

Susan, our second and last student pilgrim through the dungeons and dragons of the undergraduate college, had always loved school, she tells us in her introduction, "or at least learning." She had always been an "avid reader"; she kept two or three journals ("one personal, one is a record of my dreams, and another is just random observations"); and, like Joe, she was also majoring in English. Unlike Lisa and Charlotte, however, she does not remember being miserable as a bright female in elementary and high school. But she had come to college with certain unrealistic fantasies about contemporary American higher education in its state-college version, at universities like Rutgers: "I was the first person in my family to go away to college and my mother and I shared the same romantic expectations: ivy-covered walls, arguments about philosophy and politics in the student union, [professors who looked] like John Houseman [in *The Paper Chase*]."

The actualities of Rutgers had been rather different, but they had not thrown her, at least as she remembered them with a certain glee four years later (a remarkably tolerant mother also clearly deserves some credit):

> We were all in for a big surprise. Freshman year brought huge changes in my attitudes, behavior and language. My mother would shake her head jokingly and say: "I spent 18 years raising a lady, and look what Rutgers did in 6 months." Much of freshman year was about meeting people and socializing instead of enriching my mind. My tales of shaving cream fights, hickey patrols (in which one sneaks up on an unsuspecting male friend and tries to leave the largest mark possible upon his neck), and co-ed naps were first met with amazement and then laughter. "But when do you go to class?" my mother kept asking.

But college fun and games had not made Susan forget what she had wanted to get out of college intellectually. Even in her fun-filled freshman year,

> I usually studied on my own and my roommates and friends thought I was fun but still a little too serious. I spent a lot of time wandering around Alexander Library pulling books off the shelves that looked interesting. I read a lot about film and art during that year. Sometimes I think I learned as much in those hours lounging on the floor between racks as I did in the accumulated classroom time.

During her subsequent years at Rutgers, Susan, like Joe, went on to balance the sociable pleasures of modern college life with her friends against a more personal set of intellectual pleasures, enjoyed alone or more intimately. She recounted her private curriculum vita, in strong disagreement with my initial putdown of undergraduate life of the mind in the dorms.

> In this regard, I disagree with your general statement that freshman and sophomores spend little time discussing anything serious. I've spent every year here involved in late night conversations about a lot more than who was sleeping with who. As a freshman, one of my friends on the floor was a member of Hassidic Youth and a Zionist. I left knowing the Middle East situation inside out, at least from the Isreali viewpont. Friends on other floors were political science or philosophy majors and we spent time trying to figure things out.

Sophomore year I spent most of my time off-campus as I was involved with an older man. We spent a lot of time museum-hopping and in this way I also learned a great deal. Junior year I met my current apartmentmate, Julie, and spent a lot of time discussing politics and feminism. . . . In the spring of my junior year I was in England and learned a great deal from the people I was travelling with. The whole field of literary theory, before unknown to me was opened up and explained along with communism and Marxism.

What, in the end, was this bright young woman's overall assessment of the undergraduate college on the eve of her graduation as a senior? Clearly, in her opinion, she had benefited in most ways from her four years in a state university. She saw no obvious contradiction between the juvenilities of undergraduate student culture in the dorms and the higher educational ideals she felt she had also been able to fulfill at Rutgers; they were complementary parts of college in her underlying assumptions about it (see chapters 2 and 6). Not even sex and culture had apparently been in conflict for her (museum-hopping and that "older man"). Nor did she have any complaints about being harassed for her love of learning by her peers; quite to the contrary.

She was apparently depressed by her belief that the only way she could go on being an intellectual after four years in modern American higher education was to continue into graduate school, down the road of academic specialization:

I don't know if my enamourment of academic would ever prompt me to become a professor or not. It seems to me that at a school as large as Rutgers, professors tend to become too specialized, and the thought of studying early American literature for thirty years both bores and terrifies me.

Whatever she did with her life after graduation, however, Susan wrote in conclusion, she could not ever imagine doing it without a college or a university like Rutgers somewhere near her to do it in:

I still haven't read half of what I expected to when I came here four years ago. I plan to spend the next year or so catching up on a lot of the books that I have written down as "Must Reads." . . . I [also] plan to spend the next year or so in close contact with the college community, still attending lectures or movies. When I eventually settle somewhere, I plan to make it near a university town so that I can always return . . .

Further Comments

1 / Since this chapter is more about the official purposes of higher education than many of the preceding chapters have been, its contents are likely to be particularly sensitive, perhaps even more sensitive than the material in chapters 5 and 6. My overall feeling is that educationally Rutgers is not doing all that badly by its undergraduates. This judgment is only possible, however, if one cuts away much of the customary rhetoric about higher education and looks at the actual social structure of American public universities in the late twentieth century—and at the larger American culture (and economy, and polity) in which colleges and universities are embedded—more realistically. Though the undergraduates' point of view on this subject may come as a shock to some readers, this *is* what I am trying to do in this chapter.

It would be a valuable outcome, on the other hand, if some of the lowdown on higher education from the students' point of view emphasized here made a difference in contemporary undergraduate teaching. But it would be a mistake to use this chapter as a stick to beat only Rutgers with. For, as indicated in passing here and elsewhere in this book, there is every reason to believe that Rutgers is typical of American higher education in the late twentieth century—when it comes to the nature of its current trade-off between research and teaching and when it comes to the often only marginally intellectual mentality of many of its students (but see also appendix 2 on the typicality of Rutgers).

Meaningful institutional reforms, if considered necessary, must therefore be aimed more at all of American higher education than at one college and university open-minded enough to allow an anthropologist to poke around in it freely for a number of years. As the recent Carnegie Report suggests, new national agendas on undergraduate education may be necessary: more money and social prestige for undergraduate teaching, revised institutional relationships between research and the rest of college in all or most American colleges and universities, and tougher-minded stratifications of research-oriented and teaching-oriented institutions and professors (see Boyer 1987). These reforms would have to affect higher education and the academic professions at a national level in order to be effective in any particular college or university. If

Rutgers, for instance, suddenly announced that it was going to make undergraduate teaching count as much as research, it would no longer have much chance of attracting the best young academics; trained in research, they would go off to other, more normal places instead. And the best established scholars already on the Rutgers faculty would probably make arrangements to do the same.

Other conceivable reforms would require types of social and cultural change that do not seem within the realm of likelihood in late-twentieth-century American society, in this anthropologist's opinion at any rate—the de-bureaucratization of American life, for instance, or a reversal of the growing hegemony of an aural and visual popular culture over literate culture, a hegemony driven by a smart, cynical marketplace whose central purpose is to sell more products.

2 / Unless otherwise identified, the quotes in this chapter are taken from various academic and intellectual self-reports, which Rutgers undergraduates wrote for me in large classes in 1986 and 1987. As in previous chapters, these student papers are quoted without correction.

The assignment for these "life of the mind" reports resembled the one for the sexual self-reports used in chapters 5 and 6, though the topic was not as sensitive, and these reports were not anonymous. How do you study? What are your daily, weekly, and semester-long patterns? What is your opinion of classroom learning at Rutgers? How have you changed academically and intellectually in your years in college? How else do you use your mind at Rutgers besides in your studies? Is there much spontaneous intellectual talk among the students, in your experience? Is undergraduate Rutgers an intellectual place? What other kinds of students are there at Rutgers, academically and intellectually speaking? And so on.

3 / The Rutgers question asked students if they were "generally satisfied" with their overall education. Nationwide reactions to a similar but not identical question were a little lower. According to "Student Opinion Survey Normative Data," collected by the American College Testing Service between 1983 and 1985, 79.3 percent of the students nationwide were satisfied with their particular college. At universities of over ten thousand students, 82.9 percent of the undergraduates were similarly satisfied. (Material subscribed to by the Office of Institutional Research, Rutgers University, produced by the American College Testing Service, Iowa City, Iowa.

311

My thanks to Rod Hartnett and Ellen Kanarek for making this and other information from the Office of Institutional Research available to me.)

4 / The apparent non-vocationalism of American undergraduates in the sixties may have been a special case, a deceptive baseline of comparison for the seventies and eighties. For the sixties themselves look increasingly like a historical fluke in retrospect. Three intersecting causes of the political and cultural radicalism of the period stand out twenty years later. The first was the temporary demographic bulge in the college-age cohort as the baby-boom generation reached late adolescence; there were fewer older authorities around relative to the numbers of college-age youths during those years than has been the case at any other time in the twentieth century (see Elder 1980). Youth was therefore, demographically, uniquely in the driver's seat during those years. Second, college-age males were vulnerable as cannon fodder in a very unpopular war between about 1965 and 1972, and thus ripe in a way they had not been before and have not been since for politicization by the small minority of "protestors" whom Horowitz has shown could be found on most American campuses after about 1910 (see Horowitz

1987, chapters 7 and 10). Third, the overheated American economy seemed always to be moving into yet a higher gear in the sixties. One felt one could be as idealistic as one wanted in college and still come up with a good job after college (and the subsequent career patterns of many of the activists of the sixties has verified this optimism).

Vocationalism, in any case, has always existed among American college students, as Horowitz has also shown (Horowitz 1987, chapter 8). And political and cultural idealism has not been its principal alternative on campus in the past, nor has scholarly-mindedness. Since 1850, the biggest nonvocationalists in American colleges have been the aficionados of the adolescent pleasures of "college life."

5 / They did this so efficiently, in fact, and they then defended the boundaries of their chunks of the intellectual world so carefully, that the basic disciplinary divisions in which they happened to fall between about 1880 and 1910 are still frozen into the organization of American higher education in the late twentieth century, despite all the changes in expert knowledge in intervening years (my thanks to sociologist Andrew Abbott for this point, made in an interdisciplinary

faculty talk at Rutgers in April 1986).

6 / In a recent review article of the work of Richard Sennett, historian Jackson Lears has eloquently sketched the cultural appeal of "being a professional" in late-twentieth-century American middle-class culture:

> Autonomy [has been an American cultural ideal since the late nineteenth century], but the basis of autonomy has shifted from ownership of a business to ownership of knowledge. "I want to get enough knowledge so that no one can tell me what to do," says an ambitious 19-year-old. Expertise confers badges of ability on the successful and an aura of mystery [on] the policies of the powerful ("They have their reasons."). But the expert is also the quintessential autonomous man: he is needed more than he needs others; like the nineteenth-century artist, he seems a fully developed, unified self." (Lears 1985:92).

7 / The relationship between the undergraduate colleges (Rutgers College and a number of others) and the faculty units at Rutgers-New Brunswick was very complicated, the product of a long history and of many trade-offs between different pedagogical interests and philosophies. By the mid-1980s, most of the older liberal arts faculties (humanities, social sciences, and mathematical sciences) resided in the New Brunswick–wide Faculty of Arts and Sciences. Rutgers College undergraduates could major in all of these FAS disciplines. They could also major in communication, one of the disciplines in the separate School of Communication, Information and Library Studies, but not in other disciplines. Likewise for the Faculty of Professional Studies: yes for Health, Physical Education, and Sport Studies; no for most other FPS disciplines. Finally, engineers, pharmacists, and students in a school of the performing arts and in a new business school were said to belong to their own separate colleges with their own separate faculties; but, since these "colleges" had no campuses, these students were permitted to enjoy residence life in the Rutgers College dorms (or in any of the other three residential colleges at Rutgers-New Brunswick). See appendix 2 for a fuller explanation of some of these local complexities.

8 / Undergraduate preferences at Rutgers College were very much in line with nationwide trends. Between 1963 and 1983, for instance, the percentage of bachelor's degrees awarded in business nationwide went from 12.5 percent to 23.4 percent of the

total degrees awarded, and new fields such as computer science, communication, and criminal justice grew from 14.6 percent to 30.6 percent of the total. Psychology also expanded in these years, from 2.7 percent to 4.2 percent. Most of the older arts and sciences, on the other hand, declined: foreign languages, 2.4 percent to 1.0 percent; philosophy, 1.0 percent to .4 percent, English, 7.4 percent to 2.6 percent, social sciences, 15.9 percent to 9.8 percent, mathematics, 3.9 percent to 1.3 percent; and physical sciences, 4.0 percent to 2.4 percent (figures reported in Hacker 1986).

9 / The following description of the pecking order of the majors is a least-common-denominator account of some general undergraduate attitudes. A careful cognitive anthropologist might find it too monolithic—might discover, using finer-tuned methods, more variations in student perspectives than I am indicating here. Students who read over this sketch for me, on the other hand, have said that it does capture the average climate of opinion among the undergraduates quite well.

10 / Back in 1978, I had a sophomore roommate on Erewhon Third who was trying to major in bio-sci. One day he came back to our room worried because he had received a low grade in one of his difficult initial prerequisite courses. What would he do if he could not "make it" as a premed? His comment, as much to himself as to me, indicated the close connection in his mind between the two top vocational choices among the undergraduates at Rutgers, between the highest in prestige and the most common. "I can feel," he muttered, "that old business-managerial feeling coming over me."

11 / *Gut:* an easy course. The term is a general one in American college culture, and, according to a number of slang dictionaries, dates from around 1950. None of the three or four dictionaries I consulted, however, suggests why *gut* in this context connotes something easy; most of the other connotations of the word have to do with authenticity or toughness or important essentials. Given the date, the word may have come out of military slang. Could it be an elliptical abbreviation of *gutless?*

12 / Between about 1960 and 1980, *throat*—short for "cutthroat"—was a Rutgers undergraduate term for a hard-working, aggressive student. It seems to have been Rutgers-specific; it did not seem to exist in other American colleges. It died out among the students between

my years on Erewhon Third in the late 1970s and on Hasbrouck Fourth in the mid-1980s, however.

13 / Lots of students could not read, many of the faculty were convinced—in the sense of knowing how to really read a text in a critical way, distinguishing fact from opinion, information from interpretation, one's own quick sense of what the text means from what the author might really have meant.

14 / My thanks to Professor Randy Smith of the Department of Sociology at Rutgers for passing this student text on to me in 1979.

15 / Sometimes professors in the easier departments tried to claim they were such good teachers that their students learned much more and thus deserved to earn higher grades. It was probably true that professors in these departments did, on the average, put more into their teaching than those in the bigger, more overburdened departments. The students did not uniformly rate professors in these departments as their best teachers, however; they certainly did not think their classes were as difficult as classes in many of the more vocationally prestigious fields; and it is unlikely that differential teaching quality would have produced such systematically scaled results across a wide range

of faculty members as table 7.2 indicates.

There are some interesting anomalies in table 7.2, however. I cannot explain the relative difficulty of Medieval Studies, for instance. Art history, another subject in the humanities that is too difficult by my reasoning, had, according to one senior member of that department, established a departmental tradition that A's were not to be given out easily, that there was a real corpus of knowledge to be mastered before a student could earn an A. Perhaps the Department of Art History could afford to be tough-minded because the average undergraduate often thought of art history courses first when she or he decided it was time to pick up a little culture in college.

English, on the other hand, would probably have been higher on the list, "easier," if it were not for the thousands of grades in freshman composition that its departmental averages apparently included—a requirement for all the freshmen and hence a course whose grading could be reasonably tough.

As for economics, I have said that the students considered it no more difficult than the other social sciences, yet it is down among the most difficult subjects according to this list. It did require more mathematics than the average social science, yet some very indifferent students somehow managed to stay alive in it. The lack of any real writing requirements in its large classes may have helped. But perhaps the department could maintain tough grading standards *and* large classes because the students were so eager to major in economics that they were willing to remain in the department even when their grades were lower than would have been considered acceptable in some social sciences. Or even in a harder science— there was no point in staying in biological sciences with low grades, for example, since you would never get into a good medical school. Many economics students, on the other hand, probably had no particular postgraduate plans. They might just have figured that they would not be in bad shape after college as long as they had any kind of bachelor's degree in economics, regardless of their grade point average.

16 / Meteorology actually only became available as a mini in the sciences in the late 1980s, and I do not in fact know how easy or challenging it was. Prior to that, however, crafty undergraduates could avoid the tougher sciences with the help of the two-course mini Baby Bio plus Drugs and Plant Hallucinogens, in bio-sci.

17 / One of the biggest sources of student complaint, according to the *Survey of Student Satisfaction* released by Rutgers University in 1986, was the advising system. A number of students disliked what they saw as the rudeness and ignorance of many of the general advisers and the low availability of the departmental advisers (see Rutgers University 1986). Even if these flaws in the system were corrected, however, I would predict that peer-group opinion of professors and courses would still be a much bigger determinant of course selection than any official advice the students might take. The reason is simple. The undergraduates in fact know more about the overall undergraduate curriculum than virtually any of the overspecialized adults in the college or university do, or are likely to know.

18 / *Combined SATs:* combined scores of the *verbal aptitude* and *math aptitude* college entrance exams (Scholastic Aptitude Test) given by the Educational Testing Service of Princeton, New Jersey. The range on both of these nationally administered tests was 200 to 800. The lowest possible combined score was thus 400; the highest, 1600.

19 / Of all the undergraduates, disadvantaged youths in the Equal Opportunity Program (EOP)

tended to be the least alienated from college adults. Their EOP counselors really did look after them on a careful, personal basis, they often indicated with some gratitude.

20 / My thanks to Professor Richard P. McCormick for this memory of undergraduate Rutgers in the 1930s.

21 / There was, in fact, a wide disparity between different departments on this matter. Faculty in some departments in the humanities and social sciences had been soldiering along with three-course loads for years. Others had figured out ways of effectively reducing their load to two courses or even fewer. Teaching loads tended to be particularly light in some of the resource-rich sciences.

22 / Odd survivals of older Rutgers pedagogy still lay scattered through the modern curriculum like dinosaur bones, however. A maximum full load, for instance, was eighteen credit hours, or (on the fiction that two eighty-minute meetings per week in each ordinary course amounted to three hours of classroom contact) a six-course load. Why eighteen credit hours? Probably because in the nineteenth century everyone attended classes together for three hours a day, six days a week—for eighteen classroom hours, in other words. (Similarly, the word *class*,

which refers both to all the students who entered college in a given year and to a given group of students studying a given subject with a given professor at one time, is probably also a throwback to older, much smaller scale times when all the youths who came to college in a given year *did* sit through all the same subjects together, with the same professors, for all four years in higher education.)

23 / "Teaching effectiveness" was one of three "major criteria" in faculty promotion packets at Rutgers in the 1980s. But the other two were "scholarly and creative activities" and "research accomplishments." Except in a few of the arts, however, where creative activities were distinct from published research, no one could ever explain the difference between these two latter criteria. On the promotion committees I knew, they tended to be taken to mean that research was to be counted twice (or it was simply widely understood that research was really most important, regardless of what the paper criteria said).

Moreover, it was widely argued that teaching could not be evaluated as objectively as research, which was validated by peer review and publication with the best journals and scholarly presses. It certainly was the case that Rutgers had no system in place in the 1980s that might have made a similarly objective evaluation of teaching possible: regular visits to classrooms by impartial faculty observers, for instance (though some departments did do this with some conscientiousness internally), and student evaluations administered and collected every semester by administrative offices rather than by the professors and the departments in question. (Very few colleges or universities nationwide had anything like this in the 1980s either, it should be noted.)

Finally, in the early 1980s, as Rutgers increased its drive for a faculty of national and international reputation, a quiet message went out in most departments to young professors who did not yet have tenure. Do your teaching as efficiently as possible. Avoid all other institutional commitments (committees, for example). Put all your remaining energies into your research. One to two books with the best university presses, plus X number of journal articles, was now the minimum requirement for promotion to tenure at Rutgers. Your reputation in your wider scholarly community also depended on your research, and a key to major career advancement was being offered a job by more than one university.

Against all these incentives, there were some merit awards for distinguished teaching at Rutgers, with small increments of money attached to them, controlled by various chairs and administrators. Some faculty members tried hard to get them. But in the absence of a legitimate, universitywide system for teaching evaluation, their conferral often appeared to be capricious. You were more likely to get them, many professors believed, by adroit politics in your department or in the wider university than by giving yourself over heart and soul to your teaching.

24 / The survey was actually given to undergraduates in all the colleges in the New Brunswick system. And the important subaggregate data discussed in the following note were not broken down by college. The aggregated Rutgers College responses to these key questions, however, were reported to be within one percentage point of the universitywide undergraduate responses. (See Rutgers University 1986.)

25 / The key survey question was phrased, "How many of the faculty you've had at Rutgers would you say are superior teachers?" The reported "majority" of the undergraduates who answered "about half" or more than half was

actually a majority of one percent, however, 51 percent versus 50 percent. And what was the meaning of "superior" likely to have been to the students? Compared to what? Did it mean the opposite of "inferior"; did it mean "above average"? Were about half the students thus saying that half or more of their professors were above average? If so, this is an unusually neat result, which apparently reflects the literal meaning of *average.*

Even stranger, the answers were aggregated inconsistently, in a way that served to make mixed responses look better than they probably were. First of all, the actual percentage of responses to each of the choices provided ("almost all" my professors have been superior, "more than half," "about half," "less than half" and "none") never appears in the report. Rather, the first *three* responses ("almost all," "more than half," and "about half") were added together and compared to the last *two* ("less than half," and "none").

Figure 7 in the report suggests what the universitywide responses in each disaggregated choice might have been, though the disaggregated percentages have to be estimated by eye off the odd bar graphs. According to these graphs, about 4 percent of the students said "almost all" of their professors

were superior teachers; about 14 percent chose "more than half"; about 32 percent chose "about half"; about 48 percent chose "less than half"; and about 2 percent chose "none."

Thus, whatever "superior" meant to the students, if these responses are redrawn with five side-by-side bars, the actual pattern appears to be skewed to the right, toward "inferior" professors. Alternately stated, if the 32 percent of the students who answered "about half" is considered to be the middle of the curve, or a neutral response, then only 18 percent of the students were actually saying that a clear majority of their professors were "superior teachers," versus 48 percent who were saying the opposite.

The same odd graphic treatment was given to answers to the question, "How many of the faculty you've had at Rutgers would you say are genuinely interested in students and their problems?" The asymmetrically stacked bars in this case seem to show more positive responses than negative ones, 56 percent versus 44 percent rather than about fifty-fifty. But the disaggregated responses indicate the same negative skewing: about 7 percent said "almost all," about 16 percent said "more than half," about 34 percent said "about half," about 43 percent said "less than half," and about 2 percent said "none." See Rutgers University 1986: introductory pages, table 5B (the second line in the label for this table is erroneous) and figure 7 (the key to the graphics reverses the identity of "almost all" and "about half," it was admitted on inquiry in 1987).

26 / The university's survey also asked for further comments, and printed fifteen pages of them for Rutgers College alone. Very few of these comments praised the teaching at Rutgers; or if they did so, it was with many qualifications. Far more of them made the same sorts of mixed or negative evaluations that the students in my classes did:

> "Some of the teachers in this University are not quite up to the caliber I expect at a major University. I actually feel these instructors are not as qualified or as well-read in a subject as they should be."

> "I think the problem with the curriculum lies in the lack of interest and enthusiasm that professors (and T. A.s) display when teaching introductory courses (i.e., the first two years at Rutgers)."

> "I am dissatisfied with most science and math courses. The classes are too large, the teachers are inadequate and the grading system does

not show one's true intelligence. The main goal seems to be failing as many people as possible . . ."

> "I found it very refreshing to find teachers who took a sincere interest in their students. I came across a few such teachers but not many . . . it took me nearly 2½ years . . ."

> "In the field of academics, Rutgers has many fine teachers. They are, however, often overshadowed by the extremely poor ones. It has always puzzled me why the students are given teacher evaluations in only certain classes . . . and if they are distributed why any negative comments never seem to have any effects . . ."

> "I regret coming to Rutgers. The student are treated like shit. . . . The trend towards research is going to mess things up even more for undergraduates. We need teachers not researchers."

Etcetera. See Rutgers University 1986: last pages on Rutgers College (the document is unpaginated).

27 / To the open-ended question, "What [in your opinion] is the worst thing about the formal or classroom education at Rutgers?" over a quarter of more than two hundred students in a class in 1987 said that the classes were too big, and another one in

five deplored the "impersonality" of academic Rutgers, "being a number," or the "Rutgers Screw." Another one in five singled out particular inept professors, variously described as "bad," "boring," "terrible," "illiterate," "droning," "wandering," "rotten," "uncaring," "prejudiced," "old," "slow," "snotty," and "don't know how to teach" (many such responses). And in progressively smaller percentages, the students answered: too many teachers with marginal English; mechanical or routinized teaching; stressful exams; particular bad departments; getting by without learning anything; being taught "irrelevant" information; and, finally, as an aficionado of college life put it with a certain clumsy eloquence, "Class is the tediousness that the student body goes through between weekends."

I asked the opposite question as well, "What is the best thing about the formal or classroom education at Rutgers?" To this question, about two out of five of the students could think of nothing at all to answer. About one in four mentioned particular courses, subjects, professors, or departments they liked. About one in ten cited small classes with lots of discussion. And the rest responded, both seriously and cynically: the cheapness of the education, the diversity of the curriculum, the diversity of the students you could meet in class; the good "guy-watching" or "girl-watching" opportunities in the bigger classes, the availability of lots of "guts," sneaking out early, not having to come in the first place, having a good place to catch up on your sleep; and finally, "it beats working."

28 / And these smaller sections still ran to thirty students or more in many courses. Truly small seminar groups, six or eight students for instance, were almost unheard of at the undergraduate level outside some of the smaller departments (where, given the constant pressure from the dean's office to keep enrollments up, they were usually unintentional).

29 / American undergraduates have always had creative ways of getting through college with as little work as possible, of course; they did not all work hard back in the good old days when the professors knew them better. In fact, they may well work harder in the late twentieth century than they did in the past, for there is now more vocational pressure on them to get good grades than there once was. The anonymity of contemporary Rutgers requires a student to make up her or his own mind about how hard to study, probably a more legitimate motivation in

the minds of most late-twentieth-century American adolescents than closer personal supervision by adults. The pedagogical losses in the movement toward mass education, then, probably have less to do with how hard the students study, on the average, than with the actual quality of their educations—if one thinks that some sort of steady personal guidance or example of how to think is what teaching is really all about.

More systematic social historical research about how students actually used their time in past undergraduate generations could be done. Student diaries are one good source of evidence. The economy of supply and demand is another. In the 1880s, for instance, Rutgers was so desperate for students that a president took pride in having *raised* admissions standards to the point where Rutgers only accepted three-quarters of its applicants. And in the same years, the entire graduating senior class had grades averaging about 88. Average study times are not likely to have been extravagant in such an environment. Throughout the nineteenth century, American higher education was overexpanded and student-poor (with less than 5 percent of "college-age youth" going to college). With the educational booms after World War I and World War II, colleges were under-expanded, which led to tougher grading. In the 1980s, by contrast, Rutgers College seniors had "cums" averaging 2.768, roughly in the B− range. The recent grade inflation followed the overexpansion of higher education after the 1960s.

30 / In the "life of the mind" papers written for me in 1986, eight of the forty-two student writers, 19 percent, reported that they were unmistakable workaholics. Two were in stereotypically tough majors, premed and electrical engineering; three were in economics; and the remaining three were in communication, graphic design, and anthropology, respectively.

31 / *To blow [something] off* (slang from the mid-1980s; I did not hear it in the late 1970s): to skip it or miss it, to goof off.

32 / If "losing it" was the central trauma (and drama) of the students' sex lives (see chapter 5), "pulling all-nighters" was the most dramatic act in their academic lives. Most of the students had tried all-nighters at least once in college. About two-thirds of them concluded that they did them more harm than good.

33 / My percentages are approximate and my sample study times are illustrative. There was, of course, a continuum between

those students who hardly studied at all and the maximum grinds, who could have been working as much as (who knows what went on at the outer reaches of the science campus?) twelve hours a day, seven days a week.

34 / Undergraduate cheating is also a grand old tradition in American higher education, of course. An odd piece of evidence for the antiquity of the practice at Rutgers is the derivation of the unusual name of the Rutgers campus newspaper, *Targum*, founded by the undergraduates in 1869. In mid-nineteenth-century student slang at Rutgers, by a complicated derivation, a *targum* was one of the "trots" or "ponies" that the students commonly sneaked into their classes with them at the time. And the first *Targums* were written in such a way—through allusion, euphemism, and the use of slang— that they surreptitiously conveyed lots of student-to-student information, which adult readers could not decode (see Moffatt 1985b: 62).

More recently and more generally, 50 percent of a sample of students in a nationwide survey published in 1964 admitted that they had copied someone else's exam, used crib notes, plagiarized, or turned in someone else's paper as their own at least once during their college career (William

Bowers, *Student Dishonesty and its Control in College* [New York: Bureau of Applied Social Research, Columbia University], cited in Becker, Geer, and Hughes 1968:101 n. 4). A variety of surveys done in the 1970s indicated a wider range of rates around the same general average: Stanford, 30 percent; Johns Hopkins, 30 percent; Amherst, 43 percent; Dartmouth and University of Michigan, between 50 percent and 60 percent (see Levine 1980: 66–67). Since it is the institutional structure of American higher education as much as any free-floating pure morality or immorality among the students that generates cheating, contemporary Rutgers is probably in the same ballpark.

35 / Comment of a Rutgers College undergraduate, quoted in *Survey of Student Satisfaction* (Rutgers University 1986).

36 / *Nerd:* a socially inept youth. The term dates from about 1960. Its origins are unclear, though one slang dictionary speculates that it came from "nuts," by the derivation "nuts to you!" "nerts to you!" "nerd!" (*The New Dictionary of American Slang,* ed. Robert L. Chapman [New York: Harper, 1986]). Since nerds are by definition obtuse about the all-important norms of adolescent style generated by mass consumer

culture, they are easy to spot. Nerdiness is always externally manifested:

> Certain traits are indicative of nerdhood . . . sneakers worn with black socks; polyester button-downs; glasses—thick lensed smeared, or perhaps broken; armfuls of textbooks even when not needed; a math/science orientation; unwashed, greasy, or dandruff-rife hair; wan complexion; severe slimness—accounting for the term "pencil necked."—Sophomore male, short paper on *nerd*, 1987

> Math/science/engineering majors; radical Sylvia Plath-types; greasy hair; body odor; ill fitting clothes; complete ignorance of the American popular sub-culture known as "teenager," i.e. sex, drugs and rock and roll; dull; academic to the point of constant study; generally an underbuilt male.—Sophomore male, short paper on *nerd*, 1987

In general undergraduate opinion at Rutgers in the 1980s, nerds were not invariably intelligent, but excessive use of the mind could generate nerdiness; smart students had to be especially careful to guard against the tendency. Most students believed that someone could be intelligent without being a nerd, however.

37 / Undergraduates who were (as one honors student put it) "known brains" sometimes transformed the basic rules of dorm banter in interesting ways. Consider the following description of informal talk among four males on a special dorm floor reserved for honors students on the College Avenue Campus. (My thanks to Theresa L. Reynolds for this account, written for a Rutgers honors class in ethnographic method in 1987.)

> At first they didn't know what to talk about. Someone suggested "chicks." Matt replied, "I like it when they waddle after their mother . . ."
> Scott began to converse seriously: "I think it's stupid how people try to make [the modern world] fit into religious prophesy. I mean, the king of the north is really the Soviet Union and Ronald Reagan is the seven phallused dragon. I mean, come on!"

> *Matt:* "Religious prophesy was really intended as propaganda for the oppressed Christians of Rome."

> *Jeff:* "The Christians weren't oppressed."

> A small argument ensued as to whether Christians were oppressed by the Romans or not. It somehow led into everyone telling what religion they were.

Jeff: "I'm kind of nothing."

Matt: "I'm a Christian, but of no particular denomination."

Scott: "I'm of the ten dollar denomination."

Andy: "I'm a Taoist Agnostic Utilitarian."

Another discussion about utilitarianism and John Stuart Mill started. Someone mentioned a comparative essay on Mill and Marx. Scott commented that he once did a paper on Haley Mills and Groucho Marx. . . .

Andy reentered with the statement that "you need four limbs to drive a manual transmission" . . . [and he] began to read a passage from V by Thomas Pynchon (his favorite author . . .). The passage concerned a stickshift . . . [as] it was used erotically by a woman. . . . As a result conversation switched to one concerning cunnilingus . . .

What was going on here? On the one hand, these intellectually oriented young men were signaling that they were better read than the average student. The level of their references aside, however, they were playing by exactly the same rules of Undergraduate Cynical as students on ordinary dorm floors. Like other, more 'normal,' male undergraduates at Rutgers, they were competing with one another in their display of rapid, dismissive vulgar wit.

38 / This is obviously a very approximate judgment on my part. Many more students, somewhere between a half and two-thirds, undoubtedly felt themselves to be genuinely interested in some part of their formal educations, usually in their majors. The one in ten to one in five were those who struck me (professorially) as youths for whom intellect somehow seemed to be at the core of their identities, as youths who, if I had a chance to know them as a teacher in a small seminar class, I thought might impress me as outstanding or unusual students.

39 / This student was undefensive in his intellectual self-report about being homosexual. Perhaps because of the prejudice directed against them by most undergraduates at Rutgers, gay students had little to lose by being intellectual as well. In 1984–1985, I attended several meetings of the undergraduate lesbian-gay association and visited with large and small groups of homosexual students half a dozen times. Many of them were strikingly more aware of political issues, the arts, and the New York cultural scene than the average heterosexual student at

Rutgers. As one perceptive heterosexual male on Hasbrouck Fourth put it in 1984, with a certain hyperbole:

> You almost *have* to be gay these days at Rutgers to be a really interesting person (I'm not).—Sophomore male

40 / One of these two males was actually in the hard-working category. There were no easily detectable differences in the distributions of females and males between work-oriented and play-oriented students in these forty-two intellectual self-reports, by the way. Nor did there seem to be differences in the much more numerous twenty-four-hour time reports (I did not cross-correlate reported study times with sex, in part because there were such wide distributions in each sex that it did not seem worth the effort).

41 / By a small-world coincidence, this was the same Ruth who had lived on Hasbrouck Fourth the year I studied that floor, the hard-working sophomore woman on the low side (see chapter 3).

42 / A further mark of her sagacity, or of her preadaptation to an academic life, was that she was rarely fooled by certain faculty blowhards who often sounded good to naive undergraduates but had long since been written off by their colleagues. She was unfailingly intellectually attracted to professors who were both good undergraduate teachers and well-respected by their peers.

43 / To be fair to my own discipline, there are many anthropologists who analyze Third World cultures in this second, politically critical vein. It doesn't sell nearly as well at the undergraduate level, however; the average Intro student seems to like the fairy-tale approach much better. And it is often hard to resist providing what the market demands, especially when one is continually being judged for one's enrollments.

Appendix One
On Method

Once upon a time, an anthropologist's discussion of method could consist of a little story about how she or he achieved rapport with the natives, and perhaps of some notes on the quantity and nature of the data collected. No longer. For in the last decade, the writing of ethnography—of cultural descriptions—has become a much more problematic, self-conscious activity in American and British anthropology. In a series of subtle meditations about the sort of "experience-near" knowledge that participant observation actually produces at its best, Clifford Geertz has been a leading influence on this new self-critical mood in the discipline (see, especially, Geertz 1973, 1976, and 1988). The simplest points Geertz has made in these essays are negative ones—how traditional western cultural anthropology has mystified its readers with its implicit claims to actually *re*present the native point of view; how the participatory strategy of "Being There" does not in fact answer all the important questions about how ethnographers know what they know or about how they tell what they know to their readers. As Geertz argues in his first revision of older, unreflective views about the nature of ethnographic knowledge:

> [When we say] that descriptions of Berber, Jewish or French culture must be cast in terms of the constructions we imagine Berbers, Jews or Frenchmen to place upon what they live through [this does not mean] that such descriptions are themselves Berber, Jewish or French—that is, part of the reality they are ostensibly describing. . . . [Rather], anthropological writings are themselves interpretations, and second and third order ones to boot. By definition, only a "native" makes first order ones: it's *his* culture. (1973: 15)

But where do we go from here? One direction—a virtual subfield of ethnographic experimentalism in cultural anthropology in the last decade—has been toward more-tentative ethnographic writing, especially toward descriptions that are more "dialogic" and "reflexive"; that is, descriptions that include the anthropologist's and the subjects' talk and argumentation in the descriptions, that try to involve the subjects in the interpretative process, that reflect back on one's own cultural presuppositions as the source of what one sees and thinks about in an alien culture (see Marcus and Cushman 1982; Clifford 1983; and Clifford and Marcus

327

1986). I have attempted to draw some of these new values into some of the essays in this book. In chapter 1 and especially in chapter 3, for instance, I try to distinguish in the writing between what I saw and heard, and what I inferred from these perceptions. And in chapter 5, I could think of no other honest way of presenting such sensitive material except by problematizing the interpretative process to the extent that I did.

I have included as much of myself in these essays as I have for two reasons. It is a convenient way to get certain kinds of description done (see Geertz 1988: 101 n. 15). And I wanted to reveal enough of the details of my research methods in the dorms to allow the reader to evaluate what I am presenting.

Too much of this tentativeness and reflexivity, on the other hand, makes for wearisome reading. It also tends to shift the focus of an ethnography away from what still ought to be anthropology's proper subject, other peoples and cultures, to "wonderful, empathetic, dialogic *me* (studying them)." In any case, in order to keep the focus on the students in this book, I tried to get out of the way in other chapters, resorting to an older descriptive language about what the students evidently believed or thought about certain subjects in an averaging, estimating sort of way. Or I have done what structuralists do; I have attempted to look beneath the surfaces of the students' spoken mentalities for the unconscious or tacit principles by which they apparently thought or experienced things.

The essays in this book are not dialogic in the most experimental senses reviewed by James Clifford (1983); the controlling voice here is always my own, I think. (Whether the author of an ethnography that presents itself as more dialogical ever really cedes ultimate control over it is another question.) They are dialogic, however, in containing my own voice and in introducing many student voices. As for reflexivity in a slightly different sense of the term—reflecting one's initial interpretations off one's subjects and listening to what they have to say in reply—I am not aware of any other anthropologist who has checked his conclusions with as many of his "natives" as I have done during the course of this research and who has further modified them accordingly. I have had unusual opportunities to do so, of course, since I have been continually in "the field," my natives have been literate, and I have had the privileged position in their lives of "professor."

In any case, I taught preliminary versions of my conclusions to large and small classes of Rutgers undergraduates between 1985 and 1988; students read and commented on earlier drafts of all the chapters in this book except 5 and 6 (to which they listened, and on which they also commented). Also, I elicited more than a thousand student self-reports on sex, life of the mind, and other personal topics. I have read and reread perhaps a quarter of these self-reports intensively and have skimmed the remaining three-quarters to check conclusions from the first batch.

The classroom assignments for some of these papers were optional. Others asked the students to do local ethnography as part of the process of learning what anthropology is all about, since anthropology was what they had signed up to study. In all instances, the students were told before they wrote them that their papers might contribute to my research. And they always had the option of telling me not to use *their* papers in this way. Perhaps 95 percent of my students seemed willing or even eager to be part of this process of collective self-study, interested that a college professor would actually be interested in them in these specialized, far-from-the-undergraduates days, flattered when I asked any one of them for permission to use some piece of one of their own papers. (For more details on how I elicited and handled the most sensitive and numerous of these student papers, see chapter 5).

In what instances that I am aware of did student responses to my initial characterizations affect my eventual conclusions about them? In making me aware of the degree to which student friendship networks were fluid, open arrangements, not tight little mechanisms of automatically functioning "cliques" (chapter 3; Varenne 1982 also sensitized me on this point); in stressing the hidden currents of aggression and competition on dorm floors, not just the surface rhetoric of "friendliness" (chapter 3); in continually reminding me that every dorm floor had its own idiosyncratic history (chapter 3); in pointing out the degree to which the structure of the sections determined the racial dynamics on Erewhon Third (chapter 3); in pointing out some of the less-liberal sides of the black students' possible motivations on Erewhon Third (black student readers gave me this invaluable help with chapter 4); in continually protesting that the students were generally more variable than I tended to represent them as being during my earlier, participant observation research; in listening to the sexual materials in chapters 5 and 6 with an interest and openness that contrasted strongly with the reactions of many older readers and convinced me that I really was dealing with something close to the students' own mentalities about this hot but fascinating topic (students also gave me helpful opinions in sorting out fact from fiction in some of the sexual self-reports); and in protesting against certain ways in which I denigrated them as intellectual beings in chapter 7. And, of course, much of the substance of what is presented and reinterpreted in chapters 5 through 7 was directly produced by the students themselves.

To answer the most common question people who have heard casually about this research over the years have asked, did I really think the students acted naturally when I was around them: yes and no. Anthropologists conventionally try to deal with this problem, technically referred to as the "control effect," by their method, by acting as unobtrusive and nativelike as possible, by being around so much that the subjects of study become somewhat habituated to their presence. Another corrective technique, which ethnographers do not like to brag about as much, is "eavesdropper" or "spy." Although, given proper ethics, you almost always try to present yourself honestly to your subjects as a researcher, there are always moments in which the subjects do not know you are around just then, when you overhear something unintentionally, or when you meet a stranger who takes awhile to figure out who you really are. By comparing subjects' naive reactions to yourself to their informed reactions to same, you can sometimes actually observe the "control effect" *in* effect and figure out different ways of countering it. (For more on the control effect in the present research, see also chapters 1 and 3.) My other way of dealing with this intrinsic methodological problem of participant observation was to use other techniques of investigation as well, most notably the student self-reports.

To conclude on a more conventional topic of method, the data base, my recorded research materials from my two years of participant observation in the dorms in 1978–1979 and 1984–1985, includes field notes from all or parts of about 130 observational days, usually recorded within an hour of the event or the conversation they are about; the records of approximately two hundred semistructured interviews; more than a dozen self-administered questionnaires with returns ranging from fifty to several hundred; approximately fifty hours of tape recordings (not transcribed in toto, but sampled for key statements); several hundred of my own photos; and an uncounted number of official and unofficial documents, ranging from deanly pronouncements and other formal papers to student publications, room and door decorations, and graffiti.

Appendix Two
On Typicality

The problem of typicality is a perennial one for anthropologists because participant observation is an intrinsically microscopic technique. Clifford Geertz has tried to deal with it aphoristically by proposing that "anthropologists don't study villages . . . they study *in* villages" (Geertz 1973:22). But how do they know that *their* villages contain representative versions of the general things they are after? How much, in the present case, did Rutgers students resemble other American late-adolescents in college in the late 1970s and 1980s? No other anthropologist has applied long-term participant observation to undergraduates in American colleges, so this question cannot be answered with precision. But there are many alternate sources that suggest that the Rutgers students were far from atypical.

First of all, the generalizations in recent, more conventionally researched books about American college students elsewhere are, when they overlap with my own, generally consistent with them. Ernest Boyer's *College: The Undergraduate Experience in America* (1987) and the contemporary sections of Helen Lefkowitz Horowitz's *Campus Life: Undergraduate Cultures from the End of the Eighteenth Century to the Present* (1987) are the most useful of these sources. Mirra Komarovsky's *Women in College: Shaping New Feminine Identities* (1985) is also of value.[1]

When tapped by standard survey instruments, the attitudes of Rutgers students—their educational vocationalism, for instance (see chapter 7)—were also in the same range as those reported on a yearly basis by Alexander W. Astin in "The American Freshman: National Norms" (Los Angeles: American Council of Education and the University of California at Los Angeles). Notes on college student behavior, which occur from time to time in *Chronicle of Higher Education, Journal of College Student Personnel,* and *On-Campus Report* (a semimonthly publication of Magma Publications, Madison, Wisconsin), make it plain that what I have seen and heard in the Rutgers dorms is often national if not international collegiate or youth culture. Likewise, keeping tabs on the media makes it clear that the origin of much of the adolescent culture in the Rutgers dorms *was* general American popular culture as the students absorbed it from television, popular music, certain movies, and certain periodicals (see chapters 2, 3, and 5).

Historically, Rutgers student culture has been part of the same story as American college culture has been more widely (see chapter 2). The generality of the students' sexual mentalities is one of the main themes of chapters 5 and 6; ditto for their concepts of individualism and friendship in chapters 2 and 3 and probably for their attitudes toward racial differences in chapter 4. And there is every reason to believe that Rutgers' structure as an institution of higher education (chapter 7 again) resembles, in many important essentials, that of other large public colleges and universities in the United States in the late twentieth century. Rutgers does have some odd institutional characteristics as well, however.

In the late 1970s and mid 1980s, during the period of this research, Rutgers was a typical American state college in many ways. It provided an economically priced education to a predominantly in-state student population.[2] Most of its undergraduates came from working-class to middle-class family backgrounds, and many of them were the first persons in their families to have gone away to college.[3] The faculty was improving in its scholarly reputation; if Rutgers was somewhere in the lower half of American state universities according to this measure in the mid 1970s, by the mid 1980s the university as a whole could probably reasonably claim to be in the top twenty.[4]

And college from a Rutgers undergraduate's point of view was much like it would have been anywhere else. It resided in a geographically distinct place, on a campus (or on several campuses, for Rutgers College), with all the canonical American campus institutions: sweeps of tree-shaded, grassy lawn—less than one would have liked on the semiurban main College Avenue Campus, however—dormitories, fraternities, a student center, a commons, a library, a dean of the college, a dean of students, and, in the words of the bard, "ivy-covered professors in ivy-covered halls."[5] You went through Rutgers the same way you went through other colleges: supposedly in four years, though about 20 percent of the undergraduates at Rutgers actually took five or more years to finish and another 30 percent never finished up at all, at least at Rutgers;[6] ideally living on-campus, though about 20 percent of the college-age students commuted from home and another 16 percent lived off-campus;[7] with a ten to twelve course major and a smattering of twenty or more other courses loosely based on the old liberal arts ideal (see chapter 7). Most Rutgers graduates continued their educations after they received their baccalaureates. Many of them wound up in the professions or in business, typically at lower- to middle-management levels.

But in other ways, Rutgers College and the larger university that had grown out of it were the unusually complicated products of a peculiar local history. Most American state universities have been started from scratch. Rutgers, on the other hand, founded as Queen's College in 1766, is also the eighth oldest privately founded institution of higher education in the United States. Renamed Rutgers in 1825, the college was designated New Jersey's land grant institution in 1864, following a close contest with Princeton. But then, for nearly a century, the college and the university dithered between what might now be called a "little Ivy" identity and the identity of a public institution.[8] During their formative years, more-single-minded state universities developed on expanding, unified main campuses. Rutgers, on the other hand, muddled through the first seventy years of the twentieth century by developing as a looser and cheaper federation of separate undergraduate colleges and campuses.[9]

Thus, by the mid-seventies, Rutgers-New Brunswick, consisted of the original Rutgers College, on the main College Avenue Campus half a mile northwest of downtown New Brunswick, and with more dorms at the vast, newer, underpopulated science campus, Busch, two miles across the river in Piscataway;[10] Douglass, founded in 1918, a women's college on a pretty campus a mile to the south of the College Avenue Campus; Cook (1973), an agriculture and environment oriented college adjacent to Douglass, on the site of Rutgers' older Agricultural Experiment Station; and Livingston (1969), with a special commitment to minority and "nontraditional" students, back over in Piscataway, a mile from Busch, modernistically bleak on the site of the old army property Camp Kilmer.

Most professors at Rutgers were attached to one of these separate colleges up to 1980 and only loosely connected to other members of their disciplines at an all–New Brunswick level. The arrangement was a good one for undergraduate education; Rutgers University students worked in much smaller units of student and professors than the undergraduates at other large state universities did. By 1980, however, university leaders were beginning to feel that this arrangement was detrimental to research and to graduate education, the university functions on which nationwide prestige (and outside funding) were based. There was much needless duplication of scholarly specialties and much unproductive infighting among the members of the smaller college-level departments in any particular academic discipline, these authorities believed. So they reorganized the university, bringing the faculty members of all but one of the older colleges together at an all—New Brunswick level.[11]

But they were not quite ready to eliminate the older colleges. For the colleges did have their separate histories, their separate alumni and alumnae loyalists; and the New Brunswick campus actually consisted of their several separate campuses strewn across three miles and two townships. So each college was left with a dean of the college, a dean of students, separate residence life programs, separate college missions, and the right to maintain distinctive graduation requirements. The professors, however, no longer reported to the deans of the colleges. Their bosses became the new heads of new faculty entities—principally, the dean of the faculty of Arts and Sciences plus the deans of two much smaller faculty entities.[12] These new units of faculty organization unified the academic departments in New Brunswick and supplied undergraduate teaching to the older colleges—without belonging to any one of them. The deans of the new faculty units as teaching units reported to the provost, as did the new deans of the old colleges without professors. Poor provost.

The academic departments now had to be housed together in one place for the first time, however, which meant on one or another of the old college campuses. Working out of these locations, to whose colleges they no longer automatically belonged, the professors were supposed to circulate through all the campuses, providing convenient courses to the students, who were still in colleges. Faculty members could be involved in the activities of one of the residential colleges (in fixing its graduation requirements, for example) by voluntarily becoming a Fellow of that college. None of these professors had to have this relationship to undergraduate education any longer, however.

One thing this compromise between the needs of the colleges and the growing importance of research and graduate education meant was that a college was a more variable and indeterminate thing at Rutgers after 1980 than it was at most other American institutions of higher education. In other places, a college was either a territorial entity consisting of students, a campus, and a collection of professors and deans headed by a president, or it was a more abstract, degree-granting faculty entity embedded in a larger university (as in the College of Arts and Sciences). Three of the four residential colleges at Rutgers corresponded to some parts of this first standard meaning, except that they had no faculty members after 1980.[13] Then there were four other undergraduate colleges in the latter sense of the term: Engineering, Pharmacy, the Mason Gross School of the Performing Arts, and University College (for adult education).[14] Students at the first three of these colleges could choose to affiliate with one of the residential colleges for the purposes of student life, and their professors had a direct relationship to the granting of undergraduate degrees.[15] Most of the professors in the larger Faculty of Arts and Sciences, on the other hand, were located in no colleges at all after 1980, only in the faculty as a teaching unit.

These peculiarities in the organization of the colleges and the university at Rutgers were above the heads of most of the students. But they were not without their effects on them. How might they have influenced the typicality of what I have described in this book? In two ways I can think of. First, though undergraduates are far removed from their professors at most large, modern state universities—a high student-to-faculty ratio is one basic reason a state university can afford to offer a relatively cheap education to its students—at Rutgers by the mid-1980s, they may have been even further removed still. For many of the professors floated peculiarly free at Rutgers, with no necessary affiliations with any entity in the college or university directly responsible for undergraduate education.[16]

Second, Rutgers was, according to most administrators who moved into it from more conventionally organized institutions, an unusually complicated place. Probably more than was the case elsewhere, the left hand of its bureaucracy often did not know what its right hand was doing. Nor was there any easy way around what was locally referred to as "our peculiar geography." To handle some snafu in course registration, for instance, a Rutgers College student might have to start with some subdean on the College Avenue Campus, take a crowded bus over to an academic department headquarters at (for example) Douglass, and then take a longer bus ride to the other side of Rutgers-New Brunswick, to the "central" Administrative Services Building, back of beyond on the Busch campus—with long lines at each location, with overworked bureaucrats at the head of each line.

All these Rutgers realities probably made the undergraduate concept of Rutgers as "Rutgers Screw" more vivid than equivalent student views of bureaucracy would be at other large state universities. And the vagueness of Rutgers' organization and its administrators' constant tinkering (in hopes of finding *some* way to straighten it out *somehow*) might have mitigated against anything like genuinely felt community among its undergraduates more than was the case elsewhere.

With its unplanned suburbs melding seamlessly into one another, however, and its historically uncentered, county-dominated political system, the state of New Jersey had many of the same organizational properties as Rutgers did in the late twentieth century. Most Rutgers undergraduates were local kids who would grow up to be local adults. Whether Rutgers was entirely typical of all less-than-elite public universities in the United States in the 1970s and 1980s, it was unintentionally doing its democratic duty by its own undergraduate clients from the state of New Jersey. It *was*, to recall the undergraduate trope of "Rutgers as real world," getting its students ready for the culture and the society in which most of them would spend the rest of their lives.

Further Comments

1 / Many of Allan Bloom's authoritative-sounding characterizations of contemporary undergraduates in *The Closing of the American Mind*, on the other hand, are based on the most unscholarly kinds of anecdote-as-data. For example:

> A university teacher of liberal arts cannot help confronting special handicaps, a slight deformity of the spirit, in the students, ever more numerous, whose parents are divorced. I do not have the slightest doubt that they do as well as others in all kinds of specialized subjects, but I find they are not as open to serious study of philosophy and literature as some other students are (Bloom 1987: 120).

Even the dimmest, most routinely trained specialist in sociology might wonder what Bloom's sample size for this astonishing generalization was, what his control was, how he knew the family status of all his students, and so on.

2 / An undergraduate in residence at Rutgers in the mid-1980s could manage on a little over $6,000 a year, as opposed to $16,000 to $17,000 a year at the most expensive private colleges.

About 90 percent of the undergraduates at Rutgers College in the mid-1980s were from the state of New Jersey; most of them were from the northern half of the state, from mostly suburban hometowns less than fifty miles from New Brunswick.

3 / It is not possible to be more precise about this because, oddly for a public institution, Rutgers has not systematically collected many of its students' most basic demographic characteristics (occupations of mother and father and educational levels of mother and father, for instance, would give the university a decent measure of how well it was serving the different socioeconomic groups in the state). Likewise, the university has not done a very good job of tracking its students after graduation.

4 / It is not entirely fair to compare a state university in the Northeast with some of the great state universities in the Midwest and the West, or even with some of the average universities in those regions or in the South. Northeastern public universities have almost all grown up in the shadow of older, better-connected private colleges (the Ivy League, for example). Elsewhere, state universities have often been the only show in town. Within the Northeast, in any case, focusing on the states from Maryland up through New England, it was possible to argue by the mid-1980s that Rutgers was as good as any other public university and better than most.

5 / From "Bright College Days," *An Evening (Wasted) with Tom Lehrer* (thanks to professor of physics George Temmer for this discographic reference).

6 / Source: Ellen A. Kanarek, Institutional Research Bulletin, vol. 2, no. 2, table 2 (September 28, 1987), Rutgers University. These attrition rates at Rutgers are no worse than those at other American state universities and better than some.

7 / My thanks to Matt Weismantel for these very informed estimates.

8 / Until recently, New Jersey was one of the cheapest states in the nation when it came to the funding of education at any level. And for many years Rutgers resisted surrendering the power of its old, private Board of Trustees to the state. The state only gained real oversight with the creation of the Board of Governors in 1956, and only more recently has "The State University of New Jersey" become the invariant tag line after "Rutgers" on university masthead documents (see, for an immediate example, the copyright notice at the beginning of this book).

9 / For more on the history of Rutgers, see McCormick 1966, and Moffatt 1985b.

10 / Rutgers College also had access to two big dorms on the

Livingston Campus during the years of my research. The relevance of these dorms to undergraduate racial politics is mentioned in chapter 4.

11 / Cook managed to keep itself out of the reorganization of 1980, and it lingered on at Rutgers-New Brunswick as an undissolved remnant of the older colleges as students plus faculty members. It defined itself as a professional school under the new arrangement, so it was also possible to dichotomize the eight undergraduate colleges that existed at Rutgers by the mid-1980s in a slightly different way than will be done below: there were four "liberal arts" colleges, three residential and one not (university); and there were four "professional schools," one of them residential (Cook) and three not (Engineering, Pharmacy, and Mason Gross).

12 / The Faculty of Professional Studies (Applied Health Studies, Urban and Regional Planning, Administration of Justice, and two ROTC programs), and the School of Communication, Information, and Library Studies (the Graduate School of Library and Information Studies and the undergraduate School of Communication).

13 / Except for their Fellows. But relatively few faculty members gave their all for entities that took extra time and had no detectable relationship to the university structure that determined career success—promotion, tenure, grants—at Rutgers.

14 / The School of Social Work also offered an undergraduate program in some colleges, and there was a new School of Business in the mid-1980s.

15 / Except for the old University College faculty, most of whom had been blended into the Faculty of Arts and Sciences during reorganization.

16 / Given growing specialization, not many professors anywhere in American higher education in the late twentieth century gave much thought to general education any longer, of course. In other colleges and universities, such concerns had also devolved on much smaller faculty groups, and on academic deans in particular. The peculiar problem at Rutgers after the reorganization of 1980, however, was that the deans of the colleges had virtually no clout left with which to coerce the specialized professors into doing the work of general education, even if much smaller groups could have figured out how to do it. The provost was supposed to do this under the new Rutgers arrangement, but as of 1988, he had not

shown much ability to do so, nor much real interest in the process.

On a set of student reports written for me in 1987 on "what makes a good professor," by the way, I noticed that a disproportionate number of unknown (to me) faculty members were named from just those smaller colleges in which faculty were still directly responsible for undergraduate education.

References Cited

Allan, Graham A. 1979. *Sociology of Friendship and Kinship*. London: G. Allen and Unwin.

Baker, Ross. 1980. *Friend and Foe in the United States Senate*. New York: Free Press.

Baldares, Yanet. 1987. "Variations in Culture, Class and Political Consciousness among Latin Residents of a Small Eastern City." Ph.D. diss., Department of Sociology, Rutgers University.

Barkas, Jan L. 1985. *Friendship: A Selected, Annotated Bibliography*. New York: Garland.

Becker, Howard S., Blanche Geer, and Everett C. Hughes. 1968. *Making the Grade: The Academic Side of College Life*. New York: Wiley and Sons.

Bellah, Robert N., Richard Madsen, William M. Sullivan, Ann Swidler, and Steven M. Tipton. 1985. *Habits of the Heart: Individualism and Commitment in American Life*. Berkeley and Los Angeles: University of California Press.

Bennett, William J. 1984. *To Reclaim a Legacy: A Report on the Humanities in Higher Education*. Washington: National Endowment for the Humanities.

Berndt, Ronald M. 1976. *Love Songs of Arnhem Land*. Chicago: University of Chicago Press.

Berreman, Gerald. 1960. "Caste in India and the United States." *American Journal of Sociology* 66 : 120–127.

Blau, Eleanor. 1988. "Study Finds Barrage of Sex on T.V." *New York Times*, January 27, C26.

Bloom, Allan. 1987. *The Closing of the American Mind: How Higher Education Has Failed Democracy and Impoverished the Souls of Today's Students*. New York: Simon and Schuster.

Boffey, Philip M. 1988. "Spread of AIDS Abating, but Deaths Will Still Soar." *New York Times*, February 14, A1.

Bonacich, Edna. 1976. "Advanced Capitalism and Black-White Race Relations in the United States: A Split Labor Market Interpretation." *American Sociological Review* 41 (1) : 34–51.

Boyer, Ernest L. 1987. *College: The Undergraduate Experience in America*. New York: Harper and Row.

Brain, Robert. 1976. *Friends and Lovers*. New York: Basic Books.

Brown, Patricia Leigh. 1988. "In Era of AIDS, 'Safe Sex' Becomes the Latest Campus Crusade." *New York Times*, January 11, A12.

Calandra, Alexander. 1968. "Angels on a Pin: A Modern Parable." *Saturday Review*, December 21.

Canaan, Joyce. 1986. "Why a 'Slut' is a 'Slut': Cautionary Tales of Middle-Class Teenage Girls' Morality." In *Symbolizing America*. See Varenne 1986c, 184–208.

Chickering, Arthur W. et al. 1981. *The Modern American College: Responding to the New Realities of Diverse Students and a Changing Society.* San Francisco: Jossey-Bass.

Clifford, James. 1983. "On Ethnographic Authority." *Representations* 1 (2): 118–146.

Clifford, James, and George E. Marcus. 1986. *Writing Culture: the Poetics and Politics of Ethnography.* Berkeley and Los Angeles: University of California Press.

D'Andrade, Roy. 1987. "A Folk Model of the Mind." In *Cultural Models in Language and Thought,* ed. Dorothy Holland and Naomi Quinn, 112–148. Cambridge: Cambridge University Press.

Daniel, E. Valentine. 1984. *Fluid Signs: Being a Person the Tamil Way.* Berkeley and Los Angeles: University of California Press.

Davis, Natalie Z. 1971. "The Reasons of Misrule: Youth Groups and Charivaris in Sixteenth-Century France." In *Society and Culture in Early Modern France,* 97–123. Stanford: Stanford University Press.

Di Leonardo, Micaela. 1984. *The Varieties of Ethnic Experience: Kinship, Class, and Gender among California Italian-Americans.* Ithaca: Cornell University Press.

Dumont, Louis. 1960. "Caste, Racism and 'Stratification': Reflections of a Social Anthropologist." Reprinted in Dumont 1982, 247–266.

———. 1982. *Homo Hierarchicus: The Caste System and Its Implications.* Trans. Mark Sainsbury, Louis Dumont, and Basia Gulati. Chicago: University of Chicago Press.

Durkheim, Emile. 1915. *The Elementary Forms of the Religious Life.* London: Allen and Unwin.

Dziech, Billie Wright, and Linda Weiner. 1984. *The Lecherous Professor: Sexual Harassment on Campus.* Boston: Beacon Press.

Ehrenreich, Barbara. 1983. *The Hearts of Men: American Dreams and the Flight from Commitment.* Garden City, N.Y.: Anchor Press/Doubleday.

Elder, Glen H., Jr. 1980. "Adolescence in Historical Perspective." In *Handbook of Adolescent Psychology,* ed. Joseph Adelson, 3–47. New York: Wiley and Sons.

Elwin, Verrier. 1968. *The Kingdom of the Young.* London: Oxford University Press.

Foucault, Michel. 1980. *A History of Sexuality.* Vol. 1, *An Introduction.* New York: Vintage Books.

Frederickson, George M. 1971. *The Black Image in the White Mind: The Debate on Afro-American Character and Destiny, 1817–1914.* New York: Harper and Row.

Geertz, Clifford. 1973. "Thick Description: Toward an Interpretive Theory of Culture." In *The Interpretation of Cultures,* 3–32. New York: Basic Books.

———. 1976. "From the Native's Point of View: On the Nature of Anthropological Understanding." In *Meaning in Anthropology,* ed. K. Basso and H. Selby, 221–237, Albuquerque: University of New Mexico Press.

————. 1988. *Works and Lives: The Anthropologist as Author.* Stanford: Stanford University Press.

Gillis, John R. 1974. *Youth and History: Tradition and Change in European Age Relations 1770–Present.* New York: Academic Press.

Goffman, Erving. 1974. *Frame Analysis: An Essay on the Organization of Experience.* Chicago: University of Chicago Press.

Gold, Allan R. 1988. "Educators Seek Answers as Bias on Campus Rises." *New York Times*, January 25, A18.

Gregor, Thomas. 1985. *Anxious Pleasures: The Sexual Lives of an Amazonian People.* Chicago: University of Chicago Press.

Hacker, Andrew. 1986. "The Decline of Higher Learning." *New York Review of Books*, February 13, 35–42.

Hartman, Mary. n.d. *Sexual Crackup: Gender, Power and Identity in Western Society.* New York: William Morrow. Forthcoming.

Heath, Stephen. 1982. *The Sexual Fix.* New York: Schocken.

Herdt, Gilbert H. 1981. *Guardians of the Flutes.* New York: McGraw-Hill.

Hildebrand, M., and S. Abramowitz. 1984. "Sexuality on Campus: Changes in Attitudes and Behaviors in the 1970s." *Journal of College Student Personnel* 25: 534–46.

Hirsch, E. D., Jr. 1987. *Cultural Literacy: What Every American Needs to Know.* Boston: Houghton Mifflin.

Horowitz, Helen Lefkowitz. 1987. *Campus Life: Undergraduate Cultures from the End of the Eighteenth Century to the Present.* New York: Knopf.

Kett, Joseph F. 1977. *Rites of Passage: Adolescence in America 1790 to the Present.* New York: Basic Books.

Komarovsky, Mirra. 1985. *Women In College: Shaping New Feminine Identities.* New York: Basic Books.

Kurth, Suzanne B. 1970. "Friendships and Friendly Relations." In *Social Relationships. See* McCall et al. 1970, 136–170.

Lasch, Christopher. 1977. *Haven in a Heartless World: The Famiy Besieged.* New York: Basic Books.

————. 1978. *Culture as Narcissism: American Life in an Age of Diminishing Expectations.* New York: Norton.

Lears, T. J. Jackson. 1985. "The Two Richard Sennetts." *Journal of American Studies* 19 (1): 81–94.

Levine, Arthur. 1980. *When Dreams and Heros Died: A Portrait of Today's College Student.* San Francisco: Jossey-Bass.

Lukac, George J., ed. 1966. "The Great Landon Hoax." In *Aloud to Alma Mater*, 160–161. New Brunswick: Rutgers University Press.

McCall, George J., Michael M. McCall, Norman K. Denzin, Gerald D. Suttles, and Suzanne B. Kurth. 1970. *Social Relationships.* Chicago: Aldine.

McCormick, Richard P. 1966. *Rutgers: A Bicentennial History.* New Brunswick: Rutgers University Press.

Maltz, Daniel N., and Ruth A. Borker. 1982. "A Cultural Approach to Male-Female Miscommunication." In *Language and Social Identity,* ed. John Gumperz, 195–216. Cambridge: Cambridge University Press.

Marcus, George, and Dick Cushman. 1982. "Ethnographies as Text." *Annual Review of Anthropology* 11: 25–69.

Marriott, McKim, and Ronald Inden. 1977. "Toward an Ethnosociology of South Asian Caste Systems." In *The New Wind: Changing Identities in South Asia,* ed. Kenneth David, 227–238. The Hague: Mouton.

Marshall, Donald S. 1971. "Sexual Behavior on Mangaia." Chap. 5 in *Human Sexual Behavior. See* Marshall and Suggs 1971.

Marshall, Donald S., and Robert C. Suggs, eds. 1971. *Human Sexual Behavior.* New York: Basic Books.

Messenger, John C. 1971. "Sex and Repression in an Irish Folk Community." Chap. 1 in *Human Sexual Behavior. See* Marshall and Suggs 1971.

Moffatt, Michael. 1979. *An Untouchable Community in South India: Structure and Consensus.* Princeton: Princeton University Press.

———. 1985a. "Inventing the 'Time-Honored Traditions' of 'Old Rutgers': Rutgers Student Culture, 1858–1900." *Journal of the Rutgers University Libraries* 47 (1): 1–11.

———. 1985b. *The Rutgers Picture Book: An Illustrated History of Student Life in the Changing College and University.* New Brunswick: Rutgers University Press.

———. 1986. "The Discourse of the Dorm: Race, Friendship and 'Culture' among College Youth." In *Symbolizing America. See* Varenne 1986c, 159–180.

Myerhoff, Barbara. 1978. *Number Our Days.* New York: Simon and Schuster.

Myrdal, Gunnar. 1944. *An American Dilemma: The Negro Problem and Modern Democracy.* New York: Harper and Row.

Newcomer, S. F., and J. R. Udry. 1985. "Oral Sex in an American Adolescent Population." *Archives of Sexual Behavior* 14(1): 41–46.

Orwell, George. 1946. "Politics and the English Language." In *In Front of Your Nose: The Collected Essays, Journalism and Letters of George Orwell, 1945–1950,* ed. Sonia Orwell and Ian Angus. New York: Harcourt Brace Jovanovich, 1968.

Paine, R. 1969. "In Search of Friendship." *Man,* n.s. 4: 505–524.

Radway, Janice A. 1984. *Reading the Romance: Women, Patriarchy, and Popular Literature.* Chapel Hill: University of North Carolina Press.

Ravitch, Diane, and Chester E. Finn, Jr. 1987. *What Do Our 17-year-olds Know?: A Report on the First National Assessment of History and Literature.* New York: Harper and Row.

Rimmer, Robert. 1968. *The Harrad Experiment.* New York: Bantam.

Roll, S., and L. Millen. 1979. "The Friend as Represented in the Dreams of Late Adolescents: Friendship without Rose-Colored Glasses." *Adolescence* 24: 255–75.

Rutgers College. 1859. *The Rutgers College Quarterly*, January, 182–184.

———. 1985. "Report of the Minority Issues Committee," for the Interdisciplinary Retreat of September 20–21. Typescript.

———. n.d. *Shaping a Community: A Guide to Residence Life at Rutgers College*. Office of Residence Life, Dean of Students' Office (document distributed during freshman orientation in 1984).

Rutgers University. 1986. *Survey of Student Satisfaction*. The Office of Institutional Research.

Sennett, Richard. 1978. *The Fall of Public Man*. New York: Random House.

Shostak, Marjorie. 1981. *Nisa: The Life and Words of a Kung Woman*. Cambridge: Harvard University Press.

Smith-Rosenberg, Carroll. 1975. "The Female World of Love and Ritual." *Signs: Journal of Women in Culture and Society* 1 (1): 1–30.

Snitow, Ann Barr. 1982. "Mass Market Romance: Pornography for Women is Different." In *Powers of Desire. See* Snitow et al. 1982, 245–263.

Snitow, Ann Barr, Christine Stansell, and Sharon Thomson, eds. 1982. *Powers of Desire: The Politics of Sexuality*. New York: Monthly Review Press.

Stocking, George. 1968. "Lamarckianism in American Social Science." In *Race, Culture and Evolution: Essays in the History of Anthropology*, 234–269. New York: Free Press.

Stone, Lawrence. 1977. *The Family, Sex and Marriage in England, 1500–1800*. New York: Harper and Row.

Suttles, G. 1970. "Friendship as a Social Institution." In *Social Relationships. See* McCall et al. 1970, 95–135.

Turner, V. W. 1957. *Schism and Continuity in an African Society: A Study of Ndembu Village Life*. Manchester: Manchester University Press.

Vance, Carole. 1982. "Gender Systems, Ideology, and Sex Research." In *Powers of Desire. See* Snitow et al. 1982, 371–384.

Varenne, Hervé. 1982. "Jocks and Freaks: The Symbolic Structure of the Expression of Social Interaction among American Senior High School Students." In *Doing the Ethnography of Schooling*, ed. George Spindler, 210–235. New York: Holt, Rinehart and Winston.

———. 1984. "Collective Representation in American Anthropological Conversations about Culture: Culture and the Individual." *Current Anthropology* 25: 281–300.

———. 1986a. "Creating America." In *Symbolizing America. See* Varenne 1986c, 15–33.

———. 1986b. "'Drop in Anytime': Community and Authenticity in American Everyday Life." In *Symbolizing America*. *See* Varenne 1986c, 209–228.

———. 1986c. *Symbolizing America*. Lincoln: University of Nebraska Press.

Walkowitz, Judith R. 1986. "Science, Feminism and Romance: The Men and Women's Club 1885–1889. *History Workshop* 21 (Spring).

Weeks, Jeffrey. 1977. *Coming Out: Homosexual Politics in Britain*. New York: Quartet Books.

Weis, David L. 1985. "The Experience of Pain during Women's First Sexual Intercourse: Cultural Mythology about Female Sexual Initiation." *Archives of Sexual Behavior* 14: 421–437.

White, Constance C. R. 1987. "The New Racists." Campus Times News. *Ms.*, October, 68.

Whitehead, Harriet. 1981. "The Bow and the Burden Strap." In *Sexual Meanings*, ed. S. B. Ortner and H. Whitehead, 80–115. New York: Cambridge University Press.

Index

abortion, 181, 224, 231, 242 n. 39
academic marketplace, college as, 280–
282, 315 n. 15
academics: advising system, 316 n. 17;
cheating, 296–297, 323 n. 34; choosing
courses, 284–286; class size, 292; as
complementary to college life, 29–34,
54, 294, 309; "gut" courses, 285–286,
314 n. 11. *See also* intellectual values;
knowledge; liberal arts values; majors;
professors; specialization; studying;
teaching; vocationalism
accounting (major), 277
adolescence, invention of, 38
adolescent development. *See* coming of age
advising system, 316 n. 17
age, student attitudes toward, 6, 8, 9, 17,
100, 183, 265 n. 2
AIDS, 201–202, 228, 231 n. 1, 241 n. 35,
245 n. 50
alcohol, 6, 50, 65 n. 13, 80, 82, 83–
85, 88, 100, 123–124, 129 n. 15,
139 n. 48, 155–156, 192
"all-nighters," 322 n. 32
Alvin (student name), 96, 142
American culture, 18–19, 23 n. 10, 40–
41, 52–53, 67 n. 23, 129 n. 13,
134 n. 31, 153, 155, 162, 165, 168,
173 n. 17, 174 n. 19, 178 n. 32, 197,
201, 227–228, 229, 230, 240 n. 29,
251, 310 n. 1, 313 n. 6, 331, 332. *See
also* campus culture; community; friendship; gender; individualism; popular
culture; race; ritual; sexual mentalities;
youth culture
Andrea (student name), 78
Animal House, 37, 52–53
anthropology: anthropologist in the dorms,
1–20, 74, 91–95, 100–101, 111, 113–
114, 117, 123, 126 n. 6, 129 n. 16,
139 n. 47, 146, 155, 159, 160,
173 n. 18, 235 n. 13 (*see also* method:

control effect; method: reflexivity); close
to home, 1, 18, 19, 20 nn. 1, 2,
23 n. 10; student views of, 16, 17, 152,
276, 305, 326 n. 43. *See also* method
anti-intellectualism, 292, 303–304; relative rarity of, 298–299. *See also* intellectual values
Art (student name), 78
art history (major), 283, 315 n. 15
Asian-Americans, 168 nn. 1, 2
Astin, W., 331
attrition, student, 69 n. 32
autonomy: and anonymity, 252–253,
292–293, 320 n. 27; of fraternities,
39–40; and Secret Santa, 117–118; of
students, 34–37; and vocationalism,
313 n. 6

bathrooms, in coed dorms, 6, 82, 148, 158,
172 n. 11
Becker, Howard S., et al., 287
Bellah, Robert, et al., 41
Berreman, Gerald, 177 n. 29
biological sciences (major), 6, 277
birth control, 49, 81, 109–110, 181, 184,
186, 231, 242 n. 39, 257, 263
bisexuality, 227, 228
Black students. *See* race, racism
blaming the victim, 179 n. 35
Bloom, Allan, 271, 272, 303, 336 n. 1
"blow-it-off," 33, 34, 293, 322 n. 31
Bob (student name), 77
Bonacich, Edna, 177 n. 27
Boyer, Ernest, 64 n. 11, 271, 310 n. 1, 331
"boyfriend," 183
Brain, Robert, 68 n. 25
Brian (student name), 77
"bull session," no longer named, 133 n. 27,
298. *See also* intellectual talk
bureaucracy, 12–14, 41, 44, 59, 273–274,
310 n. 1, 335–336. *See also* college;
Rutgers

buses, campus, 25–26, 285
"busting," 11, 43, 67 n. 21, 83, 86, 90, 94, 122, 168, 296, 299

campus culture, 50–53; history of, 52–53, 332
Carrie (student name), 78
caste and race, 177 n. 29
Catholicism: and sex, 194, 196, 203, 253
Charlotte (student name), 303
cheating, 296–297, 323 n. 34
Chris (student name), 77
Chronicle of Higher Education, 331
Chuck (student name), 8
class, college, 317 n. 22; distributions in dorms, 127 n. 7; history of, 53, 69 n. 29; sexual behavior by, 248, 266 n. 2; stereotypes, 53–54; studying styles by, 295–296
class, social, 30, 50–51, 59, 123, 159, 164, 171 n. 9, 176 nn. 24, 25, 177 nn. 27, 28, 278, 332, 337 n. 3
classroom size, 289, 292, 321 n. 28
Clifford, James, 327, 328
cliques, 96–98, 102–103, 114–116, 127 nn. 8, 9, 155; on Erewhon Third, 157; on Hasbrouck Fourth, 95, 115
clothing styles of students, 1, 47, 50–51, 100, 182, 234 n. 6
college: as academic marketplace, 280–282, 315 n. 15; anonymity in, 5, 12, 16, 252–254, 273–274, 289–290; as a balance of academics and college life, 15, 29–34, 251, 271, 294, 309; different views of, 25–28, 62, 92; impersonality of, 5, 12, 252–254, 273–274, 289–290, 292–293 (*see also* bureaucracy); as an institution (*see* Rutgers); and personal identity, 51–52; as the real world, 59, 336; student satisfaction with, 272, 311 n. 3; typicality and atypicality of Rutgers as, 331–336
college life, 29–62, 73, 161, 312 n. 4; as complementary to academics, 29–34, 251, 271, 309; history of, 29–30, 34,

37–38, 39, 50, 53, 59; as informal learning, 54–61; sexuality at the heart of, 30, 48–49, 229
coming of age, 28–29, 41, 53–61, 75, 251, 263–266, 269 n. 13
communication. *See* discourse; language, types of
communication (major), 277, 313 n. 8
community, 64 n. 11, 71–73, 122–125, 144, 156, 336; interracial, 144, 159–161; noncommunity, 253–254 (*see also* college; impersonality of)
computer science (major), 277
control effect. *See* method: control effect
courses, choosing, 284–286, 316 n. 17
cultural differences: and race, 141, 146, 159, 160, 166, 172 n. 13, 174 n. 19, 178 n. 32, 179 n. 35
culture: tacit, 19, 23 n. 10, 123, 182, 328. *See also* American culture; campus culture; popular culture; youth culture
"culture," student concepts of, 151–153, 174 n. 19, 178 n. 32
curriculum, organization of, 275–282

Dan (student name), 75
D'Andrade, Roy, 42, 172 n. 14
data, from dorm research, 330
Davis, Natalie Z., 137 n. 41, 253
Deanly Officialese (language), 71–72, 90, 132 n. 25. *See also* "low talk"
deans (of Student Life): attitudes toward race relations, 144, 171 n. 6, 179 n. 35; authority over students, 34–37, 63 n. 8, 64 n. 9, 71–72, 73, 124; dorms, interventions in the, 83–84, 104–106, 117, 120, 137 n. 45, 144; fun, views of, 105, 124; invention of, 38; ritual used by, 4, 134 n. 31; staff of, 36, 64 n. 9
"Dean Wormer," 37
departments, academic. *See* majors
Di Leonardo, Micaela, 126 n. 4
disciplines, academic. *See* majors
discourse: modes of, 90–91; in dorm lounges, 234 n. 8. *See also* Deanly Offi-

cialese; locker-room; Private-Sincere; Undergraduate Cynical

Don Juans, 205–206

dorms

—coed, 9, 47, 181–185, 232 n. 2; bathrooms in, 6, 82, 148, 158, 172 n. 11; and gender, 6, 47, 48, 80, 81; history of, 232 n. 2; lack of incest taboo in, 185; and Secret Santa, 106, 134 n. 31, 136 n. 40; sexual fantasy about, 256–259; sexual restraints in, 9, 45–49, 181–185, 234 n. 11

—floors in, 36, 73, 79–83, 88–90, 111, 122–125. See also cliques; Erewhon Third; Gates Third; Hasbrouck Fourth

—freshman, 137 n. 45

—rooms in: deans' authority in, 35; decor of, 51, 80–82; sexual intercourse in, 259–260, 268 n. 11

drinking. See alcohol

drug use, 5, 50, 51, 148, 250

Dumont Louis, 165, 177 n. 29, 242 n. 38

Durkheim, Emile, 134 n. 31

Dwayne (student name), 112

Dziech, Billie Wright, and Linda Weiner, 238 n. 22

economics (major), 276, 283, 300–301, 315 n. 15

Ed (student name), 121

education, higher: meaning to students and professors of, 28–29, 272–274; quality of teaching, 291–292, 318–321; student satisfaction with, 271, 272. See also academics; college; intellectual values; liberal arts values; Rutgers; vocationalism

Ehrenreich, Barbara, 231

Elder, Glen H., Jr., 312 n. 4

Elwin, Verrier, 182

engineering (major), 279

English (major), 277, 282, 307, 313 n. 8, 315 n. 15

Equal Opportunity Program (EOP), 316 n. 19

Erewhon Third, 21, 143–162

Ernie (student name), 96, 142

ethnicity, 69 n. 31, 75, 164, 168 nn. 1, 2, 169 n. 4, 177 n. 28

ethnic stereotypes, 153, 177 n. 28

ethnographic writing, 327–338

experimentalists, sexual, 215–221, 257

extracurricular groups, 32, 38–39, 64 nn. 10, 11, 65 n. 13, 69 n. 31

feminism, 48–49, 68 n. 26, 223–225, 240, 245, 302, 309

floor awards night, 121

folklore, student, 88

football, the original game, 39

Foucault, Michel, 195, 240 n. 28

fraternities, xvi, 8, 39–40, 48, 65 n. 13, 77, 80, 87, 95, 205, 206, 207, 260–262, 284, 298; autonomy of, 39–40; gang bangs, 261, 262; hazing in, 65 n. 13; as "meat markets," 209, 261; Neanderthals in, 261–262; sex in, 205, 206, 207, 216, 260–263. See also sexism

Fred (student name), 9

Frederickson, George M., 178 n. 30

freshmen, 54, 74; academic adjustments by, 287–289; initial impressions of college, 88, 253–255, 308; orientation, 1–20; special dorms for, 137 n. 45

friendliness, 7, 43–45, 67 n. 22, 178 n. 32; on dorm floors, 66 n. 17, 72–73, 88–90, 111, 125, 140 n. 49, 147, 149–150, 160, 166; naturalness of, 152, 178 n. 32; and Secret Santa, 134 n. 31. See also students: animosity between

friendly fun, 33, 82

friendly smile, 67 n. 23

friendship, 41–42, 66 nn. 17, 18, 19, 67 nn. 20, 21, 95–98, 102, 183, 329; close reciprocated, 98, cross-sex, 45–47, 68 nn. 24, 25, 114, 116, 136 n. 39, 182, 184, 185; interracial, 142, 156, 162–163, 166, 168, 176 n. 25; making, 3, 10, 66 n. 17, 133 n. 30, 156–157. See also cliques

"gang bangs," 205, 250, 261, 262
Gary (student name), 77
Gates Third, 3–20, 21 n. 3
gay males. See homosexuality
Geertz, Clifford, 327, 328, 331
gender (see also sex)
—convergence: on coed dorm floors, 6,
    47; in Secret Santa, 104, 107–108; in
    sexual relations, 203–204, 212, 213–
    214, 215–216, 220, 221–222, 223,
    224. See also friendship: cross-sex
—divergence: on coed dorm floors, 47–48,
    80, 81, 136 n. 39; in fraternities, 261–
    262; in sexual relations, 204–211, 213,
    220–221, 230–231. See also sexism
Gillis, John, 38, 137 n. 41, 269 n. 13
"girlfriend," 183
Goffman, Erving, 46
grades, 6, 13, 132 n. 24, 287, 321 n. 29;
    by department, 280–282, 315 n. 15
"grease trucks," 244 n. 48
grinds, 34, 50, 174 n. 21, 293, 322 n. 30
guilt, sexual, 201, 203, 211, 267 n. 8
"gut" (course), 15, 285–286, 314 n. 11

Harlequin romances, 212, 243 n. 44
Harry (student name), 78
Hartman, Mary, 46
Hasbrouck Fourth, 21, 71–125, 185; his-
    tory of, 101–102, 127 n. 7; race on,
    141–142
hazing, 4, 12, 21 n. 6, 65 n. 13, 67 n. 21,
    85–88, 102, 105, 142
Heath, Stephen, 195, 200
Henry (student name), 146
"Henry Street guys," 84, 101
herpes, 201
higher education. See education, higher
Hildebrand, M., and S. Abramowitz,
    266 n. 2
Hirsch, E. D., Jr., 271
Hispanics, 169 n. 4. See also Latins
history, and this research, 27–28
history (major), 277, 307

'homosexual ironic' (behavioral style),
    46, 77
homosexuality, 224, 226–229, 250,
    325 n. 39; heterosexual attitudes to-
    ward, 46, 108, 174 n. 22, 226, 231 n. 1,
    245 n. 50, 260, 268 n. 11
Honors Program, 284, 287, 288, 303, 304
Horowitz, Helen Lefkowitz, 29, 30, 38, 50,
    52, 66 n. 18, 272, 312, 331
housing lottery, 119–120, 126 n. 6,
    127 n. 7, 145
Howie (student name), 86
humanities, 278

identity: centrality of sexual, 195; as col-
    lege student, 51–52. See also individual-
    ism; self
incest taboo, on coed dorm floors, 185
India, 1, 18, 19, 36–37, 72, 79, 177 n. 29,
    242
Indians (south Asians), 152, 168 n. 2
individualism: and bureaucracy, 274; and
    community, 73; and "culture," 151–
    153; dilemmas of, 165–168, 230,
    245 n. 52; and diversity, 60; and friend-
    liness, 43–45, 152, 178 n. 32; and
    friendship, 41–43; naturalness of,
    178 n. 32; privatized, 41, 65 n. 15; and
    race, 165–168, 177 n. 29, 178 n. 32; in
    rooms, 80; and sexuality, 230, 245 n. 52
in loco parentis, 35, 63 n. 6, 84, 253, 289
intellectuals, student, 300–309, 324 n. 37,
    325 n. 38
intellectual self-reports, 311 n. 2
intellectual talk, among students, 298–
    300
intellectual values, 8, 28, 330; and sexual
    values, 251, 267 n. 6, 271, 299, 309;
    and Undergraduate Cynical, 91, 299. See
    also academics; anti-intellectualism

Jane (student name), 202
Japanese-Americans, 75–77
Jay (student name), 79

Jim (student name), 78
"jock," female, 96
Joe (student name), 306
John (student name), 4
Journal of College Student Personnel, 331
Judy (student name, Gates Third), 8
Judy (student name, Hasbrouck Fourth),
96
juniors, 53

Kett, John, 38, 269 n. 13
knowledge: student views on, 278–279
Komarovsky, Mirra, 65 n. 16, 331
Kurth, Sylvia, 67 n. 22

language, types of: Deanly Officialese,
71–72, 90, 132 n. 25; locker-room,
48, 128 n. 10, 183, 213, 215–221,
234 n. 8, 243 n. 46; Private-Sincere,
234 n. 8; sexual, 7, 183, 188; Undergraduate Cynical, 7, 15–16, 41, 90–
96, 119, 131 nn. 21, 22, 132 n. 25,
147, 234 n. 8, 299, 324 n. 37. *See also*
discourse
Latins, 82–83, 86, 110, 129 nn. 13, 15,
142, 168 nn. 1, 2, 169 n. 4, 171 n. 5
learning. *See* academics; education, higher;
intellectuals, student; intellectual values;
liberal arts values
Lears, T. J. Jackson, 313 n. 16
Leo (student name), 86
lesbians. *See* homosexuality
Levine, Arthur, 272
liberal arts values, 12, 282–284, 332
liberals: racial, 154, 159, 162, 164,
172 n. 13, 174 nn. 20, 22, 176 n. 23,
177 n. 28; sexual, 204, 218, 221–223,
226
Lisa (student name, intellectual), 300
Lisa (student name, Hasbrouck Fourth),
96
literacy, student, 236 n. 16
literary references, in dorm banter,
128 n. 10

locker-room (language): men's, 48,
128 n. 10, 183, 184, 213; women's,
215–221, 243 n. 46
Louie (student name), 96
love, sexual, 192, 202, 210–211, 212, 213,
214, 229. *See also* sex: with affection
"low talk" (dean's term), 125 n. 3

McCormick, Richard P., 317 n. 20, 337 n. 9
majors, 128 n. 11, 313 nn. 7, 8; difficulty
of, 278–282; hierarchy of, 6, 276–282,
314 n. 9. *See also* individual subjects
Maltz, Daniel N., and Ruth P. Borker, 47,
244 n. 47
Marcus, George, 327
marriage, student ideas of, 264–265,
269 n. 13
Marriott, McKim, and Ronald Inden,
178 n. 30
Marshall, Donald S., 182
masturbation, 184, 194, 199, 228, 241 n. 32
mathematics (major), 277–278, 313 n. 8
"meat-markets," fraternities as, 209, 261
Melanie (student name), 4
men, 9. *See also* gender; sex
method, 20 nn. 1, 2, 21 n. 4, 27–28, 186,
327–330
—anthropologist in the dorms, 1–20,
74, 91–95, 100–101, 111, 113–
114, 117, 123, 126 n. 6, 129 n. 16,
139 n. 47, 146, 155, 159, 160,
173 n. 18, 236 n. 17
—control effect: defined, 330; possible
instances of, 11–12, 16–17, 100–
101, 117–118, 122, 123, 133 n. 27,
136 n. 37, 139 n. 47, 173 n. 18, 193,
240 n. 29, 241 n. 33, 298–299, 330
—data, from dorm research, 330
—participant observation, xv, 139 n. 47
—reflexivity, 138 n. 46, 139 n. 48, 184,
234 n. 10, 238 n. 20, 328–330
—student quotes, 21 n. 4
—student self-reports, 187–193, 237–
238, 239–241, 311

race, 141–180, 329; attitudes of "white" students, 146, 148–153, 162–165, 176 nn. 23, 24, 25, 26, 177 n. 28; and cultural difference, 146, 166, 172 n. 13, 174 n. 19; and individualism, 165–168, 179 n. 34; and interracial community, 159–161; and music, 136 n. 33, 146, 150–151, 156, 161; relations, history of, 149, 166, 169 n. 4

racism, 17, 96–98, 102, 113, 120, 123, 136 n. 38, 138 n. 46, 142, 148, 155, 159, 160, 163–164, 165, 168 n. 2, 169 nn. 3, 4, 176 nn. 23, 24, 25, 26, 177 nn. 27, 28, 178 nn. 30, 31, 261; blaming the victim of, 179 n. 35; incidents involving, 154–155, 163, 169 n. 4, 173 nn. 15, 16; reverse, 155, 173 n. 17; in wider society vs. in college, 147, 153–154, 164–165

radicals, sexual, 223–229

radio station, campus, 39

"ralphing," 124, 140 n. 50

rape, 48, 202, 216, 254

Ravitch, Diane, and Chester E. Finn, 271

reading, students on, 279, 315 n. 13

"real world, the," 40, 59, 65 n. 14, 66 n. 17, 92, 336

reflexivity: definition of, 328; instances of, 138 n. 46, 139 n. 47, 184, 234 n. 10, 238 n. 20, 328–330

"relationship," 96, 183, 234 n. 7

religion, 16; Catholicism, 194, 196, 203, 253

representativeness: of Rutgers as college, 332–336; of Rutgers as place for late-adolescence, 331–332; of sexual self-reports, 188, 237–238

research methods. See method

Reynolds, Theresa L., 324 n. 37

Rimmer, Robert, 232 n. 2

ritual: convocation as, 14; floor awards night as, 121; in fraternities, 40; of friendship and friendliness, 134 n. 31; interracial party as, 160–161; orienta-tion as, 4; Secret Santa as, 104–111, 134 n. 31, 136 n. 40

Robeson, Paul, 169 n. 3

Robeson section and club, 143–144, 155, 169 n. 4, 171 nn. 5, 6, 7, 9, 172 nn. 11, 12, 13, 174 n. 22

Roll, S., and L. Millen, 67 n. 20

romance, 183, 185, 202, 229, 230. See also sex: with affection

romantics, sexual, 212–215

Rutgers: academic organization of, 280, 284–285, 313 n. 7; academic quality of, 272–273, 310 n. 1, 337 n. 4; diversity of curriculum, 275, 288, diversity of students, 59–61, 69 n. 31, 74, 141, 153, 179 n. 35, 247; history of, 62 n. 2, 333, 337 n. 9; impersonality of, 5, 12, 252–254, 273–274, 289–290, 292–293 (see also bureaucracy); institutional complexities of, 16, 59, 171 n. 7, 333–336, 338 nn. 11, 15, 16; map of, 2; its president as a friendly guy, 44; as a public institution, 59, 141, 290, 305, 310 n. 1, 335, 337 n. 3; racial history and composition, 168 n. 1, 169 n. 4; sexual "map" of, 250; student character-istics at, 69 n. 31, 177 n. 28, 287–288, 336 n. 2, 337 n. 3; student opinions of, 13–14, 58, 59–60, 252–253, 273, 274, 292–293, 307, 311 nn. 2, 3; typi-cality and atypicality of, 331–336. See also college

"Rutgers Screw, The," 13–14, 31, 32, 59, 335

Ruth (student name), 78, 303, 326 n. 41

"scoping," 215, 289

Secret Santa, 104–111, 117–118, 124, 134 n. 31, 135 n. 32, 139 n. 48, 156, 182, 256

self, the, 41. See also identity; individualism

self-reports, student. See intellectual self-reports; sexual self-reports

sex, 16, 48–49, 181–270. See also abor-